The
Fiscal Crisis
of the States

Lessons for the Future

Georgetown University Press, Washington, D.C.
© 1995 by SUNY Central Sponsored Programs Office. All rights reserved.
Printed in the United States of America
10 9 8 7 6 5 4 3 2 1   1995

Library of Congress Cataloging-in-Publication Data

The fiscal crisis of the states: lessons for the future / Steven D.
  Gold, editor.
      p. cm.
      1. Finance, Public—United States—States. 2. Fiscal policy—
  United States—States. 3. Intergovernmental fiscal relations—
  United States. 4. Government spending policy—United States.
  5. State governments—United States.   I. Gold, Steven D.
HJ275.F552   1995
336′.01373—dc20
ISBN 0-87840-574-7. — ISBN 0-87840-575-5 (pbk.)   94-32275

Figures

Acknowledgments

This book reflects the contributions of many people and organizations. Research for it was funded by a grant from the Ford Foundation, which enabled us to contract with six researchers to prepare reports about the policies of the states in which they are located. The states selected had serious fiscal problems and claimed to have adopted innovative policies or abandoned business as usual. Another consideration was the availability of skilled researchers who could analyze these problems and policies.

This book draws upon the research conducted by the Center for the Study of the States, the leading independent national research organization devoted to studying state fiscal problems and policies. The Center is part of the Nelson A. Rockefeller Institute of Government, the public policy research arm of the State University of New York.

Among the people who contributed importantly to the making of this book are: Michael Lipsky, our Program Officer at the Ford Foundation; Richard P. Nathan, director of the Rockefeller Institute; persons who commented on drafts of certain chapters, including Corina Eckl, Harold Hovey, Iris Lav, Leighton Ku, Charles Palmer, and Gary Sasse; and the staff of the Center for the Study of the States, Jennifer McCormick, Jill Ross Schmelz, and Mischelle Valcourt.

Two people deserve special thanks. In addition to contributing two of her own chapters, Sarah Ritchie made innumerable helpful comments on many others, especially mine. Richard Nathan provided encouragement and wise counsel based on his experience with similar projects.

S.D.G.

PART I

The National Picture

1

Introduction

Steven D. Gold*

States play a vital role in our federal system. Although most people think of Washington, DC when they hear the word "government," state and local governments actually provide most of the services that people use. States raise about half of the money for public schools, operate the great majority of public colleges and universities, run most prisons, build and maintain thousands of miles of highways, decide how generous welfare benefits will be, and are key decision makers in the health care system.

The early 1990s were stressful years for state governments. Several governors described the fiscal crisis as the most severe since the Great Depression. In response, many states raised taxes and announced cuts in spending and employment, with some particularly dramatic reductions in higher education and welfare programs.

Unfortunately, relatively little detailed information is available describing and evaluating how states responded to this fiscal crisis. That is what this book is about. It delves beneath the rhetoric and public relations smoke screens to tell the real story of how state governments responded to the challenges they faced.

It reviews state fiscal conditions and policies during the first five years of the 1990s, focusing particularly on five sets of questions:

- How did states respond to fiscal stress? What changes did they make in tax and spending policies? How did states treat

*Steven D. Gold is Director of the Center for the Study of the States at the Nelson A. Rockefeller Institute of Government, which is the public policy research arm of the State University of New York. Gold is also Professor of Public Administration in the Graduate School of Public Affairs at the State University of New York in Albany.

3

local governments? Was it "business as usual," or did states adopt significant new approaches in the spirit of "reinventing government?"

• Who were the winners and losers as a result of state policies? To what extent were poor people the victims of state austerity?
• What role did federal policies play in state fiscal travails? Was the federal government a help or a hindrance?
• How did the political situations in these states vary, and what difference did politics make in state policies?
• What do the experiences of the early 1990s imply about prospects for the rest of the decade? Is the improvement of fiscal conditions in 1993 and 1994 a harbinger of good times to come, or are states in store for a continued period of fiscal stress?

Although these questions have been phrased as though one can generalize about all states, that is far from the truth. Fiscal conditions varied from good to atrocious, and state policy responses also differed tremendously.

These questions can be answered in two ways, with information for all fifty states and by intensive case studies of a small number of states. This book uses both approaches. Part I provides a fifty-state overview of state fiscal conditions, policies, and politics. Part II presents case studies of six states, along with introductory chapters that provide a framework for comparing them and that tell how the fiscal and political systems of those six states compare to each other and to the other forty-four states. Five of these states—California, Connecticut, Florida, Massachusetts, and Michigan—had severe fiscal problems and high-profile governors who were prominent on the national stage. The sixth state, Minnesota, had less severe fiscal problems but has a strong progressive tradition of being among the most innovative states in the nation.

In each of the five states with severe fiscal problems, the governors (Wilson, Weicker, Chiles, Weld, and Engler) took the posture that the state had to abandon business as usual. We want to find out: *Did states change their policies in fundamental ways? Can other states learn important lessons from their experiences?*

A subtheme of this book is that researchers concerned with understanding state financial policies must reach beyond the kinds of information that has conventionally been used to write about them. The preferred approach will be illustrated throughout the book, and the principles that should be followed in future research on these issues are discussed.

This book is written for several different audiences. It should be useful to state officials by providing objective descriptions and analysis of how other states coped with serious fiscal problems. But while much of what follows is already known to state fiscal professionals, it should be news to others who are concerned about state policies (such as the media and students of political science, public administration, and economics). For example:

- The state fiscal crisis was caused by a combination of factors. While some were beyond the control of state officials, others were the legacy of misguided policies pursued in the 1980s.
- Many states do not actually have to balance their budgets when they are in fiscal crises; and they don't.
- Faced with a prospective deficit, states have many more choices than merely raising taxes and cutting spending.
- Federal aid increased sharply in the early 1990s, providing a big help to state budgets.
- Some tax increases really are temporary.

2

State Fiscal Problems and Policies

Steven D. Gold

This chapter provides an overview of the state fiscal crisis and how states responded to it. It begins with a discussion of the causes of the fiscal crisis and then analyzes state fiscal conditions, tax policy, spending policy, and policies affecting local governments.

CAUSES OF THE FISCAL CRISIS[1]

Many factors contributed to the fiscal crisis. They can be divided into those that were beyond the control of states and those that were brought on by state policies. This distinction is blurred because some problems reflected a combination of influences, only some of which states could control. In any case, the relative importance of the factors that caused the crisis varied considerably from state to state, as the next chapter will demonstrate.

Among the problems that were beyond the control of states were the recession, the explosive growth of Medicaid, federal mandates, increases in school enrollment, court decisions, and voter initiatives.[2] Self-inflicted problems included excessive spending during the 1980s, dysfunctional tax systems, and large increases in the number of prison inmates. Contrary to widespread belief, recent federal aid reductions were not a cause of the fiscal crisis. In fact, federal aid rose sharply and helped states to cope with budget problems caused by other factors.

Recession. The most important cause of the fiscal crisis was the recession, which reduced state tax revenue and led to increased demand for welfare and higher education. Although the national recession officially lasted only nine months, from July 1990 to March 1991,

some individual states felt its effects for a much longer period. Employment started to fall in several northeastern states during the winter
and spring of 1989, although in most states it did not peak until mid-
1990.

The recession was very severe in the Northeast and California
but had relatively little impact in many states. In fact, twenty-three
states never experienced an employment decrease as large as 1 percent, so they escaped from its serious effects. Figure 2–1 illustrates the
varying impact of the recession by showing examples of employment
fluctuations in four states: one where there was no significant drop;
another where there was a drop followed by a rebound to a new peak;
a third where employment as of October 1993 was trending higher
but was still lower than it was before the recession; and a fourth where
employment was still falling as of late 1993.

Figure 2–2 demonstrates how the recession affected revenue
by showing the fluctuations of state tax collections after eliminating
inflation and the effects of legislated tax increases. From mid-1990
until mid-1992, state tax revenue on that basis was lower than it had
been the previous year. As the economy pulled out of the recession,
this was eventually reflected in positive growth rates of tax revenue.

Another important effect of the recession was to cause a large
increase in welfare caseloads. Between July 1989 and January 1992,
the number of recipients of Aid to Families with Dependent Children
benefits rose 24.8 percent.

Medicaid. The second most important fiscal problem for the states
was the explosive growth of Medicaid, the main program that provides
health care for poor people. Medicaid spending from state general
funds went up, according to the National Association of State Budget
Officers (NASBO), by 16.7 percent in 1991 and 19.6 percent in 1992.
Among the main reasons for this increase were the recession (which
increased poverty), health cost inflation, and federal mandates.[3]

Federal mandates. The federal government added to state fiscal
problems by expanding eligibility for Medicaid and requiring that
states provide more services than many of them had offered previously. Although these mandates were enacted between 1985 and
1989, before the recession began, their full impact was not felt until
the early 1990s.

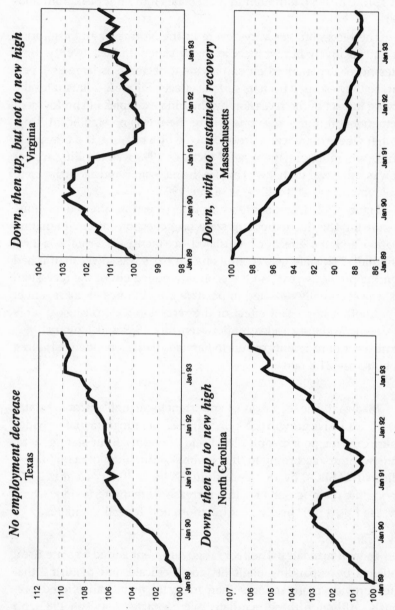

Figure 2–1. Representative States' Employment Changes, January 1989 to October 1993.

8

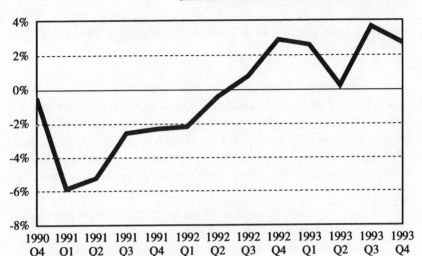

Source: Gold and McCormick, "State Revenue Report" (Albany, NY: Center for the Study of the States, February 1994).

Figure 2–2. Real State Tax Revenue Increases Excluding Legislated Changes, 1990 to 1994.

Federal mandates affected many other areas, such as environmental programs and access for handicapped people, but their main impact on state budgets in recent years has been on Medicaid. Environmental mandates have had much more effect on local governments than on states. Unfortunately, only piecemeal estimates are available of the cost to state and local governments of complying with federal mandates.

School enrollment. Increases in the school-aged population have an important effect on state and local budgets because elementary-secondary education is the biggest component of spending at both levels of government.

In the early 1990s, school enrollment was increasing 1.7 percent or more annually. This is in contrast to the situation a decade earlier, during the previous recession, when school enrollment was falling about 1 percent annually.

These enrollment increases would have been a more significant cause of fiscal stress if states had maintained their previous pattern of increasing school aid. In fact, however, states reduced their share of school costs, putting more pressure on local school districts to raise their own taxes.

Court rulings. Another uncontrollable cause of fiscal stress was federal and state court decisions that increased state costs or reduced revenues. The most widespread decisions forced states to spend more on mental health programs and on prisons to reduce overcrowding. A majority of states were affected by decisions in those areas. Other areas where court rulings had significant fiscal impacts include:

- *Health,* where decisions forced states to provide larger payments to health care providers.
- *Education,* where several states had their school finance systems overturned on the grounds that they disadvantaged students from poor school districts.
- *Taxes,* where the federal courts ruled that many states had unconstitutionally provided less favorable treatment to the pensions of federal retirees than to those of retired state and local employees.

Voter initiatives. Another important cause of fiscal stress in some states was the legacy of voter initiatives that cut taxes, limited spending, or otherwise restricted budgeting flexibility. Although most voter initiatives have not been highly restrictive, there are some exceptions, particularly those in California, Massachusetts, and Oregon. Some new restrictions approved by voters in the 1990s will also have severe effects over time, for example, in Arizona, Colorado, Oklahoma, and Washington, but they were not a major source of fiscal stress in 1991 and 1992.

Excessive spending. Probably the most important self-inflicted fiscal problem was the legacy of overspending in the 1980s. This was not a general phenomenon but rather one that particularly affected some states. With revenue booming because of a robust economy, they expanded spending to unsustainable levels.

Connecticut, Massachusetts, and New Jersey stand out. They ranked first, second, and fifth in per capita state-local spending increases between 1984 and 1988, with increases of 51 percent, 47 percent, and 44 percent respectively. The median state-local increase was

31 percent, which was also the median increase of per capita income. The inflation rate was 18 percent.

Dysfunctional tax systems. Many states have failed to reform their tax systems to reflect changes in the economy with the result that their revenue grows more slowly than personal income. In the parlance of tax analysts, the elasticity of the tax system fell, where elasticity is the percentage increase in revenue resulting from a 1 percent growth of personal income.

This is most serious with regard to the sales tax. Most states tax services much less than they tax goods, even though our economy is increasingly service-oriented.

Likewise, the personal income tax has become less responsive to economic growth. In the 1980s, many states either indexed the tax to offset the effects of inflation or reduced the progressivity of income tax rates. These actions made the tax less elastic. Many other states have not revised their tax rates in twenty years or more, so a large proportion of taxpayers are in the highest tax bracket, which also leads to a low elasticity.

Corrections policy. The fastest growing part of state budgets in the 1980s was corrections spending, which quadrupled in that decade. The main cause of this increase was not higher crime rates but rather tougher sentencing laws and the war on drugs. The probability of being incarcerated, even for a nonviolent offense, was much higher than it used to be.

Federal aid.[4] It is well known that President Reagan persuaded Congress to make substantial reductions in federal aid to state and local governments in 1981, his first year in office, and that he continued to propose cuts throughout his terms. What is not as widely recognized is that Congress rejected most of his proposed reductions after 1981, and that aid increased considerably during the Bush administration. Some of that increase occurred simply because of the recession, which boosted Medicaid and welfare rolls, but it also reflected the fact that President Bush did not fight as hard to hold down spending as President Reagan did.

Federal aid to state and local governments soared from $122 billion to $194 billion between 1989 and 1993. Medicaid accounted for 57 percent of the total increase during those four years. As discussed below, a significant part of that increase reflected state strategies to shift costs to the federal government without burdening the state budget through provider taxes, intergovernmental transfers, and transfer of other health programs into the Medicaid fold.

Thus, recent decreases in federal aid were not a cause of the state fiscal crisis of the early 1990s. In fact, federal aid increases helped states. Four caveats are important: First, local governments lost much more federal aid in the 1980s and did not share significantly in the post-1989 increase. Second, the legacy of the aid cutbacks of the early Reagan administration may have played a role in setting the stage for the crisis. States used some of their own funds to replace the lost federal revenue, and the cost of this commitment grew over time, adding to state expenditures. Third, federal mandates were a factor in increased fiscal stress in the 1990s. A large proportion of state spending reflects responsibilities related to federal requirements. Fourth, federal aid is nearly all categorical, directed more at federal priorities than goals established by states. Little of it provides general support for state budgets.

Summary. There were many causes of the state fiscal crisis. Any simple explanation of its roots is inadequate. The causes can be distinguished not only according to whether they were beyond the control of the states, but also according to whether they were cyclical or structural. The severity of the crisis was exacerbated by the business cycle, but in many states there was an underlying structural deficit. This means that revenue would have lagged behind the growth of spending needed to maintain current services even if there had been no recession. The following chapter will illustrate how the causes of the crisis differed, using the six states that are the focus of this book. The distinction between cyclical and structural problems leads to the question of whether states endured merely a short-term crisis or an episode of a continuing long-term crisis. That question will be addressed in the final chapter of this book.

FISCAL CONDITIONS

The most readily available indicator of state fiscal conditions is the year-end balance in the general fund and rainy day funds, expressed

TABLE 2–1 Total State Year-End Balances in General Funds and Rainy Day Funds

Year	Total Balance ($ in billions)	Total Balance (as % of expenditures)
1994	$ 8.5 (est.)	2.6% (est.)
1993	10.1	3.3
1992	5.3	1.8
1991	3.1	1.1
1990	9.4	3.4
1989	12.5	4.8
1988	9.8	4.2
1987	6.7	3.1
1986	7.2	3.5
1985	9.7	5.2
1984	6.4	3.8
1983	2.3	1.5
1982	4.5	2.9
1981	6.5	4.4
1980	11.8	9.0
1979	11.2	8.7
1978	8.9	8.6

Source: National Association of State Budget Officers, *Fiscal Survey of the States: April 1994*, p. 14.

as a proportion of general fund spending. As Table 2–1 shows, this proportion fell to 1.1 percent in 1991, the lowest level since the National Association of State Budget Officers (NASBO) began to report it in 1978. It rebounded to 1.8 percent in 1992, still a relatively low level, and rose further to 3.3 percent in 1993.

This is indicative of a high level of fiscal stress, but it does not necessarily prove that conditions were worse than in 1983, when the proportion was 1.5 percent. One problem with this indicator is that a small number of states may have a disproportionate impact on the national average. California, for example, reported deficits of $2.9 billion and $2.2 billion at the end of fiscal years 1991 and 1992. In fact, twenty-one states had balances below 1 percent at the end of 1991, but seventeen states had balances above 5 percent.

Year-end balances are a useful but imperfect indicator. All states do not use the same methodology in reporting to NASBO. States can avoid reporting a deficit simply by failing to pay their bills until the start of the next fiscal year or by accelerating tax collections. Massachusetts avoided a deficit in 1991 only by virtue of a $450 million windfall of federal aid for past Medicaid outlays.

In other words, a serious problem with year-end balances as an indicator is that they show where a state wound up without explaining how it got there. In this respect, a better measure is the prospective deficit or surplus that a state confronted. In April 1991, the National Conference of State Legislatures (NCSL) reported how each state estimated its deficit for the current fiscal year and the next one. Table 2–2 summarizes those estimates, with updated data for California and New York.

Were fiscal conditions really worse in 1991 than in 1982, as some governors and media analyses asserted? The answer varies from state to state. The most important determinant of fiscal stress is the severity of the recession. It was much worse in 1991 than in 1982 in the Northeast and California but considerably less severe in the Midwest.

For the country as a whole, the recession of the early 1990s was much less severe than the one that occurred a decade earlier. The national unemployment rate in 1991 was 6.6 percent, much less than the 9.5 percent rate of 1982 and 1983. The argument that the fiscal crisis of the early 1990s was worse depended on the proposition that pressures for higher spending in the 1990s were much stronger than they were a decade earlier. As discussed above, elementary-secondary school enrollments were increasing and Medicaid and corrections costs were growing at much higher rates. None of these pressures was as strong in the early 1980s. How states dealt with these pressures will be discussed below in the section of this chapter on spending policies.

TAX POLICY

Changes in tax revenue can be divided into two parts, fluctuations due to the economy and legislated changes. They are inversely related: when the economy depresses revenue, states are more likely to legislate tax increases.

Impact of the economy. The recession had a devastating effect on revenue in the first half of 1991, with revenue growing just 0.9 percent in the first quarter and 2.0 percent in the second quarter of the year. Without legislated changes, revenue would have been at least 1 percent less than it was a year earlier. In real terms, this represented a reduction of more than 5 percent.

Legislated changes. The tax increases in the four years under consideration here were volatile: $9.2 billion in 1990, $14.4 billion in 1991, $1.4 billion in 1992, and $1.2 billion in 1993.[5]

Table 2–3 shows the size of legislated tax increases for each year since 1964. It reveals a number of important points:

- The peak years for tax increases were 1967, 1969, and 1971, with increases of 7.8 to 9.7 percent. The cost of educating the baby-boom generation placed tremendous stress on state finances in that period.
- Large tax increases tend to occur in the wake of recessions. This contributed to the increase in 1971 and was especially important in 1983 and 1991.
- Other things being equal, increases are larger in odd-numbered years, which follow legislative and gubernatorial elections in most states.

The fluctuations in legislated tax increases from year to year reflect at least four factors: the impact of the economy, which hit especially hard in 1991; the state election cycle; special factors that contributed to tax increases in 1990; and the proliferation of health care provider taxes in 1992.

- *Impact of economy*: The relatively large increase in 1991 is consistent with the historical pattern of large increases in the wake of recessions.
- *Election cycle*: 1991's increase is also consistent with the pattern of big increases in the year following elections. The relatively large 1990 increase is partially attributable to New Jersey, which had the largest tax increase that year. New Jersey is one of the two states where gubernatorial elections occur in odd-numbered years.
- *Special factors*: Four of the 1990 increases were related to efforts to reform school finance systems. Kentucky and New Jersey faced state Supreme Court rulings requiring more aid to poor

TABLE 2-2 Estimated State Budget Deficits, FY 1991 and FY 1992

(Millions of $)

	Fiscal 1991				Fiscal 1992			
	Deficit	General Fund	Deficit As % of GF	Rank	Deficit	General Fund	Deficit As % of GF	Rank
New England								
Connecticut	$-747	$6593	11.3%	4	$-350	$1569	22.3%	2
Maine	-110	1627	6.8	12	-350	1569	22.3	3
Massachusetts	-850	11279	7.5	8	-1800	11530	15.6	9
New Hampshire	-45	624	7.2	10	-130	665	19.5	6
Rhode Island	-241	1450	16.6	2	0	0		
Vermont	-46	630	7.3	9	-120	662	18.1	8
Mid Atlantic								
Delaware	-28	1223	2.3	26	0	1205	0.0	
Maryland	-553	5959	9.3	5	-192	6512	2.9	18
New Jersey	-703	12217	5.8	13	812	13918	5.8	16
New York	-1150	29204	3.9	19	-6500	29145	22.3	4
Pennsylvania	-836	12322	6.8	11	2500	13090	19.1	7
Great Lakes								
Illinois	-500	13748	3.6	20	0	14178	0.0	
Indiana	-92	5820	1.6	27	-490	5741	8.5	12
Michigan	-1169	7590	15.4	3	0	8057	0.0	
Ohio	-477	10251	4.7	17	-825	10179	8.1	13
Wisconsin	0	6355	0.0		-356	6367	5.6	17
Plains								
Iowa	-15	3137	0.5	29	-230	3358	6.8	15
Kansas		2501	0.0			2902	0.0	
Minnesota	-197	7274	2.7	23	-600	7413	8.1	14
Missouri	-235	4280	5.5	14		4442	0.0	
Nebraska	-40	1489	2.7	24	-20	1489	1.3	19
North Dakota		523	0.0			583	0.0	
South Dakota		483	0.0			519	0.0	

Southeast								
Alabama	−90	3450	2.6	25		1938	0.0	
Arkansas	−8	1862	0.4	30		11522	0.0	
Florida	−878	10539	8.3	7		7900	0.0	
Georgia	−359	7632	4.7	16		4676	0.0	
Kentucky	0	4286	0.0		−921	4554	20.2	5
Louisiana		4498	0.0	15		2136	0.0	
Mississippi	−105	1960	5.4	18	−779	7787	10.0	11
North Carolina	−355	7762	4.6			3649	0.0	
South Carolina		3453	0.0	21		4491	0.0	
Tennessee	−140	3857	3.6	1		6074	0.0	
Virginia	−1100	6246	17.6			1986	0.0	
West Virginia		1914	0.0				0.0	
Southwest								
Arizona	−95	3382	2.8	22		3540	0.0	
New Mexico		1926	0.0			2024	0.0	
Oklahoma		2992	0.0			3128	0.0	
Texas	0	14247	0.0		−2250	17259	13.0	10
Rocky Mountain								
Colorado		2654	0.0			2763	0.0	
Idaho		935	0.0			993	0.0	
Montana		459	0.0			576	0.0	
Utah	−15	1745	0.9			1777	0.0	
Wyoming		422	0.0	28		405	0.0	
Far West								
California	−3600	41720	8.6	6	−14300	43282	33.0	1
Nevada		939	0.0			1068	0.0	
Oregon		2371	0.0			2548	0.0	
Washington		7286	0.0			7415	0.0	
Alaska		2288	0.0			2378	0.0	
Hawaii		2796	0.0			2763	0.0	

Source: National Conference of State Legislatures survey (April 1991).

17

TABLE 2–3 Net State Tax Changes by Year of Enactment, 1964 to 1993

Calendar Year	Billions of Dollars	Percent of Annual Collections
1993	$1.2	0.4%
1992	1.4	0.4
1991	14.4	4.8
1990	9.2	3.5
1989	3.5	1.3
1988	0.6	0.2
1987	4.5	1.9
1986	1.1	0.5
1985	−1.3	−0.6
1984	2.3	1.2
1983	8.3	4.8
1982	2.9	1.8
1981	3.8	2.5
1980	0.4	0.3
1979	−2.0	−1.6
1978	−2.3	−2.0
1977	0.2	0.5
1976	1.0	0.9
1975	1.6	2.0
1974	0.4	0.5
1973	0.5	0.7
1972	0.9	1.5
1971	5.0	9.7
1970	0.8	1.7
1969	4.0	9.5
1968	1.3	3.6
1967	2.5	7.8
1966	0.5	1.7
1965	1.3	5.0
1964	0.1	0.5

Note: The second column shows tax increases legislated during a calendar year as a proportion of total tax revenue during the fiscal year which ends during that calendar year. Tax increases do not include extension of temporary increases scheduled to expire or taxes on health care providers.

Source: Steven D. Gold, *Tax Increases Shriveled in 1993* (Center for the Study of the States), based on information from the Tax Foundation for years prior to 1984, and the National Conference of State Legislatures thereafter, with some modifications for years after 1988.

schools; Oklahoma was responding to a perceived need to increase school funding, and Nebraska used most of the increase in state tax revenue to provide property tax relief. An anticipated court ruling regarding school finance was also the major factor behind Kansas' 1992 tax increase.

- *Health care provider taxes*: The tax increases reported here do not include taxes imposed on hospitals, nursing homes, and sometimes other health care providers to help finance Medicaid. These taxes played a growing role in state finances over this period, and they were particularly important in helping to avoid other tax increases in 1992. They are discussed in a later section of this paper.

As in the case of deficits, national aggregate figures on tax increases can be heavily influenced by developments in one or two large states. That was certainly true in 1991, when California accounted for more than 40 percent of the national increase in tax revenue.

Table 2–4 summarizes the major tax increases each year, those that increased total state tax revenue by at least 5 percent. The number of large increases was ten in 1990, twelve in 1991, six in 1992, and three in 1993. Since four states (New Hampshire, Montana, Rhode Island, and Vermont) enacted large increases in two different years, the total number of states with at least one large tax increase is twenty-seven.

New Jersey's large 1990 tax increase triggered a major tax revolt that resulted in a Republican sweep of the state legislature in 1991. This reaction was, however, the exception rather than the rule. In the other states with large tax increases, no tax revolt occurred. In fact, the large number of tax increases in 1991 and 1992 had little effect on the results of the November 1992 elections.[6]

The two most important factors affecting the magnitude of state tax increases were the severity of the recession and spending increases during the economic expansion of the 1980s. Tax increases tended to be larger in states that had big reductions in employment and in states that had the largest increases in spending from 1983 to 1990.[7]

States differed considerably in terms of how they raised taxes. As Table 2–4 shows, the most common pattern was to rely on both of the major state taxes, the personal income tax and the general sales tax. The only states to rely completely on sales tax increases were Arkansas (where three-quarters of the legislature is needed to raise

TABLE 2–4   Large State Tax Increases, 1990 through 1993

State	Amount of Increase (millions)	Percent of Total Revenue	Large Tax Increases
1990 Arizona	$215	5.3%	Personal Income
Florida	1085	8.7	Miscellaneous
Kentucky	585	14.5	Sales, Personal Income
Massachusetts	1157	12.8	Personal Income
Nebraska	190	13.1	Sales, Personal Income
New Hampshire	58	9.5	Other
New Jersey	2825	26.9	Personal Income, Sales
Oklahoma	484	6.1	Sales, Personal Income
Rhode Island	105	9.0	Sales
Vermont	36	5.8	Personal Income
1991 Arkansas	$245	10.8%	Sales
California	6393	14.8	Sales, Personal Income
Connecticut	1066	20.2	Personal Income
Delaware	76	6.7	Corporate Franchise
Maine	176	11.3	Sales, Personal Income
Nevada	92	5.8	Sales
New Hampshire	62	6.6	Other
North Carolina	606	7.7	Sales, Personal Income
Pennsylvania	3167	24.0	Personal Income, Sales
Rhode Island	127	10.3	Personal Income
Texas	852	5.8	Motor Fuel
Vermont	86	12.9	Sales, Personal Income
1992 Iowa	$258	7.5%	Sales
Kansas	353	12.6	Sales, Personal Income
Maryland	395	6.1	Sales, Personal Income
Mississippi	166	6.7	Sales
Montana	41	5.1	Other, Personal Income
Tennessee	252	5.8	Sales
1993 Missouri	$319	6.4%	Personal Income
Montana	60	7.3	Personal Income
Wyoming	68	10.7	Sales

Sources: Center for the Study of the States: *How Much Did State Taxes Really Go Up in 1991?*, *The Anatomy and Magnitude of State Tax Increases in 1992*, and *Tax Increases Shriveled in 1993*.

National Conference of State Legislatures: *State Budget and Tax Actions 1990*, *State Budget and Tax Actions 1991*, *State Tax Actions 1992*, and *State Tax Actions 1993*.

the income tax); Nevada, Tennessee, and Wyoming (which have no broad-based income taxes); and Iowa (which already had a much greater reliance on the personal income tax than the sales tax).[8]

There was a tendency for states to make their tax systems more balanced. If a state already relied heavily on the income tax, it tended to put more emphasis on the sales tax. If it placed a bigger responsibility on the sales tax, it usually raised the income tax more.[9]

The probability that a state would enact a large tax increase was much greater if it was one of the thirteen states that did not impose both a sales and a broad-based income tax in 1990. Only four of those states (Alaska, Oregon, South Dakota, and Washington) avoided a large tax increase in the 1990–1993 period. This reflects the fact that states are financially more stable if they have a well-balanced tax system.

Many states included reforms in their tax increases. Especially notable were trends to restructure income tax rates and expand the sales tax base. Broadening the income tax base was a minor theme, and tax relief for the poor also occurred in many states.[10]

Income tax progressivity. In nearly every case, states that increased their income tax made it more progressive. Pennsylvania was the only exception; it has always had a flat tax, and it continued to use that type of tax.

Most increases took the form of simply imposing a higher tax rate on affluent taxpayers, but some were more comprehensive changes that reduced tax burdens or increased tax rates less at lower income levels. A few states increased progressivity by eliminating deductions that were most beneficial to high income groups:

- *Arizona* (1990) repealed the deduction for federal income taxes, which is much more valuable for high-income taxpayers than for those with lower incomes because the federal income tax is progressive. Although it reduced tax rates at the same time, the net effect was to increase revenue and make the income tax more progressive.
- *California* (1991) increased the top tax rate from 9.3 percent to 10 percent for returns with taxable income over $200,000 and to 11 percent for income over $400,000.
- *Colorado* (1992) repealed the deduction for state income taxes.

- *Kansas* (1992) restructured rates, increasing the tax burden for returns with income above $44,000 and reducing it at lower income levels.
- *Kentucky* (1990) repealed the deduction for federal income taxes without changing its tax rates.
- *Maine* (1991) imposed a two-year surcharge on incomes above $75,000.
- *Maryland* (1992) increased the top rate from 5 percent to 6 percent for returns with income over $150,000. This increase was in effect for three years.
- *Minnesota* (1991) increased the tax rate from 8 percent to 8.5 percent above approximately $172,000.
- *Mississippi* (1992) repealed the deduction for state income taxes.
- *Montana* (1993) completely overhauled its income tax, repealing all deductions (including a deduction for federal income tax payments), increasing its personal exemptions and standard deductions, and adopting a flat tax rate instead of a nominally progressive rate schedule. The result was to increase progressivity at low income levels. This reform was suspended pending the result of a November 1994 referendum.
- *Nebraska* (1993) increased the top tax rate from 6.92 percent to 6.99 percent and used the additional revenue to reduce taxes at low income levels.
- *New Jersey* (1990) increased the top tax rate from 3.5 percent to 7 percent. It did not raise rates at all for joint returns with taxable income under $70,000.
- *New York* phased out the benefit of tax rates below the maximum rate for returns with taxable income above $100,000. In effect, all income over $150,000 is taxed at the top state tax rate of 7.785 percent.
- *North Carolina* (1991) increased the top rate from 7 percent to 7.75 percent for returns with income over $100,000.
- *Ohio* (1992) increased the top rate from 6.93 percent to 7.5 percent for returns with income over $200,000.
- *Oklahoma* (1990) added a 7 percent tax rate for income above $10,000.
- *Rhode Island* (1992) imposed a two-year surcharge on returns with federal tax liability above $15,000 (approximately $90,000 of taxable income).

- *Vermont* (1991) imposed a three-year surcharge on taxpayers with income above approximately $89,000.

Sales tax base broadening. Twenty-three states eliminated some sales tax exemptions, with services being the most frequent target. Other exemptions that were eliminated in several states involved snack foods and products that are normally taxed elsewhere.

Most of the sales tax base broadening involved relatively small amounts of revenue, but Connecticut, Maryland, New Jersey, and Pennsylvania made more far-reaching efforts. For example, the exemptions repealed in Connecticut raised as much revenue as a 0.4 percent rate increase.

In 1990, Massachusetts passed a broad sales tax on business and professional services, but it was repealed the day after it took effect in March 1991. Repeal was strongly backed by William Weld, the newly elected governor.

Tax relief for the poor. States often accompanied general tax increases with some tax breaks targeted at low-income households. Examples:

- Iowa reduced income taxes at low income levels in 1992 when it raised its sales tax rate.
- Kansas expanded eligibility and increased benefits for its property tax circuit breaker and cut income taxes at low income levels in 1992, along with sales and income tax increases.
- Maryland extended eligibility for its circuit breaker to nonelderly renters when it broadened the sales tax base in 1992.
- Oklahoma provided a new refundable sales tax credit when it increased sales and income taxes in 1990.

Business tax reform. There were no outstanding trends from a national perspective, but three states took important new initiatives. First, in 1991 Texas made its franchise tax depend not only on a company's invested property but also on its net income. This makes it like the corporate income taxes in a number of other states. Thus, it can be said that Texas turned its tax into a corporate income tax. Second, in 1991 Nevada imposed a new tax based on the level of employment of a company. Finally, in 1993 New Hampshire enacted a business enterprise tax to supplement its business profits tax. The new tax is on the wages, dividends, and interest paid by companies, whether they are incorporated or not.

The most common change of business taxes, especially in 1993, was provision of new tax incentives to attract and retain business investment. For example, many states adopted investment tax credits. This trend was a reaction to the intense competition among states for economic development. The effectiveness of these tax incentives is highly controversial.

SPENDING POLICY

One of the most important responses of states to the fiscal crisis was to reduce the growth rate of spending. As Table 2–5 shows, general fund spending rose 4.5 percent in fiscal year 1991 and 5.1 percent in 1992. After subtracting inflation, these are the smallest increases since 1983. The 1991 increase represented approximately constant real

TABLE 2–5 Nominal and Real General Fund Budget Increases, 1979 to 1994

Fiscal Year	Nominal Increase	Real Increase
1994	5.1% (est.)	1.6% (est.)
1993	3.3	−0.2
1992	5.1	1.5
1991	4.5	−0.1
1990	6.4	1.7
1989	8.7	3.5
1988	7.0	2.9
1987	6.3	2.6
1986	8.9	3.7
1985	10.2	4.6
1984	8.0	3.3
1983	−0.7	−6.3
1982	6.4	−1.1
1981	16.3	6.1
1980	10.0	−0.6
1979	10.1	1.5

Note: The state and local government implicit price deflator was used for determining real changes.
Source: National Association of State Budget Officers, *Fiscal Survey of the States: April 1994*, p. 4.

spending, and the 1992 increase implied a real increase of about 1.5 percent. Spending increases in the following two years were also relatively restrained.[11]

Two points need to be considered about the national average spending increases. First, they mask the fact that cutbacks were much more severe in some states than others. Second, as mentioned above, they occurred in an environment where strong upward pressures were being exerted on spending by Medicaid, corrections, and school enrollment.

Before discussing spending policies, it should be explained that the available information is less than perfect. Census data does not go beyond fiscal 1992, and NASBO data for individual spending categories goes only through 1993 (and that is on a preliminary basis subject to substantial revision). For 1994, the only information available for some kinds of spending is NCSL estimates of appropriations increases. For a better understanding of particular spending areas, data from these sources has to be supplemented by information from organizations that focus on particular areas, like K–12 education or higher education. In some cases, major inconsistencies exist among these alternative information sources. Table 2–6, which summarizes spending increases in major budget categories, uses eclectic sources, relying on whichever data source appears most plausible. The Appendix presents and compares estimates from various sources. All of the figures cited below are for spending financed by state tax revenue, with federal aid excluded.

Budget restraint affected all major spending areas, but not to the same extent:

- School aid, the largest part of most state budgets, rose 7.1 percent in 1990–1991, 3.5 percent in 1991–1992, and an estimated 3.0 percent in 1992–1993.
- Higher education took the worst beating of any major spending category, with spending virtually unchanged over the three-year period. Appropriations in 1992–1993 were less than 1 percent higher than in 1989–1990.
- Corrections spending slowed from its double-digit increases of the 1980s. NASBO reported growth of 9.2 percent in 1991, 4.3 percent in 1992, and 6.9 percent in 1993.
- AFDC spending rose 9.0 percent in 1991 and 9.8 percent in 1992, but only 4.9 percent in 1993.

TABLE 2–6　State Spending Increases in 1991, 1992, and 1993

Category	1991	1992	1993
Total			
NCSL	5.2%	5.4%	4.6%
NASBO	4.5	5.1	3.3
School aid	7.1	3.5	3.0
Higher education	1.8	0.5	−1.5
Corrections	9.2	4.3	6.9
AFDC	9.0	9.8	4.9
Medicaid, all state funds,	21.4	34.4	12.7
General fund	16.9	19.6	10.2
Transportation	7.3	2.6	2.4

Note: Estimates are drawn from a variety of sources and use inconsistent conceptual frameworks.
Sources:

Totals	NCSL, *State Budget Actions*
	NASBO, *Fiscal Survey of the States* (October 1993)
School aid	National Education Association, *1993–94 Estimates of School Statistics* (March 1994)
Higher education	Edward R. Hines, *State Higher Education Appropriations, 1993–94* (State Higher Education Executive Officers, February 1994)
Corrections	NASBO, *Expenditure Report* (1992 and 1993)
AFDC	NASBO, *Expenditure Report* (1992 and 1993)
Medicaid	NASBO, *Expenditure Report* (1992 and 1993)
Transportation	NASBO, *Expenditure Report* (1992 and 1993)

- Spending of state general fund dollars for Medicaid went up, according to NASBO, 16.9 percent in 1991 and 19.6 percent in 1992. Increases were much larger if spending from provider taxes and other unconventional sources is included.
- Transportation spending fared relatively well in 1991, with an increase of 7.3 percent, but it rose only 2.6 percent in 1992. Because it is usually funded from earmarked motor fuel taxes, it is not affected as much by general state fiscal stress as are the other major spending categories.

To understand how these various figures add up, it is helpful to consider not just the percentage increases but also the absolute increases. School aid accounts for close to one-third of state general fund spending, so even a relatively small percentage increase involves a substantial amount of revenue. Corrections spending, on the other hand, usually accounts for 5 percent or less of general fund spending.

Each major spending category warrants further discussion.

Elementary-Secondary Education

Considering that enrollment rose in these three years by 1.7 percent, 1.7 percent, and 1.8 percent, the state spending increases represent virtually no change per pupil in real dollars. In reaction to the sluggish increase in state aid, local property taxes grew more rapidly. Local school revenue rose 7.7 percent in 1991, 5.7 percent in 1992, and 5.9 percent in 1993. In the latter two years, the growth rate was at least 2.2 percentage points greater than the increase in state aid.[12]

Higher Education

Just as property taxes increased in response to state aid trends, higher education's meager state support also resulted in very large increases in tuition. The average tuition and required fees for undergraduates at public four-year institutions jumped 36.6 percent between the 1989–1990 and the 1992–1993 school years.[13]

Corrections

A significant deceleration occurred from the 12 to 15 percent increases in corrections spending throughout most of the 1980s, although it still increased faster than spending for most other programs. Three factors underlying the slowdown are the reluctance of states to open new prisons because of the substantial operating costs involved, cuts in inmate services such as education, and smaller increases in salaries of prison employees. NCSL reports that appropriations for corrections programs rose more than any other major program in fiscal year 1994 budgets. With the popularity of "three strikes and you're out" sentencing rules (life sentence after three convictions for violent felonies), big corrections increases appear likely to continue.

Welfare

The rate of increase of spending for Aid to Families with Dependent Children depends on two factors—growth in the number of recipients and changes in state policies concerning benefit levels and eligibility. Although the number of recipients rose sharply in response to the recession, the AFDC program was not a major source of pressure on state budgets because it accounts for a small proportion of state spending, approximately 3.4 percent in 1992.[14]

AFDC caseloads started to increase in 1989, a year before the national recession officially began. After growing 4.8 percent in 1990, the number of recipients jumped 10 percent in 1991 and 8.2 percent in 1992. The rate of increase varied widely, with the fastest growth occurring in New Hampshire, Florida, Arizona, Alaska, and Nevada (with increases of 112 percent to 61.7 percent).[15]

In most states, AFDC benefits failed to keep up with inflation. Between 1990 and 1994, only four states raised the maximum benefit for a family of three persons enough to keep real benefits from decreasing. Another twenty-two states raised benefits by less than inflation, seventeen states made no change in nominal benefits at all, and seven states reduced benefits. The reductions were in California (12.5 percent, with cuts each year from 1991 through 1993), Maine (7.7 percent), Maryland (7.8 percent), Michigan (5.2 percent), Oklahoma (0.3 percent), South Carolina (2.9 percent), and Vermont (3.2 percent).[16]

General assistance, which provides benefits to people ineligible for other welfare programs, was more of a target than AFDC. Of the twenty-eight states with statewide programs, seventeen eliminated eligibility for some or all recipients or cut benefits in either 1991 or 1992 or both years. Cuts were particularly deep in Michigan (which terminated its program in 1991), Ohio (which cut its program in half in 1991), Massachusetts, Illinois, and Maryland.[17]

Medicaid

Medicaid was at the heart of state fiscal policy during these years. The U.S. Health Care Financing Administration (HCFA) reports that state Medicaid spending rose 26.9 percent in 1991 and 27.9 percent in 1992.[18] It is hard to conceive how such huge increases can be accommodated within a budget whose total growth is only 5 percent or less. The federal spending figures do not tell the whole story.

The causes of Medicaid's explosive increase are not fully understood, but a study by the Kaiser Commission on the Future of Medicaid goes a long way toward explaining it. Examining the period from 1988 to 1991, the study found that four factors affected the magnitude of the increase:[19]

- More Medicaid recipients because of the recession, federal mandates that expanded eligibility, and other factors like enhanced outreach efforts (34.1 percent of the total increase);
- Increases in general medical care costs (31 percent);
- Greater use of services per beneficiary and provider payment increases above inflation (28.4 percent); and
- Higher premium payments for Medicare and HMOs (6.5 percent).

While most of the Medicaid spending increase during this period was uncontrollable from the states' viewpoint, a significant portion resulted from deliberate state initiatives. States increased Medicaid spending as part of a strategy to shift costs to the federal government in three ways:

- Many health programs that were formerly funded entirely from state revenues were transferred to Medicaid. Examples include mental health, developmental disabilities, and maternal and child health. (This shift was not a new development, but it continued in the early 1990s.)
- Most states initiated health care provider taxes or donation programs that enabled them to obtain more federal aid without burdening providers. Here is how such a scheme might operate: A state would increase payments to hospitals by, say, $100 million. This would entitle the state to at least $50 million of federal aid because Medicaid spending had increased, and the federal government matches state spending at least dollar for dollar. (In poor states, the federal government provides as much as $4 for each $1 of state Medicaid spending.) The state could then levy a tax on hospitals equal to $95 million. Hospitals would be ahead $5 million and the state would have an extra $45 million.
- After the federal government restricted provider taxes in November 1991 legislation, states increasingly turned to intergov-

ernmental transfers. These involve transfer of money from hospitals operated by local governments or state universities, with the funds being used as a match for federal Medicaid money. After receiving the federal payment, states return the money to the hospitals; although the hospitals receive more than they originally transferred to the state, substantial money is left over for the state to use for other health programs. In other words, intergovernmental transfers are like the donations that are no longer allowed, except that they can come only from government hospitals.

An estimated three-eighths of the increase in state Medicaid spending in 1992 was attributable to provider taxes and donations, generating almost $11 billion of federal aid.[20] That year is not typical of state efforts to shift costs through such mechanisms to the federal government because (a) in earlier years a smaller number of states used these mechanisms and (b) federal legislation in November 1991 curtailed the use of provider taxes and prohibited donations. Previously states could guarantee that no hospital would pay any more tax than it received back from the state. Such "hold harmless" provisions were prohibited by the 1991 legislation.[21]

It is important to emphasize that the nature of the Medicaid program changed markedly in the early 1990s, as many states realized the potential from provider taxes, donations, and intergovernmental transfers. States can obtain revenue for Medicaid from either the general fund, which is supported by conventional state taxes, or other sources, which are mainly provider taxes. As Table 2–7 shows, in

TABLE 2–7   Sources of State Medicaid Funding, 1990, 1991, 1992, and 1993 (Billions of Dollars)

Year	General Fund	Other Funds	Total	Percent Other Funds
1993	$38.7	$10.3	$49.0	21.1%
1992	35.1	8.4	43.5	19.3
1991	29.4	3.0	32.4	9.3
1990	25.1	1.5	26.7	5.8

Note: Funds from federal aid are excluded. 1993 figures are estimates.
Source: Melanie Nowacki, 1993 State Expenditure Report (National Association of State Budget Officers, 1994), p. 85. Melanie Nowacki, 1992 State Expenditure Report (National Association of State Budget Officers, 1993), p. 75.

1990 only 5.8 percent of state support for Medicaid came from sources other than the general fund. The following year, that proportion jumped to 9.3 percent, and in 1992 it doubled to 19.3 percent (with a further increase to 21.1 percent in 1993). According to NASBO, total state spending for Medicaid rose 21.4 percent in 1991 and 34.4 percent in 1992. But general fund support rose only 16.9 percent and 19.6 percent in those years. Support from nongeneral fund sources doubled in 1991 and was 2.8 times as high in 1992 as in 1991.

To make the situation even more complicated, states vary widely in the extent to which they took advantage of provider taxes and donations and shifted other health programs into Medicaid. As of April 1993, NASBO reported that only twenty-six states imposed taxes on health care providers.[22]

To summarize, the growth of Medicaid costs was a serious burden on the budgets of many states, but it was less of a problem than the figures for the total increase in Medicaid spending suggest.

It is noteworthy that Medicaid was generally spared from large state budget cuts during the fiscal crisis. Although provider reimbursements were often reduced, and some cuts in minor optional services and eligibility were adopted, relatively few major reductions were adopted. The major exception was in states that sharply reduced their general assistance programs. People who were eliminated from general assistance often lost eligibility for Medicaid and similar state-funded programs.[23]

State Employment

Although many states reduced employment, officials often exaggerated the magnitude of the decreases by announcing cuts in authorized general fund positions. They sometimes failed to note that many of the authorized positions were already vacant. Some states also shifted workers from general fund positions paid for by taxes to positions funded by fees and charges, which are not included in the general fund.

Consequently, reductions in state employment were much smaller than many media accounts implied.[24] On a seasonally adjusted basis, state employment reached a peak in June 1991, just before the start of a new fiscal year in most states. It then fell for three months, declining from 4,355,000 in June to 4,336,000 in September, a total decrease of only 19,000. In the following year, employment rose to a new peak, 4,401,000 in September 1992. In the next six months, no further advance occurred; in fact, employment decreased slightly, to 4,395,000 in March 1993.

These national averages of course obscure a great deal of variation from state to state. Between June 1990 and June 1993, employment rose in thirty states and fell in sixteen (with two states having unchanged employment and no data available in two other states). Eight states cut employment by at least 5 percent: Illinois, Massachusetts, Michigan, Montana, New Hampshire, New York, Pennsylvania, and Vermont. On the other hand, eighteen states increased employment by at least 5 percent.[25]

An important impact of the fiscal crisis was to slow the rise of employee salaries. In fact, in many states most employees went without any raises at all for several years. State employee salaries went up much more slowly than in the 1980s and less than increases in the private sector.

Summary

The major findings about spending policies during the fiscal crisis are:

- Spending increases slowed but remained above the inflation rate in most states. Much of the increase went for Medicaid and corrections, resulting in real decreases for other programs.
- School aid was under pressure. After adjusting for inflation and enrollment growth, it increased little if at all. As a result, local property taxes picked up more of the cost of education.
- Higher education suffered more than any other major part of the budget, with small reductions in state support in two years. This resulted in large tuition and fee increases.
- Corrections spending slowed from its double-digit increases of the 1980s, but it still grew faster than average.
- Welfare spending increased sharply in 1991 and 1992 as caseloads swelled but increases were much smaller in the next two years. Many states slashed general assistance programs, and numerous states also cut AFDC benefit levels; most states made no adjustments in benefits for inflation.
- Medicaid was by far the fastest growing component of state budgets, although part of the increase was due to state maneu-

vers to increase federal aid. Even excluding the effects of those actions, Medicaid spending was a major budget problem for most states.

- State employment rose nationally at a slow rate, although it fell moderately in many states. Employee salary increases slowed.

POLICIES AFFECTING LOCAL GOVERNMENTS

Aid to cities and counties was not a high priority for states. With states having great difficulty maintaining balance in their own budgets, they were often tempted to adopt policies that shifted fiscal stress to local governments. This was truly a period of "fend-for-yourself federalism."[26]

One significant indicator of how the intergovernmental system is changing is the rate of increase in tax revenue at various levels of government. Although it does not have a great deal of visibility, more and more of the tax burden is being borne at the local level. In every year since 1985, local taxes have risen faster than state taxes. The largest increases have occurred among counties, but city and school district tax increases have also exceeded those at the state level.[27]

One contributor to this trend has been state aid policy. With Medicaid and corrections taking most of the relatively small increase in revenue, little was left over for local financial assistance. Between 1990 and 1992, aid to local governments rose more slowly than state spending for other programs in more than forty states. The most useful kind of aid, that which can be used for any purpose, was hit especially hard.

Many states compensated for aid cutbacks by relaxing the restrictions that they placed on the taxes that local governments could use. Twelve states, for example, provided more flexibility in use of local sales taxes.[28]

In general, states did not devote much attention to reforming state-local relations. Some states relieved cities and counties of certain functions, but others thrust new responsibilities on them. A few states enacted new restrictions on their own ability to impose unfunded mandates, but most states continued to increase the number of mandates, just as they complained of the federal government doing to them.

CONCLUSIONS AND QUESTIONS

States came through the fiscal crisis of the early 1990s with major changes in higher education (less state support and more reliance on tuition) and in some cases scaled down welfare programs (especially in states that formerly had relatively generous programs). They also were devoting a bigger share of their resources to health programs because of the growth of Medicaid. In terms of taxes, there was some reform and some significant increases, but most states had a tax system in 1993 that was very similar to that of 1989 (except that they had introduced new taxes on health care providers).

Is that all that changed? Unfortunately, we do not know a great deal about how state programs changed in the early 1990s. One of the paramount questions addressed in this book is: *How much did states restructure their programs to enhance efficiency and effectiveness?* Widespread discussion was stimulated by the best-selling book *Reinventing Government*, which recommended overhauling the way services are provided by relying more on markets, incentives, and decentralization.

NASBO maintains that ". . . many states are making fundamental changes in the way state government is organized and managed and in the way services are delivered to improve quality, increase efficiency and reduce costs. . . . States have eliminated programs and have launched initiatives to reorganize state government, consolidate agencies, evaluate privatization of services and otherwise improve productivity."[29]

Dall Forsythe, former New York State budget director, has a different view of this issue:[30]

> Logic might suggest that an environment of scarcity would intensify efforts to provide services through more efficient, customer-oriented models. However, the record of the last few years provides little support for this hypothesis. More typically, tight budgets in state and local governments seem to lead to disruption which drives out innovation and undercuts efforts to reorient service delivery.

The six states discussed in this book provide an excellent basis for evaluating these contrasting views. The governors of five of these states (Chiles, Engler, Weld, Weicker, and Wilson) have been in the forefront of the movement that questions the traditional way of doing business. Minnesota's Governor, Arne Carlson, also made reinvention rhetoric a major theme.

Another important issue will be considered in the six case study states: Who were the casualties of the state budget and tax policies of the 1990s? It appears that students at state institutions of higher education, poor people, and state workers have often borne the brunt of state fiscal strategies. To what extent is this perception accurate? Are there other groups that have been systematically disadvantaged?

A period of recession cannot serve as a basis for extrapolating future fiscal conditions. But the prediction that the 1990s would be much more fiscally challenging than the 1980s relied on a variety of assumptions that can and should be reviewed:[31]

- *Aid for elementary-secondary schools would have to increase because of higher enrollments.* States have not increased aid much, instead allowing local governments to pick up a bigger share of school costs.
- *Increases in Medicaid spending would place a severe strain on state budgets.* While this has occurred to some extent, the ability of states to shift costs to the federal government has significantly helped them to cope with this problem.
- *Big increases in prison populations would continue to push up corrections spending.* States have slowed prison construction and failed to use some newly constructed prisons, while cutting services in prisons. But corrections spending remains one of the fastest growing parts of state budgets.
- *The federal government would add to state fiscal problems by imposing new mandates and failing to increase aid significantly.* Federal aid has actually increased considerably as a result of the explosive growth of Medicaid and other developments.
- *Weak economic growth would slow increases of revenue.* This has occurred.
- *Court decisions would add to state fiscal problems.* This is occurring. For example, courts have recently issued rulings overturning the school finance systems in Alabama, Missouri, North Dakota, and Tennessee. A solution to Texas' school finance problem continues to be elusive. There is no apparent letup in

adverse court rulings in other areas, such as requiring that hospitals be given more generous reimbursements (as required by the Boren Amendment).

To summarize, in two major areas, school aid and prisons, states have slowed the growth of spending. In Medicaid, the states have been able to shift many costs to the federal government and in some cases obtain federal aid that helped with the finance of nonhealth programs. Will these trends continue? We will return to these questions in the final chapter of this book.

APPENDIX

COMPARISON OF SPENDING INCREASE DATA FROM VARIOUS SOURCES

In many cases, the estimates from various sources were relatively close, but in some instances there were large discrepancies. Table 2–6 reported the estimate judged to be most credible or the number free of distortions caused by shifting of appropriations between fiscal years. In some cases, the best choice among sources was not clear.

In all cases, note that the increase in 1993 is for appropriations, with an estimate for a fiscal year that was not complete at the time of reporting. Increases for 1992 were estimates made within a few months of the end of the fiscal year, so they are subject to revision.

Total General Fund Spending

NCSL and NASBO estimates were close. General fund spending is a better measure of how tax revenue was used than all funds spending, which reflects earmarked revenues, especially health care provider taxes.

Source	1991	1992	1993
NCSL	5.2%	5.4%	3.0%
NASBO	4.5	5.1	3.3

School Aid

Table 2–6 uses data from the National Education Association because it is free of distortions caused by deferral of appropriations from one year to another. NEA data also include state funding of teacher pensions, which is not included by the other sources. Because it focuses exclusively on this area of spending, it is assumed to be more accurate. NEA data were also collected at a later date than the other two.

Source	1991	1992	1993
NEA	7.1%	3.5%	1.3%
NCSL	3.8	4.4	4.3
NASBO	3.6	5.5	4.0

Higher Education

Table 2–6 uses data from Illinois State University's Center for Higher Education, *The Grapevine*, which reports appropriations of tax dollars for higher education operating expenses. Because it focuses exclusively on this area of spending, it is assumed to be more reliable. A problem with NASBO's data is that it includes tuition increases in some but not all states.

Source	1991	1992	1993
Grapevine	1.8%	0.5%	−1.5%
NCSL	−0.2	2.2	−0.2
NASBO	−1.0	3.3	2.1

Corrections

There is a major difference in 1991 and 1992 between NCSL and NASBO, with little basis for choosing between them. For the combined two-year period, they are very close. NCSL's data is for the general fund, NASBO's for all state funds.

Source	1991	1992	1993
NCSL	16.5%	2.0%	4.5%
NASBO	9.2	4.3	6.9

Aid to Families with Dependent Children

There is a large difference between NCSL and NASBO in 1991, with NCSL's increase being judged to be implausibly low. Therefore, NASBO's estimates are used for those years.

Source	1991	1992	1993
NASBO	9.0%	9.8%	4.9
NCSL	2.4	1.2	4.7

Medicaid

Table 2–6 uses NASBO's estimates, although there was no clear superiority for them compared to NCSL's. The NCSL increase for 1993 is likely to be much too low, reflecting underestimates in budgets enacted by states.

Source	1991	1992	1993
NASBO, all funds	21.4%	34.4%	12.7
General fund	16.9	19.6	10.2
NCSL	14.4	28.5	6.2

Transportation

The only available information was NASBO's estimates.

NOTES

1. This analysis draws heavily on Steven D. Gold, "The Federal Role in State Fiscal Stress," *Publius* 22 (Summer 1992), pp. 33–47.

2. The growth of Medicaid spending and court decisions were not completely beyond the control of states. As discussed below, Medicaid increases were partially due to state policies to maximize federal aid. Harold Hovey argues that many court decisions were consistent with the agenda of state officials who desired to pursue the policies required by judges.

3. As discussed below, the increases reported by NASBO somewhat exaggerate the magnitude of the Medicaid problem for states, but even using more appropriate figures, it was a serious burden on their budgets. Teresa

A. Coughlin, et al., *Medicaid Since 1980* (Washington, DC: The Urban Institute, 1994).

4. This section draws heavily on Steven D. Gold, "Trends in Federal Aid to States since 1989: Not What Many People Assume," *State Tax Notes* (June 18, 1993). It has been updated to reflect revisions reported in the federal budget released in February 1994.

5. These measures of the size of tax increases do not include taxes on health care providers or extension of temporary tax increases that were scheduled to expire. For a discussion of measurement issues, see Steven D. Gold, "The Anatomy and Magnitude of State Tax Increases in 1992," *State Tax Notes* 4 (January 18, 1993), pp. 136–140; and Steven D. Gold, "Tax Increases Shriveled in 1993," *State Tax Notes* 5 (December 27, 1993), pp. 1547–1550.

6. Steven D. Gold, "What Did the 1992 Election Results Say about State Fiscal Policy?," *State Tax Notes* 3 (December 14, 1992), pp. 897–900.

7. Paul R. Blackley and Larry DeBoer, "Explaining State Discretionary Tax Increases in Fiscal Years 1991 and 1992," *National Tax Journal* 46 (March 1993), pp. 1–12.

8. Although North Carolina is shown as relying primarily on the sales tax, it did increase the income tax for returns with income above $100,000.

9. Steven D. Gold and Jennifer McCormick, "State Tax Reform in the Early 1990s," *State Tax Notes* (May 2, 1994), pp. 1146–1161. The conclusion that most states increased the balance of their tax systems excludes states that already had balanced tax systems and states that did not impose both the sales and income taxes. Among the remaining states that had a large tax increase in the early 1990s, six of eight relied more heavily on the tax that was previously underutilized.

10. For a summary of where significant reforms occurred and where shifts away from reform took place, see Gold and McCormick, "State Tax Reform in the Early 1990s."

11. The 3.3 percent increase in 1993 was heavily influenced by California, which substituted local property taxes for state school aid. Excluding California, the increase was 4.8 percent.

12. National Education Association, *1993–94 Estimates of School Statistics* (Washington, DC: 1994), p. 22.

13. The College Entrance Examination Board, *Annual Survey of Colleges*.

14. National Association of State Budget Officers, *State Expenditure Report 1992*.

15. U.S. House of Representatives, Committee on Ways and Means, *The Green Book, 1992*.

16. Four other states reduced benefits in some years even though benefits in 1994 were nominally higher than they were in 1990: Alaska, Nevada, Ohio, and Tennessee.

17. Ibid.

18. U.S. Congressional Research Service, *Medicaid Source Book: Background Data and Analysis (A 1993 Update)*, p. 83.

19. John Holahan, et al., "Explaining Recent Growth in Medical Spending," *Health Affairs* (Fall 1993), pp. 177–193; and Judith Feder, et al., *The*

Medicaid Cost Explosion: Causes and Consequences (Baltimore: Kaiser Commission on the Future of Medicaid, 1993); Teresa Coughlin, *Medicaid since 1980* (Washington, DC: The Urban Institute, 1994).

20. Estimates from Vic Miller and the Health Care Financing Administration cited in Feder, pp. 24–25.

21. Coughlin, *Medicaid since 1980*, pp. 81–99.

22. This is very likely an undercount of the number of states with provider taxes. A survey by the American Hospital Association reported that as of July 1992, thirty-three states had tax or donation programs. (Memorandum dated August 21, 1992 to AHA affiliates from the Financial Policy and Capital Finance units of AHA.) In November 1993, NCSL reported that thirty-five states had provider taxes. Corina Eckl, et al., *State Budget Actions 1993*, p. 38.

23. Debra J. Lipson and Steven D. Gold, *State Budget Crises and Their Effect on State Health Care Access Initiatives* (Portland, ME: National Academy for State Health Policy, 1992); Isaac Shapiro et al., *States and the Poor* (Washington, DC: Center on Budget and Policy Priorities and Center for the Study of the States, 1991); Iris Lav et al., *States and the Poor* (Washington, DC: Center on Budget and Policy Priorities and Center for the Study of the States, 1992).

24. NASBO's fiscal surveys are somewhat misleading because they report changes in authorized general fund positions. See, e.g., Stacey Mazer, *Fiscal Survey of the States* (April 1993), p. 15.

25. Sarah Ritchie, "State-Local Employment Continues to Grow," *State Tax Notes* (December 13, 1993).

26. This phrase was coined in the mid-1980s by John Shannon, former executive director of the U.S. Advisory Commission on Intergovernmental Relations.

27. Steven D. Gold, "Local Taxes Outpace State Taxes," *State Tax Notes* (August 2, 1993).

28. Steven D. Gold and Sarah Ritchie, "State Policies Affecting Cities and Counties, 1990–1993: De Facto Federalism," *Public Budgeting and Finance* (forthcoming, Summer 1994).

29. Mazer, p. 31.

30. Dall W. Forsythe, "Financial Management and the Reinvention of Government," *Public Productivity and Management Review*, forthcoming.

31. Steven D. Gold, *The State Fiscal Agenda for the 1990s* (Denver: National Conference of State Legislatures, 1990), ch. 3.

PART II

The Fiscal Crisis in Depth

3

A Framework for Viewing State Policies

Steven D. Gold

Several of the major concepts used throughout this book may have varying meanings, so the sense in which they can be used has to be discussed. The three major issues are what is meant by the term *crisis*, how the strategies of the states should be classified, and how to analyze priorities and identify winners and losers in budget battles.

THE MEANING OF *CRISIS*

The dictionary has several definitions of *crisis*. One is "a turning point in the course of anything; a decisive or crucial time, stage, or event." Another is "a crucial situation; a situation whose outcome decides whether possible bad consequences will follow; as, an economic *crisis.*"

As applied to state governments, a fiscal crisis is usually precipitated by a significant prospective imbalance between revenues and expenditures. A *short-term* fiscal crisis exists when a state faces a large deficit in its budget for the current or the next fiscal year. This may be distinguished from a *long-term* crisis, which occurs when a state has a structural deficit.

States have a structural deficit when the revenue produced by their current tax system (along with revenue from other sources) is insufficient to allow them to maintain the existing level of services. Whether or not a state has a structural deficit depends on many factors:

- *The nature of its tax system.* Revenue from the personal income tax tends to grow faster than the economy, but other taxes usually lag behind economic growth. Therefore, the more a state depends on the income tax (and the more progressive that tax is), the faster its revenue will grow, other things being equal.

- *The rate of economic growth.* Even an inelastic tax system (that is, one where revenue grows more slowly than the economy) will produce substantial increases in revenue if the economy booms. This revenue windfall may be only partly offset by the fact that a growing economy requires more government spending to maintain services.
- *Demographic changes.* States vary considerably in how fast their school enrollment is increasing. This is particularly important because school aid is normally the largest program in state budgets. Other demographic factors that affect the demand for government services include the size of the populations in the sixteen to twenty-four-year-old group (which influences the crime rate and higher education enrollments) and senior citizens (which affects the demand for nursing homes and other services). The number of immigrants and members of minority groups also affects service demands.
- *Federal policies.* Increasing federal aid can reduce structural deficits, but unfunded federal mandates can increase them.
- *State spending practices.* Policies that determine spending by formulas or indexation of benefits and initiatives such as imposing strict sentencing of criminals or establishing liberal eligibility for programs affect the level of future spending. Policies affecting the productivity of employees, such as civil service reform and other "reinvention of government" themes, could also have a major impact.
- *Inflation.* If health costs rise much faster than the general price level, this tends to make spending increase faster than revenue.

The distinction between a short-term and a long-term fiscal crisis is an important one. The short-term crisis of the early 1990s ended by 1993 in most states as the economy expanded and the growth of Medicaid costs slowed, but many states are still believed to have long-term structural deficits.[1]

It is important to emphasize that the definition of crisis discussed above is based on maintenance of the existing level of services. Those citizens who feel that services are too generous would not object to a reduction in services if that were needed to bring the state budget into balance. On the other hand, some citizens may believe that a crisis exists in a different sense—namely that services are inadequate, for example, that schools are not properly preparing children for the future. That kind of a crisis could exist even if there is no structural deficit.

STRATEGIES TO CONFRONT CRISES

There is a great deal of loose talk about how states should pursue innovative policies. One definition of an innovation is "something newly introduced; a new method, custom, device, etc." Another is "a change in the way of doing things." The subtle difference between these two meanings accounts for considerable confusion.

Used loosely, one can say that one state's bold new innovation is another's hallowed old custom. In this sense, a policy is innovative if it is a change in the way of doing things in a particular state even though other states have already adopted it. On the other hand, in a strict sense, a policy can be said to be innovative only if it has never been used before.[2]

When states are in fiscal crises, it is not really necessary for them to adopt innovative policies in the strict sense. They should abandon "business as usual," but in doing so they can usually adopt policies that other states have already had in effect. As one of the key legislators in Connecticut observed after the short-term fiscal crisis had passed, "None of the things we've done as reforms are new ideas . . . [it's] just that the time has come in Connecticut."

In fact, often innovative policies are of little if any value because they are nothing more than gimmicks. If no state has ever adopted a certain policy, it could be because they rejected it, rather than because they had not thought of it or lacked the courage to adopt it. Or it could be beneficial but only marginally so. For example, in mid-1994 an innovative policy proposed in Ohio was for the state to establish a mutual fund that would invest in Ohio companies. This was touted as a way to stimulate savings, help Ohio companies raise capital, and generate profits that would avoid the need for tax increases. Realistically, such a mutual fund would do little to stimulate savings or generate capital, and the profits would have an insignificant effect on the state budget. But it would compete with private mutual funds and create a false impression in some people's minds that it would help keep taxes down. Many innovations are like this.

Currently a great deal of interest has been stimulated by the book *Reinventing Government*, which urges that state and local governments adopt numerous reforms such as decentralizing, privatizing, deregulating, becoming more enterprising, and reforming budgeting to make it results-oriented rather than input-oriented. None of these ideas are innovative in the strict sense. They have been tried in the past, some successfully and some unsuccessfully. For example, all governments already rely to some extent on the private sector to provide them with certain services. Many states have tried to implement performance budgeting[3] with little or no success.

But the fact that these policies are not really new does not imply that the reinvention movement is off base. Many states could benefit from overcoming inertia and adopting policies that have already been used successfully elsewhere.

Performance budgeting is different from some of the other reinvention themes in that it may be more feasible now because of new developments in technology. The proliferation of low-cost computer technology is a big potential help in efforts to track the results of government programs. But the problems of measuring the impact of services remain formidable because many environmental factors affect outcomes.

States really have three alternatives in dealing with fiscal crises— cutting spending, raising revenue, and adopting gimmicks that allow them to postpone facing up to problems. Each of these alternatives can be further distinguished according to whether they improve state fiscal operations: Do they merely help the state muddle through the current crisis, or do they contribute to making spending or taxation more efficient or equitable?

Cutting Spending

The politically easiest policy is often to cut across the board because that can be rationalized as sharing the pain evenly. Other easy policies are to cut programs that benefit those who do not vote much, like poor people, and to cut activities that do not produce visible short-term benefits such as maintenance of buildings.

A better approach is to cut spending while implementing reforms that enhance efficiency. This could involve some of the reinvention themes mentioned above (like privatization) or less esoteric policies like shifting from providing services in an institutional setting to less costly alternatives like community-based services.

Another positive approach is to reorder priorities in a way that recognizes that all programs are not equally important. Many states, for example, claim to place a higher priority on preventive services than on programs that merely react to problems. For example, improving health care for pregnant women helps to reduce the number of low birthweight babies.

Increasing Revenue[4]

If a state has a structural deficit, it makes sense for it to raise taxes in a way that increases the responsiveness of the tax system to economic growth. Another desirable approach is to close loopholes (or, more abstractly, to broaden the tax base) rather than to increase tax rates. If a state underutilizes an important potential tax base, it should favor increasing the tax on it rather than raising a tax that is already relatively high.

Gimmicks

Gimmicks—policies that provide a one-shot injection of revenue or one-time savings on expenditures—are not necessarily undesirable. For example, if a state refinances bonds to take advantage of lower interest rates, it is mimicking homeowners who refinance their mortgages. If pension funds are more than fully funded, there is nothing wrong with reducing contributions to them. If a state facility is no longer needed or competes with a private business, it makes sense for such an asset to be sold. Likewise, sometimes it is possible to shift costs to the federal government, substituting federal for state dollars. It would be foolhardy not to do so.

But many gimmicks merely shift costs to a later period, when they will be higher, to the private sector, or to local governments. States sometimes temporize by borrowing funds rather than balancing their budget each year. Although shortchanging pension funds is not normally reported as debt, unfunded pension liabilities have similar effects in that they shift burdens to the future.

What Is a Reform?[5]

A reform is a change in the normal way of doing business that represents an effort to improve. Thus, it gets away from "business as usual" and is inherently value-laden. One person's reform may be another person's backward step. In this sense, a reform in one state may be a well-established practice somewhere else.

Reforms in different states may go in opposite directions. For example, one state may exempt food from the sales tax in order to make its tax system less regressive, while another state may repeal that exemption to broaden its tax base. One state may adopt civil service protections to reduce the influence of patronage while another state liberalizes civil service rules to give administrators more flexibility in hiring.

In terms of spending, reforms may try to implement some of the *reinventing government* themes, or they may reorient budget priorities. In terms of taxation, reforms may aim to make the tax system more fair or favorable to economic development or to increase the neutrality, stability, or elasticity of the tax system. In state-local relations, reforms may give local governments more flexibility in raising revenue, target aid more effectively, reduce state mandates, or change incentives to increase accountability. These examples are not exhaustive but merely illustrate some of the common kinds of reforms that states can undertake.

ANALYZING PRIORITIES

It is not as easy to evaluate a state's priorities as it appears at first glance. For example, suppose that during a certain period one program grows from 10 percent to 12 percent of the budget while another falls from 30 percent to 29 percent. In a sense, one could call the first program a budget "winner" and the second a "loser" and say that the state was placing a higher priority on the first program, but those conclusions could be considered superficial.

What if the caseload of the first program grew substantially and its costs were subject to a higher rate of inflation, while the caseload of the second program decreased? To deal with these issues, many states use "current services" or "baseline" budgets. These budgets measure how much a state would have to spend to maintain the existing level of services, taking changes in workload and inflation into account.

Medicaid (the federal-state program that provides health care for some but not all low-income people) is a prime example of why this matters. After 1990 its costs grew sharply, in part because of more people being eligible and the high rate of inflation in health costs. As discussed in Chapter 5, Medicaid consumed a larger share of the budget in all six states discussed in this book. But that does not necessarily mean that Medicaid recipients were "winners" in the battle for state resources. An individual Medicaid recipient did not receive 20 percent more service just because the state and federal governments spent 20 percent more on him or her.

An important change in Medicaid during this period was that many low-income children and pregnant women became eligible for the first time. They can certainly be classified as "winners," but that does not necessarily imply that their state deserves any credit (although numerous governors took credit for expanding preventive programs). The federal government mandated this expansion in eligibility (although states did have discretion about how far above the poverty line to expand coverage).

Thus, a strong argument can be made that state priorities should be gauged by analyzing how states departed from maintenance of previous service levels, taking federal mandates into account. If Medicaid eligibility, services, or reimbursement rates were cut, that would imply that spending was reduced in terms of current services even though it increased in real dollars or as a share of the budget.

But determination of priorities is not that simple. A counterargument is that the decision to maintain current services is itself an important judgment about priorities, one that could require raising taxes. Many governors during this period advocated abandonment of current service spending projections as part of the budget process, calling instead for budget deliberations to begin with the actual spending in the previous year.

The hypothetical example at the start of this section referred to the shares of the budget devoted to different programs as a measure of priorities. That is a relative measure. During a recession it is not uncommon for a program to become a larger share of the budget even though its funding is decreasing in inflation-adjusted dollars. A program could be a relative winner and an absolute loser.

Aid to elementary-secondary schools is the largest program in most state budgets. In the example at the start of this section, it could be the program that fell from 30 percent to 29 percent of the budget. Whether that represented an increase or a decrease as a budget priority depends partly on what is happening to enrollment. In the early 1990s, enrollment trends varied widely from state to state, increasing sharply in some states while falling in others.

Another issue in analyzing priorities is whether to consider all spending including federal aid or just spending of state funds. If the federal matching rate increased,[6] as it did in many states during this period, a state could cut its own contribution without reducing a program's total budget.

Likewise, a distinction could be made between state funds from conventional taxes and money from innovative gimmicks like hospital taxes and intergovernmental transfers. As discussed in Chapter 2, these innovative gimmicks provided a method of obtaining more federal aid without taking anything away from other state programs. A strong case can be made that the state spending paid for by revenue from these gimmicks should not be counted in analyzing state priorities.

The bottom line is that there is room for disagreement about how to analyze state priorities. In many cases, several different perspectives are valid, although some views are more appropriate than others. The case studies in this book do not all employ the same framework, but the discussion in this section should be helpful in placing the varying perspectives in an overall context.

NOTES

1. A report published in 1994 by the leading organizations of state officials argued that many states have structural deficits and therefore should reform their tax systems. A survey of legislative leaders in late 1993 found that half of them believed that their states would have difficulty balancing their budgets in five years unless they made significant changes in tax or spending policies. See National Governors' Association and National Conference of State Legislatures, *Financing State Government in the 1990s* (Washington, DC: December 1993); also, Raymond C. Scheppach, statement to U.S. House of Representatives Committee on Governmental Operations, Subcommittee on Human Resources and Intergovernmental Relations, October 6, 1993.

2. The Ford Foundation honors particularly successful innovative state and local programs. To be eligible, a program has to "take a new approach to a pressing social need or significantly improve an existing program." One of the selection criteria is the "program's novelty, judged by the degree to which it demonstrates a leap of creativity."

3. Performance budgeting involves projecting what government programs will accomplish and then measuring how well they meet these projections. According to national authorities, Texas and Oregon are currently two of the most advanced states in attempting to use this budgeting approach.

4. These ideas are discussed in Steven D. Gold, *Tax Options for States Needing More School Revenue* (Washington, DC: National Education Association, 1994).

5. For discussions of state tax reform options, see Steven D. Gold, ed. *The Unfinished Agenda for State Tax Reform* (Denver: National Conference of State Legislatures, 1988); for state-local reforms, see Steven D. Gold, *Reforming State-Local Relations: A Practical Guide* (Denver: National Conference of State Legislatures, 1989); for spending reforms and condensed discussions of the other kinds of reforms, see Steven D. Gold, *The State Fiscal Agenda for the 1990s* (Denver: National Conference of State Legislatures, 1990).

6. The federal matching rate determines how much of a program's cost is paid by the federal government. For Medicaid and Aid to Families with Dependent Children, it is based on a moving average of a particular state's per capita income compared to the national average per capita income. Between 1986 and 1992 it rose in many states because the dispersion of state per capita income was increasing. Victor J. Miller, "State Medicaid Expansion in the Early 1990s: Program Growth in a Period of Fiscal Stress," in Diane Rowland et al., *Medicaid Financing Crisis* (Washington, DC: American Association for the Advancement of Science, 1993), pp. 124–25.

4

How Typical are These States?

Sarah Ritchie*

The six states examined in this book were chosen because of the severity of their fiscal crises during the early 1990s and the possibility that their policies might be particularly innovative and instructive for other states. They are not a representative cross section of all fifty states. They tend to be larger and have higher taxes and spending than most states. They were also affected more severely by the recession than "typical" states. They all elected new governors in 1990.

There are some significant differences among the states. Florida has lower taxes and spending than the others. The four states with Republican governors during this period—California, Massachusetts, Michigan, and Minnesota—were formerly relatively liberal in their fiscal policies. California and Massachusetts were the sites of the most severe tax revolts between 1978 and 1980, leaving them with strict tax limitations (Proposition 13 and Proposition 2 1/2, respectively). Michigan had a major tax revolt in 1983, resulting in the recall of two Democratic state senators and the shift of control of the senate to the Republican party. Fiscal conservatism has not had as much effect in Minnesota, although state tax cuts in 1985 had a major impact on slowing the growth of its spending.

This chapter examines the states in seven ways—their demography, income level, spending patterns, tax systems, fiscal policies during the boom of the mid-1980s, degree of fiscal stress, and changes in state-local employment levels. In most cases statistics used are for fiscal year 1991, a period that came early enough so that it was not influenced much by policies adopted in response to the fiscal crisis.

*Sarah Ritchie is the Assistant Director of the Center for the Study of the States at the Nelson A. Rockefeller Institute of Government.

The figures discussed in the text are found in Table 4-1 at the end of this chapter.

DEMOGRAPHICS AND INCOME

All of the states except Connecticut have larger population than the median state. In fact, California, Florida, and Michigan are among the ten most populous states. In 1991 California had the largest population with 30.4 million residents, 12 percent of the national total. Florida, with 13.3 million residents, ranked fourth in population, and Michigan ranked eighth. The remaining states ranked as follows: Massachusetts (thirteenth), Minnesota (twentieth), and Connecticut (twenty-seventh). California and Florida had rapid population growth between 1990 and 1993, 6.8 percent and 5.7 percent respectively, while Connecticut and Massachusetts were among four American states that lost population during this period. Michigan and Minnesota had population increases slightly below the national average.

The age distributions of state residents differ considerably. Florida, long a retirement haven, had the largest proportion of residents over the age of 65 in the country in 1991—18.3 percent—about 5½ points higher than the national average. On the other hand, senior citizens accounted for only one in ten California residents. School-aged children (ages five to seventeen) comprised 19.2 percent of the total population in Minnesota but only 15.7 percent in Florida and Massachusetts. (The national average was 18.2 percent.) These demographic traits are important because elderly people and school children place special demands on states and localities; children require education services and older individuals need health and welfare programs such as Medicaid.

Most of the six states have relatively high per capita income. Connecticut is the richest state in the country with a per capita income nearly $7,000 above the national average of $18,651 in 1991.[1] Per capita personal income in Massachusetts was also very high, $22,569. Per capita income in Minnesota is slightly above average while Florida and Michigan had a per capita income level slightly below the national average.

Although most of these states had below-average poverty rates, they had higher unemployment levels than the "typical" state in 1991.

In that year, Connecticut, Massachusetts, Michigan, and Minnesota had poverty rates less than the national average of 14.2 percent, while California and Florida had above average poverty. But the recession hit the states comparatively hard. Minnesota was the only state where the unemployment rate was below average. (Connecticut's unemployment rate was equal to the national average.) Michigan's economy was particularly vulnerable, and its unemployment rate was 9.2 percent, nearly two and one-half points higher than the national average.

SPENDING

Spending can be related to either population or personal income. Because most of these states have relatively high personal income, their spending levels appear lower when compared to income than to population.

Most of these states spend more than average. State-local per capita spending was at least $375 above the $3,591 national average in California, Connecticut, Massachusetts, and Minnesota. Michigan's spending was about average and Florida's was nearly 5 percent below average. But relative to personal income, Minnesota spent significantly above average, California and Michigan were about average, and Connecticut, Florida, and Massachusetts were below average.

Elementary-Secondary Education

Connecticut, Massachusetts, and Minnesota had comparatively high state spending per pupil in elementary-secondary schools. State-local per pupil spending in Connecticut was $3,000 above the national average of $4,982 in 1991, when Connecticut had the second lowest teacher-pupil ratio and the highest average teacher salary in the nation. Per pupil spending in Florida was above average, and Michigan and California were about average in this spending category.

When analyzing elementary-secondary expenditures, it is important to note that states differ in the extent to which localities contribute to school funding. Nationally, states contributed 52.6 percent of state-local K–12 expenditures. California's state portion far exceeded the national average, 72.6 percent. Connecticut, Florida, and Minnesota were within five percentage points of the national average while Massachusetts and Michigan were well below average.

Higher Education

California, Michigan, and Minnesota had above average higher education spending in 1991, in relation to both population and income.[2] These states have a tradition of strong state-supported higher education systems with large flagship universities and extensive community college programs.[3] In Connecticut per capita spending for higher education was about average while spending per $100 income was below average. Florida and Massachusetts posted below average spending by both measures. All of the states except Florida had above average tuition and fees; the two New England states had especially high tuition.[4]

Income Maintenance

Except for Florida, all of these states provided relatively high welfare benefits in 1991. While the national average Aid to Families with Dependent Children (AFDC) monthly benefits for a family of three was $367, five of these states had benefits above $500, and California provided $694, the second highest in the country. To some degree, these high benefits reflected higher than average cost of living in these states.[5]

They were also generous in terms of the two other income maintenance programs, General Assistance and Supplemental Security Income.[6] Four of the states had General Assistance benefits among the seven highest in the nation, while Michigan's was the sixteenth highest. However, Florida had no program. All six states had above-average state SSI supplements.[7]

Medicaid

Medicaid spending depends on the variety and cost of services provided and the number of participants.[8] State Medicaid spending per capita ranged from $116 in Florida to $377 in Massachusetts. Connecticut, Massachusetts, Michigan, and Minnesota were all above the national average of $156 in 1991. California and Florida had below average per capita Medicaid spending.

Corrections

Four of the six states spent considerably more than the national average of $71 per capita on corrections. Florida was about average, and Minnesota fell almost $40 below the national average. Corrections spending per capita depends on the number of prisoners and the amount of money spent per prisoner. All of the states except Florida were above average in per prisoner spending.[9] Connecticut, Florida, Michigan, and California had high incarceration rates, while Massachusetts and Minnesota had low incarceration rates. Minnesota, for instance, has traditionally favored community corrections programs over prison detention.[10] Florida is the only state in this study in which the entire correctional system is under a court order due to prison overcrowding and poor conditions. However, in the remainder of the states, at least one institution is under a similar court order.

TAXATION

Levels of State-Local Taxes

As in the case of spending, taxes can be compared in relation either to population or personal income. The two measurements tell somewhat different stories about how high taxes were in 1991. Minnesota and Michigan had above average levels of taxation by both standards. California, Connecticut, and Massachusetts had above average tax revenue per capita and below average tax revenue per $100 personal income. In other words, per capita taxes were high because of the affluence of the state, not because states and local governments were taking a larger than average share of residents' income. Only Florida had below average state-local taxes per capita and per $100 personal income.

This description of tax levels refers to combined state and local taxes. Both must be considered in comparing taxes among states.

Tax Centralization

These states differed in the degree of reliance on state taxes as opposed to local taxes. Minnesota was the most fiscally centralized, with state taxes accounting for nearly two-thirds of total tax revenue in 1991. California and Massachusetts also had above average degrees of centralization. California had been fiscally decentralized prior to the passage of Proposition 13, a voter initiative that cut local property taxes sharply in 1978. It then became centralized when the state stepped in to replace most of the lost local revenue.

Connecticut, Florida, and Michigan had comparatively decentralized tax systems in 1991, although Michigan's 1994 property tax reform made it considerably more centralized. Michigan raised the state sales tax to provide property tax relief.

State-Local Tax Structures

The national shares of state-local tax revenue were distributed in 1991 as follows: personal income tax (20.8 percent), property tax (32.0 percent), sales tax (23.9 percent), and other taxes (23.3 percent). California and Minnesota had tax systems that most closely resembled the national averages. With no broad-based personal income tax, Florida and Connecticut had unbalanced systems. Both states depended heavily on sales taxes to generate revenue, and Florida's robust tourist industry allowed the state to export some of its sales tax burden to nonresidents. State-local taxes in Michigan were dominated by property taxes, which accounted for over 40 percent of total revenue.[11] Massachusetts and Minnesota relied heavily on the personal income tax.

Nontax Revenues

Taxes account for the lion's share of revenue generated by states and localities. However, federal aid and user charges are two important nontax revenue sources.

In 1991, Massachusetts and Minnesota received federal aid in excess of the national average, $3.20 per $100 of personal income. The lowest amount of aid was received in Florida, which was 33 percent below the national average. These variations reflect the differences in spending among the states. States that spend heavily on Medicaid and welfare programs tend to receive more federal aid, other things being equal.

The amount of federal aid also depends on a state's income per capita since the federal government matches state spending for programs like Medicaid and Aid to Families with Dependent Children (AFDC) with the matching rate varying inversely with per capita income. Because most of the states in this study have high incomes, they have relatively low federal aid matching rates.[12]

None of these states collected above average amounts of user charges. Nevertheless, they are similar to most other states in that revenue from user charges has been increasing significantly. In nearly every case, revenue from user fees grew faster than from taxes between 1985 and 1991.

POLICIES IN THE 1980s

Policies during the 1980s affected the fiscal environment of the 1990s. Perhaps the most important fiscal legacy of the 1980s was the overspending that occurred in some states. Connecticut and Massachusetts were particularly notable in this regard. They ranked first and second in per capita state-local spending increases between 1984 and 1988, with increases of 51 percent and 47 percent, respectively.[13] The median state-local spending increase was 31 percent, far in excess of the 18 percent inflation rate.[14] The levels of spending were unsustainable during the recession of the 1990s.[15]

DEGREE OF FISCAL STRESS

With the exception of Minnesota, the states in this study encountered comparatively severe fiscal stress during the recession. According to an index developed by the Center for the Study of the States measuring the degree of fiscal stress in fiscal year 1991, Connecticut and Massachusetts had the third and fourth highest levels of stress in the country. California and Michigan were not far behind, ranking eighth and tenth, respectively. Florida ranked eighteenth and Minnesota, twenty-eighth.[16]

A weak economy is a principal source of fiscal stress. Connecticut and Massachusetts suffered the effects of the recession at the beginning of 1989, long before the national recession officially started in June 1990. Nonfarm employment dropped steadily for four and a half years in these New England states, leading to employment declines of more than 12 percent in both states.[17] California also experienced a drastic economic downturn between July 1990 and January 1994, with employment falling 5.1 percent. Florida and Michigan had considerably milder downturns (2.5 percent and 3.2 percent, respectively) while Minnesota had a negligible three-month employment decrease of less than 1 percent.

GOVERNMENT EMPLOYMENT CHANGES

An important indicator of how the fiscal crisis affected state and local governments is how their levels of employment changed. Massachusetts was the most extreme case, with decreases of 8.9 percent in state employment and 5.6 percent in local employment in the three years following June 1990. Connecticut and Michigan also reduced state employment, although local employment rose in both states.

In California, Florida, and Minnesota state and local government employment rose during the three-year period, with local increases outpacing those at the state level. None of the six states increased state employment as much as the 3.3 percent increase nationally, although Florida and Minnesota raised local employment more than the 5.1 percent growth for the U.S.[18]

NOTES

1. Although this chapter discusses states as if they are monolithic, it is important to remember that there are sometimes substantial intrastate differences. For instance, while Connecticut has the highest per capita income in the country, the state also includes three poor central cities—Bridgeport, Hartford, and New Haven.

2. This section refers to appropriations of tax dollars for higher education operating expenses as reported by the Center for Higher Education at Illinois State University. It excludes higher education spending paid for by tuition and federal aid.

3. This chapter does not review dramatic changes in higher education appropriations and tuition rates since the onset of the recession.

4. During the 1991–1992 academic year, the national average for resident undergraduate tuition and fees for state universities was $2,410. In these states, tuition and fee rates were as follows: Massachusetts ($4,698); Michigan ($4,044); Connecticut ($3,463): Minnesota ($2,923); California ($2,679); Florida ($1,512). (Although California is currently above average in tuition/fees it has a long tradition of heavily subsidized higher education.) Washington Higher Education Coordinating Board, *Tuition and Fee Rates, 1992–93* (Olympia, WA: Higher Education Coordinating Board, 1993).

5. For more on this, Center on Budget and Policy Priorities, *AFDC Benefits in California are now only 17th Highest in the Nation when Compared with Housing Costs* (Washington, DC: Center on Budget and Policy Priorities, 1992).

6. Supplemental Security Income (SSI) is the cash assistance program for poor individuals and couples who are elderly, blind, or disabled. General Assistance (GA) offers benefits to people, mainly single adults, who are not covered under AFDC or SSI.

7. The basic SSI payment is made by the federal government. Twenty-six states provide additional state payments. For more information, Social Security Administration, Office of Supplemental Security Income, *State Assistance Programs for SSI Recipients* (Washington, DC: U.S. Government Printing Office.

8. While there are certain services that all states must provide, there are numerous optional services that vary from state to state.

9. In 1992, spending per inmate was: Massachusetts ($49,125); Minnesota ($42,700); Connecticut ($36,903); California ($26,489); Michigan ($21,707); and Florida ($21,461).

10. Jill Ross Schmelz, *Corrections Spending in State Budgets* (Albany: Center for the Study of the States, 1994).

11. For recent changes in the distribution of taxes in Michigan, see the chapter 11 in this book by Robert Kleine.

12. Specifically, states with lower income (Mississippi or Alabama, for instance) received AFDC matching rates of 72.73 percent and 79.93 percent, respectively. California, Connecticut, and Massachusetts had 50 percent matching rates. The matching rates for the other states were Florida (54.46 percent); Michigan (54.54 percent); and Minnesota (53.43 percent).

13. The rapid spending increases were certainly influenced by the growth of personal income, which was 28.9 percent between 1984 and 1988. All of these states except Minnesota had per capita personal income growth higher than the national average. Massachusetts and Connecticut led the group with 40.8 percent and 39.3 percent increases, respectively.

14. States with the biggest spending increases did not have especially high spending in 1984. Per capita spending in Connecticut and Massachusetts—the states with the biggest increases—ranked twentieth and twenty-third in state-local per capita spending in 1984.

15. On the economic boom in New England see several articles in Charles S. Colgan and Joseph S. Slavet, eds. in *The Fiscal Crisis in the States: Lessons from the Northeast* (Portland: The University of Southern Maine, 1993).

16. The index was based both on factors that cause fiscal stress (such as nonfarm employment decreases and school enrollment increases) and evidence that stress occurred (like revenue shortfalls, budget cutbacks, prospective budget deficits, and implementation of budget reduction strategies). Steven D. Gold, "Comparing State Fiscal Stress in 1991," *State Tax Notes* (August 3, 1992).

17. Steven D. Gold and Sarah Ritchie, *Differences Among States in the Impact of the Recession* (Albany: Center for the Study of the States, 1994).

18. Sarah Ritchie, "State-Local Employment Continues to Grow" *State Fiscal Brief* 15 (January 1994).

TABLE 4-1 Economic and Fiscal Characteristics

	National	California	Connecticut	Florida	Massachusetts	Michigan	Minnesota
General Economy and Demography							
Population (millions), 1991	252.2	30.4	3.3	13.3	6.0	9.4	4.4
Percent Population, 5–17 Years, 1991	18.2%	18.1%	16.0%	15.7%	15.7%	18.9%	19.2%
Percent Population over 65, 1991	12.6%	10.5%	13.7%	18.3%	13.7%	12.1%	12.5%
Percent Increase Population, 1990–93	3.5%	6.8%	−0.3%	5.7%	−0.1%	2.0%	3.2%
Percent of Residents who are African-American, 1990	12.1%	7.5%	8.3%	13.6%	5.0%	13.9%	2.2%
Percent of Residents who are Hispanic, 1990	9.0%	25.8%	6.5%	12.2%	4.8%	2.2%	1.2%
Percent of Residents who are Foreign-Born, 1990	7.9%	21.7%	8.5%	12.9%	11.1%	3.8%	2.6%
Percent of State Population who Live in Urban Areas, 1990	79.4%	96.8%	95.7%	92.9%	96.2%	82.8%	68.8%
Per Capita Income, 1991	$18,651	$20,667	$25,484	$18,530	$22,569	$18,360	$18,731
Poverty Rate, 1991	14.2%	15.7%	8.6%	15.4%	11.0%	14.1%	12.9%
Unemployment Rate, 1991	6.7%	7.5%	6.7%	7.3%	9.0%	9.2%	5.1%
Aggregate Spending, 1991							
Per Capita State—Local Spending	3,591	3,978	4,446	3,415	4,105	3,599	4,250
Per Capita State Spending	1,464	1,272	2,376	1,156	2,296	1,510	1,535
Per Capita Local Spending	2,128	2,706	2,070	2,259	1,808	2,089	2,715
State Spending per $100 of Personal Income	7.92	6.24	9.32	6.34	10.13	8.28	8.28
Local Spending per $100 of Personal Income	11.54	13.27	8.12	12.40	7.98	11.46	14.63
State-Local Spending per $100 of Personal Income	19.46	19.51	17.44	18.74	18.11	19.74	22.91

Spending by Major Category, 1991

K-12 Per Pupil (State and Local)	4,982	5,043	8,113	5,210	6,062	4,952	5,575
K-12 Per $100 of Personal Income (State and Local)	4.40	4.03	4.58	4.01	3.72	4.58	5.10
State Revenue as a Percent of State-Local School Receipts	52.6%	72.6%	47.7%	56.9%	38.9%	37.1%	56.3%
Higher Ed Per Capita	157	192	159	119	116	158	227
Higher Ed Per $100 of Personal Income	0.85	0.94	0.65	0.51	0.51	0.87	1.23
Medicaid Per Capita	156	146	227	116	377	169	185
Corrections Per Capita	71	91	140	70	99	86	33
AFDC Benefit for 3 Person Family	367	694	680	294	539	525	532
State Cash Assistance Spending Per Capita	115	247	131	53	217	154	101

Tax System, 1991

Per Capita State-Local Taxes	2,083	2,283	2,668	1,932	2,469	2,104	2,348
Per Capita State Taxes	1,232	1,477	1,515	1,038	1,615	1,184	1,591
Per Capita Local Taxes	852	805	1,153	794	854	920	757
Shares of State Tax Revenue							
Personal Income Tax	32.0%	37.5%	9.5%	0.0%	55.2%	34.1%	42.2%
Sales Tax	33.2%	32.0%	48.9%	59.1%	19.7%	28.7%	27.8%
Corporation Income Tax	6.6%	9.9%	10.7%	4.2%	7.4%	14.3%	6.5%
Other	28.3%	20.7%	31.2%	36.6%	17.7%	22.8%	23.5%
State Taxes Per $100 Income							
Total	6.45	7.09	5.82	5.46	7.02	6.35	8.32
Personal Income Tax	2.06	2.66	0.55	0.00	3.87	2.17	3.51
Sales Tax	2.14	2.26	2.85	3.23	1.38	1.83	2.32
Corporation Income Tax	0.42	0.70	0.60	0.23	0.52	0.91	0.54
Other	1.82	1.46	1.81	2.00	1.24	1.45	1.95

Continued

TABLE 4-1 Economic and Fiscal Characteristics (*continued*)

	National	California	Connecticut	Florida	Massachusetts	Michigan	Minnesota
Shares of State-Local Tax Revenue							
Personal Income Tax	20.8%	24.3%	5.4%	0.0%	36.1%	21.2%	28.6%
Property Tax	32.0%	28.0%	42.7%	37.5%	33.6%	42.4%	30.6%
Sales Tax	23.9%	25.9%	27.8%	33.9%	12.9%	16.2%	19.0%
Other	23.3%	21.8%	24.1%	28.6%	17.4%	20.2%	21.8%
State-Local Taxes Per $100 Income							
Total	11.33	11.24	10.45	10.00	10.92	11.60	12.68
Personal Income Tax	2.36	2.73	0.57	0.00	3.94	2.45	3.63
Sales Tax	2.71	2.92	2.90	3.39	1.41	1.41	2.41
Property Tax	3.62	3.15	4.46	3.75	3.67	3.67	3.88
State Tax Revenue as a Percentage of State-Local Tax Revenue	59.1%	64.7%	56.8%	56.6%	65.4%	56.3%	67.8%
Other Revenues, 1991							
State							
Federal Aid Per $100 of Personal Income	2.80	2.77	2.49	1.82	2.93	2.82	2.93
Federal Aid as a Percentage of General Revenue	24.5%	24.2%	24.3%	20.8%	23.1%	24.9%	21.3%
User Charges Per $100 of Personal Income	0.98	0.79	0.76	0.48	0.97	1.33	1.30
User Charges as a Percentage of General Revenue	8.6%	6.8%	7.4%	5.4%	7.7%	11.1%	9.5%
State-Local							
Federal Aid Per $100 of Personal Income	3.20	3.15	2.68	2.16	3.37	3.09	3.47
Federal Aid as a Percentage of General Revenue	12.7%	14.9%	10.4%	15.9%	14.1%	12.6%	14.1%

User Charges Per $100 of Personal Income	3.58	2.86	1.31	2.81	1.93	2.77	3.33
User Charges as a Percentage of General Revenue	11.5%	7.3%	13.6%	9.3%	12.0%	12.1%	15.8%
Recent Fiscal Trends							
Percent Increase in Per Capita Personal Income, 1984–88	31.6% (Median)	34.4%	42.8%	34.4%	44.3%	34.2%	33.7%
Percent Increase in Per Capita Spending, 1984–88							
State	30.5% (Median)	37.2%	54.8%	55.6%	57.5%	32.5%	22.0%
Local	31.8% (Median)	38.0%	45.3%	28.4%	24.3%	27.9%	52.1%
State-Local	31.0% (Median)	37.5%	51.4%	41.7%	47.2%	30.7%	32.9%
Severity of Recession and State Fiscal Stress, 1990s							
Composite Stress Index (Rank), 1991	NA	8	3	18	4	10	28
Decrease in Non-Farm Employment From Recession Peak to Trough		−5.1%	−12.2%	−2.5%	−12.4%	−3.2%	−0.7%
Number of Months Between Peak and Trough		39	55	19	55	10	3
Government Employment Changes, 1990–93							
State	3.3%	1.3%	−2.2%	3.2%	−8.9%	−5.1%	2.2%
Local	5.1%	2.2%	1.0%	6.8%	−5.6%	4.9%	6.0%

Sources:

General Economy and Demography

Population—U.S. Census Bureau, Population Estimates Branch, *Current Population Report*, Series P–25 (Washington, DC: U.S. Government Printing Office, 1992).

Personal Income Per Capita—U.S. Census Bureau, *State Government Finances 1991* (Washington, DC: U.S. Government Printing Office, 1992).

Poverty Rates—Poverty in the United States: 1991, *Current Population Report*, Series P–60, No. 181 (Washington, DC: U.S. Government Printing Office, 1992).

Continued

TABLE 4-1 Economic and Fiscal Characteristics (*continued*)

Unemployment Rates—U.S. Census Bureau, *Geographic Profile of Employment and Unemployment* (Washington, DC: U.S. Government Printing Office, 1992).

Aggregate Spending, 1991

U.S. Census Bureau, *State Government Finances 1991* (Washington, DC: U.S. Government Printing Office, 1992) and U.S. Census Bureau, *Government Finances 1990–91* (Washington, DC: U.S. Government Printing Office, 1992).

Spending by Major Category, 1991

K-12 Spending (State and Local) and Pupils—National Education Association, *Estimates of School Statistics 1990–91* (Washington, DC: NEA, 1991).

Higher Education Appropriations—Edward R. Hines, Center for Higher Education Finance, Illinois State University, Electronic Data.

Medicaid—Congressional Research Service, *Medicaid Source Book: Background Data and Analysis* (Washington, DC: U.S. Government Printing Office, 1993).

Corrections—U.S. Census Bureau, *State Government Finances 1991*.

AFDC Benefit—Committee on Ways and Means, U.S. House of Representatives, *Overview of Entitlement Programs, 1993 Green Book* (Washington, DC: U.S. Government Printing Office, 1994).

State Cash Assistance per Capita—U.S. Census Bureau, *State Government Finances 1991* (Washington, DC: U.S. Government Printing Office, 1992).

Tax System, 1991

U.S. Census Bureau, *State Government Finances 1991* (Washington, DC: U.S. Government Printing Office, 1992) and U.S. Census Bureau, *Government Finances 1990–91* (Washington, DC: U.S. Government Printing Office, 1992).

Other Revenue, 1991

U.S. Census Bureau, *State Government Finances 1991* (Washington, DC: U.S. Government Printing Office, 1992) and U.S. Census Bureau, *Government Finances 1990–91* (Washington, DC: U.S. Government Printing Office, 1992).

Recent Fiscal Trends

State and Local Tax Revenue, 1984–88—Steven D. Gold, "Local Taxes Outpace State Taxes," *State Fiscal Brief* no. 11 (July 1993).

Severity of Recession and State Fiscal Stress, 1990s

Composite Stress Index—Steven D. Gold, "Comparing State Fiscal Stress in 1991," *State Tax Notes* 3, no. 5 (August 3, 1992).

Nonfarm Employment—Bureau of Labor Statistics, Unpublished Data.

Government Employment Changes

Government Employment—Bureau of Labor Statistics, Unpublished Data.

5

Spending Policies and Revenue Trends Compared

Steven D. Gold

Much can be learned by comparing the spending policies of these six states and how they changed in the early 1990s. The following chapters study these issues using information obtained directly from the states. A barrier to analysis is that budget concepts and measures sometimes vary from state to state. To provide a broader context for understanding how the states differ, this chapter uses information published by national organizations. In many but not all cases, this data provides a better basis for drawing comparisons because many of the inconsistencies have been removed.

After reviewing spending patterns, the trends in three major kinds of revenue—taxes, federal aid, and user charges—are compared. Some dramatic differences occurred in how reliance on these sources of revenue changed during this period, and there were also large variations in revenue growth among the six states.

COMPOSITION OF SPENDING IN 1990 AND 1993

Table 5–1 shows how the composition of General Fund spending differed in these states in 1990 and 1993. Because some of these states provide a large amount of school aid from non-General Fund sources, spending for K–12 education from other funds is also included. (The Appendix to this chapter explains why this is the most helpful approach to analyzing spending and discusses the problem of obtaining relevant data.)

The spending patterns in these states differ considerably. For example, in all cases K–12 education represented the largest outlay in 1990, but its prominence varied substantially. It was half of spending in Florida but less than a fifth in Massachusetts. These differences

TABLE 5–1 Composition of State General Fund Spending, by State, 1990 and 1993 (percent of total)

Program	California		Connecticut		Florida	
	1990	1993	1990	1993	1990	1993
K–12 Ed	37.8%	39.6%	27.8%	22.8%	50.0%	41.9%
Higher Ed	13.8	11.8	7.0	5.7	13.2	11.8
AFDC	5.5	6.9	3.0	3.1	1.4	3.0
Medicaid	8.7	13.1	8.1	11.7	7.0	13.1
Corrections	6.1	7.4	3.4	4.6	6.1	7.4
Other Programs	28.1	21.3	50.7	52.2	22.3	22.8

Program	Massachusetts		Michigan		Minnesota	
	1990	1993	1990	1993	1990	1993
K–12 Ed	19.6%	14.0%	29.9%	33.8%	26.8%	28.8%
Higher Ed	7.8	4.7	14.7	15.5	19.9	18.5
AFDC	3.9	4.0	5.4	4.8	1.1	2.0
Medicaid	12.5	14.5	11.5	13.7	10.6	12.9
Corrections	4.4	3.9	7.6	9.4	2.0	2.3
Other Programs	51.8	58.9	30.9	22.7	39.6	35.5

Program	United States	
	1990	1993
K–12 Ed	36.3%	36.5%
Higher Ed	14.0	12.6
AFDC	2.5	2.8
Medicaid	9.1	12.4
Corrections	5.2	5.7
Other Programs	32.8	30.0

Note: Because many states finance a large proportion of the elementary-secondary school spending from nongeneral fund state sources, for that function and for total spending, nongeneral fund spending is included.
Source: National Association of State Budget Officers, *1992 NASBO Expenditure Report* (1993). National Association of State Budget Officers, *1993 NASBO Expenditure Report* (1994).

reflect state priorities, demographics, and state budgetary practices. For example:

- Florida is generally a low-spending state, but it places a relatively high priority on schools, and the state pays a relatively large share of state-local school costs.

• Connecticut and Massachusetts have relatively small school-age populations. Since their schools are operated by cities and towns, some of the aid provided to those general purpose governments may support schools, though it is not counted as school aid.

Table 5–1 reveals some broad patterns about spending changes that are common to most of these states. The winners and losers in the battle for funds tended to be similar:

• Medicaid rose sharply in all states.
• Corrections also increased its share of the budget in five of the six states.
• AFDC became a larger share of spending in all of the states except Michigan.
• Higher education fell sharply in all states except Michigan, where Governor Engler made it a priority.

Elementary-secondary education was the only major budget category where there was no general trend. It became a larger share of the budget in three states (California, Michigan, and Minnesota) and a smaller share elsewhere.

SPENDING CHANGES FROM 1990 TO 1993

The preceding analysis relied upon reports published by the National Association of State Budget Officers (NASBO), which represent the only available data from a single source that compares actual General Fund spending during this period. While that data is invaluable for showing how the various parts of the budget interrelate, it suffers from a certain degree of inconsistency in the reporting methods employed by different states. That, for example, probably accounts for most of the large differences in the share of spending outside of the five major categories shown in Table 5–1.

Better sources of information are available for most categories of spending. They are used in Table 5–2, which shows increases in the five major areas between 1990 and 1993.

The patterns shown here are generally consistent with those in Table 5–1. Medicaid, AFDC, and corrections spending tended to grow

TABLE 5–2   Percent Change in State Spending by Major Program Area, 1990 to 1993

State	K–12 Ed	Higher Ed	AFDC	Medicaid	Corrections	All Programs
California	16.5%	−12.1%	19.0%	52.9%	24.4%	8.6%
Connecticut	12.3	−15.4	36.6	64.3	52.9	15.1
Florida	16.8	−6.1	101.1	99.6	29.2	35.0
Massachusetts	8.6	−20.3	34.9	50.8	14.1	−2.0
Michigan	32.3	9.3	0.9	19.3	22.9	−0.9
Minnesota	20.0	2.0	15.9	45.1	39.4	18.9
United States	22.1	1.0	23.8	54.0	22.2	14.1

Note: This table represents state spending for each program area as reported by the following sources. Only general funds were used from the NASBO *Expenditure Report*.
Sources:

K-12	National Education Association, *1993–94 Estimates of School Statistics* (March 1994)
Higher Ed	Edward R. Hines, *State Higher Education Appropriations, 1993–94* (State Higher Education Executive Officers, February 1994)
AFDC	Congressional Research Service, *Overview of Entitlement Programs* (Washington, DC: U.S. Government Printing Office, July 1993)
Medicaid	National Association of State Budget Officers, *Expenditure Report 1992 and 1993* (Washington, DC)
Corrections	National Association of State Budget Officers, *Expenditure Report 1992 and 1993* (Washington, DC)
All Programs	National Association of State Budget Officers, *Expenditure Report 1992 and 1993* (Washington, DC)

considerably faster than higher education spending and somewhat more than elementary-secondary spending. Some of the highlights shown include that:

- Higher education suffered a large absolute reduction in California and a small decrease in Connecticut. If inflation of 9 percent is taken into account, even Michigan, with the biggest increase, had virtually no growth.
- Michigan's increase for elementary-secondary education is much bigger than that in any other state, reflecting Governor Engler's commitment to education at all levels.
- Florida had extraordinary increases for AFDC and Medicaid, primarily because of faster population growth (including many poor immigrants with children) but also because it was affected more by federal mandates. Because the other states had more

TABLE 5–3   Growth of State Workload Measures for Major Program Areas, 1990 to 1992 (percent change)

Program	Cali-fornia	Connec-ticut	Florida	Massa-chusetts	Michi-gan	Minne-sota	U.S.
K–12 Ed (enrollment)	7.0%	3.6%	7.9%	2.5%	1.2%	4.0%	3.5%
Higher Ed (enrollment)	−1.5	−0.8	29.3	−2.7	0.9	−0.1	
AFDC (poverty)	19.3	54.6	10.6	−7.3	−4.6	5.7	9.8
AFDC (recipients)	21.3	30.7	62.5	17.6	2.9	12.4	19.2
Medicaid (recipients)	23.8	26.7	48.1	16.2	7.7	6.9	22.5
Corrections (prisoners)	12.5	8.6	8.8	21.6	13.9	20.3	13.5
All Programs (population)	3.3	−0.3	3.5	−0.4	1.3	1.9	2.3

Sources:

K–12	National Education Association, *1993–1994 Estimates of School Statistics* (March 1994).
Higher Ed	Research Association of Washington, *State Profiles: Financing Public School Education 1978 to 1992* (Washington, DC: October 1992).
AFDC	Congressional Research Service, *Overview of Entitlement Programs* (Washington, DC: U.S. Government Printing Office, July 1993). U.S. Bureau of the Census, *Poverty in the U.S. 1992* (Washington, DC: U.S. Government Printing Office, 1993).
Medicaid	Health Care Finance Administration, Division of Medicaid Statistics.
Corrections	Bureau of Justice Statistics, *Prisoners in 1991 and 1992* (Washington, DC: U.S. Government Printing Office).
All Programs	U.S. Department of Commerce press release dated 28 April 1994.

generous programs initially, the mandates did not have as much impact on their budgets.[1]

WORKLOAD INCREASES

It is interesting to compare spending changes with the growth and decline of the populations served. Table 5–3 shows several measures of these workload changes, and Table 5–4 shows how spending changes related to these workload changes. Because many of the workload

TABLE 5–4   Growth of State Spending per Recipient, 1990 to 1992 (percent change)

Program	Cali-fornia	Connec-ticut	Florida	Massa-chusetts	Mich-igan	Minne-sota	U.S.
K–12 Ed (enrollment)	4.7%	6.1%	7.0%	0.2%	17.6%	6.9%	11.4%
Higher Ed (enrollment)	7.3	−1.1	−39.5	−36.0	7.4	5.0	
AFDC (poverty)	−1.4	−21.1	37.0	22.2	−1.3	−0.6	8.1
AFDC (recipients)	−3.1	−2.4	7.5	1.3	−9.4	−7.0	0.2
Medicaid (recipients)	24.8	11.8	8.6	13.0	6.9	17.4	12.4
Corrections (prisoners)	9.5	18.1	11.9	−20.0	−2.7	6.2	1.4
All Programs (population)	8.8	7.3	16.5	−10.4	1.5	10.4	8.1

Note: This table represents state spending for each program area as reported by the following sources. Only general funds were used from the NASBO *Expenditure Report.*
Sources:

K-12	National Education Association, *1993–94 Estimates of School Statistics* (March 1994).
Higher Ed	Edward R. Hines, *State Higher Education Appropriations, 1993–94* (State Higher Education Executive Officers, February 1994). Research Association of Washington, *State Profiles: Financing Public School Education 1978 to 1992* (Washington, DC: October 1992).
AFDC	Congressional Research Service, *Overview of Entitlement Programs* (Washington, DC: U.S. Government Printing Office, July 1993). U.S. Bureau of the Census, *Poverty in the U.S. 1992* (Washington, DC: U.S. Government Printing Office, 1993).
Medicaid	National Association of State Budget Officers, *Expenditure Report 1992 and 1993* (Washington, DC). Health Care Finance Administration, Division of Medicaid Statistics.
Corrections	National Association of State Budget Officers, *Expenditure Report 1992 and 1993* (Washington, DC). Bureau of Justice Statistics, *Prisoners in 1991 and 1992* (Washington, DC: U.S. Government Printing Office).
All Programs	National Association of State Budget Officers, *Expenditure Report 1992 and 1993* (Washington, DC). U.S. Department of Commerce press release dated 28 April 1994.

measures were not available for 1993 at the time when this analysis was conducted, it focuses on changes between 1990 and 1992.

States have varying degrees of influence over how workloads change:

- For elementary-secondary education, states have the least control. They generally must provide education for all school-age children who do not attend private schools.
- Higher education enrollment is also affected by demographics, particularly the number of high school graduates. But states can control enrollment by limiting admissions and course offerings.
- AFDC and Medicaid workloads can be viewed two ways. States have relatively little control over the number of poor people, but they can have more influence over the number of recipients by changing eligibility standards. Federal laws and regulations, however, place many restrictions on the latitude of states to change these programs.
- States have considerable influence over the prison population through their incarceration policies.
- States have no influence over the growth of their total population in the short run.

The states fall into three categories with regard to how their total population changed between 1990 and 1992. California and Florida experienced rapid growth; Michigan and Minnesota had modest growth; and the populations of Connecticut and Massachusetts fell.

Public school enrollments and the number of poor people reflect the general population patterns to a considerable extent. California and Florida had relatively large increases in both cases. But there were some important differences. Connecticut had by far the largest increase in poverty (although it started from a low level), and it had the fourth biggest increase in school enrollment.

The changes in the number of AFDC and Medicaid recipients varied considerably. Florida had the largest increases, followed by Connecticut, California, and Massachusetts in that order. These increases do not appear very closely related to changes in the number of poor people, but the annual estimates of persons in poverty in each state are imprecise.

The relatively small increase in Florida's prison population reflects a policy of releasing a large number of prisoners well before their sentences stipulated. As a result, the average number of prisoners incarcerated on an average day grew considerably more slowly than the number of persons imprisoned at any time during a particular year.

Table 5–4 brings together the spending and workload data, revealing some dramatic patterns. Inflation between 1990 and 1992 was about 6.4 percent, implying that only Medicaid and corrections experienced real spending increases in many states. In numerous cases, spending per recipient fell even in nominal terms, that is, before taking inflation into account:

- Michigan is the only state where K–12 spending per pupil rose much more than inflation.
- Higher education spending per student experienced large nominal reductions in four states and a real reduction in a fifth. Only in Michigan did it remain slightly ahead of inflation.
- Medicaid spending per recipient rose much more than the general inflation rate for several reasons discussed in Chapter 2.
- Corrections spending per prisoner rose most in Connecticut but failed to keep up with inflation in three states.

Finally, changes in total spending per capita varied considerably from state to state.

- Florida had a larger increase than any other state, although it still spent less than most of the others in 1992.
- California, Connecticut, and Minnesota had increases slightly above the national inflation rate of 6.4 percent.
- Only Massachusetts and Michigan had real spending decreases, with Massachusetts' being much larger.

A strong case can be made for using a higher inflation factor than 6.4 percent because that rate does not consider the extraordinary increase in Medicaid costs.[2] But even if inflation were 10 percent, it would indicate that only two states had large real decreases in spending. In other words, this was not a period of large spending decreases in most states. Massachusetts and Michigan are the exceptions.

REVENUE TRENDS

Table 5–5 shows the changes in revenue from taxes, federal aid, and charges between 1990 and 1992. The most dramatic pattern is the

TABLE 5–5   Growth of State Revenue, 1990 to 1992 (percent change)

State	Tax Revenue	Federal Aid	Non-Hospital Charges
California	6.2%	34.3%	19.5%
Connecticut	15.0	29.5	13.8
Florida	8.4	35.2	33.6
Massachusetts	5.7	27.8	27.3
Michigan	−0.6	41.2	17.6
Minnesota	9.2	18.2	18.0
United States	9.1	34.4	20.5

Source: U.S. Bureau of the Census, State Government Finances 1990 (Washington, DC: U.S. Government Printing Office, 1991). U.S. Bureau of the Census, State Government Finances 1992 (Washington, DC: U.S. Government Printing Office, 1993).

large margin by which federal aid increases exceeded the growth of taxes. Revenue from charges also increased much more than tax revenue. If states had relied solely on tax revenue, they would have had a much more difficult time coping with the fiscal crisis.

As discussed in Chapter 2, several factors accounted for the explosion of federal aid. The recession increased the number of people eligible for Medicaid and AFDC, and those increases caused aid to grow. In addition, while the federal government did not have a policy of stimulating the economy by increasing aid, it did expand some programs, such as Head Start. Finally, states were able to obtain a substantial amount of aid through creative financing of Medicaid.

The most important cause of the growth of revenue from user charges was increases in higher education tuition and fees. Charges at state-operated hospitals also increased sharply, but they are excluded from the table because many hospitals operate with considerable autonomy.[3]

The increases in tax revenue among states reflect both the size of legislated tax increases and the relative weakness of each state's economy. All of the states except Michigan enacted substantial tax increases—Massachusetts in 1990 and the other four states in 1991. Among the five states with tax increases, Connecticut's was the largest as a proportion of its total tax revenue, while Minnesota's was the smallest.

The size of revenue increases differed among states in predictable ways. Connecticut had the largest revenue increase because its legislated increase was the biggest, while Michigan actually had lower revenue in 1992 than in 1990. It is noteworthy that, except for Connecticut, none of the states had revenue increases bigger than 9.2% despite passing substantial legislated increases. The relatively small increases reflect the depressing effect of the recession.

It is not a coincidence that Michigan had the largest federal aid increase and the only tax decrease. Michigan was particularly aggressive in pursuing strategies to increase federal aid.[4]

CONCLUSION

This chapter reveals that there are broad similarities in how spending patterns changed during this period. Medicaid, corrections, and AFDC increased much more than higher education spending in most states.

But significant differences also existed. Two major examples:

• California and Florida had to contend with much greater increases in workloads.
• Massachusetts and Michigan had much more austere overall spending policies.

In summary, each state was different, although some generalizations apply broadly to most states.

APPENDIX

PROBLEMS WITH TRACKING STATE SPENDING TRENDS

This Appendix consists of two parts. First, it discusses some conceptual issues related to different measures of spending. Second, it compares various sources of data about state spending.

Conceptual Issues

The most appropriate data for analyzing state spending depends on the purpose for which it is to be used. If one is concerned about the entire scope of state activity or the impact of state spending on the economy, a broad measure is called for. On the other hand, the main focus in this study is on the budget decisions that states made with the revenue that their tax systems produced. This calls for a more limited measure of spending, one that excludes spending paid for by federal aid and user charges. Thus, for example, the higher education spending considered here is solely that paid for by taxes, even though an increasing proportion of higher education spending is financed by the tuition and fees that students pay.

The emphasis on spending paid for out of tax revenue leads to a focus on General Fund spending, since that is where most state taxes are deposited. General Funds may also receive some nontax revenue, but most of their revenue is from taxes.

The concentration on the General Fund is, however, inappropriate for elementary-secondary education because numerous states have large special school aid funds distinct from the General Fund. Michigan, for example, earmarks most of its sales tax revenue for such a fund. In 1992, the school fund accounted for two-thirds of education spending. Therefore, we include all state funds for school aid, not merely the General Fund.

The concentration on General Fund spending has an important implication for Medicaid. As explained in Chapter 2, after 1990 states increasingly relied on health care provider taxes and other creative financing devices to finance this rapidly growing program. The spending paid for by these taxes does not come largely at the expense of other programs. Moreover, it is usually not included in the General Fund. Thus, the figures for Medicaid spending discussed in this chapter are considerably lower in many states than those reported by the federal government's Health Care Finance Administration, which reflect all state spending on Medicaid.

It is important to emphasize that General Fund spending is considerably different from general spending as defined by the U.S. Census Bureau. In 1992, General Fund spending was approximately $300 billion,[5] while general spending was $612 billion. The major sources of this difference are spending from federal aid, user charges, and miscellaneous revenue. In addition, general spending reflects all state activities except liquor stores, utilities, and insurance trust transactions. It includes activities by independent state authorities that are not in the General Fund as well as highway spending, which is usually financed from an earmarked fund that receives motor vehicle fuels taxes and other highway-related revenue.

Data Sources

Three organizations report data on all of the major categories of state spending: the U.S. Census Bureau, the National Conference of State Legislatures, and the National Association of State Budget Officers.[6] In addition, other organizations report data for individual budget categories.

The U.S. Census Bureau exerts the greatest effort to achieve a consistent methodology in reporting among states. However, its reports have some serious drawbacks. (1) They ignore state fund structures, sometimes making it difficult to isolate spending out of tax revenue. (2) They do not report Medicaid spending separately, dividing it into vendor payments for medical care and hospital spending. (3) They are available only with a considerable time lag. For example, data for fiscal year 1992 was not be published until the middle of fiscal year 1994. Moreover, even Census reports sometimes have serious reporting errors.[7]

The National Conference of State Legislatures provides the first information available about state spending policies, with a preliminary report on appropriations increases available a few weeks after the start of the fiscal year. While this information is invaluable because of its timeliness, it does not provide a historical record of actual spending, which may differ considerably from appropriations.[8]

The National Association of State Budget Officers provides the most useful data on spending, reporting information for three past years. It divides spending into four categories—General Fund, other state funds, federal funds, and bonds.

While the best information available for a broad perspective on state spending trends, NASBO's data has two major problems: (1) Data for the most recent year is subject to large revisions in some cases; (2) states do not report their expenditures on a consistent basis. For example, some states include tuition in "other state funds" for higher education, and others do not. Some states include federal human service block grants in their income maintenance spending, while most do not.

There are also inconsistencies in reporting for particular states in different years. For example, in the *1992 Expenditure Report*, Massachusetts reported most of its school aid in 1991 and 1992 under "other state funds," but in 1993's report, it included all of its school aid in the General Fund. More significantly, Massachusetts fails to allocate an unusually high proportion of its spending to any of the six categories of spending, strongly suggesting that it is using different definitions than other states. In 1992, 58.8 percent of total spending was unallocated, the highest in any state. The following year, 47.2 percent was unallocated, a level exceeded by only two other states. In the *1992 Expenditure Report*, Massachusetts' 1991 General Fund spending was reported to be $9.49 billion; in the *1993 Expenditure Report*, General Fund spending in that same year was listed as $11.154 billion. For this reason, the data reported in this chapter for Massachusetts is not completely reliable.

Because of the inconsistent methodology of reporting in NASBO's reports, where better information is available this study substitutes information about particular budget categories from other sources.

- *Elementary-secondary education*: National Education Association, *Estimates of School Statistics*;
- *Higher education*: State Higher Education Executive Officers and the Center for Higher Education at Illinois State University; and
- *AFDC*: *The Green Book* published by the U.S. House Ways & Means Committee.

For Medicaid and corrections, NASBO data is used. For Medicaid, it is the only source of information that separates out spending paid for by provider taxes and other creative financing devices.

In some cases there are inconsistencies between the data included in this chapter and the information provided in the state case studies that follow. For analysis of a particular state, the best data is tailored to its unique institutions. Data for individual states is usually available on a more timely basis than fifty-state data. But for making the interstate comparisons necessary to place states in an overall context, the data discussed above is the best available.

This discussion suggests how difficult it is to compare state spending and policies. But there are only fifty states. With sufficient effort and care, much better comparative information can be developed than has been available previously.

NOTES

1. The mandates expanded Medicaid services for children and pregnant women and required that states have an AFDC program for two-parent families where the head was unemployed.

2. The 6.4 percent figure is based on the implicit GDP deflator for state and local purchases of goods and services, averaging calendar years 1989 and 1990 for fiscal year 1990 and calendar years 1991 and 1992 for fiscal year 1992.

3. States did not rely on higher hospital charges to substitute for tax support in the same way that they relied on increased tuition and fees for higher education.

4. At the start of the Engler Administration, Gerald Miller left his position as executive director of NASBO to become director of Michigan's Department of Social Services. He is extremely knowledgeable about opportunities to shape state policies to qualify for federal assistance.

5. The National Conference of State Legislatures and the National Association of State Budget Officers reported General Fund spending in that year of $299 billion and $302 billion, respectively.

6. U.S. Census Bureau, *State Government Finances*; Corina Eckl et al., *State Budget Actions* (Denver: National Conference of State Legislatures); and Melanie Nowacki, *State Expenditure Report* (Washington, DC: National Association of State Budget Officers).

7. For example, Census reported that New York's aid for education rose sharply between 1990 and 1992 even though that was not accurate.

8. NCSL does report an estimate of actual spending for the previous fiscal year, but that estimate often does not reflect a final accounting that incorporates information on unspent funds, referred to as reversions. NCSL also reports information for only two years at a time (appropriations for the year just begun and "actual" spending for the past year), raising the possibility that its figures on actual spending in various years may be reported on an inconsistent basis.

6

The Political Environment

Sarah Ritchie

Recent fiscal decisions were made in the midst of complex political environments. In this chapter, politics is construed broadly to include topics relating to governing institutions, processes, and behavior. This chapter will concentrate on the executive and legislative branches; state courts will not be discussed. Five subject areas and sets of questions are considered:

- *Political Culture and History.* What is the state's political culture and ideological temperament? What historical developments affect contemporary political processes?
- *Political Parties.* Are the legislature and governor controlled by the same political party? Are state parties strong and competitive? How is party competition changing?
- *Electoral Politics.* What issues and events were prominent in recent gubernatorial and legislative elections? To what extent did the governor enter office with an electoral mandate?
- *Citizen Participation and Public Attitudes.* Are direct election mechanisms available to voters? What are the public attitudes about elected officials, government institutions, and public policies?
- *Institutional Characteristics.* What are the institutional capacities and limitations of the governorship and the legislature? What is the division of authority between the two branches?

This chapter is divided into two parts. The first section discusses political characteristics, noting differences and similarities in the six states. The second section describes each state's political system and how it affected fiscal decisions in the early 1990s.

DIFFERENCES IN STATE POLITICAL ENVIRONMENTS

Political Culture and Ideology

Longstanding cultural and ideological differences exist among these states. State political culture—the beliefs, perceptions, and expectations that people have about their government—evolves through historical, economic, and social developments. In a dynamic process, political culture and ideology influence the configuration of governing institutions and the character of state politics.

Political Subcultures

Daniel Elazar's important typology is a benchmark for comparing the political cultures of these states. Elazar identified three primary political subcultures: individualistic, moralistic, and traditionalistic.[1]

- Florida has a *traditionalistic* political culture with *individualistic* influences. The *traditionalistic* culture, an outgrowth of the plantation economies of the antebellum South, views government as a defender of the existing social order. Political participation in the *traditionalistic* culture has typically been limited to elites. This cultural persuasion prefers to address social and economic problems through non-government entities, such as the family. In addition, bureaucracy is viewed negatively as it depersonalizes public policy.
- Connecticut and Massachusetts have *individualistic* cultures, and both have a *moralistic* influence. The *individualistic* culture seeks government institutions that provide order in the marketplace. Political competition is usually partisan and bureaucracy is perceived as a means of deterring the spoils system. Compared to the *traditionalistic* culture, this perspective anticipates greater mass political participation, mainly through voting.
- Michigan and Minnesota have *moralistic* political cultures and California has a *moralistic* culture with an *individualistic* influence. The *moralistic* culture views government as a positive tool to achieve the "common good." Incorporating republican ideals, this culture encourages citizen participation through

voting and public service and promotes nonpartisan politicking. This culture has a strong commitment to a neutral bureaucracy.

Political culture and ideology are inextricably linked. With the exception of Florida, the states in this study hold liberal public attitudes and public policies vis-à-vis other American states. Liberalism is typically associated with activist government policies, high taxes, and generous expenditures. According to a study by Wright, Erickson, and McIver, Massachusetts has the most liberal policies and attitudes of the six states, followed by California, Connecticut, Michigan, and Minnesota.[2] On the researchers' scale measuring opinion and policy liberalism, Florida is in the middle range of the fifty states.

Political Parties and Interest Groups

Accurately comparing state parties is difficult.[3] Based on state electoral outcomes, Connecticut, Michigan, and Minnesota have competitive two-party systems.[4] California, Florida, and Massachusetts have somewhat competitive party systems that tend to favor Democratic candidates. However, Republicans are increasingly competitive in the latter three states. In terms of organizational strength, Mayhew argues that Connecticut has strongly organized parties while California, Florida, Massachusetts, Michigan, and Minnesota have weaker organizations.[5,6] Despite the differences, state party organizations have been weakening due to the increasing proportion of independent voters,[7] split-ticket voting, and candidate-centered campaigns.[8]

The weakening of parties has coincided with a proliferation of state-level interest groups.[9] These advocacy groups have not expanded uniformly across states, however. Rather, there tends to be an inverse relationship between the strength of state parties and interest groups. In a state like Florida with a weaker party system, interest groups tend to be more influential than in a state such as Connecticut with stronger parties. Thomas, Hrebenar, and their associates have classified states by the degree of influence of interest groups: dominant, complementary, or subordinate. California and Florida have dominant interest groups while Connecticut, Massachusetts, Michigan, and Minnesota have complementary ones.[10]

Direct Election Mechanisms

The six states differ in the provision of direct election measures: initiative and referendum. These mechanisms allow voters to become involved in public decision making, by proposing legislation for a public vote (initiative) or voting on measures initiated by the legislature (referendum).[11] All of the states except Minnesota allow some access to initiative and referendum devices.[12] The utilization of these direct election measures varies considerably across the six states. For example, between 1981 and 1990, California had fifty-eight statewide initiatives followed by Massachusetts, eleven; Michigan, six; and Florida, four.[13]

Executive and Legislative Institutional Authority

The states differ in the degree of institutional authority granted to the executive and legislative branches. Based on a gubernatorial power index developed by Thad Beyle, Massachusetts has a *very strong* governorship while Connecticut, Michigan, and Minnesota have *strong* governorships. California and Florida have *moderate* governorships (all of these measures are for 1990).[14] On balance, the states in this study have stronger chief executives than a "typical" American state.

With regard to the state legislatures, Karl Kurtz classified California, Massachusetts, and Michigan as having *highly professionalized* legislatures with full-time sessions, large staffs, high salaries, and stable membership.[15] Connecticut, Florida, and Minnesota have *moderately professionalized* legislatures. In other words, none of these states has an amateur, citizen legislature found in many American states.

SIMILARITIES IN STATE POLITICAL ENVIRONMENTS

National political trends have been superimposed on these states. Pertinent developments relate to citizen attitudes, state government institutions, and electoral politics.

Citizen Attitudes

Citizens are skeptical about public officials and government institutions. The 1970s ushered in a period of intense cynicism in the electorate.[16] Voters are increasingly pessimistic about the ability of government programs to solve economic and social problems. Many have noted the strong anti-incumbent attitudes of recent years; these opinions are clearly expressed in the passage of legislative term limitations in California, Florida, and Michigan.[17]

Coupled with the lack of confidence in government institutions, citizens are antagonistic about tax and spending increases. Several states in this study have passed explicit antitax measures. California approved Proposition 13 (1978), which severely limited property taxes. Subsequently, California voters passed the Gann Initiative (1979), a spending limitation, and Proposition 98 (1988), protecting funding for elementary-secondary schools and junior colleges. Michigan voters approved the Headlee Amendment (1978) to limit tax revenue. In 1992, Florida passed a limitation on property tax increases. Massachusetts passed Proposition 2½ (1980), a strict limitation on property taxes. In 1992 on the heels of the new personal income tax, Connecticut voters approved a constitutional amendment to cap state spending.[18] Tax and spending limitations can present important constraints in fiscal decision making.

Executive and legislative candidates have employed the antitax, antigovernment sentiment in electoral politics. Many state officials have run campaigns "against the government," further undermining citizen confidence. Governors Weld and Engler have been the most aggressive proponents of scaling back government apparatus and programs. Chiles proposed a "right-sizing" plan for Florida.

Election Outcomes and Executive-Legislative Relations

The governors in this study did not enter office with strong electoral mandates. With the exception of Florida's Lawton Chiles, these governors were elected by narrow margins of 4 percent or less.[19] In general, the newly elected governors did not campaign with a comprehensive, detailed electoral platform; thus, the chief executives did not enter office with a clear mandate from the electorate, reducing gubernatorial "political capital."[20]

The recent gubernatorial elections were not only close but resulted in divided state governments. In some cases, such as Massachusetts, this was a new development and in others, like California and Michigan, an ongoing trend:

- *California*. State government in California has been divided since Governor Edmund (Jerry) Brown left office in January 1983. California elected Republican Governors Deukmejian (1983–1990) and Wilson (1991–) and a Democratic legislature.[21]
- *Connecticut*. During most of the 1980s, Connecticut had a unified government controlled by the Democrats. Following the 1984 Reagan landslide, the legislature was held by the Republicans for one term, 1985–1986. From 1991–1994, the state had a divided government with Governor Lowell Weicker (A Connecticut Party) and a Democratic legislature.[22]
- *Florida*. With the exception of the Martinez administration (1989–1993), the Florida governorship has been held by Democrats during the last fifteen years. Likewise, the legislature was controlled by the Democratic party until 1993. However, over the last decade, the size of the Democratic majority has declined. Following the 1992 elections, Democrats and Republicans were evenly divided in the senate while the House of Representatives remained Democratic.[23]
- *Massachusetts*. Democrats dominated the legislature and governorship during the 1980s. However, the Bay State had a divided government with the 1990 gubernatorial election of Republican William Weld. In the 1990s, Democrats continue to outnumber Republicans in the legislature by substantial margins.
- *Michigan*. During most years in the 1980s and 1990s, state government was divided. The executive has alternated between the two major parties (Milliken-R, 1969–1982; Blanchard-D, 1983–1990; and Engler-R, 1991–). Between 1981 and 1983 both houses of the legislature were controlled by the Democrats but Republicans seized control of the senate in late 1983 when two Democratic senators were recalled in a protest against a large tax increase that year. Between 1985 and 1993, the house of representatives was controlled by the Democrats and the senate, by Republicans. During the 1993–1994 biennium, the senate was Republican and the house of representatives was evenly divided between Democrats and Republicans.
- *Minnesota*. With the exception of the 1985–1986 period, the Minnesota legislature has been controlled by the Democratic (DFL) party. The governorship has shifted between Democrats

and Republicans (Quie-IR, 1979–1983; Perpich-DFL, 1983–1991; Carlson-IR, 1991–). Between 1991 and 1994 the state had a Republican governor and a Democratic legislature.

Many believe that divided government increases the likelihood of executive-legislative gridlock such as stalled program proposals and tardy budgets. Alt and Lowry have shown, for example, that divided government at the state level is associated with budget deficits.[24] In these six states, divided government is associated with a higher use of gubernatorial vetoes.[25]

Intrastate Political Conflict

Most of these states have intrastate political struggles. California has dramatically different political environments and preferences in the northern and southern regions. In Massachusetts, Michigan, and Minnesota, political tension exists between the largest population center (Boston, Detroit, and the Twin Cities) and the "outstate region." In Connecticut, there is political and economic conflict between the wealthy New York City suburbs and the poverty-stricken cities of Bridgeport, Hartford, and New Haven.[26]

CALIFORNIA

California is *the* megastate in American politics. Since 1964, California has been the most populous state in the country, and in 1992, the Golden State accounted for 12 percent of the nation's population. The rapidly increasing numbers of immigrants, children, and poor people have strained state government services. The state has been coping simultaneously with natural disasters and declining public confidence. These conditions contrast with California's prosperous image.

The Progressive movement was profoundly important in California's development and continues to impact Golden State politics.[27] Responding to the political machines of nineteenth century railroad developers, Progressives, led by Governor Hiram Johnson (1910–1916), passed reforms including direct democracy devices (initiative, referendum, and recall), nonpartisan local government elections, cross-filing in primaries, and an extensive civil service system. The Progressive influence weakened parties and diffused political influence among many individuals and groups. Fragmented political power is symptomatic of California politics in the 1990s.

In 1990, Pete Wilson was elected in a close race against Dianne Feinstein (49 percent-R; 46 percent-D; 3 percent-Other). Wilson, the former U.S. senator and mayor of San Diego, received electoral support from conservative Southern California, while Feinstein, San Francisco's former mayor, garnered votes from the more liberal Northern California regions. As evidence of the weak party system, the major party candidates held few opposing issue stances—both were pro-choice, pro-death penalty, pro-defense spending, and against offshore oil drilling. Pete Wilson campaigned as a Republican centrist who embraced an activist state government. Wilson won by fewer than 200,000 votes, coming to office with a weak mandate from the citizens.

Wilson hoped for a cooperative relationship with the Democratic legislature in passing "preventive" policy initiatives (prenatal care, early childhood care for the poor, health care delivery in schools, and student mentoring). However, the severity of the recession made such initiatives unrealistic. Instead, officials aimed to stop the state's fiscal hemorrhaging. The governor navigated through a political mine field, angering both Republicans and Democrats.[28] The legislature, ridden with scandal and partisan infighting, was led by intransigent politicians, including the controversial Assembly Speaker Willie Brown. In addition, the Senate and Assembly were reeling from Proposition 140 (passed in 1990), which imposed term limits and reduced legislative staff by about 40 percent. In fact, the "class of '92" was the largest group of new lawmakers in nearly 30 years.[29] The governor was further restrained by an unusual constitutional requirement: the budget must receive votes from two-thirds of the legislature to pass. The stalemate led to an unusually high volume of gubernatorial vetoes.[30]

The level of citizen and interest group involvement in the process complicated political matters.[31] The number of initiatives has grown exponentially since the early 1950s.[32] During the past fifteen years, popular initiatives have cut taxes, altered state and local financing, and designated expenditure patterns in the budget. According to Jack Citrin, "plebiscitary budgeting" (or "ballot box budgeting") has arguably led to a less accountable state government, and the loss of a broad view of the state's long-term needs.[33]

In California, citizens continue to exhibit cynical and antitax attitudes. According to an October 1993 Los Angeles Times poll, only 24 percent of respondents approved of how the legislature was handling its job while 54 percent disapproved.[34] Likewise, Governor Wilson has experienced a steadily declining approval rating since the beginning of his administration. The 1991 tax increases were so controversial that Wilson focused on spending cuts to close subsequent budget gaps.

The standstill in California politics has led some to suggest that the system is ungovernable.[35] Indeed, there are many factors—divided government, weak parties, excessive citizen participation—that increase the probability of political gridlock. Reform advocates argue that the state needs a major institutional overhaul. For instance, the former California Senate Majority Leader Barry Keene and others have called for a constitutional convention to discuss issues ranging from making the legislature unicameral to dividing the state into smaller substates.

CONNECTICUT

Even though Connecticut is known as the Land of Steady Habits, the state's political economy has been unpredictable recently. The rapid economic decline of the late 1980s and early 1990s coincided with changes in political parties, the electorate, and executive-legislative relations and created unstable political dynamics.

Connecticut has generally embraced liberal political attitudes and expansive government programs. The economic base is built on corporate offices in New York City suburbs, manufacturing and defense-related industries along the coast, and insurance companies in Hartford. Party politics, historically influenced by power struggles between "Yankees" and ethnic minorities, are competitive.

While Connecticut has sustained a relatively strong party system, the political parties have weakened in recent years.[36] With the retirement of longtime party chief John Bailey in 1975, the Democrats faced a leadership void. Factionalism among the Democrats led to 1989 political coup that ousted Connecticut House Speaker Irving Stolberg. Simultaneously, voters in Connecticut have become more independent. In 1992, 38 percent of the voters registered Democrat and 26 percent registered as Republicans. A full 37 percent of Connecticut citizens registered with minor parties or with no party affiliation.

The political "dealignment" led to a fascinating gubernatorial race in 1990. Presiding over a swift economic decline and an unpopular tax increase in 1989, incumbent Governor O'Neill decided not to run for reelection. The attention of the election swirled around the worsening condition of the state's economy and the possibility of an income tax to generate desperately needed revenues.[37] The Republican nominee was Congressman John Rowland of Waterbury, who did not support the income tax. The Democratic primary pitted a decidedly pro-income tax candidate William Cibes, a state representative from New London, against Bruce Morrison, a Congressman from New Haven and the eventual Democratic nominee. Weicker, a longtime maverick Republican and tacit opponent of the income tax, ran under the label of "A Connecticut Party."[38] In the general election, Weicker received 41 percent of the vote compared to Rowland, 37 percent; and Morrison, 21 percent.[39]

At the beginning of Weicker's term—when his political capital was at a pinnacle—the governor became an open supporter of the income tax. Weicker's success was due to the sheer force of his personality. As a third-party governor, Weicker had no legislative party. The governor had to overcome extremely negative citizen and legislative attitudes through political bargains and a public campaign for the income tax.[40] In the end, the income tax passed by the narrowest of margins.[41]

The personal income tax was clearly the most dramatic proposal by Weicker. The governor was moderately successful in other program changes including revisions in income maintenance programs and intergovernmental relations. Despite Weicker's reasonably high approval ratings, he did not seek reelection in 1994.

FLORIDA

Florida is a megastate as it claims the fourth highest population in the country (13.5 million people). With rapidly increasing population, changing demographics, and economic development, "Florida is one of the states where America is meeting its future. . . . To be sure, Florida is not a replica of the nation; it is rather an exaggeration."[42]

For many decades, Florida was a low-population, politically conservative, heavily Democratic state with some agriculture and manufacturing interests. At mid-century, tourism and economic development started to flourish.[43] Rapid in-migration transformed Florida from a traditionalistic "Old South" state into a dynamic, heterogeneous, internationally significant location.

Longtime politician Lawton Chiles governed the state during the recession. After retiring in 1988 from the U.S. Senate, Chiles reentered politics and handily won the 1990 race for governor. Known as "Walkin' Lawton" (because he had once walked the entire length of the state during a campaign), Chiles enjoyed a wellspring of popular support. Chiles campaigned on a platform to "reinvent" Florida's government.[44] Republican incumbent Robert (Bob) Martinez had made some unpopular policy choices,[45] and Chiles and Buddy McKay, his Lieutenant Governor running mate, won the election, 57 percent–43 percent.

Despite Chiles's convincing margin of victory, the newly elected governor encountered political problems. The Florida governorship is a relatively weak office. The state constitution divides executive responsibility among the governor and six other independently elected officials.[46]

Chiles also faced strengthening Republican legislative opposition. Between 1980 and 1992, the percentage of legislators who were members of the GOP jumped from 33 percent to 43 percent. Republicans also benefited from legislative reapportionment following the 1990 census.[47] Between 1980 and 1992, the percentage of voters registered with the Republican party increased from 30 percent to 41 percent.[48] As one observer states, Florida is relentlessly marching toward Republicanism.[49]

Public attitudes have contributed to Chiles's difficulties. Floridians display a strong antitax sentiment.[50] Citizen-led tax reform proposals and amendments are increasingly finding their way on to the statewide ballot—measures that restrain taxes generally pass with wide margins.[51] Floridians are becoming ever more pessimistic about the capacity of the executive and legislature to govern.[52]

MASSACHUSETTS

Historically, Massachusetts has been one of the most politically liberal states in the country. The economic devastation of the late 1980s and early 1990s has been associated with dramatic changes in the political landscape. William Weld's election was an important departure from the past.

Massachusetts has a *moralistic* political culture, dating back to the Puritan settlements. Bay State politics have long revolved around ethnic competition. Throughout the twentieth century, Massachusetts politics was dominated by the Democrats, and during the 1970s and 1980s, "Massachusetts had one of the most liberal governance policies of any state in the country."[53] With a robust economy, the state passed expansive programs. The recession and Weld's election halted public sector growth.

The 1990 gubernatorial election was highly charged, yielding a 75 percent turnout rate. As the election approached, incumbent governor and former presidential nominee Michael Dukakis was very unpopular.[54] Frustrated by the state's economic nosedive, citizens turned to two "outsider" candidates: Weld and Democrat John Silber, the controversial president of Boston University.[55] Weld campaigned as a Republican who was liberal on social issues such as abortion and homosexual rights, but fiscally conservative. Silber proved to be an inept campaigner prone to sensational statements. Silber's alienation of numerous groups in the electorate assisted Weld in knitting together a winning coalition.

Weld entered office as the Massachusetts economy was in rapid deterioration. The governor's fundamental objective was to resist tax increases and scale back the size of state government; his "no new taxes" stance was popular among the citizenry. Weld enjoyed legislative successes in passing his political agenda as the heavily Democratic legislature did not build a cohesive opposition to the chief executive. The governor benefited from a veto-proof majority in the senate during 1991 and 1992, and he was able to capitalize on the fractured condition of the Democratic party.

Weld has remained popular during his entire tenure; indeed, the governor is seen as a national leader in the Republican party. In October 1991, 40 percent of survey respondents thought Weld was doing an "excellent" or "good" job. In January 1994, that percentage climbed to 54 percent.[56] Weld's administration signalled an important development in the Bay State politics.

MICHIGAN

Michigan state has experienced pronounced economic ups and downs in the last several decades. During the heyday of automobile manufacturing in Michigan, the state posted rising personal incomes and supported expansive state and local government programs, similar to *moralistic* states like Minnesota and Wisconsin. With the decline of the U.S. auto industry, policymakers are reconsidering the nature and scope of public policies.

Michigan was a birthplace of the Republican party, and until the Great Depression, state politics were dominated by the GOP. As labor unions in the auto industry flourished, the Democratic party strengthened. Michigan party politics have been class-based, pitting unions, minorities, urban residents, and university liberals against more conservative residents in out-state regions.[57]

John Engler won in a close race in 1990. Engler trailed incumbent governor Democrat Jim Blanchard in preelection polls. Engler ran on a platform of reducing property taxes, downsizing government, and improving education (including school choice). Engler's 50 percent–49 percent victory (only 17,000 votes) was partly attributable to the light voter turnout in Detroit, a traditional Democratic stronghold.[58]

Engler worked with a divided legislature to pass his agenda; the senate had a Republican majority, but the house of representatives was controlled by the Democrats during 1991 and 1992. In 1993 and 1994, the lower chamber was divided evenly between Democrats and Republicans.[59] Engler initially ran into strong opposition from the Democrats in his attempts to balance the budget and hold taxes down, but the severity of the fiscal crisis and Engler's leadership skills eventually broke the gridlock. The governor prevailed on several important proposals including eliminating General Assistance and privatizing some public services.

The antitax, antigovernment mood sustained Engler's effort to reduce government programs and hold taxes in check. Recent public sentiment in Michigan has been stridently antitax. In 1978, Michiganders passed the Headlee amendment, which tied state revenue increases to personal income. The personal income tax was increased in 1982 and 1983. In the aftermath of the 1983 increase, two state senators were recalled and party control switched in the upper chamber. In 1993, politicians responded to citizen antipathy towards the property tax. The legislative process was partly circumvented as the school finance restructuring issue was put before the voters in 1994.

MINNESOTA

Minnesota is considered the quintessential "good government state." The *moralistic* political culture encourages and expects citizen participation and perceives the government as a positive tool working in the public interest.[60] A high premium is placed on issue-oriented politics. Minnesotans support expansive, often innovative government programs and high state taxes and spending.

The state has a fairly competitive party system.[61] During the antebellum era, Minnesota was a strongly Republican state. Democrats gained strength following the New Deal. However, there continued to be a very active Farmer-Labor opposition party. In 1944, at the urging of Hubert Humphrey, the Democratic and Farm-Labor parties merged. (The contemporary party is known as the DFL.)

Arne Carlson did not enter the governorship with a strong mandate; rather, he was elected on the heels of a bizarre political scandal. Carlson, a former state auditor, finished fourth among four candidates in the two major party primaries. Shortly before the election, the staunchly conservative Republican nominee Jon Grunseth was charged with sexual improprieties with teenage girls. One week later, Arne Carlson initiated a write-in campaign. Shortly thereafter, the *Minnesota Star-Tribune* printed a woman's charge that she had a nine-year extramarital affair with Grunseth. Subsequently, Grunseth withdrew from the race.[62] Carlson defeated Democratic incumbent Rudy Perpich in the general election, 51 percent–47 percent.

Carlson entered office with a lopsided Democratic majority in the state legislature. Democrats outnumber Republicans 65 percent to 35 percent in the house of representatives and 67 percent to 33 percent in the senate.

Carlson—and all politicians in Minnesota—have also come against cynicism in the citizenry. A 1992 poll of Minnesotans showed that voters were much less confident in state government's capacity to solve problems than they were four years before. This skepticism may be due, in part, to the series of political scandals in Minnesota. In addition to the Carlson election, U.S. Senator Dave Durenberger has been accused of financial wrongdoings; two Minnesota representatives in the U.S. house of representatives were caught up in the congressional check-bouncing scandal; and the Democratic leadership of the state legislature were weakened in the 1993 "phonegate."[63]

Carlson enjoyed moderate success in passing his legislative agenda in the face of these challenges. Governor Carlson had a 50 percent legislative success rate in 1991–1992. This is a lower success rate than other Minnesota governors during their legislative honeymoon.[64]

SUMMARY AND CONCLUSION

The six states in this study have social and political differences and similarities; Table 6–1 summarizes pertinent details about each state's political system. Common trends that have profoundly affected the fiscal decisions described throughout this book are:

- *Electorate.* Citizens are cynical about government officials and institutions. A conservative antitax, antispending mood is running high. Fearing electoral retribution, many decision makers are using tax increases as a last resort. In this environment politicians have found it difficult to pass new spending programs.
- *Political Parties.* State party discipline is weakening. However, because of electoral inroads made by the Republican party, the distribution of party members is more competitive than it was a decade ago.[65] As parties appear to be on the decline, the number of special interest groups is increasing.
- *Governing Institutions.* Divided state governments are proliferating. Likewise, legislative bodies have become more formidable institutions, capable of thwarting gubernatorial agendas and developing their own initiatives.

Many of these political factors served to fragment the policy process. Declining authority of some centralizing institution like parties, increasing citizen cynicism and participation in direct election mechanisms, and persistence of divided state governments—all of these tend to decentralize and ultimately muddle the policy process.

TABLE 6-1 State Political Characteristics

	California	Connecticut	Florida	Massachusetts	Michigan	Minnesota
Political Culture	Moralistic Dominant Strong Individualistic Strain	Individualistic Dominant Strong Moralistic Strain	Traditionalistic Dominant Strong Individualistic Strain	Individualistic Dominant Strong Moralistic Strain	Moralistic	Moralistic
State Party Strength	Weaker Organizations	Stronger Organizations	Weaker Organizations	Weaker Organizations	Weaker Organizations	Weaker Organizations
Degree of Party Competition	Competitive-Favors Dems.	Competitive Parties	Competitive-Favors Dems.	Competitive-Favors Dems.	Competitive Parties	Competitive Parties
Party Registration	D—49.0% R—37.1% Other—13.9%	D—38.0% R—25.8% Other—36.1%	D—50.7% R—40.9% Other—8.4%	D—42.8% R—13.3% Other—43.8%	NA	NA
Interest Group Strength	Dominant/ Complementary	Complementary/ Subordinate	Dominant	Complementary	Complementary	Complementary/ Subordinate
Institutionalized Power of the Governor	Moderate	Strong	Moderate	Very Strong	Strong	Strong
Governor (1991–1994)	Wilson (R)	Weicker (ACP)	Chiles (D)	Weld (R)	Engler (R)	Carlson (IR)
Margin of Gubernatorial Victory in 1990	4%	3%	6%	3%	1%	4%
Gubernatorial Popularity Early in Term	2/91 36%	2/91 30%	5/91 43%	10/91 40%	4/91 41%	4/91 40%
Recent Gubernatorial Popularity	1/94 30%	3/94 36%	10/93 38%	1/94 54%	12/93 44%	9/93 45%

Professionalization of Legislature	Highly Professionalized	Moderately Professionalized	Moderately Professionalized	Highly Professionalized	Highly Professionalized	Moderately Professionalized
Term Limits	8 Years for Senators; 6 Years for Assembly-people	None	8 Consecutive Years for Legislators and Executive	None	6 Years for Representatives; 8 Years for Senators and Executive	None
Direct Election Mechanisms (Initiative and Referendum)	Initiative-Direct Referendum-Petition & Constitutional Requirement	Referendum-Legislature	Constitutional Initiative	Initiative-Indirect Referendum-Petition	Intiative-Direct & Indirect Referendum-Legislature, Petition & Constitutional Requirement	
Party Distribution in Legislature 1991–1992						
Lower House	47—D 33—R	87—D 64—R	74—D 46—R	118—D 37—R	61—D 49—R	78—DFL 56—IR
Upper House	25—D 13—R	20—D 16—R	22—D 18—R	25—D 15—R	18—D 20—R	46—DFL 21—IR
Party Distribution in Legislature 1993–1994						
Lower House	48—D 32—R	87—D 64—R	71—D 49—R	124—D 35—R	55—D 55—R	87—DFL 47—IR
Upper House	23—D 14—R	20—D 16—R	20—D 20—R	31—D 9—R	18—D 20—R	45—DFL 22—IR

Sources:

Political Culture—Daniel Elazar, *Federalism: A View from the States*, 3d edition (New York: Harper and Row, 1984).

State Party Strength—David R. Mayhew, *Placing Parties in American Politics* (Princeton, NJ: Princeton University Press, 1986).

Degree of Party Competition—John F. Bibby, Cornelius P. Cotter, James L. Gibson, Robert J. Huckshorn, "Parties in State Politics," in Virginia Gray, Herbert Jacob, and Robert B. Albritton, eds., *Politics in the American States*, 5th edition (Glenview, IL: Scott, Foresman, 1990).

Party Registration—State Election Boards.

Interest Group Strength—Clive S. Thomas and Ronald J. Hrebenar, "Interest Groups in the States," in Gray et al, *Politics in the American States*, p. 147.

Institutionalized Power of the Governor—Thad Beyle, "Governors", Gray et al, *Politics in the American States*, p. 228.

Gubernatorial Approval Rating—California, The Field Poll, San Francisco; Connecticut, *The Hartford Courant*, Hartford; Florida—Mason-Dixon Poll, Columbia, MD; Massachusetts—Opinion Dynamics, Cambridge, MA; Michigan—Public Sector Consultants, East Lansing, MI; Minnesota—Minnesota Poll, Minneapolis.

Professionalization of the Legislature—Karl T. Kurtz, "Understanding the Diversity of American State Legislatures," *Extensions of Remarks* (Newsletter of the American Political Science Association Legislative Studies Section), June 1992.

Direct Election Mechanisms—Harold W. Stanley and Richard G. Niemi, 4th ed., *Vital Statistics on American Politics* (Washington, DC: CQ Press, 1994), pp. 23–24.

NOTES

I appreciate comments and assistance from Gerald Benjamin, John Berg, Thad Beyle, Robert Carver, Jeff Chapman, Steven Gold, Dennis Hale, Robert Kleine, Carol Lewis, Thomas Luce, Susan MacManus, Suzanne Parker, Charles Price, Gary Rose, Dan Shea, Al Sokolow, John Snyder, Bruce Wallin, and Homer Williamson.

1. Daniel Elazar, *Federalism: A View from the States*, 3d edition (New York: Harper and Row, 1984).

2. Wright, Erickson, and McIver, "Public Opinion and Policy Liberalism in the American States," *American Journal of Political Science* 31 (1987), p. 989. In an interesting earlier study, William Schneider also found that Florida was far more conservative than the other five states. Schneider, "Democrats and Republicans, Liberals and Conservatives," in Seymour Martin Lipset, ed., *Emerging Coalitions in American Politics* (Berkeley: Institute for Government Studies, 1978).

3. The complexities are numerous—the national Democratic and Republican parties do not necessarily reflect state political parties. The ideological orientation of the state parties, particularly the Democratic parties, varies by region.

4. John F. Bibby, Cornelius P. Cotter, James L. Gibson, Robert J. Huckshorn, "Parties in State Politics," in Virginia Gray, Herbert Jacob, Robert B. Albritton, eds. *Politics in the American States*, 5th edition (Glenview, IL: Scott, Foresman, 1990), p. 92.

5. David R. Mayhew, *Placing Parties in American Politics* (Princeton, NJ: Princeton University Press, 1986).

6. Voter party identification (as determined through registration) is another measure of competition. In the four states that have enrollment, the divisions in 1992 were as follows: California (D–49.0 percent; R–37.1 percent; Other 13.9 percent); Connecticut (D–38.0 percent; R–25.8 percent; Other 36.1 percent); Florida (D–50.7 percent; R–40.9 percent; Other 8.4 percent); and Massachusetts (D–42.8 percent; R–13.3 percent; and Other 43.8 percent). Information was provided by state election boards.

7. According to the National Election Studies (NES), the percentage of voters who consider themselves independent increased from 23 percent in 1952 to 39 percent in 1992. Harold W. Stanley and Richard G. Niemi, *Vital Statistics on American Politics*, 4th edition (Washington, DC: CQ Press, 1994).

8. One should not overstate the case for party decline. Patterson points out that state parties are persistent organizations. Specifically, "parties are weaker in the electorate than they once were, but they are stronger and more coherent as organizations." Samuel C. Patterson, "The Persistence of State Parties," in Carl Van Horn, ed., *The State of the States* (Washington, DC: CQ Press, 1993), p. 193.

9. In extensive work on interest groups in the states, Clive S. Thomas and Ronald J. Hrebenar state that since the 1960s, there has been a dramatic expansion in the number and orientation of state interest groups. Lobbying at the state level has also become more aggressive. Thomas and Hrebenar have edited a series of books analyzing state interest group activities by region.

10. Clive S. Thomas and Ronald J. Hrebenar, "Interest Groups in the States," in Gray et al., *Politics in the American States*, p. 147.

11. On this subject see general works such as Thomas E. Cronin, *Direct Democracy: The Politics of Initiative, Referendum, and Recall* (Cambridge: Harvard University Press, 1989); David Magleby, *Direct Legislation* (Baltimore: Johns Hopkins University Press, 1984); David D. Schmidt, *Citizen Lawmakers: The Ballot Initiative Revolution* (Philadelphia: Temple University Press, 1989).

12. Specific state requirements for direct election mechanisms are found in the annual edition of *The Book of the States* (Lexington, KY: Council of State Governments, 1992).

13. Public Affairs Research Institute of New Jersey, *Initiative and Referendum Analysis* (Princeton, NJ: Public Affairs Research Institute, 1992).

14. Beyle's index is based on powers of appointment, budget, veto, tenure potential, and party control. Thad Beyle, "Governors" in Grey et al., *Politics in the American States*, p. 228. For all American states, two governors are classified as "very weak"; nine, "weak"; fourteen, "moderate"; twenty-one, "strong"; and four, "very strong."

15. Karl T. Kurtz, "Understanding the Diversity of American State Legislatures," *Extensions of Remarks* (Newsletter of the American Political Science Association Legislative Studies Section), June 1992. According to Kurtz, eight states have highly professionalized legislatures, twenty-five states have so-called in-between or hybrid legislatures, and seventeen states have citizen-led legislatures.

16. For an exhaustive survey, see Seymour Martin Lipset and William Schneider, *The Confidence Gap: Business, Labor, and Government in the Public Mind* (Baltimore: Johns Hopkins University Press, 1987); Frank J. Thompson, "Critical Challenges to State and Local Public Service," in Frank J. Thompson, ed., *Revitalizing State and Local Public Service* (San Francisco: Jossey-Bass, 1993), pp. 1–38.

17. California (1990) limits senators to two terms and assembly members to three terms of election. Florida (1992) restricts legislators and executives to eight consecutive years of service. Michigan (1992) limits representatives to six years of tenure while senators. Gerald Benjamin and Michael J. Malbin, eds., *Limiting Legislative Terms* (Washington, DC: CQ Press, 1992).

18. To activate the limitation, the legislature must adopt a statute to specify the limit. As of the 1993 legislative session, no statute had been passed.

19. The margins of victory were as follows: Wilson (California) 4 percent; Weicker (Connecticut) 3 percent; Chiles (Florida) 6 percent; Weld (Massachusetts) 3 percent; Engler (Michigan) 1 percent; Carlson (Minnesota) 4 percent. As discussed later in the chapter, the election of some of these governors (such as Carlson of Minnesota) was virtually unexpected.

20. Governors, like the President, often gain political capital during times of crisis—the "rally around the flag phenomenon." Through the exis-

tence of a fiscal crisis, gubernatorial authority was enhanced to some degree or other.

21. California has a long tradition of GOP governors. Since 1899, California has elected three Democratic governors: Culbert L. Olson (1939–1943); Edmund G. Brown (1959–1967); and Edmund G. Brown, Jr. (1975–1983).

22. Between 1991 and 1994, Democrats outnumbered Republicans in the upper house (20–16) and the lower house (87–64).

23. A Democrat presided over the chamber during one year of the session and a Republican during the other.

24. James E. Alt and Robert C. Lowry, "Divided Government and Budget Deficits: Evidence from the States," forthcoming in the *American Political Science Review*.

25. The proliferation of divided state governments is associated with an increasing use of the gubernatorial veto or negative lawmaking. During the 1980s and 1990s, the states in this study recorded a higher percentage of vetoes during periods of divided government compared to periods of unified government.

26. By contrast, Florida has population centers throughout the state: Miami (3.2 million); Orlando (1.2 million); and Tampa-St. Petersburg (2.1 million). In earlier years, political differences between the northern and southern regions of the state were more pronounced.

27. The Progressive movement sought to make government more efficient and democratic. Leaders aimed at two targets: corrupt political parties and wealthy businesses. The movement has been associated with increasing citizen participation in politics, improving working conditions, regulating the concentration of economic power, and reducing corruption in government. On California see John H. Culver and John C. Syer, *Power and Politics in California*, 3d edition. (New York: Macmillan, 1988).

28. During the recession, Wilson "wound up with the worst of both political worlds—too confrontational and conservative to please most Democrats, too compromising and committed to government action to please many Republicans, too much in the center of controversy and confusion to please most voters." Michael Barone and Grant Ujifusa, *The Almanac of American Politics 1994* (Washington, DC: National Journal, 1993), p. 80.

29. Charles M. Price explains, "The Class of '92 is different from the vets." The class is divided nearly equally between women and men (twelve women and 14 men) and party (fourteen Democrats and twelve Republicans). About one-fifth of the class is Latino. Only two members were former legislative staffers, and many had previous local government service or positions in the business community. Charles M. Price, "The Class of '92: The Proposition 140 Babies," *California Government and Politics Annual, 1993–94*, pp. 52–55.

30. In 1991, Wilson vetoed 21.4 percent of the number of enacted bills; 1992, 24.3 percent; 1993, 9.4 percent. Council of State Government, *Book of the States* (Lexington, KY: CSG,‹various years›) and unpublished data from the Council of State Governments' States Information Center.

31. Thomas and Hrebenar state that "California has an interest group system that more closely resembles Washington, D.C. than it does most other states." Thomas and Hrebenar, in Gray et al., *Politics in the American States*, p. 135.

32. From the 1950s and the 1990s, the number of initiatives filed has nearly doubled. More initiatives were filed in 1990 than for the entire period between 1910–1960. Charles Price and Robert Waste, "Initiatives: too Much of a Good Thing," in Thomas R. Hoeber and Charles M. Price, eds. *California Government and Politics* (Sacramento: California Journal Press, 1993).

33. Professor Jack Citrin, University of California, Berkeley, "Budgetary Politics and Welfare Reform in California," unpublished manuscript, 1993.

34. This compares to a 34 percent approval (and 45 percent disapproval rating) in 1991.

35. It is reported that Republican political strategist Stu Spencer tried to discourage then-Senator Pete Wilson from running for governor in 1990. Spencer argued that the state was ungovernable. Richard W. Gable, "California: Pete Wilson, A Centrist in Trouble," in Thad Beyle, ed., *Governors in Hard Times* (Washington, DC: CQ Press, 1992).

36. Gary L. Rose, *Connecticut Politics at the Crossroads* (Lanham, MD: University Press of America, 1992).

37. In 1990, Connecticut was one of only ten states that did not have a broad-based income tax. The income tax was a political taboo in the Nutmeg State. Even powerful liberal Democratic governors such as Abraham Ribicoff and Ella Grasso did not support the tax.

38. Weicker did not support the income tax during the campaign. However, his intentions were clear when he appointed Democrat Cibes to be his main tax advisor.

39. Weicker served four terms in the U.S. Senate, when he was defeated by Democrat Joseph Lieberman in the 1988 general election.

40. In the wake of Governor Weicker's income tax legislation, 40,000 Connecticut residents carried signs that called for everything from impeachment to lynching for the governor and his budget officers. Anne Case, "Taxes and the Electoral Cycle: How Sensitive Are Governors to Coming Elections?" *Business Review: Federal Reserve Bank of Philadelphia*, March–April 1994, p. 17.

41. Despite the public fury over the passage of the income tax, most of the legislators who voted for the tax were reelected in 1992. However, at least thirty-eight incumbents decided not to run after the difficult income tax debate. See Steven D. Gold, "What Do the 1992 Election Results Say about State Fiscal Policy?" *State Tax Notes* 3 (December 14, 1992), pp. 897–900.

42. Barone and Ujifusa, *The Almanac of American Politics 1994*, pp. 269–270.

43. For a good review see Robert J. Huckshorn ed., *Government and Politics in Florida* (Gainesville, FL: University of Florida Press, 1991).

44. Chiles "called for streamlining government, eliminating duplication in function, and reducing the bureaucracy and the relative size of administration." See Susan MacManus's chapter in this book.

45. Among Martinez's most serious political gaffes, the governor passed a very unpopular sales tax on services in 1987. Although the tax change had the potential to raise large amounts of money, the reform was very unpopular and was repealed nearly immediately.

46. These officials include the secretary of state, attorney general, commissioner of education, comptroller, treasurer, insurance commissioner, and commissioner of agriculture. The governor presides at weekly cabinet meetings and has a vote equal to that of the other elected officers. A majority vote is required to pass any policy decision.

47. Susan A. MacManus and Lesa Chihak, "The 1992 State Legislative Reapportionment: An Overview of the Outcomes Under the New Plan," *Governing Florida* 4 (Fall/Winter 1993), pp. 3–16.

48. In 1980, two-thirds (64 percent) of voters registered Democratic while 30 percent registered Republican (6 percent were unaffiliated or registered with a third party). In 1992, 51 percent of the voters registered Democratic; 41 percent registered Republican; 8 percent were unaffiliated/third-party registrants.

49. Phil Duncan, *Politics in American 1994* (Washington, DC: CQ Press, 1994), p. 320.

50. MacManus explains that even though Florida state taxes are low when compared to other states, Floridians have been angry about the *rate* of increases.

51. Negative attitudes about state taxes are on the rise. In 1982, 68 percent of Floridians opposed the adoption of a state personal income tax. The percentage increased to 74 percent in 1993. *Florida Annual Policy Survey*, various years.

52. In 1980, 36 percent of the respondents thought the Florida legislature was doing a fair or poor job while 44 percent thought the body was doing an excellent or good job. In 1993, 62 percent of Floridians thought the legislature was doing a fair or poor job and only 24 percent thought the legislature was doing a good or excellent job. In 1980, 48 percent of respondents said they usually trust government. That number had dropped to 30 percent in 1993.

53. Barone and Ujifusa, *The Almanac of American Politics 1994*, p. 595. This statement should not negate the prominence of notable Republicans in Massachusetts such as Henry Cabot Lodge, Joe Martin, Ed Brooke, and Silvio Conte.

54. According to Dennis Hale, "the voters, in poll after poll, expressed almost unbelievable hostility toward the state's political establishment."

55. Because of the growth of independent voters, the candidates "anointed" by the parties—Massachusetts house member Steven Pierce for the Republicans and former state attorney general Francis X. Belotti—were not nominated.

56. Weld is the only governor in this study who had a steadily *increasing* public approval rating during his term. Data are from MassInsight survey conducted by Opinion Dynamics Corporation of Cambridge, Massachusetts.

57. Like other states in this study, Michigan can be divided into a principle city and outstate areas. Detroit, with a population of 4.3 million, clearly dominates the political and economic landscape of the state. While there has been an out-migration of individuals in recent years, the Motor City is still a prominent force in Michigan politics. Detroit, Lansing (the state capital and home of Michigan State University), and Ann Arbor (home of the University of Michigan) generally vote Democratic while the western regions of the state are Republican-leaning.

58. Low turnout in Detroit is linked to the rocky relationship between Blanchard and Detroit Mayor Coleman Young.

59. The parties alternate each month in leading the senate.

60. Carolyn M. Shrewsbury and Homer E. Williamson, *Perspectives on Minnesota Government and Politics*, 3d edition (Minneapolis: Burgess, 1993).

61. According to Homer Williamson, "the organizational strength of Minnesota's parties is declining. Minnesota derived its strong party organization classification based mainly on the effectiveness of pre-primary endorsements by party conventions. However, for statewide office the endorsement is no longer an automatic guarantee of primary success. Governor Carlson lost the endorsement by a landslide this year (to a much more conservative Christian fundamentalist) but he will probably win the primary."

62. Under state law Carlson was placed on the state ballot by a Republican party committee after a ruling by the Minnesota Supreme Court on proper procedure to replace Grunseth.

63. The House majority leader's son was accused of allowing the member's telephone calling card number to be used for nearly $90,000 in calls. In addition, the member allegedly knew of the abuse and did not prevent the child from using the card. For details, see Dane Smith and Dennis McGrath, "Humphrey Ascribes Blame for Phonegate; Well Hit Hardest; Others Criticized," *Minneapolis Star Tribune*, June 8, 1993, p. 1A.

64. Homer E. Williamson, "The Minnesota Governor: Potential for Power," in Shrewsbury and Williamson, p. 200. In the first year in office, Governor Perpich had a 61 percent success rate; Quie, 54 percent; Anderson, 52 percent; Levander, 65 percent.

65. The following state chambers were more competitive in 1992 compared to 1982: Connecticut (senate), Florida (house and senate), Massachusetts (house and senate), and Michigan (house). The following chambers were equally competitive in 1982 and 1992: California (assembly), Connecticut (house), and Michigan (senate). Only the Minnesota house and senate and California senate were less competitive in 1992.

7

California: The Enduring Crisis[1]

Jeffrey I. Chapman*

INTRODUCTION

In 1990, the state of California began to face a set of difficult and stressful fiscal conditions that are still ongoing. In response, state and local governments initiated a series of actions, some of which were routine while others were a break from past policies. This chapter will give a brief overview of these conditions and state government policies in the California public finance arena from 1990 through 1993.

The first section of the chapter will establish the economic context of this period. It will discuss the sources of California's crises and will conclude with a description of the overall trends in its revenues and expenditures.

The next section will identify the state's strategies and responses, first from an overall perspective and then in a year-by-year discussion. The last part of this section will present brief case studies of education, welfare, and local government revenues.

The third section will identify breaks from past behaviors and the fiscal innovations that California implemented. In particular, the state's focus on realignment, restructuring, and reinventing government; the increased concern for economic development and the business climate; the establishment of prevention programs; and the recognition of a multi-year budget will be analyzed.

The fourth section of the chapter will identify some of the short-run winners (of which there were very few) and losers (of which there were many). The final section will draw some overall lessons from this multi-year experience.

---

*Jeffrey I. Chapman is Professor and Director of the Sacramento Center, School of Public Administration at the University of Southern California.

SECTION I: THE CONTEXT

During the 1990–1991 through 1993–1994 fiscal years, California state government faced one fiscal crisis after another. In part, these reflect the movement of the state from a high spending and high tax state to more of an average spending and average tax state. But this movement was not done smoothly or consciously but rather in response to a series of stressful events. The state government has faced one short-term crisis after another.[2]

The Sources of Fiscal Stress

Fiscal stress came to California from three distinct sources: natural events, other events beyond the state's control, and events that were induced by California citizens.

Three types of natural catastrophes have contributed to the fiscal stress. The drought of 1987–1992 (and which apparently has recurred in 1994) has cost California farmers about $3–$4 billion; the Loma Prieta quake of 1989 resulted in about $10 billion in direct and indirect losses, with net losses after federal aid being about $6 to $7 billion; and property losses from the 1991 Oakland fire and the 1993 Southern California fires were about $4.7 billion.[3]

There are three exogenous events that are consistently mentioned in any discussion of the stresses on the state's economy: the recession that began in 1990; the cut in defense expenditures, including the closing of many military bases; and the immigration of undocumented aliens.

California is very slowly emerging from the most significant recession since the 1930s. In June 1990, California employment peaked at slightly over 14.5 million. In August 1993, it reached its trough of about 13.8 million. The number of unemployed was about 729,000 in June 1990 and had erratically grown to nearly 1.6 million in January 1994.[4] All sectors of the economy have been affected, with the hardest hit being aerospace, construction, and retail trade. Further, while all regions of the state have been influenced by the recession, the south coast region, which accounted for 50 percent of all wage and salary jobs, has realized 73 percent of the job loss.

Some argued that the loss of jobs reflected a structural weakness in the state's business climate, while others believed that the recession and defense cutbacks were the principal causes. The Commission on

State Finance believed that both explanations were partially correct: about 50 percent of the jobs were lost because of the national recession, about 25 percent of the jobs were lost because of direct and indirect impacts of defense cutbacks, and about 25 percent of the jobs were lost because of other reasons, including high land costs, congestion, environmental concerns, and multiple regulations.[5]

California experienced a large number of base closings during the military cutbacks. During the 1988 and 1991 rounds of base closings, eighteen California bases were closed. During the 1993 round of closings, there were twelve additional California bases listed. Defense outlays in California peaked in 1988 at $63 billion (in 1993 dollars). Under the 1993 Clinton proposal, outlays would fall to $33 billion in 1997.[6] It was also estimated that about 162,000 defense-related jobs were lost between January 1988 and January 1993, while an additional 125,000 jobs were estimated to be lost by the end of 1997.[7]

The 1986 National Immigration Control and Reform Act granted amnesty to some specific groups of undocumented immigrants and also established the State Legalization Impact Assistance Grant (SLIAG) program to provide $3.5 billion to reimburse state and local governments for a variety of basic health, welfare, and education services for the three million newly legalized citizens. California has more of the newly legalized residents than all of the other states combined—an estimated 54 percent.

California's share of the $3.5 billion was more than proportionate, $2.1 billion, reflecting the state's high costs and large undocumented population. The state developed a spending plan for these funds spread out over seven years. However, since 1989, the national government has provided less than the full SLIAG financial support promised. The cumulative deficit for California is now over $500 million.

In addition to the disappearing SLIAG funding, since 1986 the national government has steadily reduced and ultimately eliminated funding for several services that are complementary to the immigration problems. For example, prior to 1986, the national government paid for all categorical program costs for refugees, including AFDC, SSI/SSP, and Medicaid for thirty-six months.[8] The original thirty-six months dropped to thirty-one months, then twenty-four months, then four months, and by January of 1991, it had disappeared.[9]

California's fiscal problems are not all exogenous. In particular, caseloads increasing faster than population growth, a fiscal and regulatory environment perceived by business to be hostile to growth, and a series of initiatives and legislative responses are also responsible for the current fiscal situations.

Caseloads for welfare and corrections have been increasing faster than the rate of population growth.[10] At least some of this increase is uncontrollable, and is a direct function of the high unemployment caused by the recession. However, some of the increase has occurred because of state legislative decisions, such as increased penalties for different types of crimes. Also, at least some of the dollar costs (for example Medicaid benefits or costs associated with increased incarceration rates) are at least partially under the control of the state.

California's business climate has often been criticized as hostile. Its strict environmental and endangered species regulations have been in place since the early 1970s and the mid 1980s. Its workers' compensation plans had rates that were among the highest in the United States while the benefits were among the lowest. There are perceptions of a clogged regulatory and permitting process. Yet, all of these factors existed during the time of rapid growth in California during the 1970s and 1980s. During this time there has been some discussion, but little data, on an exodus of firms from California.[11]

California's recent history is closely tied to a series of initiatives, legislative responses, and legislative and executive inability to make difficult decisions. Key to much of this is the Proposition 13 initiative of 1978.

California residential property values rapidly increased in the mid to late 1970s.[12] The state legislature was unable to decide between the competing property tax relief strategies of (a) pure relief versus (b) income redistribution relief, and so did nothing as the legislative session closed in November 1977. Howard Jarvis and Paul Gann immediately gathered twice as many signatures as necessary to qualify an initiative, and in June 1978, Proposition 13 passed with over 60 percent of the vote.

Proposition 13 did several things: it limited the property tax rate to one percent of market value except as necessary to pay for previously approved debt; it rolled back assessments to March 1, 1975, or to the date that the property changed ownership or was newly constructed; it limited annual property value adjustments to 2 percent per year; it prohibited the state and local governments from imposing any taxes on the sale of real property; and it required a two-thirds vote in each house of the legislature or of the electorate to increase taxes used for special purposes (i.e., not General Fund purposes). The passage of Proposition 13 cut back local property taxes by about $7 billion.

The legislature quickly passed a local government relief bill that gave block grants to cities, counties, and special districts and established a property tax allocation system. Then, during the next year, the legislature rewrote much of this legislation under the new rubric of AB 8. AB 8 is still in effect, although much changed over time.

While extraordinarily complex (it was 108 pages long), the principal effects that AB 8 had on the current set of budget problems result from two basic actions. The first was that the state dramatically increased its share of the funding of K–12 education. This meant that the local property tax was supplanted by state funds. This allowed more of the (greatly reduced) property taxes to be available for cities, counties, and special districts. The state also "bought out" a major share of the county health and welfare programs.[13] The state was able to fund these activities out of its accumulated surplus.

In 1979, another constitutional amendment, Proposition 4, was passed by the voters. This limited tax-financed appropriations by all California governments to the prior year's amount, adjusted for changes in population and inflation. Importantly, however, it was possible to exceed the limit for higher levels of service financed by user charges.[14]

Proposition 98 passed in 1988 and was later amended by Proposition 111 of 1989. Together, these initiatives earmarked a minimum level of revenues for K–12 and the community colleges—about 40 percent of the State's general fund at that time.[15] This funding is currently based on three tests: two for normal or high revenue-growth years and one for low revenue-growth years. Minimum funding guarantees can also be suspended for one year for any reason. By earmarking 40 percent of the budget, these propositions guaranteed a stable source of revenues for schools but also constrained the legislature's options for other budget items.

Even though the governor must submit a balanced budget, California has recently adopted the technique of running annual budget deficits, which were rolled over into future years. This was done by overestimating revenues and underestimating expenditures.[16] The closing budget balances of five of the last seven years were negative, reaching a maximum of a $3.3 billion deficit in 1991–1992. The 1993–

1994 estimated deficit was $683 million.[17] By continually carrying forward budget deficits, the state makes solving the fiscal problem increasingly difficult.

Some Overall Trends

Table 7–1 shows a matrix of state government expenditures. Despite protestations to the contrary, total state spending generally rose from 1990–1991 through 1993–1994. This occurred principally because of the rapid increase in federal funds. However, for purposes of this analysis, only general fund expenditures will be examined, since they are directly under the control of the state.[18] With this focus, general fund spending in 1993–1994 will decline by almost 4 percent from 1992–1993, and over 9 percent from its peak in 1991–1992. In fact it will be less than was spent (in nominal dollars) in 1989–1990. After adjusting for inflation and population growth, the decline is even more significant—more than 20 percent since 1989–1990.[19]

State employment has slightly increased, by about 3.1 percent since 1990–1991. This slight increase masks two trends: (1) a continuous increase in corrections coupled with a decline in higher education and (2) a major increase in 1993–1994 for all but higher education.[20] Local employment has just about remained the same during this time, except for cities that have seen a 3.6 percent decline. All of this should be taken in the context of a 6.3 percent population growth.

The four principal areas of spending in the budget are K–12 education, higher education, health and welfare, and adult corrections. Table 7–2 shows the relevant data. A detailed discussion of some of the trends in these expenditures will occur in Section II, Responses and Strategies.

As Table 7–3 indicates, the revenue system for California is heavily pro-cyclical, with about 90 percent coming from the personal income tax, the sales and use tax, and the bank and corporate income tax. It is not surprising, then, to observe that nominal total general fund revenues have been declining at about 2½ percent per year since 1991–1992. Further, when put into per $100 of personal income terms, the decline has been even greater, almost twice as fast. This has been principally driven by the large decline in sales and use tax revenues, which have been falling at the rate of over 7 percent per year.[21]

TABLE 7-1 California State Expenditures (in Billions)

Budget Type	FY90–91	FY91–92	FY92–93	FY93–94	% Change FY92–FY91	% Change FY93–FY92	% Change FY94–FY93	% Change FY94–FY91
State General Fund	$40.3	$43.3	$40.9	$39.3	7.6	-5.5	-3.9	-2.3
State Special Funds	8.6	11.2	11.7	12.9	30.7	4.1	10.9	51.0
State Total	48.8	54.5	52.6	52.3	11.7	-3.5	-0.5	7.2
Federal Funds	21.5	26.7	29.6	31.8	24.4	10.7	7.4	47.8
Total including Federal Funds	70.3	81.2	82.2	84.1	15.6	1.2	2.3	19.6

Source: Governor's Budget Summary, Selected years, Schedules 1 and 2. Note that these figures do not include the "Selected Bond Fund Expenditures" from the Governor's Budget. Fiscal year 93–94 are projections.

TABLE 7–2 Major General Fund Expenditures, California (Dollars in Billions)

Program	FY91	FY92	FY93	FY94	% Change FY92–FY91	% Change FY93–FY92	% Change FY94–FY93	% Change FY94–FY91
K-12, Gen. Fund	$15.5	$16.3	$16.2	$14.6	5.2	-0.6	-9.9	-5.8
K-12 Caseload (000)	5,273	5,416	5,520	5,581	2.7	1.9	1.1	5.8
Higher Education	$5.5	$5.4	$4.7	$4.2	-1.8	-13.0	-10.6	-23.6
Community College	$1.7	$1.7	$1.3	$0.9	0.0	-23.5	-30.8	-47.1
Calif. State Univ.	2.1	$1.6	$1.5	$1.5	-23.8	-6.3	0.0	-28.6
University of Calif.	$1.7	$2.1	$1.9	$1.8	23.5	-9.5	-5.3	5.9
Com. Col. Caseload (000)	841.1	952.74	927.4	887.9	13.3	-2.7	-4.3	5.6
CSU Caseload (000)	278.5	270.7	258.4	246.5	-2.8	-4.6	-4.6	-11.5
UC Caseload (000)	155.86	156.4	154.3	151.7	0.4	-1.3	-1.7	-2.6
Major Health and Welfare	$9.3	$11.1	$10.7	$9.8	19.4	-3.6	-8.4	5.4
AFDC	$3.0	3.0	2.9	3.1	0.0	-3.3	6.9	3.3
Medicaid	$4.0	5.8	5.4	5.8	45.0	-6.9	7.4	45.0
SSI/SSP	$2.3	$2.3	$2.3	$2.1	0.0	0.0	-8.7	-8.7
AFDC Caseload (Average Monthly Recipients)	2,048	2,266	2,415	2,597	10.6	6.6	7.5	26.8
Medicaid Caseload (000)	4,002	4,550	5,051	5,374	13.7	11.0	6.4	34.3
SSI/SSP Caseload (000)	687	916	961	992	33.3	4.9	3.2	44.3
Adult Correction	$2.1	$2.4	$2.4	$2.8	14.3	0.0	16.7	33.3
Caseload (000)	174.6	188.0	199.4	212.9	7.6	6.1	6.8	21.9

Sources: Governor's Budget, Misc. years; Legislative Analyst's Office, State Spending Plan, various years; Department of Social Services, "Data Index," December, 1993.

TABLE 7–3 California General Fund Revenues (in Billions)

	FY91	FY92	FY93	FY94	% Change FY92-FY91	% Change FY93-FY92	% Change FY94-FY93	% Change FY94-FY91
Personal Income Tax	$16.8	$17.2	$16.8	$16.9	2.3	-2.8	0.8	0.3
per capita	$562.08	$562.55	$535.75	$529.33	0.1	-4.8	-1.2	-5.8
per $100 of income	2.73	2.76	2.62	2.55	1.1	-5.1	-2.7	-6.6
% of General Fund	44.1	41.0	40.9	42.4	-7.0	-0.2	3.7	-3.9
Sales and Use Tax	13,303	16,146	15,110	14,256	21.4	-6.4	-5.7	7.2
per capita	443.79	526.86	483.01	446.52	18.7	-8.3	-7.6	0.6
per $100 of income	2.16	2.59	2.36	2.15	19.9	-8.9	-8.9	-0.5
% of General Fund	34.8	38.4	36.9	35.8	10.3	-3.9	-3.0	2.9
Bank and Corporate Tax	4,508	4,494	4,850	4,900	-0.3	7.9	1.0	8.7
per capita	150.39	146.64	155.04	153.48	-2.5	5.7	-1.0	2.1
per $100 of income	.73	.72	.76	.74	-1.4	5.6	-2.6	1.4
% of General Fund	11.8	10.7	11.8	12.3	-9.3	10.3	4.2	4.2
Other	3,554	4,146	4,222	3,819	16.7	1.8	-9.6	7.5
per capita	118.56	135.29	134.96	119.62	14.1	-0.2	-11.4	0.9
per $100 of income	.58	.66	.66	.58	13.8	0.0	-12.1	0.0
% of General Fund	9.3	9.9	10.3	9.6	6.5	4.0	-6.8	3.2
Total	38,214	42,026	40,942	39,875	10.0	-2.6	-2.6	4.4
per capita	1,274.82	1,371.34	1,308.76	1,248.94	7.6	-4.6	-4.6	-2.0
per $100 of income	6.20	6.73	6.39	6.01	8.5	-5.1	-6.0	-3.1

Source: Governor's Budget, Misc. Years, Schedules 1 and 3.

SECTION II: RESPONSES AND STRATEGIES FOR DEALING WITH FISCAL STRESS

The state faced an immense gap between desired expenditures and received revenues for FY91 through FY94. The aggregate magnitude of this gap between these years was approximately $37.1 billion.

An Overall Look at FY91 through FY 94

The state engaged in four basic strategies to attempt to fill the gap. It shifted responsibilities to other levels of government, it engaged in deferrals and smoke and mirror budgeting, it reduced programs, and it raised taxes. Table 7–4 indicates how these decisions were attempted.[22] While the last three years will be analyzed below, some general conclusions can be drawn.

- About 54 percent of the total budget gap has been addressed through either programmatic reductions or increasing resources. About 23 percent has been addressed through shifting responsibilities to either local jurisdictions or to the national government. Eighteen percent fall into the smoke and mirrors category.
- The extent to which the gap was closed varied by year. Over time, there seems to be an increasing tendency toward shifts and deferrals and away from hard decision making. In fiscal year 1990–1991, 83 percent of decisions related to either funding reductions or resource increases. By fiscal year 1994, perhaps as much as 76 percent of the gap closing might be categorized as shifts and deferrals.
- The total numbers are staggering. Over $12 billion in program reductions and nearly $8 billion of increased resources over the four-year period are not inconsequential. For example, the $8 billion dollar adjustment in FY94 should be seen in context of the almost $40 billion of General Fund revenues.

The following discussion should help in illuminating the California experience. Most of this discussion will center on the 1991–1992 budget, since its implementation involved changing many of the ways that California did its business. Because of the complexity of the discussion of the yearly changes, short case studies of education,

TABLE 7–4   California Budget Decisions Implemented[a]

Fiscal Year	FY91	FY92	FY93	FY94	Total
I. Shift to Other Levels of Gov't		**2.7**	**2.3**	**3.7**	**8.7**
To Local		2.4	1.7	2.8	6.9
To Federal		.3	.6	.9	1.8
II. Deferrals, Accounting Changes, etc.	**.6**	**1.7**	**1.9**	**2.4**	**6.6**
Proposition 98		—	—	.9	.9
Retirement Deferrals	.6	.7	.2	.3	1.8
Accounting Changes, Other		1.0	1.7	1.2	3.9
III. Funding Reductions	**2.1**	**4.1**	**5.1**	**1.1**	**12.4**
Fund Shifts		.7	.7	.5	1.9
Health/Welfare	.3	—	.8	.3	1.4
Prop. 98 Recalculation		1.9	1.9	(.1)	3.7
Employee Compensation		.4	.2	—	.6
Higher Education		—	.7	.1	.8
Other	1.6	1.1	.7	.3	3.7
Not Classified	.2				.2
IV. Increased Resources	**.9**	**5.6**	**.6**	**.8**	**7.9**
Tax/Revenue Actions	.8	5.1	.5	.5	6.9
Fees		.5	.2	.2	.9
Other	.1	—	—	.1	.2
V. Miscellaneous		**.2**	**1.3**	**—**	**1.5**
Total	**3.6**	**14.3**	**11.2**	**8.0**	**37.1**

[a]1990–91 difference from LAO: Retirement contributions changed from funding reductions (LAO) to deferrals, etc. 0.6 billion.
1991–92 differences from LAO: moved fund transfers from increased resources (LAO) to program reductions (LAO's in 1993–1994) (0.7 billion); moved accounting changes from increased resources (LAO) to deferrals, etc. (0.7 billion)
Subheadings do not always total to headings because of rounding.
Realignment based tax increases at local level are in the shift (I) category (not increased resources).

welfare, and local government funding will be presented after the year-by-year analysis.

The 1991–1992 Budget and Implications

Against the advice of some of his friends, Republican Pete Wilson left his relatively secure U.S. Senate seat, ran for and was elected governor, taking office in January 1991.[23] His first budget, the 1991–1992 budget, was submitted almost immediately. It was presented in the context of a preceding 1990–1991 budget that was exemplified by major expenditure cuts; an anticipated $1.9 billion General Fund deficit at the end of the 1990–1991; and a deepening recession.

The fact that there were continuing budget problems was not a surprise. The Assembly Committee on Revenue and Taxation had held hearings six months earlier, in June 1990. The hearings concluded that revenues were falling short of expectations and expenditures were higher than expected because of population growth, inflation, and new programs. Given the Democratic composition of the committee, its conclusion was not unexpected:

A basic principle of public finance provides that revenue structures should finance a given level of service demanded, **revenue structures do not determine the level of service required** (emphasis in original).[24]

It was in this environment that Governor Wilson's first budget was considered.[25]

Governor Wilson immediately faced a $7 billion gap between the workload budget and available revenues.[26] This gap arose from his estimate of $1.9 billion to pay off the 1990–1991 deficit, $3.7 billion to fund the current levels of services in the 1991–1992 budget year, and $1.4 billion to fund the state's reserve fund. He proposed to fill the gap through a variety of means, most of which were relatively small, but in the aggregate did add up to the $7 billion. The principal proposals involved across-the-board cuts, eliminating cost-of-living allowances (COLAs) and decreasing AFDC payments, increasing fees, recalculating K–14 education expenditures, shifting some revenues and program responsibilities to the counties (to be known as "realignment"), increasing taxes, and changing accounting methods.

Despite the budget squeeze, the governor did propose some shifting of resources to begin to address some long-term problems, with the emphasis being on prevention. In particular, the governor suggested three other long-term reforms: extending perinatal and well-baby services to uninsured women, expanding childrens' health services, and restructuring welfare. However, the total amount of money allocated for all of these programs was under $200 million out of a $43.3 billion General Fund budget.

The Legislative Analyst is principally responsible for the formal reaction to the governor's budget. Soon after the release of the budget, the Analyst issued her overview. She found that the total budget gap was closer to $9.9 billion, not the $7 billion that had been announced only two weeks earlier.[27]

The Analyst was also pessimistic about the long-run ability of the state to close the funding gap. She argued that about half of the gap was due to cyclical phenomena and would close as the economy recovers. This meant that half of the gap was due to structural causes, with demands for expenditures increasing faster than revenues, even when the economy is healthy. Therefore, without long-run structural change, the gap would not disappear.

In California, after the governor introduces the budget in January and the Legislative Analyst presents the detailed analysis in February, little happens until May, when the Department of Finance revises the expenditure and revenue estimates for the upcoming year. This occurred during the spring of 1991.

Because of the declining economy, revenues received never reached the Department of Finance's projections. In addition, caseloads for health, welfare, education, and institutional population also exceeded projections. While some of the caseload increases occurred because of population growth, others occurred because of the recession.[28] By June, the gap reached $14.3 billion, the number ultimately utilized for budget purposes. It had more than doubled since January.

The ultimate gap closing relied upon three traditional steps and one nontraditional attempt. In so doing, it raised the possibility of some long-run developments that could influence future budgets.

Traditional step 1: Raise taxes. Both state income tax rates and state sales tax rates and base were increased. Two additional brackets were added to the state income tax.[29] In addition to the old top rate of 9.3 percent beginning at about $58,000 (for a joint return), the state added a 10 percent rate for taxable incomes in excess of $200,000 and 11 percent for taxable incomes over $400,000 (both for joint returns). The means test for the renter's credit on the state income tax was also increased,[30] along with increased conformity with the federal tax laws, a two-year disallowal of carry forward of net operating loss, an extension of the sunset on the research and development tax credit, and an increase in the alternative minimum tax rate from 7 percent to 8.5 percent.

The sales tax was increased by 1.25 cents. Of this, one-half cent was a temporary tax for the state general fund, one-fourth cent was a permanent sales tax increase for the state, and the last one-half cent was a permanent increase for the counties, allocated on a point-of-sale basis. The sales tax base was also broadened to include candy and snack foods, aircraft and ship fuel, bottled water, and newspapers and periodicals.[31]

In addition, vehicle license fees and college and university fees were increased to yield an additional $865 million.

Traditional step 2: Cut expenditures from projected levels. Even though it appears as if there were an expenditure cut of about $4 billion, total general fund expenditures were estimated to increase by about $3.1 billion and total state expenditures (including federal funds) by about $11.1 billion. The cut was only from levels projected under a no change in legislation assumption.

The principal budget cuts from the caseload levels were in the unallocated trigger reductions[32] (about $800 million), employee compensation savings (about $400 million), K–12 education (about $1.6 billion), and a variety of structural changes in AFDC, foster care, and Medicaid programs (about $600 million). In addition, the budget played a complex game of shifting and loaning funds to K–14 education, which gave the appearance of both maintaining constant expenditures as well as saving about $1.3 billion.

In addition to the above cuts, the budget made reductions in several social service and Medicaid programs. AFDC benefits were reduced by 4.4 percent, there was a five-year suspension of automatic cost-of-living allowances for a number of entitlement programs, and Medicaid eligibility would continue to be determined based on the old AFDC payment. Also included in these reforms was a change in the way that AFDC grants were to be calculated for recipients with income. The effect was to establish a work incentive for recipients, because the amount of income they will be allowed to keep without offsetting grant reductions was increased.

Traditional step 3: Smoke and mirrors. The typical California budget is full of special fund transfers, constantly changing accounting methods, assumptions of increased federal funding, and optimistic economic scenarios. The 1991–1992 budget utilized all of these techniques. One in particular caused a good deal of political infighting, a statutory change in the state pension system funding. Here, the state restructured the pension plan by arbitrarily assuming increased yields in investments so that the state contribution could be reduced. In addition, the state established a two-tier retirement system. These saved about $700 million.

Nontraditional step 4: Realignment. There was a realignment of responsibilities and revenues between the state and the counties. The counties would receive extra revenues and in return would absorb some responsibilities from the state. The original intent was to generate about $900 million toward solving a $7 billion gap. With the gap growing to $14.3 billion, realignment had become significantly more complex and important, with it ultimately becoming over a $2 billion transfer. Realignment will be discussed in more detail in Section III.

The 1992–1993 Budget and Implications

The recession did not end as predicted. In November 1991, Prudential Securities issued a report on the California economy that was notable for its pessimism. It concluded that the California economy was in a worse recession than the rest of the country, that the recession would last through 1992 at least, and finally, that California should lag the U.S. for several years in terms of escaping from the recession.[33]

Also in that November, a new focus of debate emerged. The California Department of Finance prepared a report entitled "California's Growing Taxpayer Squeeze." This brief report argued that California's major tax "receiver" groups—students, welfare recipients, prisoners, and Medicaid clients—were growing more rapidly than its "taxpayer" group—people 18 to 64 years of age. The net result would be a long term $20 billion shortfall in the budget by the year 2000, unless the California business climate improved, the growth in government spending was reduced, and prevention of problems was emphasized.[34] Although the demographic projections were heavily criticized as being inconsistent with projections done by other public and private researchers, and that people in the taxpayer group might also be in the receiver group, the thrust of the report emphasizing economic growth and fiscal conservatism seemed a relatively straightforward statement of the governor's philosophy.[35]

By December 1991, it was already clear that (1) realignment revenues would be less than budgeted so counties would be facing serious shortfalls, (2) solving the $14.3 budget gap for 1991–1992 did not solve the state's budget problems, and (3) the state would end up going into 1992–1993 with a budget deficit. The LAO estimated that the budget deficit for 1991–1992 would be about $2.2 billion and the total funding gap for 1992–1993 was estimated to be $6.6 billion.[36]

In January 1992, the governor presented a budget that reduced programs by $2.8 billion, shifted funds by $.5 billion, reduced the reserve to $105 million, and slightly increased revenues through a variety of small changes. There were to be no general tax increases. About $1 billion of the budget gap solutions would be realized in 1991–1992, reducing the carryover deficit to about $1.8 billion.

The May revisions did not help. The governor recognized that the recession had not ended in the first quarter of 1992, and now predicted a fourth quarter ending as well as slow growth for 1993–1994. This resulted in new estimates of revenue shortfalls and expenditure increases, so the governor then estimated a new total gap of about $10.8 billion. And even this was highly risky, since the economic impact of the Los Angeles riots was not considered, and the SLIAG funds and federal waivers for the welfare reforms had still not been obtained.

The adoption of this budget was extraordinarily difficult. It was finally signed on September 2, 1992, sixty-three days after the statutory deadline. During that time, the state paid some of its bills and many of its workers with I.O.Us (technically, registered warrants) instead of immediately cashable paychecks.[37] In August, after the Department of Finance admitted that it would be 1993 at the earliest before any meaningful state economic recovery would occur, the governor and the majority and minority leaders of the assembly and senate met in continuing conferences to produce a budget document. At that time, the participants believed that they were closing a $7.9 billion gap, although after a more careful analysis, it turned out that the gap was really $11.2 billion.[38] The gap was almost entirely covered by expenditure cuts and tax shifts.

Principal Expenditure Reductions

1. Higher Education Funding[39]
   The budget provided about $224 million less in general fund support for the University of California. It was anticipated that up to $72 million of this cut would be offset by increased student fees. The UC Regents' response was an increase in fees as well as the implementation of an early retirement program for faculty and staff.

   The California State University system was cut by about 7.5 percent, or about $123 million. The Legislative Analyst estimated that with a fee increase, the CSU system could recoup about $55 million. Again, both fee increases and an early retirement program were implemented.

   The community colleges were provided with a 2.5 percent increase in funding, or about $66 million. However, this actually reflected a decline of $430 million from the general fund, a loan of $241 million, which is to be repaid over the next two years, and an increase of $49 million from student fees.

2. Personnel Savings
   State employees faced an eighteen-month-long personal leave program that consisted of a mandatory one-day-per-month reduction in pay with no reduction in work, and of course, no pay increase. However, employees would earn one day of credit per month, and at the end of the eighteen-month period, would be eligible to receive either a cash payment or time off. Further, after the eighteen months, employees would receive a 5 percent pay increase (in January 1994) and a 3 to 5 percent increase in January 1995. The state's contributions for health benefits and pension funds were also changed for a net savings of about $330 million.

3. Judiciary and Criminal Justice Funding
   Even criminal justice programs faced funding reductions of a total of about $242 million or 6.2 percent. However, more than half of the cuts were in trial court funding, which put

additional funding on the counties because they must come
up with the balance of financial support.

4. Health and Welfare Funding
   Health and welfare programs were reduced by $967 million
   from 1991–1992. AFDC benefits were reduced by 5.8 percent
   and a residency requirement was implemented, Supplemental Security Income/State Supplemental Program (SSI/SSP)
   grants were also reduced by 5.8 percent, legislation was enacted to help counties control general assistance costs, and in-
   house supported services were reduced by about 12 percent.

A tax shift for K–14 funding. Through a series of loans and recalculations, the state was able to keep per pupil expenditures constant in
nominal terms. Included also was a property tax shift of about $1.1
billion from local jurisdictions to schools. This reduced the state's
share of school financing. The case study of local government funding
will provide more detail.

The legislature also consolidated and then reduced almost all K–
12 categorical program spending into one "mega-item" ($4.5 billion).
This was an across the board reduction of 2.1 percent, with some
discretion for school districts to redirect up to 5 percent of funds
allocated to specific programs to other categorical programs.

The 1993–1994 Budget and Implications

As California careened from one fiscal year to the next, the 1993–1994
budget reflected a continuation of several past trends as well as the
introduction of additional possibilities. Originally, the Legislative Analyst forecasted an $8.6 billion budget gap between current services
budgets and revenues received.[40]

Because of the deficit carryover, the nominal expenditure cutbacks were more dramatic: total general fund expenditures were
budgeted to fall by nearly $2 billion. There were three components
to these initial proposals: a general expenditure cutback, an additional
shift in resources from local governments to school districts, and the
elimination of the ½-cent sales tax that had been added in 1991–1992.

The governor proposed an additional shift of $2.6 billion in prop-
erty tax collections from cities, counties, and special districts to school
districts. Through this shift, the state would have to spend $2.6 billion

less of its revenues for schools, and would therefore have the revenues available for other state expenditures.

A series of temporary taxes were enacted as a partial solution to the 1991–1992 budget gap. Among these was a ½-cent sales tax that was to expire on June 30, 1993. At the time of its adoption, the widely held view was that the California economy would be out of the recession by that time and so the tax would not be needed. That view was wrong.

As part of the governor's May revision proposals, he admitted that the additional ½-cent sales tax should not expire. However, rather than have the state continue to impose the tax, the governor proposed that it be allowed to expire at the state level but counties could reimpose it at the county level. After some negotiations, the final outcome was a statewide sales tax increase earmarked (but with no maintenance of effort requirement) for the counties' spending on public safety that was passed by the electorate in November 1993.

To the surprise of many, Governor Wilson was able to sign the budget on time, June 30, 1993. The budget was designed to pay off the $2.8 billion carryover from 1992–1993 over a two-year period, with most of it being paid off in 1993–1994.[41] An $8 billion gap was closed by four basic actions: (1) there was a shift to other levels of government of $3.7 billion ($2.3 billion to local governments and $1.4 to the federal government); (2) cost deferrals, loans, and revenue accelerations saved $2.3 billion; (3) program reductions saved $1.2 billion; and (4) increased resources contributed about $800 million.

Principal Expenditure Reductions

1. Welfare Cutbacks

   AFDC maximum grants were reduced by 2.7 percent from 1992–1993 levels (maximum grant for a family of three dropped from $624 to $607 per month). In addition, SSI/SSP maximum grants were also reduced by 2.7 percent. The federal COLA for SSI/SSP was not be passed through to be added to the grant, but rather the state's contribution declined by that amount, leaving the net grant unchanged, but saving the state about $65 million.

2. Higher Education

   The University of California system was cut by $84.4 million, but of that, increased student fees were anticipated to increase to offset $63.1 million, leading to a net cut of $21.3 million. The California State University system, after factoring in increased student fees, saw an actual increase in revenues of almost $10 million. Finally, the community colleges, including student fee increases, realized an increase of $32.3 million.

3. General Government

The principal savings in this category came from the two-year suspension of the Renter's Tax Credit program. This program provided a "refundable" income tax credit to moderate and low-income renters. Savings were $390 million in 1993–1994 and are estimated to be $445 million in 1994–1995.

4. Smoke and Mirrors

The usual smoke and mirrors also appeared. Special fund transfers of about $345 million and loans of about $92 million were utilized. Unallocated general programmatic reductions of $50 million were implemented. And, the state contribution to the retirement system was shifted to be one year in arrears rather than six months.

Three Case Studies of Specific Strategies

Education. Proposition 98, passed in 1988 and amended by Proposition 111 in 1989, established a minimum funding guarantee for K–14 education. While initially intended to be a floor for spending, it has become much more of a ceiling with the governor and legislature typically attempting to satisfy minimally the requirements and then move on to other areas. A major element of the state's response to the fiscal stress during the 1991–1992 through 1993–1994 fiscal years involved a series of recalculations of past expenditures, prepayments for future expenditures and shifting funds from local governments: The total amount involved in the loans and recalculations was about $3.1 billion.[42] The total amount of money shifted from local government was about $3.9 billion.

Part of this structure began to collapse in the fall of 1993. In *California Teachers' Association et. al v. Gould*, the superior court ruled that schools are **not** required to repay either recaptured funds or prepayment loans. However, only the loans are counted in the Proposition 98 base. At a minimum, it appears as if future state obligations to schools might be increased by nearly $800 million.[43]

Because of the Proposition 98 loans, repayments and recapture effects and because of the property tax shift from local governments to school districts thus replacing state aid, it can appear as if total expenditures on education have fallen. This is not true. Table 7–2 indicates that state General Fund aid has declined; however, with increasing enrollments and constant expenditures per pupil, total expenditures have increased. However, with constant nominal expenditures per pupil, real expenditures per pupil fell by about 10.5 percent.[44]

Finally, during this entire time period, enrollment in California schools has become far more heterogeneous. In 1990–1991, K–12 enrollment was about 34 percent Hispanic, 9 percent black, and 46 percent white. Three years later, enrollment was about 37 percent Hispanic, 9 percent black and 42 percent white.[45]

There have been large fee increases for all three major public institutions of higher education in California. University of California fees and community college fees have more than doubled while California State University fees have gone up by about 85 percent since 1990–1991.[46] Coincident with this is a decline in enrollment of about 2 percent of UC, about 12 percent for CSU, and about 9 percent for the community colleges.[47] Several facts should be noted about these relationships.

First, the state does not set University of California fees; they are set by the UC Board of Regents. The regents have chosen to increase fees to fund the reduced state funding; other choices such as increased workload or program elimination could have been utilized to a greater extent.

Second, declining enrollment could also reflect general economic conditions as well as increased fees. Remember, this time period was one of increased unemployment and recession in California.

Finally, all of these fees are either the lowest or among the lowest in the U.S., even after their increases. Compared to other states, California is still a bargain for higher education.

Welfare.[48] California has several welfare programs, including General Assistance, SSI/SSP, food stamps, Medicaid, and AFDC. The latter is the largest program for able-bodied adults and their children.[49] Solving the budget problems of the past several years has required several changes in the California system that reflect many compromises. Three types of program reforms were emphasized: grant reductions, work incentives, and education and training programs.

Although the majority in the legislature resisted grant cuts, the ultimate compromise year after year involved their reduction. The typical argument was that California is a high grant state and was attracting migrants from other states and illegal immigrants from other countries. The net results were total AFDC cuts of 14.9 percent, tightened eligibility rules, including a twelve-month waiting period to obtain California level benefits, and changing county General Assistance requirements allowing reductions in these county programs. In addition, the statutory cost-of-living allowances were suspended until FY 97.[50] During the last three years of grant reductions, a family of three would have seen a nominal decline of 8.4 percent in its grant.[51]

Work incentives and educational assistance played a much smaller role in the welfare reforms. In addition to the GAIN program, the state applied for and received federal waivers that allowed them to disregard two provisions of federal law that are believed to reduce work incentives.[52] In addition, some child care support was increased indirectly and a program was implemented that allowed some to remain eligible for Medicaid and child care benefits even if they refused an AFDC grant. Included under educational assistance is the "Cal Learn" program that gives cash bonuses for scholastic performance and graduation and implements cash sanctions for poor academic attendance.

Most of the changes reflect efforts to contain the program costs that were projected to be increasing rapidly because of the economic climate. Between fiscal year 1991 and fiscal year 1994, caseload increases for AFDC, Medicaid, and SSI/SSP ranged from 27 to 44 percent; yet only Medicaid expenditures rose dramatically, and AFDC rose only marginally.

Local government funding. Local governments have sometimes claimed that the state had solved its budget problems on their backs. There is some truth to the accusation.

The principal effect on local government in 1992–1993 was the $1.1 billion property tax shift from local governments to schools. This increased school district revenues and allowed the state to reduce the funds it gave the schools. Cities (a loss of $200 million), counties (a loss of $525 million), special districts (a loss of $206 million), and redevelopment agencies (a loss of $200 million) were all affected.

This process continued in 1993–1994. The state permanently took $2.6 billion from local agencies from the local property tax revenues and again gave it to schools. Nearly $2 billion would come from counties, $288 million from cities, $244 million from special districts, and $65 million from redevelopment agencies. These are permanent cuts. For redevelopment agencies, this is a temporary reduction and will not be in effect in FY 96.

In order to fund these cutbacks, the final state budget incorporated several revenue enhancing possibilities for local government. The two most important were the sales tax extension and increased vehicle license fee revenues. These were included as part of the realignment reform. Without realignment, this new source of relatively stable funding for local government might not have been possible.

As part of the final budget, the ½-cent sales tax that was to expire on July 1 was extended for six months. In November, the voters decided to make this extension permanent, with the revenues allocated to maintaining public safety activities at the local level. In a change from the past in which sales tax revenues were allocated on the basis of point of sale, these funds will be allocated on the basis of property tax losses.

In addition to increased revenues, the state also implemented mandate relief for a variety of programs, including the justice system and some health and welfare programs. It also revised state guidelines regarding general assistance grant levels, allowing counties to reduce the value of General Assistance grants to 40 percent of the 1991 county poverty level for a period of twelve months.[53] The net impact of the property tax shift, sales tax extension, and mandate relief was predicted to be between a 1 and 2 percent cut in net revenues for cities and counties.[54]

SECTION III: SHARP BREAKS AND INNOVATIONS

Perhaps the most dramatic innovation that the state implemented was the 1991–1992 realignment of responsibilities and revenues among the state and counties. The ultimate program reflected a compromise between both political parties as well as state and local governments. Without the pressure of the immense FY92 deficit, it probably would not have occurred. This legislation included three major components: (1) program transfers from the state to the counties; (2) changes in state/county cost-sharing ratios for selected health programs and social services; and (3) increases in the state sales tax and the vehicle license fee earmarked to support the new financial responsibilities of the counties.

Realignment

The realignment measures eliminated a total of $1.7 billion in projected General Fund expenditures for the transferred programs and increased county costs through changing cost-sharing ratios by about $469 million, for a total increase in county expenditures of $2.2 billion. The revenues were to be generated by the increased sales tax (½ cent) earmarked for counties as well as the increase in the Vehicle License Fund (through a modified depreciation schedule). These came to be about $2.2 billion, leaving the county shortfall (presumably to be funded through administrative savings) originally estimated at $21 million. Additionally, a set of complex formulas were developed to allocate growth in the various revenue sources to specific programs, further earmarking resources.

The small projected county shortfall became much larger as the recession deepened. Ultimately, for FY 1991/92, the actual revenues were $241.8 million less than their original estimate, for FY 1992/93, the actual revenues were $229 million below their estimate, and by January 1994, revenues were already $64.3 million below their estimate of the previous six months. In fact, revenues have still not risen to the original estimate for FY 1991/92.[55]

Although it might appear that county expenditure discretion increased during these transfers, there were several strings attached. For example:

- Counties can transfer only up to 10 percent of funding from one major program area to another.
- Counties can transfer only an additional 10 percent from health programs to the entitlement-driven programs if increased caseload costs exceed the amount of revenues available in the social services account.
- Maintenance-of-effort requirements for some mental health programs required counties to make up the full amount of the current-year shortfall in the health account from their general purpose revenues if they wish to continue to receive other funds.[56]

Realignment has been considered a success by many of the participants. It did take expensive programs away from the state and it did provide a steady stream of revenues to the counties toward specific services with more flexibility in the use of those revenues. Many also claim that even with the less than expected revenues, county social services are still better off than they would have been because if the state had directly cut services, the cuts would have been far more draconian. There is also some evidence that service levels changed; for example, some mental health practitioners have claimed that the stability of revenues has allowed for better use of resources in that area. There has also been a decline in the use of some of the more expensive interventions in the foster care programs (which may not necessarily indicate more efficiency). However, a complete and formal analysis of the total realignment program has not yet been undertaken, nor is there any funding available to do so.[57]

Restructuring Government

Realignment generated a new focus on the appropriate role of the different levels of California government and a discussion of the entire intergovernmental system. And, although California does not have a state ACIR, it does have a plethora of analysts who are concerned with intergovernmental problems.

Principal among these is the Legislative Analyst. In *Perspectives and Issues*, published in February 1993, under the rubric of "Making Government Make Sense," she identified a series of problems that plague California's intergovernmental arena. These problems include counterproductive fiscal incentives, inappropriate assignment of responsibilities, inappropriate use of administrative oversight, unproductive competition for resources, and erosion of local control. They propose that governments in the state be reorganized in order to:

1. Maximize separation of state and local government duties,
2. Match redistributive programs with redistributive revenue sources at the highest level of government,
3. Recognize program linkages and restructure to promote service coordination and removal of barriers to innovation,
4. Rely on financial incentives to promote coordination.[58]

With this set of principles, local governments would transfer some programmatic responsibility to the state and vice versa while their share of the property tax would be increased while access to the sales tax would be reduced.

Restructuring government is a long-term project and subject to a great deal of political discussion and change. It is not clear whether it is truly meant to be taken seriously, although the Speaker of the Assembly has appointed a subcommittee to examine these potential changes and the governor has appointed a Constitutional Revision Commission.

Reinventing Government

The governor's 1993–1994 budget adopted the idea of "reinventing government." This is to consist of four components: (1) a downsizing of state operations (a reduction of 15% in selected state operations, legislative funding, and the judiciary); (2) an introduction of performance budgeting (in lieu of the automatic workload budget) in four pilot programs; (3) a reorganization of the executive branch, including the consolidation and elimination of many commissions, some departments, and the privatization of either Hastings School of Law, Boalt School of Law, the UC Davis Law School, or the UCLA Law School and the privatization of the California Maritime Academy; and, finally, (4) the expanded use of information and communications technologies to reduce management costs by expanding the span of control and improving the quality of service delivery. In 1993–1994, most of these suggestions remained only suggestions. The privatization has not occurred and performance budgeting has not yet been implemented. However, the latter is likely to go into effect for the next budget cycle.[59] Further, recently discovered information technology problems have led some computer-using state agencies to throw away their software. For example, the Department of Motor Vehicles has written off a $44.3 million system and the Student Aid Commission has started to believe that its $37 million system is not usable.[60]

Future Economic Development and Business Climate Programs

The recurring budget problems have forced the state to focus on its underlying economic structure. In 1992, the governor named a team of private entrepreneurs to come up with a statement of what should be done to improve the state's economic climate. This commission was headed by Peter Uberroth, of Los Angeles Olympic fame. The assembly Democrats, not to be outdone, also conducted a study of the business climate.

Both studies came up with quite similar conclusions. In addition to both urging reform of workers' compensation and streamlining the regulatory and permitting processes, both also urged improved education and job training programs and the provision of incentives for long-term investment and business development.

Given license to provide tax breaks, both Democrats and Republicans saw opportunities to fill in those details. During the 1993–1994 legislative session, nearly 60 tax-break bills were introduced, all justified by a supply-side belief that each would generate enough jobs so that enough income would occur so that enough taxes would be collected to offset the tax reduction. Ultimately, the legislature passed and the governor signed a series of tax credit measures that would generate about $400 million of tax relief for businesses.[61]

In addition to the tax reductions, a package of bills reforming worker's compensation were also signed. These bills contained medical-legal reforms, health treatment cost-containment provisions, and vocational rehabilitation benefits. They also required an overall rate reduction of 7 percent in insurance premiums. In addition, higher standards of "predominant cause" in compensation and tougher fraud-prevention measures were included. Finally, some benefits were increased by over 20 percent. Total savings to the workers' compensation system were anticipated to be about $1.5 billion.[62]

The Establishment of a Variety of New (but Small) Programs Oriented Toward Prevention of Children's Problems

Several new programs were established throughout this period that were oriented toward preventing children's health problems from developing. Some examples are:

- A perinatal insurance program;
- A multi-year program designed to expand the availability of state-subsidized preschool;
- Programs to refer children in grades K–6 to public health and social service providers;
- Programs to reduce the number of teenage pregnancies in California;

- Programs for family planning and providing mental health counseling in schools.

Nearly $200 million is included in these and some additional programs. These programs are still alive, but at low funding levels. *

A Movement to a Multi-year Budget Solution

Although California has really been in a multi-year budget solution framework for several years, it is only now being publicly discussed. The governor, in his 1993–1994 May Revision, has proposed a set of optimistic revenue forecasts and a set of savings in the health and welfare budgets in order to achieve a balanced budget by 1994–1995.

In addition to the governor's attempt to move to a multi-year framework, at least one powerful Democrat has also introduced the same notion: the Chair of the assembly Committee on Ways and Means has urged a two-year budget with an additional three years of economic forecasts, to provide a total of a five-year outlook.[63] (Of course, it might be noted that in 1988, no one was predicting the 1993 problems.)

SECTION IV: LOSERS AND WINNERS

A variety of strategies to close the gap between caseload driven expenditures and the tax revenues generated by the existing tax system have been utilized over the past four years. Within these solutions, there were far more losers than winners.

Some losers

1. K–14 Education
   Nominal, not real, dollars per ADA were kept constant during this time period. It might be that the increasing heterogeneity of the California student body should encourage increasing, not constant, ADA expenditures. Finally, the mega-item block grant, while allowing more flexibility among school expenditures, could lead to the recipients of previously earmarked funds to lose access to that money.

2. University of California/California State University/Community Colleges

   Higher education was a multiple loser. Programs and courses were cut, student fees were increased, and bonus retirement programs encouraged the retirement of the established faculty. Both the institutions and the students were affected.

   The public attitude toward the UC system also became negative. The stories of several hundred thousand dollar retirement bonuses surrounding the president and some of the other high level administrators generated a good deal of negative publicity.[64] In addition, workloads became a matter of public debate, and the high costs of both the UC and CSU system became public.[65] In the long run, this discussion could be more significant than the dollar cutbacks.

3. Local Government

   Local governments were principally hurt by the forced shift in property tax revenues. While the ½-cent sales tax continuation helped to offset this shift, it did not cover the total loss. There is some anecdotal evidence that local governments moved to more intensive use of charges, utilized personnel in different ways (e.g., community services officers rather than sworn police), and let maintenance slide on some projects. Further, those special districts that are property tax dependent (for example, library districts) have continually cut hours of service to make up for this loss. In addition to these service cutbacks, this loss of revenue has raised questions by rating agencies concerning the quality of credit of local government.

   Evidence is mixed on the affects of realignment. Revenues are smaller but more secure and, while the level of some services may have fallen and jurisdictions have adjusted their service mix, it is still unclear whether these reflect more efficient use of resources.

4. Politicians

   Both the governor and the legislature have often looked foolish during these budget discussions, especially during the sixty-three day delay of 1992. Public opinion polls showed little love for either side during this fight. Although the participants appeared to have learned this lesson because they were able to complete the 1993–1994 budget on time, they still have not risen in the eyes of the public.

5. Welfare Recipients

   Welfare recipients faced continued cuts in their benefits. Nominal levels of support were reduced. This was a major change from the past in which welfare benefits were sacrosanct.

6. State Analysts (Legislative Analyst's Office, Commission on State Finance)

   When messengers bring bad tidings, they sometimes pay a price. This may have happened to both the Legislative Analyst's Office (LAO), which experienced deep cuts, and the Commission on State Finance (COSF), which was eliminated.[66] The LAO is funded by the legislature and so is under the voter-mandated cutback provisions with the level of its staffing subject to legislative provision. The Analyst has been consistently more accurate than the legislature in its budget estimates and its staff has been consistently cut back. In February 1990, the LAO staff was at 104; by February 1994, the staff had dropped to fifty-four. The COSF was under the direction of the state treasurer (currently a Democrat). It too has been considerably more accurate than the Republican governor in its revenue and expenditure projections. The governor vetoed the appropriation necessary to keep the commission alive.

Some winners

1. Corrections

   Corrections was one element of the budget that showed increases. While these basically represented increasing caseloads rather than additional per capita resources, the Department of Corrections did receive an increase of almost 33 percent over the time period, while caseload increased by 22 percent.

2. Some Working Poor Welfare Recipients

   Although welfare payments were cut in nominal terms in most of the welfare programs, there were some allowances made for the working poor who were attempting to get off welfare. In particular, the amount that could be earned before welfare payments were reduced was increased, and thus the incentive to work was also increased.

3. Poor Pregnant Women and the Very Young
Throughout this period, several programs were instituted for prenatal care for poor women and health care for the very young. Although funded at extremely low levels, these programs recognized that prevention activities could ultimately save far more than they cost. These programs are still continuing.

SECTION V: SOME OVERALL LESSONS

For the most part, California followed strategies of expenditure cuts, tax increases (at least once), and smoke and mirrors. Tax expenditures remained the same and the cuts were essentially in health and welfare, education, and general government. The gimmicks were traditional—change accounting systems, reexamine pension contributions and change pension earning assumptions, underestimate the extent of the recession (this may not have been deliberate), recalculate school expenditures, and continue reliance on federal funds some of which never appeared.

The governor and legislature only learned modestly from these experiences and they still refuse to grapple with the state's structural problems. The 1994–1995 budget again was based on a two-year plan and balanced with assumed aid from the national government that no one truly believes will occur and a very modest expenditure growth. It took veiled threats from a debt-buying consortium led by Bank of America to force a trigger mechanism that will cut spending automatically (but allows taxes to sunset) in either 1994–1995 or 1995–1996. The result of these actions was a downgrading of California debt within two weeks of the budget's passage.

Despite the above, California did engage in a few thoughtful actions that might be useful for other states to consider. These include:

Change the Vocabulary. Although the "gap" between caseload budgeting and revenues is still a term used by the Legislative Analyst, the governor has recasted the budget in terms of an expenditure constraint—continually arguing that we must live within our means, even if it implies cutting sacred programs. The vocabulary of the assembly Committee on Revenue and Taxation (p. 9) has nearly disappeared. Entitlements have been marginally changed, but they are no longer always automatic.

Consider Intergovernmental Realignment. Over the last three years, some basic relationships between the state and local governments have been questioned. Services have been shifted and revenue flows have been altered. Although the new revenues have not kept up with new responsibilities, this may change as the economy improves. And truly major cuts in revenues were avoided.

Prevention Programs Can Be Considered. Even in dire financial straits, California has attempted to fund programs that, in the long run, might lead to less welfare and health expenditures because individuals have been able to break out of the system. Commitment by the governor seems necessary for these to survive.

Analyze the Entire State Economy. At the beginning of the recession, most California analysts believed that it would be short-lived. As it continued, the complaints about the regulations and state-imposed costs on business began to be taken more seriously. Many boards and commissions were abolished, a workers' compensation reform bill was passed, and some taxes focused on business were reduced.

Overall, California has encountered a major set of impacts, and has reacted by beginning a series of changes in its economic and governance structure. Whether these will be sufficient to be successful remains to be seen.

NOTES

1. I would like to thank Peter Schaafsma and Elisabeth Kersten for their analysis of the chapter, useful insights, suggestions, and corrections. Any remaining errors are, unfortunately, my responsibility.

2. David Bowman, John W. Ellwood, Frank Neuhauser, and Eugene Smolensky, "Structural Deficit and the Long-Term Fiscal Condition of the State,"in *California Policy Choices, Vol. 9*, ed. John J. Kirlin and Jeffrey I. Chapman (Sacramento: University of Southern California, 1994), pp. 25–50. This conclusion is based on aggregate government revenues.

3. John J. Kirlin, Jeffrey I. Chapman, and Peter Asmus, "California Policy Choices: The Context," in Kirlin and Chapman, *Ibid.*, pp. 6–8. The losses occurring because of the 1994 earthquake in Southern California have been estimated as high as $15 billion.

4. The duration of unemployment has also increased. In June 1990, slightly less than 54,000 were unemployed for twenty-seven weeks or more; that figure had risen to almost 369,000 in December 1993. See State of California, Economic Development Department, "Labor Market Conditions in California," February 4, 1994, p. 4 and p. 6.

5. State of California, Commission on State Finance (COSF), *Quarterly General Fund Forecast*, January 1993, p.6.

6. Defense outlays in California will be about $50 billion in 1993. COSF, "Impact of Defense Cuts on California: An Update," May 1993. p. 2.

7. *Ibid.*, p. 3.

8. AFDC is Aid to Families with Dependent Children, California's version of Medicaid is called Medi-Cal, SSI/SSP are Supplemental Security Income/State Supplementary Program (for the aged, blind, and disabled).

9. Governor Wilson's request for aid from the national government for the 1994–1995 fiscal year now goes far beyond the SLIAG reimbursement. His position is that the national government should be responsible for the *full* costs of illegal immigrants.

10. Population growth between 1990–1991 and 1993–1994 was 6.3 percent.

11. A package of laws reforming Worker's Compensation was passed in July 1993. Both parties have also agreed that streamlining regulatory and permitting processes are necessary solutions to the perception of a poor business climate.

12. For details, See Frederick D. Stocker, ed., *Proposition 13: A Ten-Year Retrospective* (Cambridge, MA: Lincoln Institute, 1991).

13. John J. Kirlin, *The Political Economy of Fiscal Limits* (Lexington, MA: Lexington Books, 1982), p. 64.

14. This ultimately led to the implementation of a multitude of local user charges on land developers as well as an increased use of cost accounting.

15. The actual formula and legislative amendments are far more complex and do allow for some leeway at the margin.

16. This was explicitly done for the 1994–1995 budget, which was designed to be balanced over two years.

17. State of California, Controller's Office. *Annual Report 1991–1992 Fiscal Year.* p. A–18; *1993–1994 Governor's Budget*, Schedule 1.

18. Some special funds are also directly controlled by the state. As Table 7–1 indicates, these have also rapidly grown during this period; however, these funds are usually earmarked for specific purposes.

19. A semantic problem exists in this discussion. In 1991–1992 there occurred a realignment of revenues and functions away from the state and to the counties. The sales tax was increased by ½ cent to be earmarked to the counties and another ¾ cent for the state, of which ¼ cent was permanent. In 1992–1993 there was an additional shift of revenues of $1.3 billion from local governments to school districts that reduced the state aid to these districts by that amount. In the 1993–1994 budget, there was an additional reduction of state expenditures on education by $2.6 billion that was financed by a property tax shift from local governments to schools. During this time, the ½-cent temporary sales tax that the state had been collecting for the counties was made permanent (through a statewide election) but was supposed to be used for local public safety. Both of these actions resulted in a reduction of the state General Fund expenditures but an increase in local expenditures. More details are in the text.

20. The 1993–1994 state employment data are projected to include over 12,000 position savings that may not occur and have not been allocated to the departments. *Governor's Budget*, Schedule 4B; State of California Economic Development Department, *Labor Market Conditions in California*, Table 8A, selected years.

21. Some of the 1993–1994 decline is attributed to the shift in the ½-cent sales tax to counties. See footnote 19.

22. There is some arbitrariness associated with some of the classifications in this table, and they are not necessarily consistent with the underlying data presented by the Legislative Analyst, *State Spending Plans*, misc. years and *Focus, Budget 1993*. Further, it should be remembered that even with this filling of the gap, the state was still consistently running deficits.

23. Wilson also faced a conflicting pressure to run in order to prevent the Democrats from dominating the reapportionment process.

24. State of California, Assembly Revenue and Taxation Committee, *Bridging the Budget Funding Gap*, June 11, 1990, p. 5.

25. In November 1990, in addition to electing Pete Wilson, voters approved six out of twenty-eight ballot propositions (and only two of fourteen bond proposals). The six that were approved included a term limit on state officeholders.

26. The workload budget is a current services budget. It is defined as the budget year cost of currently authorized programs, adjusted for changes in caseload, enrollment and population; statutory COLAs; chaptered legislation; one-time or full-year costs; federal and court mandates; merit salary adjustments and price increases for operating expenses and equipment; and constitutional program costs. *Governor's Budget Summary, 1991–1992*, p. 8.

27. State of California, Legislative Analyst's Office (LAO), "An Overview of the 1991–1992 Governor's Budget," January 23, 1991.

28. Jeffrey I. Chapman, "The Fiscal Consequences of California Policy Choices," in *California Policy Choices, Vol. 7*, ed. John J. Kirlin and Donald R. Winkler (Sacramento: University of Southern California, 1991), p. 24.

29. These were allowed to sunset in FY 95–96.

30. The 1990 renter's credit was $120 for married couples, single parents, and surviving spouses, and $60 for individuals. The 1991 budget legislation prohibited higher income taxpayers—those with taxable incomes over $42,500 (married) and $21,350 (single)—from receiving the credit from 1991 through 1995. In 1993, the credit was suspended for all taxpayers. It is scheduled to go back into effect, for all renters, in 1994. The credit is first applied to any state income taxes, with the balance refunded to the renter. If the renter has no tax liability, upon filing a return, the credit is received.

31. The candy, snack, and bottled water portions of this base broadening were repealed by initiative in the November 1992 elections. The legislature repealed the tax on free newspapers, magazines ordered by subscription, ship fuel and airline fuel used for international flights.

32. In 1990, the legislature passed and governor signed a law that mandated that General Fund appropriations were to be reduced by up to 4 percent whenever state General Fund revenues were insufficient to fund the state's "workload" budget expenditure level. These reductions were to be made on an unallocated basis, so the governor does not have to engage in across-the-board cuts.

33. Prudential Securities, *Research, California Banking Industry Outlook*, November 13, 1991. They concluded that hundreds of businesses are leaving California and that the quality of life has declined. "In short, a long era of growth and prosperity. . .has ended in California," p. 2.

However, there were still optimists in the picture. The Center for Continuing Study of the California Economy, a Palo Alto think tank, argued that 1992 growth would be modest, and the outlook for the rest of the 1990s remained strong. Center for Continuing Study of the California Economy, *The Outlook for the California Economy* (Palo Alto: CCSCE, November 1991), pp. 2–3.

34. State of California, Department of Finance, "California's Growing Taxpayer Squeeze," November 1991, pp. 1–7.

35. The report was also to give fuel to groups (and the governor) that want to eliminate public education and health care from illegal immigrants.

36. LAO, "The State's Fiscal Problem," December 1991, p. 3. The actual General Fund deficit for 1991–1992 turned out to be about $3.3 billion. See State of California, Controller's Office, *Annual Report, 1991–1992 Fiscal Year*, p. A–20.

37. This technique, when used to pay state employees, was later ruled illegal, and so is no longer a viable option. Currently, a class action lawsuit against the state has been brought by various state employee groups in federal court. Damages may be as high as $300 million.

38. See Assembly Ways and Means, "Overview of 1992–93 Budget," September 3, 1992. This describes AB 979, the budget bill that deals with the $7.9 billion deficit. Then see, LAO, *State Spending Plan for 1992–93*, November, 1992, p. 7, which identifies the $11.2 billion gap.

39. The University of California system (UC) consists of nine campuses and is the principal research University in the state. The California State University system (CSU) has twenty campuses and is predominantly undergraduate. CSU does not offer a doctorate. The 107 community colleges provide the first two years of undergraduate education as well as specialized courses.

40. LAO, *The 1993–94 Budget: Perspectives and Issues*, February 1993, p. 10.

41. LAO, *Focus, Budget 1993*, July 6, 1993, p. 3.

42. LAO, *Update California*, November 1993. Funds originally appropriated in one fiscal year as a loan, to be repaid by schools from subsequent appropriations, are called recaptures. Recaptures have occurred when there has been a midyear reduction in the estimate of the minimum amount of state school support required under Proposition 98. Prepayment occurs when the state loans funds to schools and community colleges that will be repaid out of future Proposition 98 funding. These loans have occurred when the amount required to meet a per pupil spending goal exceeded the Proposition 98 mandate.

43. *Ibid.*, p. 4.

44. Inflation from third quarter 1990 through first quarter 1994 was about 10.5 percent.

45. The remainder consisted of Native American, Asian, Pacific Islander, and Filipino.

46. Annual University of California fees have increased from $1,624 in FY 91 to $3,454 in FY 94; California State University fees have risen from $780 to $1,440 during the same period; and community college fees have risen from a flat $100 to $13 per unit. See LAO, *Analysis of the 1994–95 Budget Bill*, p. F–11.

47. See the California Higher Education Policy Center, *Time for Decision* (Discussion Draft), March 1994, pp. 2–3. It should be noted that later in this report it is disclosed that community college enrollment is actually up since 1990–1991. However, in the last two years, it has fallen.

48. Much of this section is based on David Illig, "Recent Welfare Reform," in *California Policy Choices, Vol. 9*, ed. Kirlin and Chapman, pp. 173–202.

49. The state also has a welfare-to-work program, Greater Avenues for Independence (GAIN). Most adults with no children under the age of three are required to participate in this program. In addition, the state also has a program to help collect child support payments from absent parents.

50. Illig, *op. cit.*, p. 182.

51. AFDC maximum aid for a family of three fell by 8.4 percent, from $663 a month to $607 a month during this period. *Governor's Budget*, various years.

52. The state has waived indefinitely the $30 and one-third income disregard and the 100-hour rule.

53. General Assistance payments vary by county throughout the state.

54. State of California, Senate Office of Research, *An Overview of the Budget Solution for 1993–94*. July 1, 1993, p. 6. Unfortunately for the local governments, most of the mandate relief never occurred.

55. Karen Coker Keeslar, "Realignment Data Project, Report #1," March 6, 1994, no page number. In this area, also, the promised reductions in regulations have never been realized.

56. Proposition 99, passed in 1988, established a surtax on cigarettes and tobacco products and specified that the surtax funds "shall be used to supplement existing levels of service" for indigent and mental health programs and "not to fund existing levels of service" based on 1988–1989 expenditure amounts. LAO, *The 1992–93 Budget*, pp. 119–120.

57. Realignment also demonstrated an opportunity for the legislature to engage again in arcane maneuvers to accomplish its goals. Proposition 98 required a set percentage of General Fund revenues to be spent on education. Realignment financing forced the legislature to establish a separate fund to ensure that local government received the sales and vehicle license revenues. This avoided the Proposition 98 requirements, gave a patina of more stability to local revenue, and made the budget even more difficult to follow.

58. LAO, *The 1993–94 Budget: Perspectives and Issues*, pp. 113–14. Peter Schaafsma is the principal author of this section.

59. *Governor's Budget Summary, 1993–94*, pp. 33–42.

60. LAO, "Information Technology: An Important Tool for a More Effective Government," June 16, 1994; Stephen Green, "State computer projects in disarray, analyst says," *Sacramento Bee*, June 18, 1994, p. A1.

61. Besides gutting what was left of California's unitary tax, the legislation included measures expanding research and development tax credits, adding tax credits and exemptions for companies buying new factory equipment, and partial tax exclusions for long-term capital gains on small business investment. The gross revenue cost was estimated to be $400 million.

62. *Cal-Tax News*, August 15, 1993, p. 4.

63. John Vasconcellos, Chair, Assembly Committee on Ways and Means, "The California Smart Budget," May 25, part E–5–a.

64. Faculty also did well. The final retirement offer for their defined benefit program was a three-month severance bonus, the crediting of five additional years of service, and the adding of three years to their age. Further, many of the faculty were immediately hired back as consultants.

65. Both UC and CSU instructional costs per full-time student are about 33 percent above the comparable costs of other states. *Crosstalk*, No. 1.

66. In November 1990, as part of a successful term limitation measure, there was also a mandated 38 percent reduction in legislative spending.

8

Connecticut: Surviving Tax Reform

Carol W. Lewis*

INTRODUCTION

Connecticut began systematically transforming state fiscal policy and the direction, procedures, and potential of state government in response to a budget crisis. A decade of economic boom coupled with undisciplined spending growth intensified the pain of adjusting to a worsening recession. Surfacing by 1989, the crisis peaked in 1991, when a newly elected independent governor and Democratic legislative majority confronted a cumulative deficit of almost $1 billion and a budget gap projected at over $2 billion, or about one-third the total budget for FY 1992.[1]

Only after Connecticut began FY 1992 without a budget for the first time in over a century, faced agency closings and furloughs, and ran on mini-budgets did the governmental resolution emerge: restructure the tax base, spending, and the budget process. The perceived causes of the crisis very much shaped the strategies designed to cope with it and the political and fiscal realignment and public policies that emerged from it.

The state's greatest accomplishment since 1991 is that underlying, fiscal fundamentals are sounder. Admittedly, the state did not embrace reorientation and reform but was pushed to them by the severe lessons of the crisis and the political accommodations it forced and fostered. Perhaps foremost among these is the tax overhaul and increase, and Connecticut's experience shows that it is politically possible to survive both.

---

*Carol W. Lewis is a Professor of Political Science at the University of Connecticut as well as a faculty member in the Public Affairs Program.

CAUSES OF THE FISCAL CRISIS

The fiscal crisis was caused by the legacy of past spending and revenue policies and uncontrollable factors.

Spending Policy

The crisis was induced primarily by the state's own spending and revenue policies, their mismatch, and the budgetary impacts of a deep and prolonged recession. Spending from major funds had grown at an annual average of more than 11 percent in FY 1981–FY 1990; in the five years immediately preceding the 1991 climax, expenditures had risen 156 percent, from $4.9 billion in FY 1987 to $7.7 billion by FY 1991.[2] Allowing for annual spending at FY 1987's figure, the cumulative increase over these five years added $801 million to the emerging problem.

The spending increase is attributable more to changing service demands and political responsiveness to these demands than to overall population growth. While the state's population rose only 5.8 percent in 1980–1990 to total 3.28 million by 1992, the number of households grew faster. The resulting decline in household size reflects various social changes often associated with high levels of service needs. Increases in the elderly population and single-parent families translate into caseload increases in welfare and Medicaid (more than one-half of which is expended on nursing home care in Connecticut).[3] These and similar components of the spending increase may be judged compassionate, perhaps even generous, but *not* frivolous.

Ballooning state services are evident in other areas important both financially and politically in the 1991 and subsequent budget battles. The long-term implications of the 1980s' spending spree are dramatically evident in state debt, which increased 79 percent in FY 1989–FY 1991 alone. The expedient of bonded indebtedness played a central role in 1991 and thereafter. Supported by the bonding that finances prison construction, the growth in the prison population outpaced national figures[4] and, by FY 1991, state spending on corrections was 56 percent of what it had been just five years earlier. The comparable figure for aid to localities is 42 percent. State support for K–12 education was 56 percent higher. While student enrollment during this five-year period remained stable at about 473,000, the state's share of total K–12 funding reached its high of 45 percent in FY 1990.[5]

˜evenue Policy

ncreasing revenue from all sources simply failed to keep pace with spending. Revenue growth in FY 1987–1991 averaged 6.8 percent, compared to 11.6 percent for spending. Volatility in annual revenue growth exacerbated the yield problem.[6]

The policy response in 1989 to budgetary imbalance left the fiscal structure intact and still dependent upon the sales tax as the largest single revenue source. Although the budget increase for FY 1990 was held to under 10 percent for the first time since FY 1985, the 1989 resolution drew primarily upon a revenue strategy that added almost $800 million to revenue. The sales tax rate was raised to a new national high, from 7.5 to 8 percent for $161 million, and the elimination of certain exemptions added another $231 million. The tactic of turning to the sales tax—on which the state already relied so heavily—coincided with its disappointing yield for FY 1989 and its recession-induced slide from 40 percent to 37 percent of all revenues financing general operations. Other lucrative changes made in 1989 include an increase in the tax rate on interest income and dividends ($36 million); repeal of the long-term capital gains exclusion ($73 million); a cigarette tax increase ($31 million); and a 15 percent surtax ($62 million) on the corporation business tax that also was increased 20 percent ($45 million). Dwarfing these changes, the sales tax increases of 1989 constrained politically viable alternatives available in 1991. According to the *Economic Report of the Governor, 1993–1995*, the state's sales tax collections as a percentage of personal income put Connecticut ninth among the states in FY 1991, so that the sales tax burden weighed heavier than in most other states.

Despite 1989's efforts and another net revenue increase of more than $95 million the next year, FY 1990 ended with a $259 million deficit in the general fund. Part was financed by $102 million from the budget reserve ("rainy day") fund established in 1979; this third consecutive transfer followed $116 million in FY 1988 and $28 million in FY 1989. The remaining deficit was carried over to the next fiscal year and contributed $157 million to the 1991 crisis.

Uncontrollable Factors

Several factors beyond state control exacerbated a crisis that was largely the state's own doing. Federal funding, the recession, and court-mandated spending contribute to uncontrollable expenditures (committed by law and outside current decision-making discretion) that now account for 86–88 percent of net general fund expenditures.[7] As the proportion of the operating budget available for discretionary spending and subject to the appropriations process declines, the system's short-term responsiveness and pliability necessarily also decline.

Federal funding. The deficit and projected gap that precipitated the fiscal crisis are not attributable directly to federal aid. Federal dollars increased from almost 11 percent of general fund revenues in FY 1987 to 12 percent in FY 1988, 13 percent in FY 1989 and FY 1990, and to approximately 16 percent by FY 1991. However, largely related to federal welfare and education programs, these funds are dedicated to specific purposes and often impose reciprocal state obligations (e.g., matching funds, administrative costs, and mandated standards). Illustratively, human services and education accounted for almost 60 percent of all federal funds to Connecticut in FY 1993. The structure rather than the amount of federal funding added inflexibility to and demands on the state budget and thus contributed to the crisis.

Recession's impact. Spending increases were politically cost-free as long as economic growth generated a handsome revenue dividend, but the recession made divergent spending and revenue patterns unsustainable and both confirmed and intensified the volatility and unreliability of major revenue sources. Tax revenues fell 5.6 percent from FY 1990 to FY 1991, and total revenues declined 2.9 percent. The outlook was especially grim because the sales tax, the fiscal workhorse generating about two-fifths of total revenue and one-half of all tax revenue, could no longer fund double-digit spending increases. The increase in sales tax receipts fell from approximately 18 percent in FY 1990 to 2.5 percent in FY 1991. (Its subsequent further decline reflects the introduction of the income tax rather than economic conditions.) The recession fueled the crisis atmosphere by generating personal financial insecurity that understandably affected willingness to pay increased taxes. Although unemployment rates remained at or below national rates, the employment downturn that began in 1989 (and ultimately cost 150,000 jobs) seemed all the more acute after the gain in FY 1983–FY 1989 of one-quarter million jobs (or 17.5 percent of all nonagricultural employment in the state). Moreover, as Governor Lowell P. Weicker Jr. noted in his 1993 budget address, 43 percent of the new workers in Connecticut in 1980–1988 came from minority groups. Diminished employment opportunity has especially sensitive distributional ramifications.

The state depends upon current employment to maintain its foremost ranking in personal income, 60 percent of which is furnished by wages and salaries. Solutions to the fiscal crisis were debated and developed just as Connecticut's real per capita personal income was declining. Growth in average income nationally in fact outpaced the state's in 1990–1992, and the state's relative high of more than 138 percent of the national figure was reached in 1988. Nonetheless, average personal income in the state continued to outstrip the national average by more than one-third as of 1993, and Connecticut sustained its status as the wealthiest state on this measure.

The recession also pushed distributional issues off the political agenda for the most part. Wealthy by measures of central tendency, Connecticut also has some of the poorest cities and some of the largest urban-suburban disparities in the country. In the state's largest cities of Hartford, Bridgeport, and New Haven, more than 10 percent of the population was receiving Aid to Families with Dependent Children in 1991, compared to less than 3 percent in about 150 other municipalities in the state.[8] This and other need indicators explain why some participants in the ongoing budget debate phrase issues in terms of have and have-nots, and the variability among jurisdictions suggests why urban advocates, proponents of more state-financed property tax relief, and promoters of economic development appear to pull public policy in incompatible directions.

Court orders and consent decrees. A class-action lawsuit resulted in a consent decree and, in December 1990, a federal district court ordered sweeping changes in the state's child welfare agency, known by its acronym of DCYS.[9] Caseload reductions, hiring many more social workers, enhanced training, and improved procedures were part of the package. The decree became an issue in the budget crisis and the FY 1992 budget. In the summer of the 1991, when the state was without a budget for the new fiscal year and operating under a moratorium on new spending, the agency got a court order under the consent decree to maintain private provision of emergency services.

Judicial mandates influence budgetary relationships and outcomes in Connecticut as elsewhere.[10] As the most recent of costly court orders that have touched components of services such as corrections, mental retardation, and mental health in Connecticut and around the country, the DCYS case accents the complexity of fiscal policymaking in a fragmented and fractious system. It also highlights the problems of maintaining financial and political accountability when spending decisions are made outside the regular budgetary process.

Consent decrees are a contentious issue. A statutory response in 1991 to the perceived infringement upon legislative appropriating authority set a dollar limit on the attorney general's authority to sign consent decrees and stipulations without prior legislative approval. (A bill designed to restrict authority further made no headway in the 1993 session and a resolution proposing a constitutional amendment concerning consent decrees also failed to make progress.) An impending federal court decision in the *Sheff* vs. *O'Neill* lawsuit over public school desegregation undoubtedly will transform public school financing and Connecticut's 1993 and 1994 official statements for general obligation bonds disclosed that "fiscal impact of an adverse decision cannot be determined at this stage of the case but could be significant."

Court orders and decrees further constrict current decision-making discretion and, along with the revenue and expenditure limitation (discussed below), amplify the structural realignment in state budgeting already evident. Court mandates significantly shape service provision and related staffing; minimally, they thrust cost cutting and downsizing prospects onto unprotected functions. DCYS's recent experience illustrates how, for better or worse, judicial budgeting operates to reorder spending priorities.

Public Attitudes

Public opinion in the state figured strongly in defining policy options in 1991. Tax resistance predictably characterized public opinion during and after the public debate over adopting a new tax structure to address the fiscal crisis. The proportion of respondents indicating that taxes are too high increased markedly, from 55 percent in February 1989 to 74 percent in January 1992.[11] The proportion reporting that spending was too high also increased. The negative characterization of state government as *wasteful* was selected by 38 percent of Connecticut respondents in early 1989 but by 55 percent in March 1991, when the debate was fully under way. The backdrop for the ensuing difficult decisions was this: an increasing majority considered spending and taxes too high, and government inefficient.

Public opinion in Connecticut also preferred—or at least accepted—an active, broad role for state government. In January 1992, hard on the heels of the budget crisis and income tax adoption, a *Hartford Courant*/Institute for Social Inquiry Connecticut Poll (hereafter, Connecticut Poll) asked respondents to characterize their view of what the state government in Hartford should be. Response options ran from "as limited a role as possible" to "an active role to make Connecticut as good a place to live as it can." The majority (82 percent) of Connecticut respondents identified an active state as ideal, whereas only 14 percent preferred as it as limited as possible (and 2 percent responded somewhere in the middle; another 2 percent don't know, other, etc.). According to the pollsters' interpretation,

> [T]he size of the agenda by itself is not the basic problem. . . . Evidence abounds that the public wants cuts. . . . The key, though, is that the state government has a broad mandate. . . .[T]he public—as it looks to spending reductions— remains convinced that state government is inefficient and that much can be saved before programs actually suffer. . . . Major cuts were opposed across the board. . . . Support for trimming [minor cuts] jumps a good deal. . . .

The Watershed of 1991

The stage was set by fiscal crisis, a deep recession, a broadening public perception of excessive taxation, high disposable income, and public demand for active government coupled with rejection of major cuts. However, these factors did not stimulate a bandwagon response to or legislative consensus around the governor's position that yet another hike in the sales tax would be politically unpopular, inequitable, economically counterproductive, and inadequate to the financial task in the long term. On the contrary, a bitter controversy ensued (and its refrain plays still—at lower decibel levels and around spending priorities, modifying the income tax, and property tax relief). A 1991 legislative coalition forged between conservative-to-moderate Democrats and Republicans passed three budgets based on a broadened sales tax base, only to see each vetoed by the governor.

STRATEGIES FOR COPING WITH FISCAL CRISIS

Political and fiscal turmoil, realignment, and policy changes with far-reaching implications marked 1991. Lasting several months, the 1991 special legislative session designed and then redesigned the basic strategy for coping with the fiscal crisis. Political leaders turned to a combination of tactics that reflects the political compromise needed to muster a legislative majority and the governor's consent. They ultimately instituted a statutory expenditure limit, biennial budgeting, a more stringent cap on bonded indebtedness, the Government Reorganization Commission (Harper-Hull, discussed below), and an advisory Economic Conference Board. They also bonded the cumulative operating deficit, increased unfunded accrued liabilities through pension manipulation, began trimming spending and especially its growth even in some heretofore untouchable areas, and fundamentally overhauled the state revenue system.

Revenue Strategy

In 1991, the state enacted a broad-based personal income tax, repealed the income tax on unearned income (dividends, interest, and capital gains, now subject to the income tax), and broadened the sales tax base while reducing its rate. The first impact was a net increase in yield of $1.1 billion and general fund tax revenues jumped almost 23 percent from FY 1991 to FY 1992. Another was the change in the degree to which the state relied on different revenue sources.

Income Tax

The adoption of an income tax was the single most important element in Connecticut's strategy for coping with the fiscal crisis. Now the largest single source of tax revenue, the broad-based personal income tax is projected to generate $2.7 billion in FY 1995, or more than two-fifths of gross tax receipts and one-third of general fund revenues.

(Unless otherwise specified, figures for FY 1995 are as adopted in 1993 for the FY 1994–FY 1995 biennium.)

The tax went into effect on October 1, 1991 with a 4.5 percent rate applied to earned and unearned income. With moderating elements such as personal exemptions and tax credits, the tax is effectively graduated. For example, the personal exemption for married couples filing jointly is $24,000 for returns with income under $48,000. It declines by $1,000 for each additional $1,000 in adjusted gross income above $48,000, and falls to zero for income above $71,000. Personal tax credits decrease from 75 percent for incomes of $30,000 or less to 35 percent for incomes of $40,000 and to 10 percent for incomes of $50,000–$96,000. The vanishing credits and personal exemption means that a family with an adjusted gross income of $30,000 pays at an effective rate of less than 0.8 percent (about $250), whereas a family with double the income pays at an effective rate of almost 4 percent (over $2,400). The top rate of 4.5 percent applies only at an adjusted gross income of $96,000 for the joint filer.

The income tax's effect on taxpayers was influenced by its intergovernmental context. Changes in the federal tax code in 1986 eliminated the deductibility of state sales tax payments but retained the deductibility of state income and local property taxes and the nontaxable status of most municipal bonds. Credits for income taxes paid to other jurisdictions meant that commuters from southern Connecticut into New York, where the tax rate was higher than the newly adopted Connecticut income tax, would not be paying more income taxes. In addition, the state repealed the tax on capital gains, dividends, and interest and began taxing them at lower rates under the new income tax. Some taxpayers actually saw their state tax liability reduced as a result of these factors. Some political protagonists attributed this outcome to Governor Weicker's electoral base in wealthy Fairfield County; some saw merit in a tax structure attractive to the wealthy and to high-income corporate leaders.

The lack of *steep* progressivity in the tax structure immediately stimulated efforts to revamp the newly adopted income tax. Although support for modification now crosses party lines, consensus breaks down over specifics. For example, the house Republican leaders' 1993 package offered $613 million in spending cuts from the governor's proposal, a like amount in business and individual tax reductions, many deductions and credits aimed at the middle class, and reducing the rate by 0.25 percent. On the strength of the "broad-based agreement among Democrats,"[12] and with support from the Taxpayers Alliance to Serve Connecticut and others, a version of "middle-class tax relief" passed as the first major piece of legislation in 1993. It was vetoed by the governor, who stood by his earlier promise not to shift the tax burden to higher incomes. Because so-called *tax repair* is revenue neutral and necessarily and purposefully shifts the tax burden, the result was deadlock. Without the votes to override, the leadership of the Democratic majority kept the issue alive symbolically in 1993 by putting it on the "go" list daily but it was never taken up again in caucus.[13] By 1994, the governor's opposition, his not seeking reelection, and his proposal for state-financed local property tax relief (discussed below) pushed tax repair off the agenda, at least temporarily. The 1993 and 1994 sessions were marked by no more than revenue tinkering, although the latter smoothed out the sharp income tax increases of "cliffs" by effectively creating more brackets as of January 1, 1995.

Modifying the tax is a popular position, whereas repeal has faded as a fiscally realistic option. As early as spring 1992, public support for amending the income tax surpassed support for repealing it or retaining it as enacted. A Connecticut Poll conducted in May–June 1992 asked, "What should be done with the state income tax? Should it be left in place as is, should it be modified so some people pay more and others pay less, or should it be repealed altogether?" In all, 43 percent of the respondents favored modification, compared to 22 percent supporting leaving it as is, and 33 percent opting for repeal (and 2 percent don't know, etc.). On the other hand, there is no popular support for increasing its role. A March 1994 Connecticut Poll asked about the proportion of state revenue from the income tax. Only 7 percent responded that the state should get more of its money from the income tax, whereas 48 percent preferred less, and 40 percent, the same (and 5 percent don't know, etc.).

Other Revenue Changes

Sales tax. When the income tax was introduced, the sales tax rate was reduced from 8 to 6 percent. At the same time, the base was broadened enough to recapture 20 percent of the revenue lost by cutting the rate 2 percentage points. Sales tax receipts declined almost 7 percent from FY 1991 to FY 1995 as projected. The sales tax was no longer preeminent; its yield decreased from 40 to 28 percent of general fund revenues in FY 1991–FY 1995, and a further decline is projected.

Business taxes. The corporation business tax applies to any corporation or association doing business in the state. Tax liability is the greatest amount computed under three formulas: net income of taxpayer (portion assigned to the state); additional tax on capital (insurance companies exempt); or a minimum tax of $250. The 20 percent surtax introduced as of January 1, 1989 was halved for 1992 and then eliminated as of January 1, 1993. A further reduction in corporate taxes is scheduled for January 1995. A credit against business taxes for property taxes on computers (about $60 million) was enacted in 1994, along with a cut of 0.25 percent in the tax on insurance premiums.

Reduced business taxes are a much-touted component of the Weicker administration's economic development policy aimed at job retention and creation. Many business groups such as the Connecticut Business and Industry Association, the Connecticut Policy and Economic Council, the Stamford-based Southwest Area Commerce and Industry Association, and several chambers of commerce had supported adopting the income tax for reasons of revenue stability, budgetary balance, and competitiveness. That corporation tax receipts fell as a percentage of both total revenue and tax collections is evidence of their strategic success. The corporation tax declined from 11 percent to 8 percent of general fund revenues in FY 1991–FY 1995.

Gambling revenues. Casino gambling took on political dimensions well beyond its materiality to state revenues. A 1993 compact between the governor and Mashantucket Pequot tribe provided new revenue for the state and forestalled at least temporarily the expansion of casino gambling beyond tribal lands and into Connecticut's cities. In exchange for a monopoly on slot machines, the tribe ultimately agreed to pay $113 million as FY 1994's minimum, $135 million for FY 1995, and thereafter 25 percent of gross revenues from the slot machines. Legislative resistance to the perceived preemption of public policy making by the governor was softened by his proposal to use much of money for local property tax relief, a dominant concern in the ensuing legislative session. By 1994, the casino issue was transformed from one of revenue, morality, crime, and jobs into an executive-legislative power struggle. By the session's end, the governor had signed a second compact with the Mohegan tribe (newly recognized by the federal government), renegotiated the first compact to extend slot machine privileges to this second tribe, vetoed a bill requiring legislative participation in such matters, and had seen the legislature insist upon its inclusion in future such negotiations.

Local property taxes. The accent shifted in 1994 to state-financed relief from local property taxes that state law tightly governs. Two-thirds of the $379 million tax reduction adopted is an income tax credit for local taxes on automobiles. The outcome was more modest than the governor's proposal and to be phased in over five years beginning only in 1997.

Federal funds. The state is increasingly dependent upon federal funds, which rose from 16 percent to 20 percent of total general fund revenues from FY 1991 to FY 1995. Because the state ranked eighth in total defense dollars awarded and first in awarded dollars per capita in FY 1991,[14] threatened and actual defense cuts deeply affect Connecticut's economy. So, too, do health care reform and other proposals affecting the insurance industry.

Evasive Strategy: Deficit Financing

As an alternative to raising current revenues, long-term, general obligation borrowing was the technique selected in 1991 for financing the cumulative deficit. (It had been used by the state in 1975 for a $71 million deficit.) This is a coping strategy designed to evade the problem.

The state established a five-year Economic Recovery Note Debt Retirement Fund (hereafter, ERF) in 1991, and the treasurer issued fixed and variable rate notes with a total principal payment of almost $966 million. Treated as revenue transfers from the general fund, ERF payments amounted to $139 million in FY 1993, $186 million in FY 1994, and $267 million in FY 1995. With refinancing considered, interest payments alone total almost $149 million over five years.

The legislature expressed disapproval of its own action by adopting a more restrictive debt limit in 1991. Concern over the rising level of indebtedness (related to the overhaul of state infrastructure under way since 1984) predated the ERF. The Commission to Study the

Management of State Government (or Thomas Commission, created in 1989 in response to the unfolding fiscal crisis) noted the increase in fixed costs in its 1991 final report and identified the failure of existing state law to impose discipline on bonding as "problem number one." The legislature followed through in 1991 on the commission's recommendation to strengthen the statutory debt limit and reduced the maximum permitted indebtedness from 4.5 times to 1.6 times general fund tax receipts. Short-term borrowing for cash flow purposes is excluded from the limit, along with the balances of debt retirement funds, receivables from federal grants, and indebtedness related to financing budget deficits through FY 1991.

Despite FY 1992's first decrease in bond authorizations in five years and the lowest bonding total since FY 1988, the ERF, infrastructure program, and current economic development efforts aimed at job retention have increased the state's indebtedness since FY 1991. Moody's Investors Service ranked the state in 1993 as the highest among all states in net tax-supported debt per capita and second highest in net tax-supported debt as a percent of personal income.[15] Net direct general obligation indebtedness (excluding limited or contingent liabilities, self-liquidating debt, and short-term notes) outstanding as of March 1, 1994, totaled $5.6 billion, or $1,717 for each state resident. According to the state's March 1994 official statement, the 33 percent increase in outstanding debt from 1991 to 1994 raised the ratio of debt to personal income from less than 5 percent to more than 6 percent.

The more stringent debt cap has not been triggered yet and so has had no restraining effect to date. Of course, any statutory defense against excessive borrowing and future deficit financing is subject to legislative alteration. Yankee ingenuity in fact had devised a gimmick for bonded indebtedness by 1993. The treasurer was required to transfer any *unappropriated* surplus up to $205 million annually in FY 1992–FY 1994 to the ERF and, in FY 1992, $110.2 million in surplus was transferred. In May 1993, the legislature appropriated an anticipated $84 million surplus as a one-shot *carry forward* whereby a FY 1993 appropriation reduces debt service by $52 million in FY 1994 and $32 million in FY 1995. Substituting debt service for debt retirement, the legislature converted what would normally have been a projected surplus (and therefore dedicated first to early retirement of state debt) into "a kind of self-destruct mechanism that results in the entire amount's being intercepted and spent before it can accumulate as a surplus."[16] The gimmickry is compounded as any *additional* unappropriated surplus also is deemed to be appropriated for FY 1994 debt service. FY 1993 closed with a $113.5 million surplus that was applied to the next year's debt service.

Assessment of Revenue Strategy

The revenue components of Connecticut's strategy for coping with the fiscal crisis can be assessed by three different standards: revenue yield and structure; electoral outcomes and public opinion; and the one subscribed to by budgetary decision makers, budgetary balance or deficits.

Revenue yield and structure. Because most other states already employ an income tax, Connecticut's shift in tax reliance is less important for its direction than for its abruptness and for the political lesson that it is possible to survive a major tax increase. As a result of changes since 1991, the revenue system now in place is marked by reduced regressivity and volatility, lower business taxes, and, perhaps most important in terms of the immediate crisis, higher revenue yield. The general fund's total tax revenues increased more than 44 percent, from $4.5 billion in FY 1991 to $6.5 billion projected for FY 1995. With estimates indicating that the income tax had performed on target, the governor announced in July 1993 that the fiscal crisis was over.[17] According to one assessment, the relatively small increase of less than $8 million in 1993 was made possible by unanticipated growth in revenues from taxes already in place, rather than by spending cuts.[18] The governor summed up the effect of the radical restructuring of revenue in his February 1993 budget address: "Two years later, our budget is balanced, corporate taxes rolled back 20 percent, the sales tax down 25 percent, and the sales tax base for business has been reduced."

Electoral standard. The state's own experience, New Jersey's, and the crisis immediately at hand added high drama to adopting an income tax. Since Connecticut had trifled temporarily with a personal income tax in 1971, only to have the legislature overturn it in within several weeks, prior to any revenue collections, an income tax had been politically taboo. The 1991 situation in New Jersey, where voters threatened to (and later actually did) retaliate against the legislative majority for a large tax increase, was too pointed a lesson to be ignored in Connecticut. Income tax protests peaked in fall 1991, when polls indicated that one-half the electorate intended to vote against incumbents who had voted yea on the income tax.[19]

Because adamant tax opposition by 25–35 percent of the voters crossed party lines, its electoral impact was diluted. Moreover, polls also indicated that jobs and the economy had supplanted taxes as the foremost issue.[20] *The Hartford Courant's* capital bureau chief wrote, "For months, the public howling about the income tax sent shivers up the spines of many legislators who voted for it. Few doubted that the tax issue would haunt, and probably sink, many reelection campaigns in November 1992. Now there is some doubt."[21] Williams then disclosed the results of the Connecticut Poll conducted in May–June 1992 that showed four out of ten residents did not expect an incumbent's pro-tax vote to substantially affect their ballot and also showed that more people preferred retaining or amending the tax than repealing it.

The savaging of income-tax supporters did *not* occur and, with a net loss of one seat in the house and four in the senate, the income-tax Democrats retained their legislative majority by a small margin.[22] The 1992 elections resulted in a partisan lineup of eighty-seven Democrats to sixty-four Republicans in the house and nineteen Democrats to seventeen Republicans in the senate. Measured by the standard of electoral survival, the revenue strategy apparently is a success. However, the slim senate majority prevented veto overrides, agreement on language to implement the constitutional expenditure limitation passed in 1992, timely passage of the budget bill in 1994, and more.

Negative tax attitudes persist however, and are as about as prevalent as during the fiscal crisis. Fully 72 percent of respondents to a Connecticut Poll in March 1994 indicated that taxes are too high. On the other hand, the proportion responding that taxes are "about right" doubled from results in January 1992 and approach the pre-crisis level.

Budgetary balance. The important contextual feature that triggered action—and perhaps also public acceptance—was a deficit of crisis proportions again propelling change in "the land of steady habits." As the crisis began taking shape at the end of the 1980s, this author wrote,[23]

TABLE 8-1 Connecticut General Fund Budget Balances (in millions of dollars)

	1989	1990	1991	1992	1993	1994 estimated	1995 projected
Operating Surplus (Deficit)	(28)	(259.5)	(818.5)	110.2	113.5	61.2[c]	1.7
Unreserved Fund Balance							
Budgetary Basis	0	(157.2)	(965.7)	0[a]	0[b]	61.2[c]	
GAAP Basis	(991.3)	(461.8)	(1274.3)	(476.5)	(503.6)	(460.4)	

[a]After applying the operating surplus to the Emergency Recovery Fund.
[b]After applying the unappropriated surplus to debt service in FY 1994–FY 1995.
[c]Based on unaudited information from February 1994 comptroller's report.

Source: Connecticut General Assembly, Office of Fiscal Analysis, 1993, *Connecticut State Budget 1993–1995*, p. xi; author's telephone interview with Robert Harris, Assistant Director of Office of Fiscal Analysis, September 17, 1993; and State of Connecticut's official statement of March 16, 1994, p. 42.

In a process marked by continuity, stability, and tradition, only a general assessment that something is very wrong induces change or the contemplation of change. That happened in 1971 . . . [i]t recurred in response to deficits in the early 1980s. The surplus or deficit is the single most important overall indicator by which the process is assessed, and this single figure is behind most attempts to alter that process.

By 1991, the cumulative deficit was almost a billion dollars and the rainy day fund—monies deliberately set aside to deal with an operating deficit—already had been depleted.

Budgetary balance is widely perceived as the foundation—if not definition—of fiscal prudence. Its importance leads numerous prominent members of the business community to support the income tax. For example, a balanced budget is the primary goal of the Connecticut Policy and Economic Council (an influential, private fiscal watchdog, hereafter CPEC).[24] Democratic legislative leaders similarly contend, "The first responsibility of governing is to pass a balanced budget."[25] Connecticut's voters appeared to agree when, in a 1992 November referendum, they replaced the statutory requirement for a balanced budget as adopted with a constitutional version.

By the standard of budgetary balance, the revenue strategy fulfilled its promise. After four consecutive deficits, the general fund saw a surplus in FY 1992 and thereafter. Yet, the arithmetic in the first two rows of figures in Table 8–1 disregards deficit financing, surpluses appropriated forward, and other manipulations that suggest success may be technical and more by letter than in spirit. According to the CPEC, "'smoke and mirrors' budgeting again highlights the need for the state to adopt a consistent and honest accounting system . . ."[26] The comptroller has issued an auxiliary financial report in accordance with Generally Accepted Accounting Principles (hereafter, GAAP) since FY 1988, but operations are still reported on a budgetary or *modified cash* basis. Unreserved fund balances under the current, statutorily required basis of accounting and under GAAP are shown in Table 8–1, and present an altogether different picture of budgetary balance.

Deficit financing and other recent evidence of fiscal artistry propelled several public interest organizations to support and legislators in 1993 to adopt GAAP as the budgetary basis beginning in 1996. Taken in the 1993 session after years of annual audit recommendations to move to GAAP, this step may elevate compliance with the spirit of budgetary balance, or at least reduce the range of gimmicks available for evading it. The accrued liabilities and other adjustments related to conversion are to be paid off in equal amounts over fifteen years starting in FY 1997.

SPENDING STRATEGY

The primary strategy has been to control spending growth, with attendant cost savings and cost cutting. The strategy dates to 1989, when the Commission to Study the Management of State Government was created in response to the unfolding fiscal crisis. Popularly known as the Thomas Commission, its 1991 reports helped define goals and expand options, emphasized spending control, and claimed to identify potential, cumulative, net savings of $2.6 billion through FY 1995.

The business community also endorsed spending control. Although the CPEC sees it as one of their "missions," it defines spending control as "not really less spending but less growth in spending."[27] The pollsters read the Connecticut Poll January 1992 to mean that public opinion also supported spending control, but defined it getting more for less.

> When it comes to the overall fiscal size of state government, the public clearly thinks too much comes in and too much goes out.
> . . . [T]he public remains upset about both taxes and spending.
> . . . Efficiency, more than the agenda for the state, seems to be the key. . . . [T]he public—as it looks to spending reductions— remains convinced that state government is inefficient and that much can be saved before programs actually suffer.

The immediate task in 1991 was to reduce FY 1992 outlays, but actual cuts and some gimmickry managed only to hold down the spending increase (including general fund, debt service, highway and transportation activities, and bond retirement and education funds) in FY 1992 to less than 1 percent. Of course, this was in sharp contrast to 9 percent the prior year and was the first decline in real terms since FY 1980. The longer-term design emerged especially in 1992–1993, when the governor explicitly targeted what he termed "engines of growth" irrespective of protected status (*sacred cow*) and perhaps even of political repercussions.

Restraining Spending Growth

A focus on budget growth rates instead of nominal dollars redefines the strategy as one of *restraint*. Its effectiveness is contextual: general budget expenditures grew at double-digit rates six times in FY 1980–1989, but not once thereafter. Annual growth averaged 6 percent in FY 1991–FY 1995; in FY 1991 spending grew 9 percent; in FY 1992, 0.8 percent; FY 1993 as estimated, 7.3 percent; FY 1994 as adopted, 8.2 percent; and FY 1995 as adopted, 5.4 percent. In real terms (after allowing for inflation using the implicit price deflator for state and local governments), the annual increase averaged 3 percent and actually declined by 2.1 percent in FY 1992.

An analytic shift from dollars to growth rates emphasizes long-term restructuring over short-term, sheer economy. It is germane especially in light of the governor's professed goals of rechanneling spending and restricting its growth in preference to simplistically reducing the size of the outflow. To hold down spending growth, the administration sought to reduce increases in functions and programs—some growing explosively—to levels that could not support services already being delivered.

Cuts from current services. The governor's proposed current service reductions purposefully and strategically targeted engines of growth including Medicaid, K–12 aid, a state welfare program, debt service, and corrections among others. The much-touted (or much-lamented) spending cuts since 1991 are actually reductions from current service levels, a concept that allows for changes in statute, mandates, costs, and other factors not attributable to the service level (held constant). Evaluating cuts relative to current services maintains comparability in the face of program changes such as beneficiary rates. According to the state budget director's analysis, summarized in Table 8–2, reductions in current services were $1.1 billion in FY 1992, another $1.1 billion in FY 1993, and $0.6 in FY 1994. The cumulative impact of significant reductions from general fund current services from FY 1992 through FY 1994 as adopted amounted to $3.1 billion, or 9.4 percent of the $33 billion expended in these three years.

TABLE 8–2. Significant Reductions from Prior Year General Fund Current Services Spending, Connecticut

	1992 Millions	1993 Millions	1994 Millions	Cumulative[c] Total	Percent of All Cuts
K–12 Education	$ 47.3	$ 172.6	$220	$ 439.9	14.2%
Delayed state pension payments	215	100.4		220	7.1
Teachers' retirement	168.7	188	22	378.7	12.2
Wage Deferrals	51	73.8		124.8	4
Aid to Localities	42.2			42.2	1.4
Department of Correction	13.5	10.8	38	62.3	2
Department of Mental Health	13.7	13.8		27.5	0.9
Department of Mental Retardation	35.1	17.6		52.7	1.7
Dept. of Income Maintenance					
General assistance (welfare)	24.1	75.5	44	143.6	4.6
Medicaid/Medical[a]	96.5		55	151.5	4.9
Other[b]	31.7	191.9		223.6	7.2
Higher Education		35.7		35.7	1.2
Approximate Aggregate	1,100	1,100	600	3,100	61.4

[a]Includes limited rate increases for long-term care facilities and other medical services primarily related to Medicaid.
[b]Unspecified.
[c]Calculated by author from data in cited source.

Source: Cibes, W. J., Jr., 1993, Connecticut's economic and fiscal constraints in the nineties, presentation in interest arbitration, Hartford: State of Connecticut, duplicated document, 26 July, pp. A1–A5.

Spending cap. Connecticut adopted a stringent, statutory spending cap in 1991 as part of the price tag for the income tax, so that the razor-thin legislative majority could be reassured that an enhanced revenue base would not support the state's reverting to the open-handed style of the 1980s. The governor opposed the statutory cap but signed it "as the cost of the legislative margin for the income tax."[28] The governor and Democratic leaders in addition agreed to support a constitutional limit on spending in order to get the necessary votes in the General Assembly. The constitutional cap was ratified in November 1992 by more than four-fifths of those voting on the referendum question.

The essence of both caps prohibits the legislature from increasing *general budget expenditures* "by a percentage which exceeds the greater of the percentage increase in personal income or the percentage increase in inflation. . . ." and a balanced budget is now required by statute and constitution. Super majorities in both chambers are required for a declaration of emergency or "extraordinary circumstances" that permits overriding constitutional spending limits.

The constitutional version had not been implemented by the end of the 1994 legislative session. Because a three-fifths vote in both chambers is required to define exclusions, core terminology, and the basis on which the cap is calculated, the reality was simple arithmetic: the thin Democratic senate majority (nineteen of thirty-six seats) needed Republican support for approval of implementing language. The Republican position is to support only definitions that tighten the cap's terms. As a result, the minority party was unusually leveraged on a major budget issue in 1993–1994. (One Republican legislator has filed a lawsuit to enforce the constitutional cap.[29])

The statutory version, however, has been in force since FY 1993.[30] The governor's 1993 budget submission describes its operation in the FY 1994–FY 1995 budget cycle.

> The statutory spending cap limits the growth of expenditures to either (1) the rolling five-year average annual growth in personal income, or (2) the increase in the consumer price index for the last year, whichever is greater. Certain spending—including debt service—is exempt from the cap. To preclude shifting expenditures out of the [g]eneral [f]und to other funds, the spending cap applies to all appropriated funds combined.

The cap already is getting quite tight. Predictably, some manipulation has already occurred. The carry-forward appropriation of surpluses approved in May 1993 for debt service in FY 1994–FY 1995 raised the base on which the statutory cap was calculated; 1994 saw a fruitless effort to retain in the constitutional cap certain statutory exclusions such as local aid to distressed municipalities and federal funds. As the low average growth in personal income of the recession years rolls into the cap, allowable growth is limited to 6 percent in FY 1994 and less than 5 percent in FY 1995. The budget adopted for FY 1994 was only $50 million or 0.6 percent under the cap. According to calculations from the legislative Office of Fiscal Analysis (hereafter, OFA) that include adjustments and additions to the original appropriation for FY 1995, the $9.48 billion total budget for FY 1995 comes in only $57 million under the cap.

Gimmickry

In addition to deficit financing and appropriations carried forward (discussed under revenue strategy, above), other, more customary contrivances were used to manipulate budgetary outcomes on the spending side. Shifting costs off the general fund and postponing pension payments were particularly profitable devices. Describing the 1993 legislative session, the CPEC says,[31]

> The priority of the [Appropriations] [C]ommittee was to restore all or part of spending reductions proposed by the governor. . . . In order to reach its goals the committee made some legitimate reductions . . . , utilized some temporary savings that will be repaid later (such as in teachers' retirement contributions) and relied on unspent funds from this year to pay for FY 1994 programs. Obviously the latter two mechanisms are not consistent with sound fiscal practice.

OFA's analysis of the governor's proposal for FY 1994 in its *Connecticut State Budget 1993–95* imparts some sense of the magnitude of these manipulations (some of which are legitimate and responsible, others less so). OFA's adjustments for the Economic Recovery Fund (budgeted as revenue reduction, not appropriation) and for "items moved off-budget" raised the increase in general expenditures 0.1 percent, from 7.1 to 7.2 percent of general budget expenditures in excess of $8.6 billion.

Interfund shifts. It is useful analytically and politically to separate out the general fund from other funds, especially given some speculation that the downsizing wave, the forceful spending limitation, and public service demands work in tandem to encourage interfund shifts. Some spending has been moved off the general fund, including $85 million to the transportation fund in 1992–1993. Although some such shifts may be responsible and even recommended by the state auditors, they undercut comparability and open the process to manipulation and charges of bad faith. There also is some apprehension that this device and artfully defined exclusions could undercut the constitutional spending cap.

Connecticut uses something on the order of 250 funds, a number so cumbersome from a bookkeeping perspective that the treasurer's office is undertaking a project to identify and reduce the number to simplify cash management. Professional cash managers have been trying "to impress upon legislative staff that you don't have to have a fund to have a program."[32] In 1991, funds were created to finance four minor agencies supported by fees and/or assessments, for $22 million in "savings" on the general fund. The 1993 session added yet another to account for slot machine revenues but rejected an environment fund proposed by the governor because it smacked of a (minor) tax increase.

Unfunded accrued liabilities. Unfunded accrued liabilities—legally binding promises of future payments that remain to be paid off in the future—represent the buildup of governmental IOU's. By failing to fully finance costs as they are incurred and accumulating legal obligations that must be paid eventually, the state can push current costs into the future. (GAAP is designed in part to forestall this gimmick.) With pension deferrals accounting for almost one-fifth of all cuts from current services in FY 1992–FY 1994, this short-term and short-sighted stratagem was important in coping with the fiscal crisis. (See Table 8–2.)

Executive proposals and legislative action on the state-financed retirement system for public school teachers typify the methods. They include directly reducing the funding of current costs; changing assumptions for rate earnings to permit reduced state-appropriated contributions; using "excess earnings" in the fund to finance cost-of-living-adjustment (or COLA, heretofore automatically provided by statute); increasing the participants' contribution; and requiring a municipal contribution (which the legislature rejected). For example, the $1.5 billion ultimately appropriated for state aid to public education in FY 1994 was almost $8 million less than the executive proposal, despite a series of addbacks. This arithmetic triumph evidently was achieved by applying $21.5 million in "savings" from reducing the state contribution to the fund from 100 percent to 85 percent. According to the most recent actuarial projection, the unfunded accrued liability in the teachers' retirement fund totaled $2.4 billion as of June 30, 1992.

The retirement system for state employees was also modified, with the concurrence of the State Employees Bargaining Agent Coalition (hereafter, SEBAC) representing about eighteen different public employee organizations in matters of pensions and health care.[33] The parties agreed in February 1992 to amend an arbitration award in order to reduce state funding of past service liability for FY 1992 by $15 million. In June of the same year, they replaced straight-line amortization with the percentage-of-payroll method (widely used in the private sector) so that state payments for past service liability could be much reduced.

Based on actuarial estimates of normal cost savings associated with the elimination of the COLA for future retirees, the legislature reduced the upcoming state contribution for FY 1995 by $22.3 million more than the governor had proposed. While on its face this may appear to be prudent financial management, the gimmick is that the COLA is subject to collective bargaining. Putting great pressure on unions and on any arbitration board, the retirees' COLA "has to be the number one union issue" because it pits current employees against future retirees.[34] There also was no provision for the retirees' COLA in the FY 1995 budget as adopted. While the COLA provision remains in force until another contract is agreed upon, this issue suggests how much budget dynamics—and postures—have changed.

With respect to future costs, the governor proposed to remove pension (and health benefits) from the scope of bargaining beginning July 1, 1994, when the current SEBAC contract expired. In "the only state in the country that bargains over pension *funding*—both rate and amount,"[35] the legislature, *Hartford Courant*, and public employee union leaders were all in accord on the matter of preferring negotiation to imposition. The "big win" for the unions in recent years has been just to preserve the status of collective bargaining.

The state never directly borrowed against pension funds, as the governor had proposed in 1992. Some resistance to the idea surely derived from the pension's having climbed over the last decade from 10 percent to 60 percent actuarially funded.[36] The state did stretch out (effectively, reduce) its level of contributions, however. Some of the dollar decline in state contributions (from more than $288 million in FY 1990 to $251 million in FY 1993) is attributable to the shrinking work force. According to the state's official statements for general obligation bonds, the unfunded accrued liability increased $831 million, from $2.8 billion as of June 1991 to $3.6 billion by June 1993 (the most recent actuarial valuation).

Assessment of Spending Strategy

As it turned out, the strategy did *not* reduce nominal spending. General budget expenditures increased from $7.7 billion to $9.5 billion, or more than 23 percent in FY 1991–FY 1995 (and the general fund increased from $6.6 billion to $8.1 billion). Nonetheless, spending growth rates were reined in to well below the 1980s' and cuts from current services amounted to more than $3 billion in FY 1992–FY 1994. Some gimmickry such as shifting costs among funds and pension manipulation occurred. Although the state never borrowed from pension funds, unfunded accrued liability increased substantially, a factor critical to an appraisal of the long-term consequences of the spending strategy.

The public's assessment throughout the crisis has been that state spending is excessive. A Connecticut Poll of January 1992, at the height of the crisis, elicited the response that state spending is *too high* from 78 percent of the respondents, compared to 59 percent in February 1989. When a poll conducted in March 1994 asked respondents to characterize the level of state spending, the majority (65 percent) responded in like fashion.

The state fared well on procedural criteria. Although the 1994 legislature failed to meet budget deadlines and was forced into special session, by and large it adhered to biennial budget procedures. More than one-half of the $141 million added in 1994 to the FY 1995 appropriation enacted in 1993 was for rising Medicaid caseloads and costs, and the revised appropriation authorized for the governor's youth initiative only $14 million or about one-half of what he requested for his unfinished business in his last budget.

The spending cap has been met, at least arithmetically, but it has not halted budgetary growth and, for some informed observers, thereby fails the primary test.[37] A Connecticut Poll conducted in January–February 1994 on the constitutional cap shows that Connecticut residents favor it (32 percent strongly, 34 percent somewhat) but only 19 percent judged the cap's performance at holding down state spending as good, compared to 44 percent rating it as fair and 22 percent as poor.[38] Nonetheless, the cap has *slowed* spending growth and fundamentally changed budgetary decision making by reframing the terms of the budget debate. By injecting obligatory discipline into a process now focused on restraint, the cap already has succeeded in the eyes of many key players whom this author interviewed.

INITIATIVES AND INNOVATIONS

The next logical step is to restructure and reorient governmental operations. The governor's policies took aim at welfare programs, employee benefits, and state government (downsizing, administrative costs, consolidation), and he began to restyle the state's relationship with municipalities (mandates, aid) and with business and industry (jobs, economic development). The legislature adopted major initiatives, foremost among which are a restructured revenue system, spending caps, and a stricter debt limitation, and the adoption of biennial budgeting with a long-term forecasting component.

The reorientation actually predates the Weicker administration; much of current strategy and many specific steps derive from the Thomas Commission. Commission proposals adopted during the extraordinary 1991 legislative marathon include a spending limitation (the commission had recommended capping state grants); a more restrictive debt limit; a five-year capital plan; biennial budgeting; modification of binding arbitration; and more.

To build on the Thomas Commission's foundation, the Commission to Effect Government Reorganization was established in 1991 with the statutory mission to increase government productivity while reducing the overhead costs of state services. Known as the Hull-Harper Commission, it identified four "cross-cutting issues": the need for rationalized and standardized service delivery in common regions;

the wholesale adoption of total quality management (hereafter, TQM); the need for performance measures and indicators to increase accountability and aid policy making; and, also designated by the Thomas Commission, reform of the personnel and merit system "to make it simpler, more flexible, and responsible to modern management and organization needs."

Since 1991, the state has undertaken numerous initiatives aimed at revamping decision making and reorienting service delivery. These include reorganization through regionalization into standard service regions; decentralization and downsizing; sponsoring and funding governmental innovation through capital investment and awards; creating an Economic Conference Board as a standing economic advisory council; providing business incentives, grants, loans, and guarantees while reducing business taxes and seeking job retention; building supportive relationships with business; enhancing accountability by introducing benchmarking under the Connecticut Progress Council; adopting GAAP as the budgetary basis beginning in FY 1996; and creating a chief financial officer (Office of Finance) in the central budget office.

Other efforts aim at building management capacity. Efforts have been made to standardize information technology and standardized, automated budget and personnel systems are being implemented and refined. TQM has been fully implemented in at least one-quarter of the major agencies, including central staff agencies for budget and administrative services and the agency responsible for economic development; at least twenty agencies adopted TQM to some extent. There is a heightened emphasis on quantified measures of performance and outcomes. The ideas associated with Osborne and Gaebler's *Reinventing Government*[39] have been influential in shaping Connecticut's reorientation.

Reorganization of Human Services

The reorganization of social and health services illustrates many facets of the reorientation under way. Senator Joseph H. Harper Jr., cochairman of the Hull-Harper Commission and of the powerful joint Appropriations Committee through 1994, selected the reorganization when asked by this author in July 1993 to specify a fiscal or managerial innovation. It follows from the commission's recommendations, according to Harper, and is intended "to improve the coordination, accountability and cost effectiveness of health and social services delivery systems in the state." Services from twelve agencies have been consolidated and restructured into four departments, and other agencies completely or in part were merged into a new super agency, the Department of Social Services (hereafter, DSS).

The 1993 implementation plan developed by the Office of Policy and Management (or OPM, the executive budget office) refers specifically to TQM principles (client needs, empowered employees, continuous improvement, and the team approach) and *Reinventing Government*. The goal is to "create more flexible, adaptable and innovative state government structures that strive constantly for new ways to improve services and heighten productivity."[40]

The reorganization also aims at reducing excessive bureaucracy in service delivery. According to Harper, the enabling legislation addresses the ratio of direct to indirect services in order to "maximize resources for services and reduce bureaucracy" and the overhaul is designed to foster interagency service integration. A work force reduction in DSS targets under 5 percent of the 2,500 jobs, and plans call for moving others out to regional offices. Implementation costs of about $15 million are expected to be offset in the long-term by better services.

Reorganization often stems from fiscal pressures rather than from unadulterated concern with service delivery or managerial issues. As a result, it starts off disadvantaged by the dissonant goals of cost savings and service enhancement. It sometimes even may represent a cheap, artificial, and expedient substitute for real problem solving. Of course, reorganization signals leaders' concern and, given the intractable nature of some socioeconomic problems and a realistic assessment of governmental capacity to solve them, reorganization may be preferred to no action or false promises. Although definitive evaluation is premature, the reorganization under way in Connecticut's human services appears to be more than a placebo.

Welfare Reform

The governor proposed welfare reform in his FY 1994 budget; a legislatively mandated, bipartisan task force made recommendations; and the legislature approved an AFDC reform package in 1993. The package is designed to encourage work and responsibility instead of controlling behavior. Rules now allow recipients to retain more earnings before benefits are reduced ("fill-the-gap" benefit determination), keep more of child support payments, and maintain two-parent households (married or not). The mandatory employment feature requires a federal rule waiver and asset and car value limitations are raised. Other changes such as cash replacing food stamps are designed to instill client responsibility for personal finances.

The *Governor's Budget Summary* for FY 1994 asserts that the reform "emphasizes the principle of making work pay, removing the disincentive to work and to family unity." DDS Commissioner Audrey Rowe claims that Connecticut is the first state to take on President Clinton's goal to "change welfare as we know it." [41] Although it is far too soon to attach dollars or assess outcomes, welfare reform has significant potential.

Regionalization and Decentralization

The social services model is "predicated on regionalizing administrative and programmatic support services to strengthen and bolster the service delivery system."[42] Here the administration's concerns center on client accessibility, staff efficiency, and interagency planning.[43] Approximately sixty state agencies provide a variety of services, a majority of which are in health and human services. Because some twenty-three of these agencies use regions that do not match the proposed uniform regions, much of state government will have to modify administrative operations and service delivery.[44]

Decentralization and reducing bureaucracy also affect managerial capacity. A budgetary facet of decentralization introduced in 1991 is higher education's so-called *fiscal autonomy* or block grant funding. Higher education units are exempt from the position control provisions adopted in 1992 and from budget control of objects of expense, purchasing, and contracting under $2 million. The cochairman of the higher education appropriations subcommittee in 1991 contends that this is "the only example where we have invested managers with the ability to manage."[45] From another perspective, OFA's director asks, "How do we justify [flexibility] for one area of state government and not for others, and tell them now much [in major objects of expenditure]?"[46]

Decentralization runs counter to many proposals for enhanced accountability, consistency, and integration. For example, as recommended by the Hull-Harper Commission, the new Office of Finance under an executive financial officer, as was created in 1992 within OPM to standardize and coordinate finance, budget, and information systems and policies among state agencies. One legislator observes, "We've seen half a dozen or more pieces of legislation shifting responsibilities from the agencies to OPM [including] hiring all consultants, personal service agreements over $10,000, energy . . . all management is being driven by OPM's fiscal controls. There is no true decentralization. . . ."[47]

Measuring Performance and Effectiveness

Troubled by the lack of accountability in many state programs, the Thomas Commission concluded in 1991, "There is no process in place to evaluate how large amounts of money are being spent, what needs are or are not being met, and if some services are even required." Efforts under way to change this situation include program performance measures, management and quality assessment, and benchmarking.

Seemingly echoing in policy terms that "[t]he central failure of government today is one of means, not ends"[48] and that government should shift to a more productive use of resources, the state initiated *benchmarking* in 1993. Derived from the experiences of Oregon, Minnesota, and other jurisdictions, benchmarking's objective is to improve accountability by getting and measuring outcomes as steps toward established goals. In 1993, the legislature established a Connecticut Progress Council to develop a long-range vision and appropriate benchmarks across the full range of state functions and public concerns. The act directs that OPM, "in consultation with each budgeted state agency, shall develop, for state budgeting purposes, specific biennial goals and objectives and quantifiable outcome measures, which shall not be limited to measures of activities, for each program, service and state grant. . . ." An annual evaluative report is required.

Because self-assessment is seen as a positive source of ideas for improving services and capacity, as well as part of the commitment to TQM, several other efforts to measure government performance and the difference it makes are under way. OPM is applying the Governmental Accounting Standards Board's Service Efforts and Accomplishments Reporting system, or SEA measures. The board asserts that "[t]he measurement of a governmental entity's performance requires information not only on the acquisition and use of resources, but also on the outputs and outcomes of the services provided and the relationship between the use of resources and outputs and outcomes."[49]

Privatization. Although recommendations to hire private providers for public services date back to the Thomas Commission, there has been relatively little privatization of state services.[50] Despite privatization's status as a labor concern specifically addressed in some collective bargaining agreements, the state may see less direct service delivery by government in the future. After months of debate, Hartford's Board of Education decided in July 1994 to begin contract negotiations with Education Alternatives Inc.[EAI], the for-profit Minnesota firm, to manage the thirty-two-school system. Although EAI went into twelve Baltimore schools in 1992, newspaper accounts describe Hartford as the first city in the country to privatize the entire school system and focus on issues of control, accountability, cost savings, and prospects for improved student performance.[51] A Connecticut Poll conducted in July 1994 found low public resistance to privatization (three out of five residents favoring consideration), but a majority rejected the idea for their own town's schools and were unaware of municipal services already privatized.

Assessment

OPM Secretary Cibes maintains, "The [g]overnor is absolutely and totally in favor of applying innovations and increasing productivity in state government."[52] While actually the administration has originated little or nothing, it has taken so many steps and adopted so many practices at the frontier of public management that the pattern of innovation is indisputable and impressive. Most of the reforms and lesser initiatives are less *reinventing* than rediscovering or borrowing from the experiences of other jurisdictions. According to one knowledgeable participant, "None of the things we've done as reforms are new ideas . . . [it's] just that the time has come in Connecticut."[53]

It is too early to assess fairly individual initiatives such as reorganization, welfare reform, or regionalization, but it is clear already that the reorientation touches most if not all state agencies and services. The single biggest beneficiary to date of Connecticut's new approach to service delivery and management capacity appears to be the executive central budget agency, responsible for standardized systems and the measures and controls associated with enhanced accountability. It is not surprising, then, that decentralization and reducing bureaucracy have progressed slowly. (See discussion of state employees and reorganization of human services.)

BUDGETARY OUTCOMES AND CHANGING PRIORITIES

The winners and losers over a given period customarily are assessed against their own history and against other players. Relative gains and losses are measured by percentage change and the proportion devoted to functions, programs, or agencies (budget share). Table 8–3 and Figure 8–1 detail these outcomes for major government functions and other categories that together amount to 94–99 percent of general budget expenditures each year. Reductions from current services (Table 8–2, above) is another important gauge, as is relative staffing, especially for agencies delivering labor-intensive services.

Different measures generate alternate and sometimes contradictory views of budgetary outcomes. With respect to the numbers, Governor Weicker said in his 1993 budget address,

> The sound and fury of political beliefs make for good theater. Good government, however, is the result of precisely arrayed numbers on paper that, by virtue of integrity and priority, give voice to the aspirations of a people. Far from being a dry academic exercise, a budget speaks eloquently and hopefully—elegantly— as to what all of us deem important in our lives.

But the numbers do not speak for themselves. Their meaning in politics and policy depends upon specific historical and contextual factors. For example, some functions such as human services, corrections, and debt service are characterized by significant growth, but for different reasons. The first is protected by judicial and federal mandates; the second is related to sentencing practices and crime rates outside its direct influence; and the third is a fully nondiscretionary legal obligation driven by the magnitude of current and historical borrowing.

The conventional measures of budgetary outcomes displayed in Table 8–3 focus exclusively on bureaucratic concerns internal to the process or agency. Because there is no one-to-one correlation between service provision and spending (or staffing), these measures do not

TABLE 8–3 Changes in Selected Connecticut Expenditures[a]

Fiscal	1991		1992	1993	1994	1995		1991–1995
	% Change	% of Total	% Change	% Change	% Change	% Change	% of Total	% Change
Medicaid	24.0	15.5	7.6	14.4	8.7	7.8	18.3	44.3
AFDC[b]	14.5	4.5	7.6	1.9	4.8	4.6	4.2	20.1
General Assistance[c]	57.5	1.5	46.4	9.3	–21.5	–12.8	1.3	9.6
Aid to Localities[d]	–4.9	23.0	–0.1	–1.4	8.9	2.8	20.6	10.3
K–12 Education	4.6	15.4	4.1	–2.6	5.9	2.7	13.8	10.2
University of Connecticut[e]	8.9	2.4	–1.8	6.0	6.4	2.4	2.2	13.0
Corrections	26.1	3.1	4.8	15.5	23.0	13.0	4.2	68.2
Debt Service	7.8	6.7	49.7	15.5	14.2	18.6	12.8	134.2
Personal Services	5.9	21.5	0.4	3.9	8.7	2.4	20.2	16.1

[a]Includes General, Transportation, Higher Education Tuition, Educational Excellence, Economic Recovery, and other appropriated and nonappropriated accounts. Percentage of total is calculated from figures in millions of dollars. Figures for FY 1995 are as adopted in 1994. Figures are as estimated for FY 1993 and, for FY 1994–FY 1995, as adopted in 1993.

[b]Includes AFDC-Unemployed Parent.

[c]Local welfare partially reimbursed by state.

[d]Includes state payments for teachers' retirement.

[e]When tuition funds are excluded, higher education declined as % expenditures in FY 1991–1995.

[f]Excludes employee fringe benefits and includes relevant higher education's block grants and tuition fund monies.

Source: Connecticut General Assembly, Office of Fiscal Analysis, draft documents, September 15 and 28, 1993.

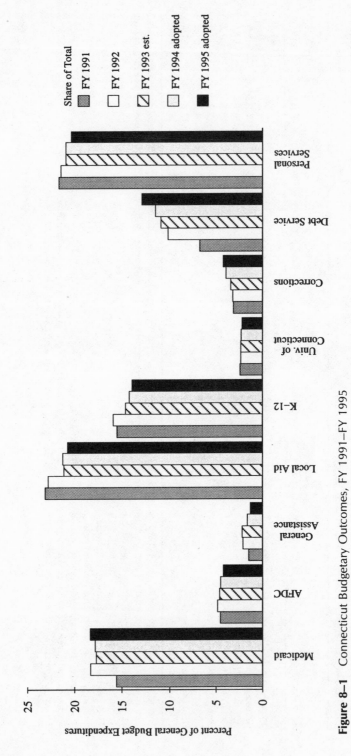

Figure 8–1 Connecticut Budgetary Outcomes, FY 1991–FY 1995

Source. Table 8.3 and Connecticut General Assembly, Office of Fiscal Analysis, draft documents, September 15 and 28, 1993.

speak directly to service quantity and quality, effectiveness, public demand, client satisfaction, and other facets of public service. To impart a sense of service impacts, the analysis that follows augments budgetary outcomes with figures on service recipients, benefit levels, and related concerns.

Taxpayers: Current and Future

Because state tax receipts are higher, Connecticut taxpayers obviously are paying part of the price for the fiscal crisis. That the public is not enthusiastic is suggested by public attitudes described above. The moderate progressivity of the income tax, tax avoidance techniques by some taxpayers, and decreases in business taxes mean that not all taxpayers pay the same price.

A classic outcome is that the largest single dollar impact falls on prospective taxpayers, who will be bearing future costs for current strategic choices. Total debt service already obligates taxpayers to more than $3.2 billion in FY 1996–FY 2000 alone. (In FY 1991–FY 1995, debt service increased by a third, from $668 million to a projected $889 million.)

The question is how large an aggregate bill future taxpayers will receive as a result of today's decisions, not the social value of investments nor the legitimacy of billing them and for what. A rough answer is that future taxpayers face obligations approaching $12 billion.[54] The bill to future taxpayers *for the fiscal crisis alone* totals something on the order of approximately $5 billion in debt, bond allocations, deferred retirement contributions, and other liabilities.[55]

State Aid to Localities

At over $500 million, state aid (grants and payments in lieu of taxes) accounts for more than one-fifth of general budget expenditures and is its single largest component. (See Table 8–3.) The Thomas Commission initiated the attack on this heretofore *sacred cow* in 1991 and observed that FY 1992's reduction over the prior year "was the first time in anyone's memory that this spending was held below the previous year's total." Table 8–3 and Figure 8–1 show that the proportion of state spending devoted to local aid decreased somewhat, but the dollar amount of aid actually increased 10.3 percent in FY 1991–FY 1995. State aid accounted for only 1.4 percent of the cuts from current services listed on Table 8–2. Municipal interests enjoyed some victories in FY 1991–FY 1995; aid in dollars increased, and changes were enacted in state policies on mandates and compulsory arbitration. Defeats include the failure to exempt local aid from the spending cap and a reduction in the state's share of a welfare program. (See General Assistance, below.)

After effective property tax rates declined in the 1970s and 1980s,[56] a flat property tax base turned local leaders toward the state. The annual growth rate of 7–10 percent in per capita spending in Connecticut municipalities in the 1980s fell to 4.3 percent in FY 1992 and then to 2.1 percent in FY 1994.[57] The Connecticut Conference of Municipalities reports a declining average annual increase in property taxes (7.6 percent in FY 1991, 4.7 percent in FY 1992, and 3.2 percent in FY 1993) and, for FY 1995, only a 2 percent increase in the local property tax base (figured on values as of October 1993).[58]

State aid frequently is a political battlefield, and wins and losses vary with the session. With municipal leaders concerned that the new state spending cap may lead to increased reliance on property taxes that already account for 46 percent of all state-local taxes,[59] the 1993 session was responsive to municipal interests and directed a large proportion of the new revenue from slot machines to local aid. State grants were reduced for FY 1994 over the previous year, and the overall increase is attributable to payments in lieu of taxes or PILOTs, monies paid by the state to partially compensate municipalities for forgone local property tax revenues on state and certain tax-exempt institutions such as colleges and hospitals. According to the Connecticut Conference of Municipalities, state law exempts over seventy types of property from local taxes and the state has established ten PILOT programs.[60]

The 1994 debate, perhaps as a hint of things to come, centered on state-financed local property tax relief. Proposed by the governor in a more generous version than was ultimately adopted, the relief is largely symbolic: a credit against state income taxes for local property taxes on motor vehicles begins phasing in at 20 percent increments in 1997; it is valued at $248 million by the turn of the century.

The 1993 mandate reform imposes a one-year delay in implementing new state mandates that require municipal appropriations, and requires aggregate cost and reimbursement statements for each legislative session, public hearings by legislative committees, and other steps geared toward comprehensive costing and disclosure. The legislation does not prohibit new or unfunded mandates, but is a step toward accountability. The report of the Connecticut Advisory Commission on Intergovernmental Relations on the 1993 General Assembly listed seventeen new or expanded mandates on local general government (and another eight on schools districts).

The 1992 modification of compulsory arbitration for local governments and K–12 education mandated that arbitrators consider a jurisdiction's ability to pay. In effect, the change gives priority to the locality's financial capacity. Arbitrators ruled against municipal and teachers' unions in several instances in 1994.

State Employees

The Thomas Commission reported in 1991 that "[t]he size of the state government work force approaches national norms. . . . Overall, it is difficult to conclude whether the work force is too large, too small, or 'just right'." Since then, reducing the state work force has been the avowed policy of just about all participants. Downsizing has proceeded largely in terms of personnel cutbacks via attrition and two early retirement programs. A focus on technology-driven productivity increases and "doing more with less" were themes repeated in interviews conducted by this author in 1993. The realities of constricted discretionary spending and the need to slow spending growth added payroll and benefits to position count on the list of concerns.

Negative public sentiment backed the tactic of targeting the state work force. A Connecticut Poll taken during the height of the fiscal crisis in March 1991 asked respondents to compare state employees to their private sector counterparts. The majority (53 percent) rendered the opinion that state employees "work less hard." State employees constituted a cutback target of choice in a January 1992 Connecticut Poll, which identified laying off state workers and sharply limiting the number of new hires (52 percent favor) as among the more acceptable steps to be taken.

Personal services did in fact drop significantly as a proportion of the general fund. Yet, despite early retirements, position freezes, high-level screening of hiring authorizations, voluntary unpaid leave programs, and other efforts, personal services declined only from 21.5 percent of general budget expenditures in FY 1991 to 20.2 percent in FY 1995, as shown on Table 8–3. The dollars increased more than 16 percent over the period.

TABLE 8-4 Connecticut State Staffing (permanent, full-time positions)

	Total	General and Transportation Funds				
	Authorized	Authorized	As Percent of Total	Filled	Vacancies	Vacancy Rate
June 1990	57,076	47,472	83%	43,767	3,705	8%
June 1991	54,586	44,241	82%	43,427	814	2%
June 1992	53,351	42,796	80%	40,085	2,711	7%
June 1993	54,439	43,031	79%	41,079	1,952	5%
January 1994	54,239	44,552	82%	42,061	2,491	6%
1990–1994 Change						
Number	−2,837	−2,920		−1,706		
Percent	−4.97%	−6.2%		−3.9%		

Source: Connecticut General Assembly, Office of Fiscal Analysis, memorandum of Spring 1994 on monthly position counts.

Position count. To what extent has the Weicker administration succeeded in reducing the number of state employees? While the precise contours of an answer depend upon the funds and dates selected for analysis, Table 8–4 shows indisputably that an overall reduction in full-time, permanent state employees has taken place. Total authorized positions were reduced almost 5 percent from the historic high in 1990. Filled positions on the general and transportation funds declined almost 4 percent. That these funds accounted for a declining proportion of all authorized positions through FY 1993 and considering selective staffing increases (associated with court decrees and hitting the general fund), these figures suggest the increasing extent to which positions are being financed through other funds.

Agency impacts. Not all agencies have been affected equally and some have seen significant increases. According to the governor's 1993 budget proposal, general fund staffing rebounded almost 4 percent between 1992 and 1993, but fully 94 percent of the added positions (or 1,356 of 1,445) was court mandated. The story was repeated in 1994–1995, with net employment increases being absorbed by DCYS and the Department of Correction. The *Governor's Budget Summary* for FY 1994–FY 1995 outlines the overall changes in the state work force.

From June 20, 1990 to June 30. 1993, the state work force has been downsized by almost 10 percent—in spite of significant growth in staff increases in the Departments of Correction and Children and Youth Services. In fact, the growth in Corrections staffing from fiscal years 1991 to 1995 is over 50%; Children and Youth Services grows at 59%. Reductions in other parts of the work force will balance out at zero percent growth in the state work force for the four years from 1991 to 1995.

Payroll. Pushed by increased staff and salaries, the state payroll increased 71 percent in FY 1984–FY 1989.[61] In 1991, the Thomas Commission reported that the state's "salary and benefit levels are among the most generous in the nation. Comparative statistics show that the average salary for Connecticut's state government employees ranks fourth highest in the nation." Since then and despite declining staffing, the payroll increased. According to September 1993 figures from the State Retirement Commission, the payroll rose 10 percent from FY 1990 to FY 1991, to almost $2 billion, and almost another 3 percent in FY 1992. Even considering wage deferrals in FY 1992 and

FY 1993 worth $125 million (4 percent of all cuts from current services shown on Table 8–2), average salaries continued to rise. Retirement Commission figures show that the average salary of $32,823 in FY 1991 had increased more than 8 percent by FY 1991 and another increase of more than 6 percent brought the average to $37,771 by FY 1992.

The governor has attempted to cut into the costs associated with the work force, and he succeeded to a limited degree, despite the higher payroll. He proposed that the 1993 session eliminate annual increments (AIs), worth 1.5 percent or less of the payroll.[62] AIs began the session as statutory, automatic step increases for time in grade, aimed at smoothing out the effects of seniority within a given job classification. Ending more than one-quarter of a century of increments that antedated collective bargaining, the 1993 session compromised by keeping statutory AIs for contracts in negotiation in 1993, but made them subject to collective bargaining thereafter. The unions lost AIs but won on the larger issue of positioning themselves for upcoming negotiations. At stake was leverage in negotiating contracts—whether terms and conditions stay in effect upon contract expiration, as they now do. Back-of-the-budget language exempted *terms and conditions* from the particular decision and they remain in force should a contract lapse.

Retaining terms and conditions soon became very important to state employees. In 1993, the governor had recommended and the legislature had adopted FY 1994–FY 1995 budgets containing no wage or salary increases beyond current contracts. In 1994, the Senate followed through and in effect froze salaries by rejecting four arbitration awards. It was the first time an arbitration award had been rejected since the introduction of binding arbitration in 1986. The statute governing binding arbitration had been modified in 1991 so that a two-thirds vote by only one chamber, rather than two, could reject an award.

Through SEBAC, public employee unions contributed to resolving (and, some would say, causing) the fiscal crisis; this is clear from Table 8–2. One union leader argued, "State-employee unions have provided $1.3 billion in contract concessions over the next five years to help balance the budget. . . ."[63] Public employee unions "worked so hard to get the income tax passed. Now the question is, at what price?"[64] By 1994, labor's relations with the governor and Democratic legislative leaders had deteriorated to recriminations, and worse. The treatment of state employees' and retirees' interests in 1993 and 1994 suggests that, by the end of the Weicker administration, the programmatic winners of the 1990 election were, ironically, the defeated Democratic income tax proponent and the defeated Republican advocating spending cuts and downsizing state government.

Economic Development

The current approach to economic development and stimulation illustrates that "a new way of doing things" does not necessarily translate into spending less or the state's doing less. After the governor proposed a broad package of assistance, services, and inducements in the winter of 1993, at least four major steps were taken to lure and retain businesses and private sector jobs in the state, enhance the state's competitive position, and in the words of the *New Connecticut* marketing campaign, to "make government user friendly." First, workers compensation was restructured to lower costs and enhance the state's competitiveness. Second, the chronically underfunded unemployment insurance system was reformed. (In both cases the legislature passed a variant of a gubernatorial proposal.) Third, in late spring, a much-touted economic development package worth $32 million began in earnest the process of preserving 2,300 jobs at beleaguered Pratt and Whitney plants. The persistently disquieting employment picture explains why employment continued to dominate everyone's political agenda into 1994.

The fourth step was a swift increase in the state's financial participation in economic development through grants, credits, loans, and loan guarantees. One instance that received popular attention but did not succeed was the governor's initiating and the legislature's approving the use of state bond proceeds to finance a stadium in Hartford, entice the Patriots to Connecticut, and revitalize the state capital's economy. According to this author's analysis of activity data from the Department of Economic Development (DED), the total dollar value of development projects in 1990–1993 was almost $240 million, of which almost 47 percent was allocated in 1993. DED provided loans, loan guarantees, or grants directly to private firms (excluding educational, cultural, and nonprofit organizations) to three projects in 1990, four in 1991, at least forty-two in 1992, and ninety-six in 1993. More than two-thirds of the almost $112 million in economic development funds in 1993 was extended to private firms to modernize, expand, or relocate into the state. State assistance (DED's activities are augmented by programs of the Connecticut Development Authority and others) totaled $393 million between January 1991 and June 1993, but went to only 242 companies representing only about 1 percent of all the state's businesses.[65]

Concern voiced over accountability, participation, effectiveness, and return to the state on investments in economic development projects led the legislature to appoint a task force in 1994, when it also revised the FY 1995 budget to add $70 million (including grants relating to displaced defense workers and the "superhighway") to DED's bond authorizations.

Higher Education

Because student costs increased substantially and full-time enrollment at state universities declined in FY 1990–FY1993,[66] students in public higher educational institutions in Connecticut number among the losers in the fiscal restructuring. FY 1995 is the sixth consecutive year of double-digit tuition increases at the University of Connecticut, whose budget and finance offices' data indicate that tuition and the mandatory general university fee increased by $1,722 or 59 percent in FY 1991–FY 1995 and total $4,636.

What students receive for the increased cost to them has been the subject of much debate. In part because of enrollment declines, student/teacher ratios improved somewhat in the university components of the system in FY 1992–FY 1993. The University of Connecticut's budget request for FY 1994–FY 1995 submitted to the board of trustees complained of the staffing decline; from FY 1991 to FY 1992, the university's permanent position count (full-time equivalents or FTEs, on all funds) dropped 323 or 7.3 percent (counting retirees under the FY 1992 retirement incentive program).

Changes in overall funding for institutions of higher education do not translate necessarily into impacts on the state budget and may mask the loss of state support if tuition funds are included (as, for example, in Table 8–3). Considering only appropriated funds, higher education declined from 5.5 to 4.3 percent of all appropriated funds in FY 1991–FY 1995. State support to higher education through appropriations declined almost 2 percent or $7.7 million, to total $390 million in FY 1995. At the University of Connecticut, as tuition and fees rose from 20 to 28 percent of total current revenues in FY 1991–FY 1995, state appropriations declined almost 6 percent, from 44 to 40 percent of total current revenues. Institutional expenditures in state universities and colleges declined absolutely in FY 1993, but not to FY 1991 levels. Higher education absorbed 1.2 percent of the cuts from current services in FY 1992–FY 1994.

Average faculty salaries increased from FY 1990 to FY 1992, from more than $45,000 to almost $51,000 in the state university system, $40,000 to $46,000 in the community-technical colleges, and $54,000 to $57,000 at the University of Connecticut. The salary "win" is offset to some extent by the figures on pensions and wage deferral figures in Table 8–2 and the freezing of many salaries when an arbitration award was rejected in 1994.

K–12 Education

State appropriations for public education increased almost 7 percent or $102 million in FY 1991–FY 1995, to total $1.6 billion. Conversely, the proportion of state appropriations going to K–12 fell, from 20 to 17 percent of all appropriations. (Note that payments to the teachers' retirement fund are treated as aid to localities in appropriation analyses and in Table 8–3.) Education's share of cuts in current services shown in Table 8–2 was about 14 percent in FY 1992–FY 1994. The 10 percent dollar increase for K–12 in FY 1990–FY 1995 was not enough to maintain its budget share and it declined from more than 15 to less than 14 percent. The state's share of total funding for K–12 education decreased from 45 percent in FY 1990 to 37 percent by FY 1993,[67] while school expenditures increased. That public education is included in the municipal budget's bottom line in Connecticut complicates matters politically and analytically.

Average teacher salary, the student census, and per pupil expenditures all rose during the fiscal crisis. As the average salary increased more than 21 percent from FY 1990 through FY 1994 as estimated, the student census rose 8.3 percent (to almost 505,000).[68] The salary increases followed years of a statewide effort to raise salaries, attract and retain excellent teachers, and improve the quality of K–12 education. From 1983 through 1993, teachers' salaries in Connecticut had increased at the highest rate in the nation, more than 133 percent compared to the national average of 69 percent; by 1993, the Connecticut average of $48,000 was $13,000 or 37 percent higher than the national average.[69] The state's average teacher salary surpassed

$50,000 in FY 1994. With binding arbitration modified, pressure on the property tax base widespread, and the salary range for teachers averaging from approximately $28,000 to $55,000, a number of arbitration rulings in 1994 went against the teachers' unions.

Corrections

The corrections function increased by $281 million in FY 1991–FY 1995, to total $682 million. This 68 percent increase raised the proportion of all appropriated funds committed to the corrections function from 5.7 to 7.3 percent. Table 8–2 shows that the department took more than $62 million or 2 percent of all cuts from current services in FY 1992–FY 1994. The legislature appropriated $21 million less than requested by the Correction Department for FY 1994 but revisions made in 1994 to the FY 1995 budget added $24 million for prison expansion and to comply with court orders.

The staffing pressure perceived by the department is evident in its following up on a 22 percent increase in funded positions for FY 1993 by requesting a 24 percent increase for FY 1994, according to figures in the governor's 1994 submission. To some extent reflecting a shift to smaller facilities, staffing has outpaced the average daily inmate population. The ratio of positions to inmates declined from 1.9 in FY 1990 to 1.7 in FY 1993; while the average daily inmate population increased 24 percent in FY 1990–FY 1994, the number of authorized positions increased 40 percent.[70] However, inmate overcrowding, delayed openings and mothballed facilities, recent prison violence and inmate unrest, guard disaffection, and management problems continue to trouble corrections.

Human Services

By the time the budget adopted for FY 1995 was revised in 1994, the budgetary impact of human services had increased dramatically since FY 1991. Counting all appropriated funds and including federal funds (appropriated through agency budgets in Connecticut), a 61 percent increase worth $1.2 billion brought the total to $3.3 billion and raised the share of total appropriations committed to this function from 28 to 35 percent. Even so, the Department of Social Services bore almost $519 million in current services cuts, or 17 percent of all reductions listed in Table 8–2.

The human services function exerts particular pressure on the budget and some program components have been vulnerable to repeated cuts. Statutorily required annual cost-of-living increases (based on the increase in the consumer price index) in AFDC and General Assistance were eliminated first in 1991 for FY 1992, in 1992 for FY 1993, and, upon the governor's recommendation, again in 1993 for both FY 1994 and FY 1995. On the other hand, some programs serving the elderly fared well. Their advocates retained a voice in the Commission on Aging within the newly established super agency, the Department of Social Services, and in 1993 the legislature restored almost all funding for the pharmaceutical assistance program for the elderly (by rejecting the assets test and yearly fee the governor proposed), but increased the co-payment 50 percent, to $15. The single largest new or expanded program for FY 1994 was $95 million to expand home care programs for the elderly and implement welfare reform. The Medicaid component of human services dominated additions to the FY 1995 budget as well.

Welfare Programs

Medicaid. Medicaid accounts for most of the welfare-related pressure on the budget. Measured as the percentage of spending in FY 1991–FY 1995 shown in Table 8–3, AFDC and General Assistance (a welfare program largely state-financed) remained almost steady at above 4 and 1 percent respectively, while Medicaid rose from 15.5 to 18.3 percent. Net state Medicaid costs (state appropriations minus federal reimbursements) rose 38 percent in FY 1991–FY 1995, to $878 million. The appropriation for Medicaid for FY 1995 had to be adjusted upward by $78 million in 1994 to cover rising caseload and costs and accounted for 55 percent of the additions made to the second year of the biennial budget cycle. The same year, the legislature also expanded Medicaid eligibility for children ages six through eleven who are poor but not on AFDC (to 185 percent of the federal poverty level) at an estimated cost of $2.8 million.

About 55–60 percent of Medicaid expenditures are for nursing home care, so the state's buy-back of certificates of need from nursing homes (to level off the number of available beds, costing an average of $150 per day) was expected to generate "significant savings" in "one of the budget busters."[71] This, according to the governor's 1993 budget recommendation, "is perhaps the single most important long-term cost-saving measure in the entire budget." This may mean future needs go unmet.

General assistance. The state reimburses local jurisdictions for the costs of providing cash and medical assistance to needy individuals ineligible for federal welfare. To reduce costs to the state (and in several instances shift them to the towns), General Assistance was revised and reorganized in 1992–1993, but considerably less so than the governor's recommendations would have done. The state reimbursement was reduced to 85 percent, effective July 1, 1992. The state was to assume its administrative functions and associated costs effective two years later, but in 1994 the legislature postponed this step another two years. Although the governor had recommended the program be reduced to serve only unemployable persons, eligibility for employable individuals survived in the legislature. Duration limits for employable recipients continue at nine months in a twelve-month period (with a three-month extension at local option) but benefit levels were reduced in 1993 to $300 and the town's share increased from 15 to 20 percent. Cuts in General Assistance translate into increased mandated local costs and have been fiercely resisted by local officials. In FY 1991–FY 1995, the program increased almost 10 percent, but Table 8–3 shows that the rate of growth was slowed considerably starting in FY 1993.

AFDC. Gross spending including the 50 percent federal matching funds for AFDC increased almost 17 percent, to $397 million by FY 1995. Based on actuals for FY 1991 and estimates behind the FY 1995 budget as adopted, the AFDC caseload increased by almost 23 percent, from approximately 47,800 to 58,600, and the cost per case decreased almost 5 percent to $564.

Assessment

Budgetary outcomes measured by percentage change since FY 1991 most advantaged Medicaid, corrections, and especially debt service. The last rose 134 percent in FY 1991–FY 1995, from $668 million to a projected $889 million. Keeping score by percent of budget discloses declines of one percent or more in wages and salaries (personal services), aid to localities, and K–12 education. Total state appropriations (including federal funds as appropriated) increased $1.86 billion from

FY 1991 through FY 1995 as adopted. Five areas account for almost two-thirds of the increase; K–12 represents almost 6 percent of the increase; corrections, more than 13 percent; AFDC, 3 percent; Medicaid, almost 29 percent; and debt service for 12 percent. Appropriations to higher education decreased and tuition costs increased substantially.

CONCLUSION

Budgetary and policy decisions were linked to economic conditions, leadership commitments and ambitions, intergovernmental dictates and opportunities, popular and popularized innovations in service delivery and governmental operations, and perceived public attitudes. The best of decisions in a representative democracy are responsive to variable political demands and public needs. In this fluid environment, predictions often are invalidated by events and assessment necessarily is provisional.

Connecticut's greatest accomplishment is that underlying fundamentals are now fiscally sound. True, the state did not rush toward reform and reorientation but was impelled by the severity of the crisis. Nevertheless, the balance induced between revenue and spending now provides fiscal stability so long as it is underwritten by the newly found fiscal prudence. In the view of the state's budget director, "One of the best indicators of a state's fiscal health is the confidence that bond rating agencies place in a state, and the receptiveness [sic] of financial markets to a state's bond issues."[72] Ratings for Connecticut's general obligation bonds in 1993 and 1994 were Aa by Moody's, AA- by Standard & Poor's, and AA+ by Fitch. Fortifying the assessment on the basis of management criteria, *Financial World* had ranked Connecticut very low (46:50) in 1991 but raised that to about the midpoint (23:50) by 1993.[73]

What lessons does one state's experience hold out for other states? Connecticut has demonstrated since 1991 that it is possible to enact a major tax reform and increase and to survive politically. Predicated upon the state's high average income, the specific revenue strategy cannot be exported readily to those many other states with significantly lower average incomes and/or an income tax in place. Crucially, the public and its leaders by and large exhibited a political willingness to exercise budgetary self-discipline. It was undoubtedly important for public acceptance that almost everyone was seen to pay something through tax increases and service cuts, although some paid more than others.

Relatively high losses were sustained by state employees and unions; AFDC and state welfare recipients; and higher education and its students, to whom costs were shifted through tuition increases, with likely consequences for access. Some budgetary outcomes apparently mirror political muscle and social and economic vulnerability. Although predictable from a perspective of *real politik*, they run counter to the progressive bent in a state budget increasingly dedicated to human services and the needy. Contrarily, programs for needy elderly and state programs for needy children (DCYS, 1994 initiative, etc.) received special care since 1991, in some measure because of the federal money and political clout behind the former and the governor's commitment to and court protection of the latter. The courts and rising crime rates advantaged the corrections function, while the recession did the same for economic development programs and business interests.

Local interests saw both gains and losses, and there is some evidence and many allegations that public education costs are shifting to the property tax. Initially, the local ramifications of the coping strategy largely were ignored. This reversed when gambling revenues offered an illusory, quick, and "free" solution in 1993 and local property tax relief eclipsed most other issues in 1994. The seeds of future tensions in the state-local fiscal system already have been planted.

The ability to finance an operating deficit through long-term borrowing and also accrue unfunded liabilities led to an archetypal outcome: the heaviest dollar burden for the fiscal crisis fell on prospective taxpayers, who bear the future costs of strategic choices both made and evaded. Expediency sometimes overruled prudence as the state depleted reserves and manipulated year-end operating balances. Here the state appears to follow prevailing custom.

> In most states, the balanced budget mandates apply to enacted budgets or to the governors' proposed budgets. Few balanced budget requirements specifically mandate year-end balance. States focus primarily on balancing the general fund . . . [and] measure general fund surplus or deficit cumulatively, carrying over surplus or deficit amounts from the prior year into current year results.[74]

Rigorous compliance with GAAP could remove some traditional techniques from the budget-balancing repertoire.

The spending strategy did reduce growth rates, but not nominal spending, and the almost $9.5 billion budget adopted for FY 1995 was $1.8 billion or 23 percent higher than the FY 1991 budget. The human services function and especially its Medicaid component continued exerting extraordinary pressure on the budget, despite earnest efforts to curb fast-growing elements. From a state budget perspective, national health reform (especially including long-term care) appears critical to a state's successfully reducing expenditure growth and controlling its own spending.

Connecticut began to discover that another approach, the spending cap, is working as planned to hold down spending growth as revenue receipts increase. The paradoxical result is reduced fiscal capacity and simultaneous spending and tax cuts. Unless the spending limitation is diluted or sidestepped, the budget soon will not have the capacity to support the broad, activist role associated with state government in Connecticut. The cap inevitably puts even more pressure on discretionary functions such as higher education, and the structural realignment in state expenditures should intensify. Disappointed beneficiaries may seek court redress, with the end result being more judicial budgeting. If a history of shifting costs to local jurisdictions is a reliable indicator, then state aid to localities may also be vulnerable and, as a result, Connecticut may undergo a tax revolt over local property taxes in the not-too-distant future.

Fiscal capacity also has been reduced because the spending cap impedes state efforts directed at countercyclical economic stimulation.[75] The gravity of this observation is moderated by the limited extent to which state government realisitcally can stimulate or guide a state economy dependent upon national and global markets, as John Carson (formerly DED commissioner and currently CPEC president) notes.[76] Although impressive in absolute terms, the sums devoted to economic development represent only a fraction of the state's economy

Connecticut also demonstrated the value of its own state motto, *Qui Transtulit Sustinet* (he who transplanted still sustains), by selectively adopting new techniques and temperament. It is too soon to assess the many budgetary and managerial initiatives undertaken since 1991, but the change of attitude and course is unmistakable. Other initiatives and policy changes are important for what is *not* spent, as the modification in state compulsory arbitration illustrates. Changes in state law governing local compulsory arbitration and the 1993 reform of state mandates on local government testify to the fact that off-budget outcomes also are consequential.

The governor announced in July 1993 that the fiscal crisis was over. Inevitably, some hard choices are yet to come; that is the enduring essence of allocating scarce resources to competing ends in any state. Does Connecticut have the capacity to make them wisely? Senate Appropriations cochairman Harper articulates a "growing disenchantment" with a process that encourages "myopic and politically practical" choices.[77] At the time of his announcement, the governor "said it would be unrealistic to say the state never will have budget problems again. 'I suspect we're still going to have some tough times ahead. . . . I don't want anyone to feel we can go back to the good old days of just spend, spend, spend. We will conduct ourselves with prudence. We'll live within our means'."[78] These comments suggest that there remains plenty of scope for future administrations and legislative sessions to add to and sustain prudent financial management, balanced fiscal capacity, and judicious budgetary outcomes.

NOTES

1. Unless specifically noted otherwise, data in this study are from annual or periodic data sources regularly published by the State of Connecticut. Among these are (1) Connecticut General Assembly, Office of Fiscal Analysis, *Revenue, Budget and Economic Data*, 1993; (2) Connecticut General Assembly, Office of Fiscal Analysis, *Connecticut State Budget, 1993–1995*, 1993; (3) *Governor's Budget, 1993–1995* and Budget-in-Brief, including diskette version; (4) *Economic Report of the Governor, 1993–1995*; (5) Reports of the State Comptroller to the Governor, 1988–1992 (budgetary basis); (6) statements of official offerings for general obligation bonds, 1993–1994; and (7) *State of Connecticut. Three Year Budget Report, 1995–1996, 1996–1997, 1997–1998.*

2. Compiled annually by the Office of Fiscal Analysis for comparability purposes, general budget expenditures and revenues combine activity in the general fund, other appropriated funds, and selected nonappropriated funds such as tuition, Educational Excellence, and Economic Recovery (debt retirement) funds. The general fund represents 89–91 percent of these expenditures in FY 1991–FY 1995 as adopted.

Note that the state appropriates gross for programs that are partially or fully reimbursed by the federal government and agency operating budgets include federal funds. The current budgetary basis is modified cash accounting for appropriated funds; revenues are recognized when received, except for specific accrued taxes and federal and other restricted grant revenues; expenditures are charged against appropriations of the year in which the charge is paid. The state accounts for pension, health care, and other employee benefits through central accounts so that these costs are not included in figures for functions, programs, or agencies.

3. According to the Department of Social Services (formerly, Department of Income Maintenance), the caseload in Aid to Families with Dependent Children (a welfare program that is partially federally financed, hereafter AFDC), increased almost 28 percent in FY 1989–1991 alone and, because the cost per case increased 9 percent at the same time, total payments rose more than 39 percent. Nursing home expenditures rose at an annual average of more than 13 percent in FY 1987–1991, for a cumulative increase of almost 83 percent. Arthur Anderson & Co., "Understanding Nursing Home Reimbursement," presentation handout, 1993.

4. Incarceration rates (per 100,000 residents) increased 350 percent in 1980–1990, compared to 209 percent for all states. T. Flanagan and K. Maguire, eds., *Bureau of Justice Statistics Sourcebook of Criminal Justice Statistics—1991* (Washington, DC: U.S. Government Printing Office, 1992). By the end of the decade, the number of sentenced prisoners under state jurisdiction was increasing at several times the average for all states. U.S. Department of Justice, Bureau of Justice Statistics, "Prisoners in 1992," *Bureau of Justice Statistics Bulletin*, 1993, p. 2. Despite theses increases, Connecticut was not among the ten states with the highest incarcerations rates or prison population in 1992, nor among the ten states with the largest percentage increase in prison population in 1987–1992. Bureau of Justice Statistics, p. 4.

5. State of Connecticut, Department of Education, "Connecticut Public School Enrollment Projected to the Year 2005," duplicated document, 1993. Connecticut Conference of Municipalities. "Testimony before the State Board of Education" (New Haven, CT: CCM, 1992), p. 3.

6. State of Connecticut, Task Force on State Tax Revenue, *Final Report— Income Tax*, 1991, pp. 3–6. The report was submitted to the Governor and General Assembly at the beginning of the 1991 session. The task force was cochaired by then Representative William J. Cibes, Jr., a Democrat defeated in his 1990 gubernatorial bid and among the most vocal of income tax advocates. Governor Lowell P. Weicker Jr., appointed him as Secretary of the Office of Policy and Management. As head of the executive's central staff for planning and budgeting, Cibes was the state's budget director.

7. Included are fringe benefits and retirement contributions, statutory payments to local governments, human services grants, debt service, and other fixed charges. State of Connecticut, official statement of March 16, 1994, p. 35.

8. Connecticut Conference of Municipalities [CCM], *Indicators of Need in Connecticut Municipalities, Measures of Municipal Distress*, vol. 1, Public Policy Report. (New Haven, CT: CCM, November 1991). Other indicators are available in volume 2, published in 1992, and the January 1994 update.

9. The Department of Children and Youth Services' [DCYS] name was changed as of July 1993 to the Department of Children and Families but DCYS is retained here to correspond to budget terminology for FY 1990–1995.

10. Eight similar suits had been filed nationally at the time of the DCYS consent decree. J. Barden, "Panel to Direct Child Welfare in Connecticut," *New York Times* December 21, 1990, pp. B1, B4.

11. Public opinion data are from *Hartford Courant*/Institute of Social Inquiry Connecticut Polls, 1989–94.

12. John Larson, author's interview on June 30, 1993, with Senate President Pro Tem, Mansfield.

13. Jonathan Pelto, author's interview on June 28, 2993 with the then state representative (D., Mansfield), cochairman of appropriations subcommittee for higher education, and former deputy majority leader and statewide political director for Democratic Party, Mansfield.

14. Economic Report of the Governor, 1993–1995, 1993, Hartford: State of Connecticut, p. 3.

15. Moody's Investors Service, Public Finance Department, *1993 Medians, Selected Indicators of Municipal Performance* (New York: Moody's, 1993), pp. 3, 5.

16. Larry Williams, "State Budget Crisis Over, Weicker Says," *Hartford Courant*, July 16, 1993, p. A1.

17. Larry Williams, "State Budget Crisis Over, Weicker Says," pp. A1, A5.

18. Larry Williams and M. Pazniokas, "State Budget on Hold After Pay-Freeze Revolt," *Hartford Courant*, May 7, 1993, p. A12.

19. Larry Williams, "State Income Tax Drawing Less Heat," *Hartford Courant*, June 6, 1992, p. C1.

20. Taxpayers Alliance to Serve Connecticut, memorandum of June 2 on income tax and the 1992 elections (Hartford: TASC, 1992).

21. Larry Williams, "State Income Tax," p. C1.

22. A 67-member freshman class sat in the 1993 legislature as a result of the 1992 election (elections are biennial except for statewide, constitutional offices) but at least thirty-eight incumbents had opted for retirement after the grueling 1991 session and its bitter tax controversy that included death threats and other incivilities; three others were lost due to redistricting, and another went down in a delegate primary. Taxpayers Alliance to Serve Connecticut, memorandum on income tax.

23. Carol W. Lewis, "Connecticut: Prosperity, Frugality, and Stability," in *Governors, Legislatures, and Budgets, Diversity Across the American States*, ed. E. J. Clynch and T. P. Lauth, Contributions in Political Science, No. 265 (Westport, CT: Greenwood Press, 1991), p. 51.

24. A balanced budget is considered better "even if revenues have to be increased a bit than to kneel at the alter of lower taxes . . . but the best solution is lower spending and taxes, in balance." Michael B. Levin, author's interview on June 29, 1993 with vice president and research director, Connecticut Policy and Economic Council, Inc., Hartford.

25. Thomas D. Ritter and T. S. Luby, memorandum of May 4 to members of the House Democratic Caucus (Hartford, CT: House Democrats, 1993).

26. Connecticut Policy and Economic Council, "Biennial Budget Moves through Legislature Smoothly," *Budget Watch* 2, 6 (May 1993): p. 6.

27. Michael Levin interview.

28. Michael Levin interview.

29. M. Nielsen (R., Danbury), "The People Voted to Cut the Budget," *Hartford Courant* June 17, 1993, p. C13.

30. Attorney General G. Richard Blumenthal opined in 1993 that the statutory cap remains in force while the constitutional cap awaits legislative compliance and that "to amend the 1991 law, or to adopt a budget that exceeds that spending cap, would require a 60 percent majority of both houses because it would [be] the same thing as enacting a bill to implement the constitutional cap." Larry Williams, "Legislature's Budget Shows Spending Cap Isn't on Tight," *Hartford Courant*, July 12, 1993, p. A4.

31. Connecticut Policy and Economic Council, "Biennial Budget," p. 2.

32. L. Wilson, Cash Management Division, Office of the Treasurer, State of Connecticut, author's telephone interview on July 13, 1993.

33. The labor-management Health Care Cost Containment Committee, with eight participating unions and dating to the previous administration, agreed to managed care by adopting preferred provider and gatekeeper or required referrals approaches for state employees and retirees.

34. Edward C. Marth, author's interview on June 24, 1993 with executive director of University of Connecticut Chapter of American Association of University Professors, AAUP representative at State Employee Bargaining Coalition (SEBAC), and trustee and member of the Commission of State Employee Retirement System, Mansfield.

35. Edward C. Marth interview.

36. Edward C. Marth interview.

37. Disallowing statutory exclusions and identifying an overall budget increase of 7.6 percent for FY 1994 as far in excess of the 5.8 percent increase in personal income over the last five years, a news analysis in *The Hartford Courant* explained, "What actually happened is what critics of the spending cap always predicted would happen: The legislature found legal ways to circumvent it." Larry Williams, "Legislature's Budget," p. A1. See also M. Nielsen, "The People Voted," on the argument that the statutory cap is "illusory."

38. A majority expect the cap to result in services cuts over the next year; 18 percent expect major cuts and 42 percent anticipate minor ones, according to the *Hartford Courant*/Institute for Social Inquiry Connecticut Poll no. 142.

39. David Osborne and T. Gaebler, *Reinventing Government, How the Entrepreneurial Spirit is Transforming the Public Sector*, Reading, MA: Addison Wesley, 1992.

40. State of Connecticut, Office of Policy and Management, *Health and Human Services Reorganization, with the Implementation Plans for the Department of*

Social Services and the Department of Public Health and Addiction Services, Oversight Report to the Connecticut General Assembly (Hartford, CT: State of Connecticut, January 1993), pp. 34–35.

41. V. Finholm, "State's Welfare System Shifts Priorities," *Hartford Courant* June 21, 1993, p. C7.

42. Office of Policy and Management, *Health and Human Services Reorganization*, p. DSS–35.

43. State of Connecticut, Office of Policy and Management, *Strategy to Establish Uniform Regional Service Delivery Areas for All State Agencies, Report to the Connecticut General Assembly* (Hartford, CT: State of Connecticut, February 1993), p. 4.

44. Office of Policy and Management, *Strategy to Establish Uniform . . .*, p. 45.

45. Jonathan Pelto interview.

46. Ralph Caruso, Director of Office of Fiscal Analysis, Connectiuct General Assembly, author's interview of June 29, 1993, Hartford.

47. Jonathan Pelto interview.

48. David Osborne and T. Gaebler, *Reinventing Government*, p. xxi.

49. Governmental Accounting Standards Board, *Preliminary Views of the Governmental Accounting Standards Board on Concepts Related to Service Efforts and Accomplishments Reporting* (Norwalk, CT: Financial Accounting Foundation, 1992), pp. iii–iv.

50. Edward C. Balda, executive budget officer, Office of Policy and Management, State of Connecticut, author's interview on June 30, 1993, Hartford.

51. Rick Green, "EAI Wins Vote to Run Hartford Schools," *Hartford Courant*, July 23, 1994, p. A1, A5, and George Judson, "As It Moves to Privatize Schools, Hartford Debates Issue of Control," *New York Times*, July 22, 1994, pp. A1, B6.

52. William J. Cibes, Jr., Secretary of Office of Policy and Management, State of Connecticut, Testimony to Appropriations Committee, public hearing of April 13, 1993, duplicated document, p. 7.

53. Joseph J. Harper, Jr., state Senator and Democratic cochairman of General Assembly's joint Appropriations Committee, author's telephone interview, July 22, 1993.

54. This total is estimated by summing the cumulative deficit of $460.4 million as figured on a GAAP basis (Table 8–1), the unfunded accrued liability in the state employees' ($3.5 billion) and teachers' ($2.4 billion) retirement funds, and the $5.2 billion in bond authorizations outstanding as of March 1994 (according to the state's official statement). The figure does not include bond authorizations approved late in 1994.

55. Bond allocations are closer in time and amount to actual issuance of debt than are legislative authorizations and, different from bundled bond sales, relate to commitments initiated rather than the cash flow needs of numerous projects as they develop. By OFA data, allocations related to general obligation bonds, revenue bonds, and special tax obligation issues totaled $5.3 billion cumulative in FY 1990–FY 1993. To avoid overstating the case, this methodology substracts the somewhat more than $1.1 billion associated with financing the deficit because this obligation has only a five-year life. The deferred payments on state employees' and teachers' retirements funds, valued at almost $600 million are added. Alternatively, the increase on unfunded accrued liability of $831 million in 1991–1993 in the state employees' retirement fund can be added (but the dated actuarial valuation precludes estimating the increase in the reachers' retirement fund).

56. Advisory Commission on Intergovernmental Relations, *Significant Features of Fiscal Federalism*, M–169 (Washington, DC: Government Printing Office, 1990), p. 102.

57. M. Swift, "Rate Slows for Per Capita Spending," *Hartford Courant* July 6, 1993, pp. B1, B7. Connecticut Policy and Economic Council, "Municipal Spending Slows; Hartford Remains on Top," *Budget Watch* 2, 7 (June 1993): p. 1.

58. Connecticut Conference of Municipalities, *The Municipal Budget Outlook for 1993–94*, Public Policy Report 93–06 (New Haven, CT: CCM, March 23, 1993), p. 1, and for FY 1995, the same source, Report 94–04r, March 28, 1994, p. 1.

59. Connecticut Conference of Municipalities, *State Tax and Expenditure Limits (TELs): Exemptions for Local Government Programs*, Public Policy Report (Hartford, CT: CCM, April 14, 1993), p. 4.

60. Connecticut Conference of Municipalities, *State Tax and Expenditure Limits (TELs): Exemptions for Local Government Programs*, Public Policy Report (Hartford, CT: CCM, April 14, 1993), p. 4.

61. Connecticut Policy and Economic Council, "Analysis of the Governor's State Budget for 1994," *Budget Watch* 2, 4 (March 1993), p. 3.

62. Edward C. Marth interview.

63. Robert Rinker quoted in *CSEA NEWS* [Connecticut State Employees Association], May 7, 1993, emphasis omitted.

64. Barry R. Williams, principal of Government Relations Consulting and lobbyist since 1981 for labor and nonprofit organizations, author's interview of June 30, 1993, Mansfield.

65. "Task Force to Review Aid-to-Business Effort," *Hartford Courant*, June 10, 1994, p. D1.

66. Full-time enrollment increased in community-technical colleges. Unless otherwise indicated, higher education statistics are from Connecticut General Assembly, Office of Fiscal Analysis, unpublished document, September 10, 1993.

67. Connecticut Conference of Municipalities, "Testimony before the State Board of Education," p. 3.

68. Connecticut General Assembly, Office of Fiscal Analysis, *Revenue, Budget and Economic Data, Fiscal Years 1972–1992* (Hartford: OFA, 1992), p. 148 and, from the same source, unpublished document of August 1993, courtesy of Alan Shepard.

69. Calculated from data in Connecticut Policy and Economic Council, *How Do Connecticut Schools Compare?* (Hartford: CPEC, February, 1994), unpaginated brochure.

70. Connecticut General Assembly, Office of Fiscal Analysis, unpublished document, September 10, 1993.

71. Edward Balda interview.

72. William J. Cibes, Jr., Secretary of Office of Policy and Management, State of Connecticut, unpublished letter on fiscal management dated March 10, 1993.

73. Edward Balda interview.

74. U.S. General Accounting Office, *Balanced Budget Requirements, State Experiences and Implications for the Federal Government*, GAO/AFMD–93–58BR (Washington, DC: GAO, March 1993).

75. S. Cunningham and W. Lott, 1994, "Connecticut's Recovery: A Step Behind the U.S.," *Connecticut Economy* 2, 2 (April 1994): 8.

76. John Carson, "A Bank to Business?" *Hartford Courant*, March 13, 1994, p. B1.

77. Larry Williams and M. Pazniokas, "State Budget on Hold," p. A12.

78. Larry Williams, "State Budget Crisis over, Weicker Says," p. A5.

9

Florida: Reinvention Derailed

Susan A. MacManus*

Florida's tax structure, with its heavy reliance on a narrow sales tax base, is particularly vulnerable to economic downturn, but the recession is not to blame for all ills. Even when the economy recovers, the economists say, Florida will not see the kind of growth that stoked the furnace in the 1980s.

Bill Moss, *St. Petersburg Times*
March 3, 1991

Government in Florida is ineffective, inefficient, and increasingly expensive, and it suffers from a lack of citizen confidence. Over the past decade, growth in the size and spending of Florida government has outstripped growth in the state's population and economic base. During the 1980s, Florida's population grew by 31 percent while the state budget increased by 224 percent. [Yet] Florida still has the nation's highest crime rate, a below average graduation rate and one of its highest illiteracy rates.

Partners in Productivity Task Force Report
July 1992

The public has lost confidence in the state's ability to spend money wisely. The state must reform itself before it can ask more of its citizens.

Florida Taxation & Budget Reform Commission
February 1991

---

*Susan A. MacManus is Professor and Chair of the Department of Government and International Affairs at the University of South Florida.

INTRODUCTION

Florida, the nation's fourth largest state, was hard hit by the recession of the early 1990s. A fast-growing, increasingly two-party competitive state, with a unique age distribution and a historical penchant for "no new taxes," Florida responded by avoiding the adoption of major new tax sources, even though a new governor pushed hard for tax reform. The legislature chose a more conservative path, tinkering with existing taxes, closing loopholes, tightening exemptions, and raising rates (although only slightly). It also turned to user fees and charges—and to a lesser extent, long-term borrowing—to fill revenue gaps and forestall spending cuts as long as possible. Short-term "borrowing" also occurred as trust funds and the Working Capital (Rainy Day) Fund were raided to bolster the state's General Revenue Fund. (Even these funds, including the rainy day fund, did not have much excess to tap into. The state's year end balance had rarely exceeded 2 percent even prior to the recession.)

These rather incremental revenue approaches allowed the state's legislators to lay claim to imposing as few *new* taxes as possible during this highly stressful period when spending demands were rising much faster than revenue intake.

Sheer population growth yielded sharp increases in the state's school-age population. The recession did little to mitigate this trend. As shown in Table 9–1, the state had experienced a 15.4 percent increase in the number of full-time equivalent (FTE) students between FY 1984 and FY 1989. It dropped only slightly during the recession (to 14.6 percent between FY 1989 and FY 1993), still a sizable enough increase to put real pressures on the expenditure side of the budgetary ledger.

A sour economy *was* a primary cause of sharply rising demands for entitlement spending in the areas of health care and social services, along with increases in the number of women of childbearing age and the birth rate. The rate of increase in Aid to Families With Dependent Children (AFDC) cases more than doubled between FY 1989 and FY 1990 (from 5.7 to 12.4 percent). The number of AFDC recipients rose from 317,875 in FY 1989 to 664,846 (up 109 percent) between FY 1989 and FY 1993, the point at which Florida's recovery from the recession begins to show up statistically. Not until FY 1994, did the rate of increase in AFDC cases drop sharply, to 2.6 percent between FY 1993 and FY 1994. (See Figure 9–1.) Spending on Medicaid (an entitlement program governed heavily by federal rules and regulations) followed the same basic pattern thereby causing the Department of Health and Rehabilitative Services (HRS) to replace the Department of Education as the most costly for Floridians in FY 1992.

The state also experienced tremendous fiscal (and political) pressures in the corrections area. While the recession no doubt contributed to a higher crime rate, it was not the primary reason for the need to spend more on corrections. Corrections-related expenditure increases were a result of a variety of factors, such as a court order to reduce prison crowding, growing numbers of juvenile offenders, heavy drug trafficking, and the public's dissatisfaction with a high incidence of early release of prisoners due to limited prison space. (The length of time an average state inmate remained incarcerated increased from 34 percent in FY 1990 to approximately 47 percent in FY 1993.)

When all politically acceptable revenue strategies had been exhausted and spending cuts became the only alternative, the legislature had little choice but to target the three most heavily funded functions—education, human services, and transportation. Like budgeters everywhere, legislators tended to focus most intensely on the standard budgetary object categories of personnel, travel, training, and capital outlays. In most instances, *delaying* the implementation of newly authorized programs, capital projects, equipment purchases, and even previously enacted employee salary and benefit increases was preferable to outright elimination. The few programs that were eliminated were newer ones, which tended to have smaller constituency bases. The general consensus of decision makers was "this, too, shall pass." After all, recessions had come and gone before. However, others were not quite so sure that the state would enjoy the same economic recovery pattern as in the past. Florida's demographic, political, and economic profile had already begun to change before the recession of the early 1990s hit full force.

THE SETTING: NO MOOD FOR MORE TAXES DURING THE RECESSION

Florida has long been recognized as one of the fastest growing states in the Union. Since it became a territory in 1821, Florida has grown faster than the rest of the nation in each decade. Between 1980 and 1990, its population increased by 33 percent, moving it from the sev-

TABLE 9-1 Comparison of Estimated vs. Actual Florida Revenues,

| | FY 1990[1] | | | |
Revenue Source	Estimate	Actual	$ Over (under) estimate	% Over (under) estimate
Sales Tax—GR	7081.0	6872.7	−208.3	−2.9
Beverage Tax & Licenses	461.2	450.6	−10.6	−2.3
Corporate Income Tax	930.9	908.1	−122.8	−13.2
Corporation Trust Fund Fees	—	—	—	—
Documentary Stamp Tax	281.9	261.1	−20.8	−7.4
Cigarette Tax	143.7	141.8	−1.9	−1.3
Insurance Premium Tax	264.8	198.0	−66.8	−25.2
Pari-mutuels Tax	80.3	69.9	−10.4	−13.0
Intangibles Tax	182.8	178.0	−4.8	−2.6
Estate Tax	203.6	257.8	54.2	26.6
Interest Earnings	124.1	108.6	−15.5	−12.5
Drivers License Fees	38.3	36.9	−1.4	−3.7
Medical & Hospital Fees	65.0	70.4	5.4	8.3
Auto Title & Lien Fees	22.0	22.2	0.2	0.9
Motor Vehicle Charges	—	—	—	—
Severance Taxes	36.3	37.4	1.1	3.0
Service Charges	107.4	110.9	3.5	3.3
Other Taxes, Licenses, Fees	109.5	108.8	−0.7	−0.6
SIF Transfer to GR	150.0	150.0	0.0	0.0
Less: Refunds	−107.4	−143.1	−35.7	33.2
Net General Revenue	10175.4	9740.1	−435.3	−4.3
	FY 1993[4]			
Sales Tax—GR	8273.3	8379.9	106.6	1.3
Beverage Tax & Licenses	523.5	527.7	4.2	0.8
Corporate Income Tax	834.6	846.6	12.0	1.4
Corporation Trust Fund Fees	87.5	92.0	4.5	5.1
Documentary Stamp Tax	360.9	369.9	9.0	2.5
Cigarette Tax	130.0	133.7	3.7	2.9
Insurance Premium Tax	220.7	231.5	10.8	4.9
Pari-mutuels Tax	58.6	67.5	8.9	15.2
Intangibles Tax	480.0	492.4	12.4	2.6
Estate Tax	292.0	307.5	15.5	5.3
Interest Earnings	81.6	96.1	14.5	17.8
Drivers License Fees	60.8	56.0	−4.8	−7.9
Medical & Hospital Fees	135.7	114.5	−21.2	−15.6
Auto Title & Lien Fees	19.9	21.6	1.7	8.5
Motor Vehicle Charges	70.8	67.5	−3.3	−4.7
Severance Taxes	28.3	29.3	1.0	3.5
Service Charges	279.2	295.4	16.2	5.8
Other Taxes, Licenses, Fees	107.5	91.5	−16.0	14.9
SIF Transfer to GR	—	—	—	—
Less: Refunds	185.7	162.0	−23.7	−12.8
Net General Revenue	11859.2	12058.6	199.4	1.7

FY 1990 to FY 1994 (in thousands)

FY 1991[2]				FY 1992[3]			
Estimate	Actual	$ Over (under) estimate	% Over (under) estimate	Estimate	Actual	$ Over (under) estimate	% Over (under) estimate
7494.9	6950.2	−544.7	−7.3	8042.4	7635.6	−406.8	−5.1
588.1	527.7	−60.4	−10.3	549.8	516.9	−32.9	−6.0
896.4	701.6	−194.8	−21.7	884.6	801.3	−83.3	−9.4
—	—	—	—	—	—	—	—
425.5	305.8	−119.7	−28.1	396.1	359.1	−37.0	−9.3
139.6	135.1	−4.5	−3.2	134.9	129.6	−5.3	−3.9
219.7	192.5	−27.2	−12.4	222.1	213.1	−9.0	−4.1
75.9	66.5	−9.4	12.4	75.4	58.3	−17.1	−22.6
348.2	290.0	−58.2	−16.7	320.8	324.5	3.7	1.2
249.8	301.1	51.3	20.5	279.2	291.4	12.2	4.4
110.0	106.6	−3.4	−3.1	102.3	89.4	−12.9	−12.6
42.7	40.7	−2.0	−4.7	63.8	60.5	−3.3	−5.2
79.7	108.0	28.3	35.5	105.2	102.9	−2.3	−2.2
21.3	23.9	2.6	12.2	22.0	19.7	−2.3	−10.6
—	—	—	—	66.4	87.7	21.3	32.3
34.3	35.3	1.0	2.9	36.9	36.2	−0.7	−1.8
189.8	204.4	14.6	7.7	251.1	262.0	10.9	4.4
137.8	125.6	−12.2	−8.9	149.7	124.5	−25.2	−16.9
150.0	150.0	0.0	0.0	—	—	—	—
136.2	150.2	14.0	10.3	163.4	201.3	37.9	23.2
11067.5	10114.8	−952.7	−8.6	11539.3	10911.5	−627.8	−5.4

FY 1994[5]			
8994.0	9006.9	12.9	0.14
482.7	476.2	−6.5	−1.34
1011.9	1047.4	35.4	3.50
103.4	101.3	−2.2	−2.09
422.0	431.8	9.8	2.33
130.6	131.9	1.3	0.96
251.0	250.6	−0.4	−0.14
58.2	63.9	5.7	9.73
547.4	529.5	−17.9	−3.27
330.0	359.0	29.0	8.79
97.3	83.9	−13.4	−13.75
53.3	54.8	1.5	2.77
129.3	113.9	−15.4	−11.89
22.5	21.9	−0.6	−2.57
63.8	60.3	−3.5	−5.44
24.3	−19.0	−5.3	−21.76
346.8	351.4	4.6	1.33
89.5	92.0	2.5	2.75
—	—	—	—
184.5	152.4	−32.2	−17.43
12973.5	13043.5	69.7	0.54

Notes:
[1] Comparison includes impact of 1989 Session and excludes 1990 Session—Sales Tax Speed Up.
[2] Estimates based on the July 1990 Revenue Estimating Conference (REC).
[3] Estimates based on the July 1991 REC.
[4] Estimates based on the July 1992 REC adjusted for legislative changes.
[5] Estimates for July 1, 1993 through April 30, 1994 based on the February 1994 REC.

Source: State of Florida, Executive Office of the Governor, Office of Planning and Budgeting, Revenue and Economic Analysis.

enth to the fourth largest state. Much of the growth was fueled by an influx of retirees from the Midwest and Northeast, foreign immigrants from Latin and South America seeking refuge from repressive environments, and young adults attracted to the state's expanding economy. As a consequence of this in-migration, Florida's age profile changed dramatically. It is an older, and more diverse population today than even a decade ago.

Of the fifty states, Florida ranks first in the percentage of persons over age sixty-five (18.3 percent in 1991) and last in the percentage of its population between five and seventeen years of age. However, both of these age groups are growing at rates faster than the state's population as a whole, which greatly affects spending needs and demands, most notably in the areas of education, health, and social services. Florida's age profile is often considered a leading indicator of what the nation's will look like in the not-too-distant future, which means that other states are closely watching its policy choices.

The state's unique age structure creates an unusual income profile. Because Florida has a proportionally greater retirement age population, property income (dividends, interest, and rent) and transfer payments (Social Security and pension benefits, among other sources of income) are relatively more important sources of income than for the nation as a whole. For example, Florida's employment income in 1992 represented 61 percent of total personal income, while the nation's share of total personal income in the form of wages and salaries and other labor benefits was 72 percent. One positive aspect of this greater diversity is that transfer payments are typically less sensitive to the business cycle than employment income and, therefore, act as stabilizing forces in weak economic periods. The negative is that a large proportion of persons on fixed incomes, especially older retirees, usually translates into political opposition to higher taxes.

Florida is also distinguished by its sizable and economically significant temporary population of tourists, visitors, and partial-year residents. These temporary residents account for a large portion of the state's economic activity in the form of jobs, income, and tax revenue. A recent report by the governor notes that this population places demands on the state's infrastructure, transportation, environment, law enforcement, emergency service, and health care policy arenas. From a political perspective, these people vote more with their pocketbooks than with the ballot, which sometimes makes them more susceptible to revenue strategies based on the principle of tax exporting (choosing revenue alternatives that shift the bulk of the burden to nonresidents).

While Florida's population is expected to experience a slower, although still positive, growth rate (19 percent) over the decade of the 1990s, the bottom line is that for many decades, population growth has been a crucial engine of growth for Florida's economy. But along with growth have come some major growing pains. Rapid population increases have pressured the state to expand services and put new or improved infrastructures in place, occasionally necessitating tax increases, primarily in sales or excise taxes, since the state is prohibited constitutionally from imposing a personal income tax.[1]

The Budgetary Consequences of Rapid Growth

Rapid growth and the problems it exacerbates often force lawmakers to spend in a reactive, as opposed to a preventive, manner. This causes less of a problem when revenues are also expanding. However, during tough times, in a search to make fewer dollars go farther, taxpayers and government officials alike begin to think more about the efficacy of spending priorities emphasizing prevention. This has been one of the most important lessons Florida learned from the recession of the early 1990s as it adopted numerous organizational, procedural, managerial, and budgetary reforms aimed at improving the efficiency and effectiveness of governmental operations, tackling problems at their root causes.

Growth-driven fiscal pressures have also been exerted on Florida's local governments, which have relatively restricted revenue raising capacity, and generally must secure voter approval before tapping new revenue sources or significantly raising existing ones. For most, the property tax remains the most important revenue source, along with fees and charges. Escalating property values, on top of incremental increases in the property tax millage rate, have created the impression among a large portion of the electorate that taxes are out of control in the state.

Younger and older voters alike are particularly hostile to property taxes, the young perceiving them as deterring homeownership, the old viewing them as threats to their fixed incomes. In November 1992, during the depths of the recession, Florida voters approved a constitutional amendment limiting the annual growth of assessments on homestead property to either 3 percent or the inflation rate (the increase in the Consumer Price Index) whichever is smaller.[2]

The intense animosity toward property taxes carried over to other local taxes, leaving cities and counties few revenue raising options other than increased user fees and charges. But the more governments turned to them, the more Floridians saw them as but another form of taxation ("fee *taxes*"). Before the recession, local government officials had already begun blaming the state (and the federal government) for putting them between a rock and a hard place. The rock was unfunded state- or federally mandated programs and facilities; the hard place, a legally restricted revenue-raising capacity, made even more onerous by a tax-hostile constituency.

The Intergovernmental Setting

Prior to the recession, the state of Florida's finances were already being impacted by various federal mandates and court orders, reductions in federal aid (either to the state or its localities), and demands for help from its localities. Federal court orders had been issued imposing minimum state service levels in areas such as corrections, mental health, and foster care. Federal mandates in the areas of education, human services, and the environment had, in the state's view, contributed to the sharp growth in the Medicaid, education (especially for exceptional and at-risk students), environmental protection, and health care portions of the budget. At the same time, federal fiscal assistance to state government to help provide newly mandated service levels and offset mandates had increased only marginally. In turn, state assistance to local governments declined, leading local government leaders to blame the state for "balancing its own budget on their backs."

Prior to the recession, local governments had been pressing the state to stop its practice of imposing more mandates on them without any monetary reimbursement or any additional revenue-raising capacity to pay for them. They endorsed a constitutional amendment to limit the ability of the state to pass unfunded mandates onto local governments. (The public overwhelmingly approved it in November 1990.[3])

Local government associations like the Florida League of Cities and the Florida Association of Counties also began pushing for more state aid to local governments (which had been rather stagnant), revisions in state shared tax revenue formulas, revision of the homestead exemption law ($25,000), elimination of voter approval requirements for local option sales taxes, and more discretionary revenue sources in general. Sentiment was fairly strong that many of the state's small and rural cities and counties, especially those in the Panhandle, were really in need of help. Many of these smaller entities had poor and declining populations, high proportions of property exempt from taxation under the homestead exemption law, and tax rates already at the constitutional limit (10 mills).[4]

School boards pushed for more discretion over lottery funds transferred to them by the state as well as revisions in the state's school finance formulas. In the latter case, it was the large school districts, with more diverse student bodies subject to federal and state mandates, making the most noise. They threatened to sue the state for its distributional formulas that they perceived to be highly inequitable and biased in favor of smaller, more rural districts. As of August 1994, a suit had yet to be filed on this issue. However, 45 counties joined the Florida School Board Association, the school superintendents, the NAACP, and three Hispanic groups in a suit against the State of Florida for imposing unfunded mandates. The suit alleged that legislative appropriations have been inadequate and will deter school districts from achieving performance objectives established in the Blueprint 2000 Act.

In summary, interjurisdictional tensions were heightened throughout the state prior to and in the midst of the recession, often driven by changes in the state's demographic and political environments. These tensions began to ease somewhat as the state's economy improved, local government revenue-raising authority was increased (although incrementally), and more decentralized approaches to expenditure prioritization were adopted, especially with regard to education and social services. But Florida officials still see a bias against the state in federal aid formulas, most notably with regard to federal assistance for newly arrived immigrants, many of whom enter the country illegally. And local government officials continue to be upset by federal and state unfunded mandates, declining levels of aid, and limited revenue-raising authority.

Changes in the Political Environment

Florida's political landscape has been altered significantly in recent decades due to the rapid influx of retirees (many of whom are lifelong Republicans) and a more conservative youth population.[5] Once labeled a typical southern one-party (Democratic) state, Florida is now a two-party competitive state. By 1990, the affiliations of Florida's registered voters by party were: Democrat (52.2 percent), Republican (40.6 percent), and Independents/Third Parties (7.2 percent). According to the 1990 Census of the Population, two-thirds of all Floridians were not born in the state.

The 1992 state legislative reapportionment plan created new districts that generally reflect the two-party character of the state.[6] In one-third of the districts in each house, the difference between the percent registered Democrats and the percent registered Republicans was 5 percent or less, indicative of high levels of party competition. Under the 1992 plan, forty-two of the 120 house districts (35 percent) were so classified; thirteen of the forty senate districts (32.5 percent).

The elections held under these newly configured districts changed the power distribution of the parties in both the senate and the house. Prior to the 1992 redistricting, Democrats held 57.5 percent of the seats in the senate, 61.5 percent in the house. After redistricting, political power in the Florida senate was evenly divided between the Democrats (twenty senators) and the Republicans (twenty senators), necessitating an agreement to rotate the senate presidency between the two parties in 1993 and 1994. A Republican (with an eye on the governor's seat) served as senate president in 1993; a Democrat, in 1994. Democrats controlled the house and the governorship during this time frame. The 1992 redistricting resulted in seventy-one Democrats in the house and forty-nine Republicans. But the party competitive nature of many of these districts kept many Democrats from endorsing major tax reform and spending expansion initiatives proposed by Governor Chiles during the recession.

Florida's legislators were somewhat more receptive to gubernatorial initiatives aimed at improving the efficiency and effectiveness of state governmental operations. They also supported decentralization efforts designed to solicit more community input and responsibility, especially with regard to schools (Blueprint 2000) and social services. With regard to the latter, the legislature approved the governor's request to create Health and Human Service Boards in fifteen Department of Health and Rehabilitative Services (HRS) regional districts and eleven regional Community Health Purchasing Alliances. (More will be said about these reforms later in the chapter.) However, even these efforts were hotly contested and hard to push through the legislature. Part of the problem was HRS's poor reputation, following numerous lawsuits alleging mismanagement, nation-leading AFDC and food stamp error rates, and repeated snafus related to a multimillion dollar computer that was supposed to alleviate these problems.

A History of Tax Reform Jitters

Florida's legislature has a history of being skittish when it comes to enacting major tax reforms, even when strongly endorsed by the governor. The legislature has reversed itself several times in recent years in reaction to strong opposition from key sectors of the public. For example, the state adopted a sales tax on services on June 6, 1986 (effective July 1, 1987). However, widespread opposition from the legal and advertising sectors and from the public-at-large resulted in its repeal in December, 1987 and its replacement with a 1 cent increase in the sales tax rate.[7]

Many then-opponents rue the day they opposed the services tax, since the service sector is now the largest part of Florida's economy.[8] Slowly, the state has begun to impose taxes on services (i.e., to broaden its sales tax base). Gubernatorial efforts to speed up this process have been received in a rather lukewarm fashion by legislators, who have to run for office more frequently than the governor and fear facing opponents who will use a tax-broadening vote against them on the campaign trail.

Public's Perception of State Government and Florida Taxes

The popularity of fiscal restraint proposals parallels the taxing and spending sentiments of Florida's voters, as reflected in a number of public opinion surveys such as the Florida Annual Policy Survey. The 1991 survey conducted in the fall showed that when asked "How much of each tax dollar that you pay to state government would you say is wasted? Would you say all of it, most of it, some or hardly any?" 34 percent said "Most" and 55 percent said "Some." A majority (57 percent) said that state government had not used the new revenues it had raised over the past several years very wisely. Another survey conducted by Mason-Dixon Opinion Research Inc. in March 1991 found that 59 percent of registered Florida voters wanted lawmakers to change their spending habits before they raised more taxes. Only 24 percent said they believed lawmakers should raise taxes first.

While many studies have shown Florida to be one of the nation's "low tax burden" states,[9] it is the *rate* of increase in taxes paid that has provoked citizen anger. A 1993 study by Florida TaxWatch, Inc. found that between 1977 and 1993, total taxes paid by Floridians to federal, state, and local governments grew 363.4 percent, outpacing the combined population and inflation growth rate of 271.4 percent. The tax growth between 1990 and 1991 was 4.4 percent; between 1991 and 1992, 4.1 percent; and between 1992 and 1993, 9.2 percent. The same study found that the average Florida family's effective buying power declined for three straight years (1991–1993). Effective buying power is after-tax income adjusted for inflation. It declined 3.8 percent in 1991, 2.7 percent in 1992, and 0.1 percent in 1993.

In a state with a substantial number of retirees on fixed incomes, these economic realities naturally provoked an anti-tax, anti-government growth sentiment among many voters. Not surprisingly, elected officials have turned increasingly to private sector dominated task forces and study groups for recommendations and advice on how to make government run more like a business. Several of these groups were already in place when the recession hit. More were formed after the economy began to improve to keep the momentum for government reform moving.

Commissions, Task Forces, and Study Groups: Prescriptions for Government

Several high-profile, high-powered commissions, task forces, and study groups were already searching for ways to make Florida's governmental officials more accountable to the public and the state's operations more efficient and effective when the recession hit hard. One, the Tax and Budget Reform Commission, was constitutionally mandated by the state's voters in 1988. Twenty-five of Florida's top lawyers, business executives, and political leaders were appointed to the commission. Its charge was to examine the appropriateness of the state's tax structure, determine the ability of the state and local governments to tax and adequately fund government operations and capital needs to the year 2000, and identify revenue needs to the year

2000. It was also charged with finding ways to effectively gather additional revenue from existing sources and to examine alternative ways of raising revenue that would be acceptable to the citizenry. It was given the authority to propose tax and budget reform-related constitutional amendments directly to the voters for approval, thereby bypassing the governor and the state legislature.

Many tax reformers hoped the commission would place a constitutional amendment calling for the imposition of a personal income tax before the state's voters. This did not happen. The commission was deeply divided on the issue and, in the end, even supporters of a state personal income tax were not willing to have it put on the ballot, fearing it would be defeated overwhelmingly. Other tax-related reform proposals, long pushed for by some proponents, also ended up not being placed before the voters. Among these were the repeal of state sales tax exemptions, granting to local governments the authority to adopt a 1-cent local option sales tax without voter approval, taxing businesses operating on government property, and imposing a taxing and spending increase cap. (There was a statewide vote on a cap amendment in November 1994, reflecting sustained interest in this idea.)

The Tax and Budget Reform Commission's efforts at *budgetary* reform were more successful than its tax-oriented activities. In 1992, voters approved four amendments placed on the ballot by the commission. One amendment dealt with a whole host of budget reforms, including an annual budget requirement, a program budget format for the general appropriations bill, an appropriations review process requiring a comparison between the agency request and the governor's recommended budget, a seventy-two-hour waiting period between introduction of the *final* appropriations bill and its passage by the legislature, faster distribution of the final budget report, abolition of more than 1200 state trust funds, a phased-in budget stabilization fund of at least 5 percent but no more than 10 percent by 1998, a requirement for a biennial state planning document to be prepared by the governor and submitted to the legislature, designation of the governor as the chief administrative officer of the state but authorization for the governor and the cabinet to balance the state budget when revenue shortfalls occur, and authorization for use of certain capital outlay funds for maintaining, restoring, or repairing existing public education facilities. A second amendment created a taxpayer's bill of rights. A third amendment authorized counties and municipalities each to levy up to a 1-cent sales tax, if approved by the voters, to be used for local government services. The fourth amendment subjected leaseholds of government-owned property entered into since 1968 to ad valorem taxation.

The effectiveness of some of these budget process reforms has recently been called into question by some former commission members and legislators. They are of the opinion that some of the budgetary process reforms "looked better on paper" than they actually worked out. Most notable were the seventy-two-hour waiting requirement and the consolidation of trust funds that the head of the house budget committee said "never really saved that much, and cost the state a lot of time and money." However, others feel that it is too soon to make conclusive judgments. Meanwhile, the governor and the legislature have continued to review and approve consolidation of trust funds, support the move toward program and performance budget procedures and formats, and multi-year forecasting. The momentum for moving in these directions has been sustained for two basic reasons: (1) the presence of persons who staffed or were liaisons to the Tax and Budget Reform Commission or other highly visible task forces among the governor's top-level Planning and Budgeting staff; and (2) passage of the 1994 Government Performance and Accountability Act.

Governor Chiles brought the Tax and Budget Reform Commission's former executive director, Dr. Robert Bradley, into his Office of Planning and Budgeting (OPB) as a deputy director. He and other high-level OPB staff were very receptive to various recommendations coming from the commission and other high-powered public-private sector task forces and study groups such as Partners in Productivity, the Productivity Measurement and Quality Improvement Task Force, and the Governor's Commission for Government By The People. The primary focus of these groups was on ways to improve government accountability and productivity. These task forces were already well into their investigations when the recession hit. The economy's sharp downturn merely reinforced the urgency of their missions.

Responding to newly elected Governor Lawton Chiles's "reinventing government" type recommendations, the legislature adopted the Productivity Enhancement Initiative in its 1991 session (FY 1992). This legislation permitted state agencies to keep a share of their productivity gains and use them for technology improvements, employee bonuses, training, workplace enhancements, and salary upgrades ($30 million of the estimated $100 million savings). While the depths of the recession made this program one of the victims of FY 1993 budget cuts, it was revived in FY 1994 as the Innovation Incentive Program. The idea, of course, had been around for quite some time, beginning with early task forces.

The 1994 Government Performance and Accountability Act continued the incentive program. It designated the year 2000 as the target date by which state agencies must fully implement performance-based budgeting. Managers are charged with showing how they are meeting performance standards and creating incentives for good work but penalties for poor performance. The act established an Office of Program Policy Analysis and Government Accountability, charged with examining what programs cost, their results, their efficiency, and the consequences should they be discontinued. It also requires the governor and cabinet, sitting as the State Council on Competitive Government, to consider whether certain state services can be best be provided by private enterprise. Finally, the act formalized the Commission on Government Accountability to the People (known as the GAP Commission), a fifteen-member task force that had been advising Governor Chiles for quite some time. The GAP Commission was charged with determining the impact of various state actions on the well-being of Florida's citizens and making recommendations for improved government-citizen relations.

The effectiveness of relying upon task forces, commissions, and study groups is another sure-to-be-long-lasting lesson gleaned from Florida's recession experience. But it is equally clear that the manner in which the state reacted to the fiscal crisis was heavily influenced by demographic and political trends set in motion long before the recession.

MAJOR REVENUE DECISIONS

The precise beginning and end of any recession are always difficult to pinpoint. In Florida, below-projected revenue patterns began appearing in FY 1990 and lasted through FY 1992. (See Table 9–1.) Sharp rates of increase in AFDC and other poverty-impacted entitlement program enrollments also began appearing in FY 1990 but extended into FY 1993 (Figure 9–1). In general, most analysts agree that FY 1991 and FY 1992 were the worst years of the recession. They also tend to

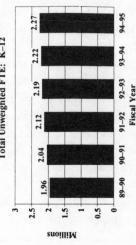

AFDC Caseload

Fiscal Year	89–90	90–91	91–92	92–93	93–94
Thousands	129.43	154.04	197.85	251.54	257.99

Source: "Florida's AFDC Program: The Facts and the Fears," Research Report (March 1994).

Total Unweighted FTE: K–12

Fiscal Year	89–90	90–91	91–92	92–93	93–94	94–95
Millions	1.96	2.04	2.12	2.19	2.22	2.27

Source: FY 89/90—FY 92/93 data from "Florida's Ten-Year Summary of Appropriations Data 1983–84 through 1992–93," Volume 15, December 1992, pp. 8 and 68. FY 93/94—FY 94/95 data from the Department of Education Enrollment Conference, July 1993, as reported in The Governor's Budget Recommendations Summary—FY 1994–1995, p. 50.

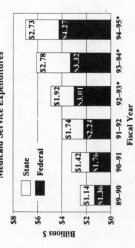

Medicaid Service Expenditures

☐ State ■ Federal

Fiscal Year	89–90	90–91	91–92	92–93*	93–94*	94–95*
State	$1.14	$1.42	$1.74	$1.92	$2.78	$2.73
Federal	$1.36	$1.76	$2.24	$3.01	$3.32	$4.27

*Estimate: November 23, 1993 Social Services Estimating Conference
Source: Agency for Health Care Administration—Medicaid Program as reported in The Governor's Budget Recommendations Summary—FY 1994-95, p. 63.

Inmate Population

Year	1990	1991	1992	1993	1994	1995
Thousands	42.73	46.23	47.01	50.6	55.07	63.28

Source: Florida Department of Corrections, Bureau of Planning and Research, December 1993, as reported in The Governor's Budget Recommendations Summary—FY 1994–1995, p. 81.

Figure 9–1 Florida Workload Indicators

agree that when the recovery began in FY 1993, it was incremental in nature, unlike past recoveries, which had been much sharper.

During the darkest days, Florida's elected officials struggled to make budgets balance as revenues lagged considerably behind expenditure needs and demands. Ever mindful of the need to heed the public's antitax, antigovernment mood but faced with record numbers of Floridians in dire economic straits, the state's legislators consistently chose the path of least resistance. The state got by with a "patchwork quilt" of incremental tax and fee increases and decremental spending reductions.

Common Revenue Strategies

Florida's revenue strategies during the recession of the early 1990s featured some "tried and true" techniques along with some fairly new approaches. The "old hat" approaches were earmarking revenue increases to popular (or mandated) programs (roads, prisons, education, health care), raising a whole host of fees and charges, relying more on "sin taxes" (tobacco, cigarette, liquor, lottery), raising tuition (claiming Floridians still get a good deal in comparison with residents of other states), and passing more taxes on to newcomers or tourists (those less likely to rebel at the polls).

Some of the newer approaches were to: (1) raise taxes that affected narrow segments of the population, allowing lawmakers to claim that they imposed no new general taxes applicable to all Floridians; (2) close sales tax loopholes and exemptions (a back door approach to the services tax that was repealed in 1987); (3) rely more on borrowing; and (4) "let the voters decide" major taxing and spending issues through local referenda or constitutional amendments. From the governor's perspective, another truism appeared to be, "If it fails with the Legislature one year, try it again the next." This assumed a governor got another chance.

Governor Martinez, a Republican, was responsible for proposing the FY 1991 budget. Governor Chiles, a Democrat who thwarted Martinez's bid for reelection in November 1990 and took office in January 1991, initiated the budgets from FY 1992 forward. Their revenue-raising proposals reflect a difference in philosophy and the point in the election cycle at which their budgets were devised. Legislative responses also reflect a great deal of sensitivity as to how their choices would impact their reelection campaigns.

FY 1991 Revenue Proposals and Adoptions
(Spring 1990 Legislative Session)

The FY 91 budget proposal turned out to be Governor Martinez's last. Knowing that he faced a reelection campaign in the fall of 1990, he worked hard to propose a tax-and-fee package he felt would be acceptable on the campaign trail (i.e., no broad across-the-board tax increases). Yet the state desperately needed to find new revenues due to lower-than-expected tax revenues as a consequence of the recession. Martinez proposed $512 million in new taxes and fees, along with some increases in existing fees. A 19-cent increase in the cigarette tax was to cover the rising costs of health care for the poor and Medicaid. Higher tuition rates were proposed to help pay for higher education. A whole host of fee increases for duplicate or replacement drivers licenses, late renewals, motor vehicle registration and licenses, and on various liquor and tobacco products was favored by the governor. Perhaps most controversial was a $195 fee to be imposed on all motor vehicles brought into the state and registered for the first time (but not on any vehicles purchased in-state). This evoked some claims of unfairness and a class action lawsuit from new residents of the state. Governor Martinez also called for greater reliance on borrowing (more than $1 billion) to fund transportation and environmental projects.

In the closing hours of a tense session, the legislature approved more than $804 million worth of new taxes on cigarettes, beer, wine, liquor, soft drinks, and various motor vehicle fees, including the controversial out-of-state resident car registration fee and an increase in the rental car surcharge, to balance the state's proposed $26 billion-plus budget. Fees and taxes were also raised on intangibles, real estate, corporations, utility bills, and gas, earmarked for road improvements.

Post-session accounts documented the plan of the governor and various legislators who had a hand in this increase to "brag during their reelection campaigns this year that they avoided a 'general' or 'statewide' tax increase." One columnist questioned this assessment. "They have a curious definition of 'general', because the aggregate of these nickel-and-dime increases represents the biggest tax increase in the state's history. That's bigger even than the services tax of 1987, which, if memory serves, an angry public forced the Legislature to repeal."

FY 1992 Revenue Proposals and Adoptions
(Spring 1991 Legislative Session)

The FY 1992 budget was Governor Chiles's first budget. He had run a high profile election campaign promising to "reinvent government"—to get it under control by "downsizing" (language soon changed to "right-sizing") government, reforming the civil service system, making government more accountable to the people, improving ethics laws, putting more emphasis on the prevention of major social problems, and reforming the state's tax structure. His initial budget called for $323 million in new and increased fees and another $111 million from other sources (lottery and sales tax collection speedup). At the heart of his fee proposals were higher tuition rates and increases in a variety of student fees to help pay for higher education, increases in fees earmarked for indigent health care, and higher fees on a variety of environmental permits, food establishment inspections, forest fire control assessments, and license plate renewals, among others.

Prior to the start of the 1991 legislative session (Chiles's first), a *St. Petersburg Times* article described the budget challenge facing the legislators.

> The state has just about run out of wiggle room. No help from the top. No help from below. Property values have leveled off. The recession has cut sales tax collections. . . . Lawmakers have wrung the cash from various fee and surcharge schemes. . . . Costs continue to go up for schools, transportation, entitlement programs, medical care for poor people and the uninsured middle class, and social services. The gap between "needs" and "means" grows ever larger.

In this constrained environment, the legislature continued its "hodge podge" approach to revenue acquisition. The major revenue hikes were on: automobile tax fees (earmarked to health care), marriage licenses (earmarked to spouse abuse shelters), the documentary stamp tax on deed transfers (earmarked to the state's Preservation 2000 land-buying program), tuition rates at both the state universities and community colleges, condominium association annual fees, lifetime hunting and fishing licenses, citrus taxes (earmarked to compensate growers whose trees were destroyed by citrus canker), fines for not putting seat belts on young children, and others. The legislature also granted permission for some counties to impose an additional sales tax to pay for indigent health care.

Not all the fees proposed by the governor made it through the session. The governor had proposed an increase in the daily car rental fee from $2 to $3.50. It failed after intensive lobbying by the car rental industry, a key element of Florida's tourism sector. And a major revision in the homestead exemption law failed. The $25,000 exemption on property taxes would have been modified to capture at least some property taxes from homeowners who now pay none because their homes are assessed at less than $25,000. Another defeat for the governor was his effort to increase hospital taxes and impose a fee on doctors to help pay for health care. Hospital and doctors' lobbyists kept this from happening. They claimed that the measure would drive up hospital costs 10 percent, force up health insurance rates, unfairly burden the elderly, add up to $750 to the average hospital bill, and require hospitals to cut services.

The budget process in the 1991 session (Chiles's first) was markedly different from that of the 1990 session (Martinez's last). One reporter described the difference:

> It was quite a contrast to the session that ended a year ago with the passage of every major piece of legislation, including a $27 billion budget and $1.6 billion in new taxes, between midnight and 5 a.m. . . . Last year, nearly 200 bills were passed the final day of the session. This year, 20 bills passed on the final day. The budget was approved four days ahead of the scheduled adjournment.

The easier-than-usual passage was a product of "[Governor] Chiles and legislative leaders saying that they had to pass a tight budget [FY 92] in order to set the table, next year or later, for a significant tax increase that would pay for all the services the public demands." This was to be Governor Chiles last "easy" budget session for quite awhile.

FY 1993 Revenue Proposals and Adoptions (Spring 1992 Session)

FY 1993 was a rather unique "happening" in terms of budgeting. The governor proposed *two* budgets, a gamble at major tax reform that failed. He first introduced what he called his "bare bones" or "reality" budget ($29.1 billion—$200 million less than the FY 1992 budget) on November 25, 1991. It included few new taxes and was described by the governor as "bleak" but "a real life scenario of where we'll be if we don't have spending reform, budget reform, reorganization and some kind of *tax* reform." (He fully expected this budget to be rejected and his alternative "investment" budget to be adopted—a serious miscalculation in the middle of economic adversity.)

Among the reforms envisioned by Governor Chiles were the merger of law enforcement agencies into a super police agency, decentralization of the Department of Health and Rehabilitative Services (HRS), revamping of the civil service system, more privatization efforts, and the "sunseting" of all sales tax exemptions. Anticipating that the legislature would adopt some of these reforms in its December special session, he began laying the foundation for support of his alternative and preferred $30.5 billion budget—his "investment budget." It was introduced on January 14, 1992 and *did* feature major revenue-raising provisions ($1.35 billion worth). The notion that everyone should pay their "fair share" was at the heart of his tax proposals. Said Chiles,

> The first thing to establish is fairness. Our current tax system is like a meat platter that has been picked to the bones by many special interests . . . the party's over. Over the decades these special interests have been up to the table getting themselves exempted from paying their fair share. The time has come to play fair and see that they are included before we ask those who have been paying to pay more.

In a nutshell, the governor's "Fair Share" tax plan called for rolling back the state sales tax from 6 percent to 5 percent and repealing about 100 sales tax exemptions, including some major corporate exemptions, in exchange for cutting local property taxes for schools by more than half. However, it also called for $1.35 billion in new or increased taxes and fees (the first year of a $2.5 billion annualized tax increase). As one reporter phrased it, this was "a lump state lawmakers just couldn't swallow."

In its annual prelegislative session analysis, the *St. Petersburg Times* forecast the FY 1993 budget deliberations as follows:

If you are into bloodshed and paralysis . . . this might be your
year. . . . We are in a recession that has reduced the amount
of money available to fight over. Thus the fight over the few
remaining crumbs could get bitter. It is a macabre scene to watch
grown men and women decide whether to put money into programs that provide liver transplants or those that help the homeless. Add into this continuing budget mess the fact that 1992 is
an election year for every single member of the house and senate
and all of them will run in districts that are being realigned in
keeping with the constitutional requirement that we reapportion
the state every 10 years."

The speaker of the house characterized it as likely to be "the session
from hell and back." It turned out to be several "hot sessions." Only
after several special sessions was the budget finally adopted.

At the end of the regular session, the legislature passed a no-
new-taxes budget of $30 billion (March 1992) closer to the governor's
original "reality" budget. The governor was quick to veto it, claiming
that "We can take this budget and make a case it will cost Floridians
an awful lot more money than the investment budget we're talking
about." Not until July, several special sessions later, was SB 26–H
passed and signed by the governor. It increased taxes and fees by
$436.1 million on an annual basis, raising $376.7 million for FY 1993.
The major increases were in the intangible tax, documentary stamp
tax, pollutant tax, the sales tax on telecommunication services and
electrical power, Agriculture Department registration and inspection
fees, university and community college tuition, and a new supplemental corporate filing fee. The sales tax was extended to detective and
burglar protection services and nonresidential cleaning and pest control services. Most controversial was a $1.50 assessment per patient
day on nursing homes scheduled for repeal on May 1, 1993 following
legislative review. It was estimated to raise $27.0 million in FY 1993
(and $33.1 million of additional federal matching aid) and was ear-
marked to go into the Public Medical Assistance Trust Fund to fund
Medicaid.

In the end, the governor had to settle for tax increases amounting
to only one-fourth of his proposed $1.3 billion. The legislative session
created battle lines along party lines and featured "some of the most
hostile political warring in years." The tensions subsided somewhat

in the next session as the revenue picture got a little brighter and the reapportionment battles were over.

FY 1994 Revenue Proposals and Adoptions (Spring Session 1993)

The governor continued his pursuit of tax reform and an expanded social reform agenda, with a strong preventive emphasis. In a speech before business and government leaders in October 1992, Governor Chiles identified four major problems that he believed would have to be tackled to fix the state's sluggish economy and ensure the long-term health of its businesses. The four were: "runaway health care and workers' compensation insurance costs; an outmoded tax system which isn't producing enough revenue; and a subpar education system, which has the highest drop-out rate in the country." These comments laid the groundwork for his FY 1994 budget proposals.

Governor Chiles continued his quest toward tax fairness. His FY 1994 budget proposal called for $662 million in new fees and taxes on services. Just as in his FY 1993 budget, he proposed eliminating hundreds of sales tax exemptions (in effect, reimposing the services tax but in a less visible manner). He proposed that all of the state's sales tax exemptions be scheduled for review over a five-year period to determine which ones should be eliminated. And as in his FY 1992 budget, he proposed extending the state's 5.5 percent corporate income tax to exempt businesses (subchapter S corporations owned by thirty-five or fewer shareholders). Chiles cited statistics showing that 80 percent of Florida's corporations are exempt from the corporate income tax because of their classification as S corporations. A small number of fee increases (amounting to $31 million of the $662 million) on such things as driver history checks, mobile home park fees, and laboratory test work for infants were included in the governor's proposal as well.

The Republican president of the senate characterized many of these new "fee taxes" as "Scuse me for living" taxes—a remark that got a lot of press coverage and probably prompted some legislators to back away from the governor's tax reform proposal. In fact, prior to the session ever beginning, newspaper stories were speculating that "Legislators aren't likely to go along with all the Governor's proposals and some think his tax increase plans are already dead because of the Republican-controlled senate." While the economy had improved slightly, the political winds were blowing in a different direction than toward tax reform.

In tackling the FY 1994 budget, legislators agreed that the three topics that would most affect the bottom line were taxes, health care, and worker's compensation insurance. Of these, the tax topic was projected to be the least problematic because the governor's major tax reform proposal was simply not on the legislature's agenda. One leading newspaper's pre-session prediction was that "Tax reform is a battle abandoned. The economic upturn is providing the politicians with one more reprieve on the day of reckoning." This forecast turned out to be right on target. By the close of the session, the legislature had rejected the governor's proposal to add taxes on fourteen personal services, including attorneys' and accountants' fees. The plan was shelved for another year. The legislature also killed the governor's plan to expand the corporate income tax to S corporations and turned its back on a plan to increase the cigarette tax by 25 cents a pack (a proposal designed by the governor to help pay for prison expansion).[10] It repealed the highly controversial $1.50-a-day tax on nursing home beds and delayed a 1-cent recycling fee on many containers.

In many ways, the FY 1994 budget symbolized a return to "normality" as the state eased out of the recession. According to one post-session analysis:

> The tax structure remains the same. It's performing as it always did. Based heavily on the sales tax, alcohol tax and other consumption taxes, Florida's tax revenues fell off dramatically when the economy faltered. Legislators cut $2 billion out of the state budget when tax revenues fell short of projections. Now that the economy is recovering, taxes are rebounding too.

The state continues to "live and die" as its sales and consumption taxes fluctuate.

Revenue Relief for Local Governments?

Not until the state was coming out of its own budgetary doldrums did it offer up any major relief for equally stressed local governments. In the 1993 session, the legislature authorized counties to impose a new local option gas tax, extended authority to levy improved local discretionary sales surtaxes, offered localities a chance to increase occupational license taxes after their reform, and mandated a significant change in the municipal revenue sharing program.

Analysts attribute the interest in expanding local government revenue-raising capacity to several factors: (1) the 1990 constitutional amendment limiting unfunded state mandates; (2) elevated legislative awareness of the overwhelming demands for local governments to provide services and infrastructure under the state's Growth Management Act (perceived by local governments as a very onerous mandate); (3) support during the session from policy commissions and statewide associations representing local governments; and (4) pre-session work by the Advisory Council on Intergovernmental Relations.[11] The ACIR recommended the continuation of the local government infrastructure surtax, the reform of the local occupational license tax, and the elimination of the 7 percent annual increase to Metro-Dade's distribution in the Municipal Revenue Sharing Program (designed to spread the money more evenly across other municipalities).

Earlier legislation affecting local government finances focused more on loosening rather stringent use strings and stimulating intergovernmental, especially interlocal, cooperation. During the 1990 legislative session, a law was passed expanding the use of the infrastructure surtax funds by allowing counties to share the proceeds with school boards, and to use the funds to buy land for public recreation, conservation, or for the protection of natural resources. In its 1992 session, the legislature passed legislation permitting small counties to levy a 1 percent sales surtax to be distributed to the county and its municipalities according to an interlocal agreement, or according to the half-cent sales taxation formulas laid out in the Florida Statutes. It also enacted a small county indigent care surtax, designed to help small counties fund a broad range of health care services for indigent and medically deprived county residents. However, the antitax environment made many county officials reticent to propose these additional taxes, in spite of their expanded legal authority. The effectiveness of using earmarking strategies to gain voter support for *new* taxes has been waning for quite some time.

Dedicated, or Earmarked, Revenues and Tax Swapping: Growing Public Hostility

Floridians have become more suspicious of earmarking strategies as a consequence of their negative experiences with the lottery and its ability to fund education. Lottery funds were used to substitute rather than enhance education—much to the dismay of the public.[12] Also not very popular are proposals to "substitute" one tax or revenue source for another. Efforts during the recession period to trade one tax for another were not very successful.[13] Subsequent surveys found that many voters feared that it would be simply a matter of time before the tax traded for was put back in place and the legislators reacted by axing any such proposals from the governor.

In spite of repeated legislative rejection of the "swap" approach to getting major new taxes or tax reform during his first term, Governor Chiles remained convinced the strategy could work. He promised to push for an expansion of Florida's sales tax base by offering the state's residents school property tax relief should he be reelected in 1994. However, the budget he introduced during the 1994 legislative session (FY 1995) abandoned the idea of sales tax reform, namely eliminating exemptions and extending them tax to a wide array of services. It was characterized by the governor himself as a "no new taxes" budget. The $39.06 million in net new revenues proposed for FY 1995 were almost all fee increases on motor vehicle registrations, tags, tag replacements, divorce, pool and bathing facility permits, brand wines, amusement device inspections, vehicle overweight fees and permits, sign permits and applications, etc. (Election years change the priorities of even the most ardent tax reformers!)

A Retrospective View: Revenue Choices and the Election Cycle

The election cycle itself explains the incremental nature of revenue reforms during the recession. The state's worst fiscal hour was between late 1990 to early 1992 (the FY 1991 and 1992 budgets). During this period, legislators were in no mood to implement major tax reform. The fear of having to face a newly configured electorate after reapportionment kept many of them from supporting the governor's proposed tax and fee increases in his FY 1993 investment budget. By the start of the 1993 session, the state's finances had improved somewhat, lessening the need for major revenue increases in the FY 1994 and FY 1995 budgets. By then, a number of legislators from both parties were interested in holding the line on tax increases as they headed into the 1994 election season.

In retrospect, it is clear that regardless of their party affiliation, neither Governor Martinez nor Governor Chiles got the magnitude or breadth of revenue increases and changes they proposed during the recession. Public opinion and the political cycle prompted a more conservative approach by the legislature. The same dynamics characterized their approach to spending, although citizen- and employee-initiated lawsuits occasionally forced a reevaluation of several legislative spending cut decisions.

MAJOR SPENDING DECISIONS

Historically, the three biggest functional spending areas in Florida's budget have been education, transportation, and human services (health and welfare). When it was necessary to make deep cuts, naturally these were the heaviest targeted. (See Table 9–2 detailing the amounts cut from each agency in the three-year period FY 1990–1992.) When cuts in these popular functions occurred or when the growth rate in appropriations lagged behind demands, usually the next step was to restore them as quickly as possible to fend off their quite vocal advocates. Cuts at one point in time were often the rationale for raising or expanding fees and charges at the next legislative session and dedicating them to a specific department or activity.

Throughout the recession period, Florida's lawmakers were faced with a slower-than-normal growth rate in revenues. The tide of public opinion was running strongly against raising taxes before cutting spending. At the same time, fast-rising numbers of recipients in the entitlement programs (especially Medicaid, AFDC, and Food Stamp) as a direct consequence of the recession forced up spending demands. And a large increase in school-age children of baby-boomer in-migrants of the 1980s put lots of pressure on the education budget. Under these conditions, it was not surprising that both the governor and the legislature were highly receptive to organizational and management reform plans designed to cut down operating costs and improve efficiency and effectiveness. Nor was it unusual that their interest in *preventive* strategies and better long-range planning was heightened. The state was most innovative in its organizational and management reforms, which will be discussed in the next section.

TABLE 9–2 Summary of Florida General Fund Reductions by Agency during Depths of Recession

Agency	Actual			Total Three Years
	FY 1990	FY 1991[1]	FY 1992[2]	
Administered Funds	2,437,655	2,608,157	13,263,432	18,309,244
Administration	346,347	366,006	203,319	915,672
Agriculture	2,199,874	6,408,497	2,944,029	11,552,400
Banking/Finance/Comptroller	779,257	1,810,602	687,909	3,277,768
Commerce	528,287	5,047,551	499,373	6,075,211
Community Affairs	276,194	3,340,113	524,208	4,140,515
Corrections	15,901,413	46,287,610	44,804,248	106,993,271
Education	161,557,223	431,110,805	274,244,499	866,912,527
Elder Affairs			23,025	23,025
Environmental	916,588	2,946,083	3,681,927	7,544,598
Game/Fresh Water Fish Commission	550,952	1,523,630	922,175	2,996,757
General Services	322,718	843,763	617,380	1,783,861
Governor	366,562	982,297	545,374	1,894,233
Health & Rehabilitative Services	68,214,586	183,323,067	139,313,534	390,851,187
Highway Safety and Motor Vehicles	4,046,130	60,749,753	5,146,166	69,942,049
Insurance/Treasurer	8,524	210,944		219,468
Judicial	3,500,666	6,670,440	9,611,675	19,782,781

Labor & Employment	565,130	1,715,985	1,166,967	3,448,082
Law Enforcement	1,696,949	3,434,581	2,980,205	8,111,735
Legal Affairs/Attorney General	456,909	1,607,366	1,086,235	3,150,510
Legislative Branch	3,286,792	9,429,021	7,385,067	20,100,880
Military Affairs	177,730	469,026		646,756
National Conf/Comm.	492	1,365	2,510	4,367
Natural Resources	894,470	3,991,677	1,139,036	6,025,183
Parole Commission	142,506	236,150	267,650	646,306
Professional Regulation		75,000		75,000
Revenue	1,417,203	3,716,883	931,408	6,065,494
State	909,509	4,852,590	1,129,040	6,891,139
Veterans' Affairs	86,424	301,008	214,040	601,873
Total	**271,587,090**	**784,059,970**	**513,334,832**	**1,568,981,892**

Notes:

¹Additional actions taken:

Transfer from Working Capital Fund	$ 172.0 M
Transfers from trust funds to GR	138.6 M
Transfer from SIF	20.0 M
Legislative reduction to appropriations	7.9 M

GR = General Revenue
SIF = State Infrastructure Fund

²Additional actions taken:

Transfer from Working Capital Fund	$ 101.9 M
Transfers from trust funds to GR	5.7 M
Transfers from Commerce/HSMV to WCF	10.2 M

WCF = Working Capital Fund
HSMV = Highway Safety and Motor Vehicles

Source: State of Florida, Executive Office of the Governor, Office of Planning and Budgeting, Revenue and Economic Analysis, unpublished.

It was rather predictable in its cutting strategies, often focusing on personnel, training, travel, and capital outlay object categories.

FY 1991: Four Rounds of Budget Adjustments

The real crunch of the recession hit the state in the fall of 1990. In October, stopgap measures had to be put in place to address the projected $544 million revenue shortfall. Nearly $215 million in obscure reserve trust funds and an early repayment by DOT of an $81 million internal state loan from the General Fund helped offset the half-a-billion tax shortfall and enabled state agencies to pare their recommended spending cuts from 5 percent to 2.3 percent. This left $260 million to be cut by the governor and cabinet from the FY 1991 budget. On October 9, 1990, they cut $155 million from the education budget, $54 million from HRS, and $17 million from the Department of Corrections, with smaller cuts scattered throughout other state agencies. Some $6.1 million was slashed from a new juvenile justice reform package and another $1.3 million from the state court system.

In the waning hours of his term, Governor Martinez imposed a hiring freeze and severe spending restrictions on state government agencies. In his executive order issued in early December 1990, he instructed the agencies he controlled to freeze vacant positions, stop buying new equipment, severely limit travel and purchase of supplies, and suspend new programs not yet been put into operation. This action followed the release of figures showing that state tax collections would fall well short of revenue projections and force another $271 million to be cut from the FY 1991 budget. (Agencies governed by separately elected cabinet members were not subjected to the order.)

On January 10, 1991, two days after taking office, Governor Lawton Chiles and the Florida cabinet had to cut $270 million from the FY 1991 budget. They were told by the budget director that by March 1, it was likely that the state's revenues would fall another $200 million short of the FY 1991 budget. At the time, the governor said he hoped to avoid more cuts in services by building up the state's emergency bank account by getting the legislature to authorize taking funds from an infrastructure trust fund that was supposed to be used for long-term needs such as new construction. (Ironically, Governor Chiles had criticized his predecessor Martinez for raiding trust funds to cover cuts as an "accounting gimmick" that paid for day-to-day operations with uncertain funding.)

Of the $270 million cut, approximately $24 million came from one-time-only projects that benefited a specific part of the state. Said one press account: "These are the often-criticized 'turkeys' that legislators put in the budget to please the folks back home." The largest portion, however, came from the biggest beneficiaries of state tax dollars—schools, $149.6 million ($107.3 from the public schools, $12.5 million from community colleges, and $25.7 million from state universities), social services, $74.5 million, and prisons, $18.6 million (including a new program to help keep troubled youngsters out of prison that had yet to accept clients).

A $21 million subsidy program for seventy-seven hospitals that provided charity care was trimmed significantly. The medically needy program was slashed by $9 million by changing income eligibility requirements so that 7,800 of the of the 80,000 people served by the program no longer qualified. The HRS deputy secretary predicted that: "A lot of those people will just incur bills until they are eligible. In the meantime, with no other way to pay, they will be forced to present themselves to hospitals for treatment. Hospitals or local governments will be left holding the bag." Eliminating the subsidy program and cutting the medically needy program resulted in an estimated additional loss of $17 million in federal matching funds.

Also cut were $921,604 in aid to mosquito control programs and a $20 million program to provide trauma care for the indigent. Some 979 state positions were eliminated although it was estimated that only 100 people might actually lose their jobs; the other cut positions were vacant.

Two truisms emerge from this and subsequent rounds of budget cuts: newly created programs were the most vulnerable, and those with the largest budgets bore the largest cuts.

Facing another $163.3 million shortfall in revenues in May 1991, the governor and cabinet authorized going into the state's rainy day fund. When they finished, there was only about $600,000 left in the fund—not even enough to run the state for half an hour.

By June 1991, further revenue shortfalls had created a deficit of $151.3 million. A special session (June 6) was called by Governor Chiles primarily to consider legislation to address executive fiscal management tools to manage revenue deficits effectively. Rather than cut the FY 1991 budget any further with just forty-eight days left in the fiscal year, the governor proposed filling the shortfall by transferring funds from trust funds into the General Fund. While the governor and the cabinet had the authority to borrow from trust funds, they could do so only if the money were repaid the same year—out of the question in this circumstance. Therefore, the governor called the special session to revise this statute, which it did.

Legislation passed during this session reduced appropriations made in previous years from the State Infrastructure Fund. Moneys from the Principal State School Trust Fund, Law Enforcement Radio System Trust Fund, and the Nonmandatory Land Reclamation Trust Fund were transferred to the General Revenue Fund. Capital outlay moneys from selected trust funds were transferred to fund FY 1992 Public Education Capital Outlays (PECOs). In a further cost-saving-oriented move, the Department of General Services was ordered to conduct a lease-purchase analysis for the Department of Corrections, Parole Commission, and HRS.

FY 1992 Budget Cuts: Three Rounds

FY 1992, like its predecessor, was a painful one from a fiscal perspective. The governor and cabinet met on October 22, 1991, and by a 5–2 vote cut $579 million from the FY 1992 budget. Of the cuts, education took $288.9 million, social services, $159.8 million, corrections $45.6 million, state pay raises $32 million, judicial system $13.5 million, legislature $7.5 million, and other agencies $31.7 million.

Initially the governor and the cabinet thought they would have to cut $622 million from the budget but the governor devised a plan that proposed to eliminate pay raises for state workers and raid the state's $195 million rainy day fund for $42.7 million to blunt the cuts. These last minute changes spared education some $40 million.

To save money, 1,830 positions were deleted (only 228 of which were scheduled to be actual layoffs). Other cuts (but not all) were made to programs aiding people with epilepsy, educating physicians and expectant parents about poisons, researching and treating childhood tumors, and providing guardians in court for abused and neglected children.

The cuts sparked two major lawsuits, one brought by a group of children's advocates challenging the right of the executive (governor and cabinet) to "de-appropriate" funds and another by a major state employees union and the union representing state university faculty and professional employees who challenged the governor and cabinet's legal right to eliminate $32 million in scheduled pay increases agreed upon earlier that year by the unions and the legislature.[14] (Plaintiffs in both suits ultimately prevailed.)

On December 10, 1991, the legislature had to be called into special session to deal with more revenue shortfalls, this time to the tune of $622 million. The Florida Supreme Court had ruled in late October that the governor and the cabinet did not have the constitutional authority to cut the state budget, thereby necessitating the special session. The initial plan called for the most cuts to hit school children, university students, Medicaid recipients, and nursing home patients.

The governor and cabinet's cutback plan called for getting $42.7 million from the rainy day fund and making $546.8 million in program cuts and delaying worker pay raises to save $32.2 million. Both the house and senate plans called for higher amounts to be raised via the rainy day fund and trust funds but less to be raised via elimination or delay of worker pay raises. They also favored less in program cuts (house $492.4, senate $491.4) and supported a $10 million cut in a plan sponsored by Chiles that gave bonuses to agencies that improved their performance.

In the end, a compromise was made to cut $513 million ($274 million from schools, $139 million from social services, and $59 million from prisons and the criminal justice system). The law deleted 1,908 state positions. A state worker pay raise was delayed forty-five days to save $8 million. The plan also took $124 million from the rainy day fund and trust funds; of this, $84 million came out of the rainy day fund. The prison cuts meant that the state would have to delay opening facilities for more than 3,000 inmates.

The governor ultimately vetoed the $8 million cut from a program offering cash bonuses, new equipment, and other incentives to improve government efficiency. As a consequence, another $8 million was taken from the state's rainy day fund, leaving it at $104 million.

In the governor's call to special session, he had also taken the opportunity to charge the legislature with addressing various spending reforms and government reorganization proposals. Among these were: reorganization of HRS to give more control to local communities; implementation of the recommendations made by the Governor and Cabinet Task Force on Governmental Efficiency to reorganize, combine, and consolidate other state agencies; reform of the civil service system to give managers more flexibility in hiring and paying workers by allowing each department to establish its own rules for salaries, recruitment, promotion, and bonuses; and writing a new law to give the governor and cabinet authority to cut budgets in the future.

During the special session, the legislature authorized exempting additional managerial positions from the Career Service System, required state agencies, in consultation with legislative standing committees, to include performance measures in their functional plans, and stated its intent to address HRS reorganization in the 1992 session. It did not adopt legislation restoring budget-cutting authority to the governor and cabinet or mandating reorganization of other state agencies.

In early February, state economists predicted a $121.4 million revenue shortfall. To make matters even worse, the forecasters estimated that the state would have to target another $81 million to make up for deficits in special accounts that fund welfare, Medicaid, and the state workers' health insurance plan. When all was said and done, the legislature approved $162 million in spending cuts and account transfers. It canceled a 3 percent state worker pay raise that was supposed to take effect only days later, took $46 million from schools that became available when the state overestimated the number of students attending public school, and used $54.5 million of the state's $98 million rainy day fund. At the same time the legislators made these cuts, they got the bad news that the revenue forecast for FY 1993 had been slashed by $263 million.

FY 1993: A Philosophical Battle—and a Delayed Budget Adoption

The struggles over the FY 1993 budget best reflect the clash between the expansionary, revisionist philosophy of the governor and the more traditional, incremental approach of a majority of Florida's legislators, especially in the senate. This was the year of the governor's "dual budgets"—the reality and the investment budget. The reality budget, introduced on November 25, 1991, proposed spending $29.1 billion, about $200 million less than the existing FY 1992 budget ($29.3 billion). The pressures created by this "bare bones" budget were intense. In spite of adding 261,000 residents, 97,000 school students, and 1.8 million new Medicaid cases, some analyses speculated the FY 1993 reality budget would: (1) drop per student public spending to $3,010 (1988 levels) and bring 1,000 more teacher layoffs; (2) cut back the governor's popular "Healthy Start" prevention-oriented health care program for pregnant women and infants; (3) eliminate the environmental-lands purchase program Preservation 2000; (4) eliminate funds aimed at cleaning up polluted waterways; (5) further cut the state work force by 2,371 positions; and (6) give no raises to teachers or state employees.

A whole host of other possible cuts was also laid on the table. One was a $2.9 million cut in operating funds for the National High Magnetic Field Laboratory (a highly competitive National Science Foundation grant-funded project that the state had managed to capture). Another was a $6 million cut to community art and historic preservation programs. Cuts were also scheduled for an $880,000 computer network designed to help the state collect more taxes, and in the program that paid for the hospital care for working families who made too much money to quality for Medicaid but had no insurance to cover long-term hospital care.

Under the reality budget, the legislature would have had to trim about a half a billion dollars from projects just to provide existing services without spending beyond their present means. School enrollment growth and escalating Medicaid rolls were the source of intense pressures on the budget.

The governor's investment budget ($1.3 billion), introduced to the legislature on January 14, 1992, placed a high priority on expanding spending for schools, health care, public safety, the environment, growth management, and economic development. Prevention and early intervention programs were emphasized as long-term cost-savings approaches.

In the education arena, Chiles' budget plan called for $603.1 million to improve education, from kindergarten through graduate school. It laid out $28 million for pre-kindergarten classes, $6 million for dropout prevention, $3.4 million for breakfasts for needy school children, and moneys to restore past budget cuts that hit the community colleges and state universities. The Governor proposed to spend almost $155 million for a "lottery buyback" program to return to schools money for enhancements that was supposed to come from the lottery (a proposal that had failed in the past).

In the health and family services areas, Chiles proposed $45 million for his Healthy Start programs stressing prevention and early intervention. The money was to go to immunizations, school-based clinics, satellite clinics in high risk neighborhoods, and children's medical needs. The largest amount ($207 million) was earmarked for the medically needy, rural health care, and other community services.

His child welfare proposal included $81 million for foster child care, child therapy, family day care homes, and child protection services and $57 million for community-based programs for the elderly and adult mental health. He requested $29.6 million to cover juvenile justice system shortfalls that had prompted a lawsuit charging the state with neglecting its responsibilities.

For the environment, Chiles proposed spending $36 million in general revenue and $387 million from bonds on the Preservation 2000 land-buying program, state parks, coastal protection, and beach restoration.

In the public safety area, he called for a $128 million to help pay for putting new prisons on line, adding a violent crime squad to the Department of Law Enforcement, supporting a crime lab, and expanding the judiciary system.

The governor's investment budget was a tough sell from the beginning. Many of his critics preferred his original reality budget. Said the president of the senate (a Republican), "The solution is, take the money you have, tighten your belt, just like the people are doing." "The Governor himself should trim down his own personal staff, which is bloated, and he should demand the same of every agency of state government." Many of his Democratic counterparts agreed. That's why passing the FY 1993 budget turned out to be so long and difficult a process and required several special sessions to get the job done.

The special session: March 23–April 1, 1992. During this special session, the legislature restored budget reductions for the period April 1, 1992 through June 30, 1992, to the Medicaid Medically Needy Program by transferring $11.2 million from the Public Medical Assistance Trust Fund and $13.5 million from the Medical Care Trust Fund to HRS. The same appropriations act transferred $11.2 million from the General Revenue Fund to reimburse the Public Medical Assistance Trust Fund. The FY 1993 budget was not on the special session agenda nor on that of the next.

Special session: April 1, 1992. The sole purpose of this special session was to enact legislation to abolish the Department of Administration, transferring its power and duties to the Department of General Services and to rename it the Department of Management Services (DMS). DMS was to be created January 1, 1993 and to include twelve divisions: Administration; Building Construction; Communications; Facilities Management; Information Services; Motor Pool; Personnel Management Services; Purchasing; Retirement; State Employees' Insurance; Administrative Hearings; and Capitol Police. The authorization required the new department to reduce funds expended for salaries and benefits by 5 percent in FY 1994 and by 10 percent in FY 1995.

Special session: June 1–July 10, 1992. This was the session at which the FY 1993 budget was finally passed. In the end, the Governor reluctantly signed a $31.8 billion budget that didn't reach his proposed investment budget level but still raised state spending more than $550 million above the "bare bones" budget the legislature had passed earlier (that he had vetoed). Chiles said that the prospect of a partial shutdown of state services and state employees missing their paychecks weighed heavily on his signing the bill. The legislators "sent me a state budget and tax package that falls woefully short . . . but vetoing them would have hurt Floridians," said the governor. Things got brighter for him in the FY 1994 budget—but not until Hurricane Andrew hit Florida in August 1992. Ironically, Hurricane Andrew helped boost the state's economy with the infusion of federal funds and insurance payouts.

The FY 1994 Budget: Better, Although Not Great, Times

With brighter budgetary forecasts on the horizon, Governor Chiles proposed a $34.9 billion budget on December 14, 1992—a 9.6 percent increase over the previous year's budget. Calling it his "Putting People First" budget, he continued his push for more prevention-oriented spending increases, most notably in the health and human services and educational areas, especially his Healthy Start program aimed at expectant mothers and their babies.

A brighter revenue picture put legislators in a much better mood to consider expansionary spending during their 1993 session than they had been in previous years. Still, there were marked differences of opinion as to what would be the best approaches to spending the revenue "windfalls." After much debate, the legislature approved an

FY 1994 budget that increased spending for schools by $111 per student, financed more than 7,000 new prison beds, gave state employees a 3 percent pay raise, covered the costs of the fourth year of Preservation 2000, expanded the governor's Healthy Start program, and adopted several welfare and juvenile justice reform programs. (A May special session appropriated $211 million more to build 10,700 more prison beds—short of what the governor wanted. But the legislators were still a little anxious about the true extent of economic recovery.)

FY 1995: An Election Year Budget

On December 21, 1993, Governor Chiles proposed a $38 billion FY 1995 budget (a 7.2 percent increase over the FY 1994 budget). It was a classic election year "no new taxes" (but lots of fee increases) budget, with high spending priorities for prisons, schools, and welfare reform. One press account described this metamorphosis as the governor's effort to "stage another political comeback" (his support had waned considerably among the public-at-large) "by positioning himself as tough on crime, and as a born-again fiscal conservative." However, Chiles continued his emphasis on prevention and even labeled the FY 1994 budget his "Lifeline" budget because it proposed putting more money into programs "that strengthen families and enhance the progress of children through school and into their work careers." Among these were a programs aimed at juvenile offenders, Medicaid-eligible or working-poor mothers and their babies, pre-kindergarten-aged children, and foster children, among others. But without question, attacking violent crime in Florida, especially that perpetrated by juveniles, was the governor's top priority and also that of most legislators. The struggle was over how best to remedy the problem.

In the end, the legislature adopted a $38.6 billion budget with stricter, more punitive, approaches to juvenile crime than that offered by the governor. It also rejected his proposal for health care reform expansion (state-subsidized health care insurance for the poor) in a special session, expressing skepticism over his claims that it could be funded by savings generated by Medicaid reforms. As one newspaper account concluded: "Prevention of crime and disease took a backseat to punishment as lawmakers look[ed] ahead to November elections." By FY 1995, the need to *cut* spending had passed; the new emphasis was on *controlling* spending and living within the state's revenue means.

Redirecting Policy: Difficult During a Recession

Florida's experiences during the recession of the early 1990s demon-strate how difficult it is to accomplish radical budgetary reform on either side of the budgetary ledger in the midst of a recession. Repeat-edly, the governor pushed for major tax reform and considerably more spending on "investment" and prevention-related programs. A more conservative legislature was not at all supportive of major tax reform and only marginally receptive to spending more in the short term, even if it might save in the long term. However, they were not as antagonistic toward prevention-oriented spending as they were toward spending increases *per se*. Legislators were more receptive to innovations, particularly in the area of organizational and manage-ment reforms.

INNOVATIONS IN THE MIDST OF A RECESSION

Governor Chiles came to office with an aggressive, textbook-like "rein-venting government" agenda. In his election campaign, he had "called for streamlining government, eliminating duplication in function, and reducing the bureaucracy and the relative size of administration" be-fore "asking the citizens of Florida to pay more taxes to invest in Florida's future." Soon after taking office, he developed The Gover-nor's Strategic Plan for Florida 1992–1996 with five priorities: enabling every family to be self-sufficient, improving education through part-nerships with communities, ensuring public safety for Floridians, safe-guarding the quality of life, and making government work for Florida. His goals for making government work better were to revitalize gov-ernment's ability to perform and make government more accountable.

From his first budget, Governor Chiles emphasized administra-tive reform. What initially captured the public's attention, however, was his pledge to "downsize," then "right-size" and reorganize the governmental bureaucracy. The governor got off to a bad start with his "downsizing" pledge, which the average citizen took to mean he would reduce the number of state employees. His credibility in this area was rather quickly challenged when one of the state's major newspapers did an analysis of the state payroll and found little evi-dence of payroll reduction. While that analysis may have been done too quickly, an analysis based on fiscal years 1990 through 1994 shows that only in FY 1992 was there a reduction in the number of state employees (see Table 9–3). (The governor counters this statistic by citing figures showing that in terms of state employees per capita, Florida ranks forty-eight out of fifty.)

Without question, the bad publicity the governor got over his failure to "downsize" quickly or deeply enough made his job of selling organizational and management reform to the legislature more difficult. But his determination, and the ensuing demand from prominent citizen-dominated commissions, juxtaposed on a deteriorating economy, warmed them up to the idea.

By 1993, the governor and legislature had adopted a number of innovative approaches that led Ted Gaebler, coauthor of *Reinventing Government*, to characterize Florida as one of five states in the forefront of reforming and redesigning state government. He specifically mentioned the state's decentralization of the Department of Health and Rehabilitative Services and its Blueprint 2000 plan to reform public schools (emphasizing local control) as evidence of major reform. It is important to note, however, that Gaebler's comments were limited to the *adoption* of key reform ideas rather than their implementation or assessments of their effectiveness. As of August 1994, many of these reforms had not yet been fully implemented.

To date, the evidence is quite mixed on the impact of the numerous reforms adopted by the legislature, mostly in its FY 1993 budget. Audit and evaluation efforts thus far have noted difficulties in sorting out precise impacts due to inadequate time lines, baseline data, and the absence of rigorous empirically based performance indicators in the affected agencies and programs. Few, however, question the innovativeness of the ideas behind these reforms and the influence of the *Reinventing Government* principles.

Managed Health Care

Florida is constantly touted as a state in the forefront of health care reform. Clinton administration officials have examined the state's plan closely and are said to have borrowed heavily from it, which might be one of the reasons the legislature resisted proposals by Governor Chiles to expand the state's move toward universal health care during its 1994 legislative session. State legislators were facing reelection battles and had seen polls showing Floridians' declining support levels for Clinton and health care reform.

TABLE 9–3 Changes in Population, Economy, and Government: State of Florida, FY 1990–94

Type of Change	FY 1990	FY 1991	FY 1992	FY 1993	FY 1994
Population	12,686,340	13,132,744	13,369,500	13,568,356	13,868,400
Percent change	2.4	2.1	1.8	1.5	2.2
Consumer Price Index					
(1982–84 base)	127	134	138.3	142.6	146.6
Percent change	4.7	5.5	3.2	3.1	2.8
State Government					
Positions	131,833	137,216	134,135	137,657	141,371
Percent change	6.1	4.1	–2.2	2.6	2.7
Total Spending (thousands)	$23,211.52	27,743.52	28,862.66	31,722.29	35,466.30
Percent change	9.2	19.5	4.0	9.9	11.8

Source: Florida's Ten-Year Summary of Appropriations Data 1984–85 through 1993–94. Vol. 16, October 1, 1993, pp. 6–7.

In 1992, the legislature had enacted the Health Care Reform Act, which consolidated health care financing, purchasing, planning, and regulation of health care facilities, professionals, and cost containment into one agency, the Agency for Health Care Administration. The Agency then developed a Florida Health Plan. In 1993, the legislature passed the Health Care and Insurance Reform Act, directing the state to begin implementing health care reforms based on a managed competition model. Eleven Community Health Purchasing Alliances ("Chippas") were created and charged with assisting small businesses in pooling their purchasing power to purchase more affordable health insurance. Membership in the nonprofit alliances is voluntary and open to businesses with fewer than fifty employees. The alliances themselves do not sell insurance. They merely act as brokers and benefits managers between businesses and insurers.

Innumerable controversies arose over the composition of these boards, the most common being that they were too partisan and closely aligned with the health care industry. The final appointments were not completed until the fall of 1993, which delayed their review and selection of insurers until the spring of 1994. At the time this paper was written, there were no data available on the plans selected or the level of employer interest and participation.

In his FY 1995 budget, the governor had proposed going one step further and funding subsidies permitting uninsured Floridians to purchase insurance. This would have allowed him to achieve one of the goals of his Strategic Plan, namely the establishment of a system to ensure that all Floridians have access to quality and affordable primary health care by December, 1994—a universal coverage goal not likely to be met. His plan did not make it through the regular 1994 legislative session or a subsequent special session. One of the basic criticisms was that it came too quickly on the heels of the previous year's reforms, making it impossible to determine whether what had been done had been cost-effective.

Civil Service Reform

In its December 1991 special session, the legislature mandated reform of the state's Career Service System. It identified classification and pay, performance appraisal, and recruitment and selection as problem areas. The legislature authorized the development of a broad-based job classification system, elimination of cumbersome rules and procedures, establishment of better interagency communication, increased flexibility for agencies to manage, promotion of training in modern management principles such as Total Quality Management (TQM), merit-based performance rewards, and use of modern technology, among others.

These reforms have proceeded much more slowly than anticipated due to some union and employee resistance to changes concerning attendance and leave policies, work force reduction practices, position and pay reclassifications, quality management procurement, and merit rewards. These controversies surfaced during the deliberations of an appointed Civil Service Commission mandated by the legislature to report back recommendations to it by the end of 1991. According to one study, "There were real differences about what deregulation and decentralization would mean in practice, what kind and degree of reforms were feasible, and how reform would ultimately be carried out."[15] The pace of reforms was also slowed down by the normal delays accompanying organizational restructuring of a key departmental player (the merger of the Departments of General Services and Administration into one agency, the Department of Management Services).

Departmental Reorganizations and Management Reforms

An underlying premise of these reforms is that they can reduce unnecessary layers of management and eliminate or modify programs that have not provided necessary services to the public effectively and efficiently. The inference is that they will streamline the bureaucracy and improve agency productivity.

The high profile the governor's "downsizing" and "right-sizing" priorities received during the early days of his administration focused a great deal of attention on changes in state employee levels. His FY 1995 budget proposal summary reports that during FY 1992 over 7,000 FTE were cut, primarily as a result of the loss of revenue during a nationwide recession, followed by a reduction of 1,655 FTE in FY 93 and 823 FTE in FY 1994. In terms of fixed (no part-time) positions, there was a decline of 2.2 percent in FY 1992 but a 2.6 percent increase in FY 1993 and 2.7 percent in FY 1994. However, the governor has argued that even these increases were less steep than in previous years. But his critics pointed to more positions at higher salaries, negating the cost savings from cutting positions.

There were also complaints that departmental reorganizations and mergers soon resulted in requests for expanded, rather than streamlined, work forces. A FY 1995 budget request submitted to the legislature by the new Department of Environmental Protection (created by the merger of the Departments of Environmental Regulation and Natural Resources) requested 500 new employees. This agitated a number of lawmakers, including Democrats, who said they were not inclined to approve any new positions until the merger shows some substantive savings. The jury is still out on the effectiveness of the 1993 merger of the Department of Business Regulation with the Department of Professional Regulation to form the Department of Business and Professional Regulation. But the governor's FY 1995 budget indicated he intended to keep using the reorganization strategy.

Management flexibility pilot projects, authorized by the 1991 legislature and expanded by the 1992 legislature, have also generated mixed reviews thus far. The Departments of Revenue and State, and the Division of Workers Compensation in the Department of Labor and Employment Security, were granted temporary exclusion from restrictive state personnel and budget procedures. Managers were instructed to focus on outcomes, encouraged to determine the true costs of programs and to reduce waste, and given more flexibility over resources. The ultimate goal was to determine whether productivity could be improved under these conditions. Early evaluations concluded it was impossible to measure any productivity improvements because of "failure to establish and consistently use baselines and benchmarks and to devise measurement tools prior to the implementation of the pilot flexibility project." Nonetheless, the legislature has continued to support these projects, banking on the eventual success of a Productivity Advisory Group and the GAP (Government Accountability to the People) Commission, charged with devising adequate performance indicators and measurement techniques.

Educational Reforms: Blueprint 2000

The 1991 Florida legislature adopted distinct accountability acts for each of the educational delivery systems—public schools, community colleges, and the state university system. The major public focus has been on the plan for reform of the public schools known as Blueprint 2000. This plan created a statewide system of goals designed to return the responsibility for education to those closest to the students—the schools, teachers, and parents. The central component of Blueprint 2000 consists of seven goals:

- *Readiness to Start School.* Communities and schools collaborate to prepare children and families for children's success in school.
- *Graduation Rate and Readiness for Postsecondary Education and Employment.* Students graduate and are prepared to enter the work force and postsecondary education.
- *Student Performance.* Students successfully compete at the highest levels nationally and internationally and are prepared to make well-reasoned, thoughtful, and healthy lifelong decisions.
- *Learning Environment.* School boards provide a learning environment conducive to teaching and learning that includes appropriate educational materials, equipment, and pupil/teacher ratio.
- *School Safety and Environment.* Communities provide an environment that is drug-free and protects students' health, safety, and civil rights.
- *Teachers and Staff.* The schools, district, and state ensure professional teachers and staff.
- *Adult Literacy.* Adult Floridians are literate and have the knowledge and skills needed to compete in a global economy and exercise the rights and responsibilities of citizenship.

The act expanded the size and responsibility of the Commission on Education Reform and Accountability created by the legislature in its 1990 session. The commission was charged with such duties as observing the development and implementation of the school improvement plans, reviewing and analyzing the schools' initial needs assessment, and involving business in training teachers, administrators, and parents. It was mandated to recommend to the legislature and state board of education by October 1, 1992, such things as performance standards for indicating progress toward state and local goals, methods of measuring progress, guidelines for dealing with schools that do not improve after three consecutive years of assistance and intervention, and identifying statutes, rules, and policies that stand in the way of school improvement and should be repealed or modified.

Each school was assigned the responsibility for coming up with specific plans for how they intended to achieve the seven goals and how they would measure improvements. Teams of teachers, staff, parents, and community representatives spent months examining the school's needs before writing a plan. Each school was mandated to produce a needs assessment and needs response plan to the commission by November 1991. The commissioner of education was assigned responsibility for reporting to the legislature by January 1, 1992, the costs of accountability and the need for new assessment procedures and information systems.

The inaugural year of Blueprint 2000 was academic year 1993–1994. Just five months into the school year, the state's GAP Commission asked schools to conduct a midyear review of the program. Many school officials were upset, as represented in these comments of one: "To walk in in December or January or February and expect to find any tangible outcomes, that's ludicrous. Real school improvement, not quick fixes or blitzes, is going to take longer than that. Maybe three years, maybe five years." While there are some signs the program is working, the state still lags behind the nation in high school graduation rates, SAT scores, and other outcome indicators. School violence, dropouts, the influx of immigrants, inadequate instructional materials, and health of the student population remain major concerns. The good news is that Floridians strongly approve of putting more state funds into education. The bad news is that there's also evidence they are losing patience with the public schools and, to a lesser extent, institutions of higher education. This makes it difficult to argue for higher taxes earmarked for education.

Decentralization of HRS

The "too soon to tell" conclusion regarding the effectiveness of other reforms also applies to efforts to decentralize HRS. The overall purpose of decentralization of the Department of Health and Rehabilitative Services, approved by the legislature in its 1992 session, was to "move decision-making authority to the lowest practical level within the agency to improve services to clients through increased stakeholder and community ownership of the Department and its programs." HRS expanded its district offices from eleven to fifteen service districts and created Health and Human Services Boards in each district that were designed to be the focal point for district program and planning, budget development, and fiscal management as well as community involvement. Delays in creating these boards deterred decentralization, making any evaluations difficult.

Similar criticisms have been aimed at these boards as at the Chippas—too many "political" appointees with possible conflicts of interest. HRS continues to be plagued with a bad enough reputation that before the 1994 legislative session, the governor recommended a name change for the agency. The proposed name, Department of Family Services, was ultimately rejected by the legislature because it would cost too much and cause a lot of confusion. As it was, HRS was stripped of responsibility for two major functions: handling teenage crime and collecting child support from deadbeat parents. (The latter was transferred to the Department of Revenue and the former to a new Department of Juvenile Justice.)

Welfare Reform Experiments

Long concerned with sharply rising AFDC rolls, especially during the recession, the governor and legislature approved the Family Transition Program in the 1993 legislative session. The purpose of this program is to "move AFDC participants from dependence on society to independence that comes with self-sufficiency through employment." Two demonstration projects were authorized, one in Alachua and another in Escambia County (mandatory in the first, voluntary in the second).

In these counties, parents on AFDC are assigned randomly into the new program. They are given job training and receive child care and medical coverage. They can keep the first $200 they earn each month, plus half the rest, with no cut in their welfare check, compared to keeping $30 and one-third the remainder under current rules. They are permitted to accumulate up to $5,000 and have up to $8,150 equity in a car, so they can get themselves on their feet before leaving welfare. After two years, they will be taken off AFDC and will not be able to reapply for three years. The bottom line is that Florida, like other states and the president, is moving in the direction of giving welfare recipients an ultimatum: "Get a job, or hand over your welfare check."

These pilot programs were not put in place until early 1994, making any assessments of their effectiveness impossible at this point in time. (The first status report was not due until November 1, 1994.) This effort, like the state's managed competition health care reform, is perceived by national leaders as being quite innovative. In fact, the experiments required federal approval, granted in January 1994. The state's plan was carefully studied by federal officials devising President Clinton's welfare reform plan.

Sentencing Reforms

In May 1993, the legislature passed the Safe Streets Initiative, the first major reform of Sentencing Guidelines since their inception in 1983. It was primarily an effectiveness-oriented reform, designed to reserve prison space for violent and repeat offenders and to place nonviolent offenders (mostly first time drug users) in treatment programs. But its most notable change was to eliminate basic gain time for violent and repeat criminals. Under the old system, basic gain time reduced an offender's sentence by ten days for each month of the sentence. The reforms, which took effect January 1, 1994, reward gain time only for participation in education or other rehabilitative programs, exemplary of the state's effort to *prevent* recidivism. Estimates are that it will effectively increase the time inmates serve in prison by 33 percent. This means that these reforms will not save much, if any, money and, in effect, will take money away from spending for other state functions as the number of prison beds will likely expand. But it reflects attentiveness to strong public support for keeping violent criminals in jail.

These innovations are but a few of the major efforts the State of Florida has engaged in to improve its accountability and operational effectiveness and efficiency. There is little doubt that the state's fiscal crisis of the early 1990s prompted a closer look at how to make things work better. The crisis certainly highlighted the fact that the state had little performance data or objectives in place with which to evaluate itself and lagged behind the private sector in its adoption of new management techniques emphasizing team building from the grassroots up. The major fear is that many of these organizational and managerial approaches will not *really* significantly increase productivity unless genuine civil service reform takes place. But it is clear that these reforms *have* altered program structures and priorities. Strategic planning is making it easier for the public and elected officials to determine who the real winners and losers are under various budget proposals. It was not always so clear during the recession when virtually every agency could cite huge demand, or need, statistics.

THE RECESSION'S WINNERS AND LOSERS

It is hard to say there are any true winners when a state is experiencing a deep recession, particularly a fast-growing state where demands already outstripped revenues. However, there is a fairly strong consensus that state employees, public schools, community college and university students, and the in-need dependent populations, children and the elderly, were the biggest losers. There is also general agreement that the delays in major capital improvements and equipment were sure to cost Florida's taxpayers in the long-term. But they were the most politically palatable cuts to make at the time, all things considered.

State employees experienced "small or nonexistent" salary increases over this period. State employee salaries and benefits as a percent of the total budget fell each year from FY 1992–1995 (from 16.0 to 15.0, 14.2, and 14.0 percent), reflecting both salary freezes and personnel reductions, primarily through attrition. State employee salary increases did not keep pace with inflation at any point during the recession. State employee training, travel, and personal development opportunities were also cut back significantly. The governor's FY 1995 budget proposal reported that state agencies experienced substantial cuts in their training budgets during the recession. It also reported that since the state had adopted a requirement for supervisory training in 1988, only 6 percent of approximately 15,000 supervisors had received any training due to limited funds.

Florida's students, regardless of level, suffered considerably when deep budget cuts prompted cuts in the amount of money available from state and local funds for instructional materials. Library, including multimedia, and equipment funds were a prime target of the budget slicers from the elementary through the university levels. There is some evidence that tuition hikes kept some students from attending community colleges and universities. Following a significant tuition hike between FY 1991 and FY 1992, enrollment headcounts at four of the state's nine universities declined, including its two largest resident campuses (Florida State, University of Florida). There is also evidence that loss of funds for adjuncts and new hires reduced course availability, making it take longer to get complete a degree program.

Programs aimed at small, but needy, youth and elderly populations were among those most likely to feel the effects of budget reductions. As previously noted, a new program designed to keep troubled youth out of prison was axed before it was implemented. Changes in the eligibility requirements for a medically needy program provided at seventy-seven hospitals immediately rendered 7,800 of the people previously served by the program ineligible. A health care program aimed at providing trauma care for the indigent was cut. Prison educational programs were slashed, having a disproportionate impact on younger inmates. Planned programmatic expansions of the Department of Elder Affairs were put on hold. Cost-containment policies affected elderly access to nursing home care.

Rising caseloads for all the state's social services, in combination with hiring freezes and cutbacks, often meant poorer, less expeditious assistance to those in need, even when program funds were not cut. However, the state did everything possible to avoid making cuts until absolutely necessary, after virtually all plausible revenue alternatives had been exhausted. It also avoided total elimination of programs and opted for piecemeal reductions in a wide variety of programs. To their credit, the state's elected officials supported some prevention-oriented programs, especially in the education, health, and juvenile justice areas. But, inevitably, deserving and needy persons and localities suffered.

FLORIDA'S LESSONS FROM THE RECESSION OF THE 1990s

When individuals are having difficulty making ends meet, they tend to be more critical of government taxing and spending—and of the elected officials who must make such choices under the worst of circumstances. This was certainly the case in Florida. The worse the economy got, the angrier the public became. Job performance ratings of the governor and the legislature plummeted. Survey after survey found that the public preferred cutting spending first before raising new revenue. Of course this was not possible but this preference unquestionably affected the choices that lawmakers ultimately made in response to the fiscal crisis. It certainly explained their preference for a "reality" as opposed to an "investment" budget when posed with a choice between the two.

On the revenue side, the choice was to make only incremental changes in tax policy. It is clear from this study that even the deepest of recessions will not prompt major tax reform in the State of Florida. (Will there ever be a good time?) Discussions of imposing a state income tax got nowhere. Likewise, a plan to lift a whole slew of exemptions to the state sales tax (the premier revenue source) got little support when proposed en masse. It appears that the only way to lift these exemptions is to remove them a few at a time. This incremental, "back door" approach to the reimposition of a state sales tax on services that was revoked in 1987 appears to be the only politically viable one.

The state's lawmakers relied on many of the standard revenue enhancement techniques. Among these were: raising numerous fees, fines, and charges incrementally; hitting the "sin taxes" (cigarette, liquor, lottery) hardest; eliminating exemptions and loopholes; earmarking tax increases to popular programs, most notably roads, prisons, and education; and sharply increasing taxes and fees that hit the "constituents" least likely to have the political clout to fight them (tourists, newcomers to the state, college students).

Anything that allowed elected officials to claim that they had not raised or imposed taxes that would hit the electorate-at-large (only narrow portions thereof) was popular. Borrowing also emerged as a revenue-raising alternative. Prior to the 1990s, Florida was not a very heavy user of bonds to finance public improvements. It still is not, but borrowing, which began in earnest under Governor Martinez, has continued under Governor Chiles.

The study also shows that Florida may be headed down the same path as California in terms of citizen-led initiatives and referenda. The number of constitutional amendments with a fiscal restraint flavor is increasing. The state's legislators are increasingly willing to "let the voters decide" when the choices are really tough. More and more, citizen groups are up to the challenge of putting issues directly on the ballot. Fiscal constraint measures that make it to the ballot usually pass handily.

On the spending side of the budgetary ledger, it was obvious that the cuts were made where the money was. The bulk of Florida's budget is allocated to three functions—education, human services, and transportation. (In 1993, human services surpassed education largely as a function of steep growth rates in the entitlement programs, especially Medicaid.) Thus, when deep cuts had to be made, these functions were targeted most intensely. Typically, the pattern was to restore cuts made in one legislative session the next session, then cut in "new" areas— a "moving target" approach to cutting. Rarely were cuts made to the exact same programs in subsequent sessions.

Of course many of the specific budget cutting techniques were the old "tried and trues": eliminating vacant positions, freezing or canceling scheduled pay raises, delaying infrastructure improvements, changing eligibility requirements and funding formulas, delaying or canceling equipment purchases, and eliminating newly created programs lacking ardent constituencies. The "robbing Peter to pay Paul" syndrome also prevailed, as time after time, one fund was raided to cover deficits in another.

Perhaps most surprising was the receptivity of legislators to new program emphases. It was apparent that new spending aimed at employee productivity enhancement, better workload and cost-per-unit data collection and analysis, risk avoidance, prevention (especially in the education, social service, and criminal justice areas), and more efficient financial administration had a fairly good chance of being adopted, at least in part, if proposed. At this point, it appears that one of the most significant outcomes of the state's fiscal crisis was support for the notion of preventive, rather than just reactive, spending.

Once the recession hit, it quickly became apparent to lawmakers that to make wise choices, they needed more detailed information on program efficiency and effectiveness than was normally available. The consequences of inadequate contingency plans and long-range forecasts also became quite clear. Many of the private sector members of the various task forces formed during this period to address the state's many problems were mind-boggled at the absence of "bottom line" figures and workload statistics.

The utility of large appointed task forces was another important lesson learned from this period. Without question, the Florida Taxation and Budget Reform Commission, the Governor's Commission for Government by the People, the Partners in Productivity Task Force on Productivity Measurement and Quality Improvement, the GAP Commission, and others with narrower foci conducted studies that were of extremely high quality and filled with incredibly detailed recommendations. Many of these suggestions made their way into the governor's budget proposals, the legislature's appropriations acts, and the Florida Statutes. Their suggestions resulted in significant changes in state government operations, especially in the budgeting and financial management arenas. While some legislators may not believe these changes have improved the budget process noticeably, users of financial and budgetary information, such as academics, advocacy groups, and common citizens have applauded improvements in the format, quality, and timeliness of the data available for analysis. Major taxpayer watchdog groups like Florida TaxWatch have strongly endorsed the trend toward program budgeting, productivity measurement, and outcomes assessment.

It is still too soon to know what the real long-term effects of the multitude of reorganizations, management and program reforms, and incentives adopted during this period will be. It may well be that the greatest impact will be on improving decision-making processes and enhancing accountability to the taxpayers rather than real cost savings.

In summary, Florida's experiences during the recession of the 1990s, while extremely painful, taught the state some important lessons that should help it avert going down the same path when the next one hits.

NOTES

1. Around 70 percent of the state's general revenue comes from sales taxes, followed by the corporate income tax (7 percent), and beverage taxes (4 percent), intangibles taxes (4 percent), miscellaneous others (4 percent), documentary stamp taxes (3 percent), insurance premium taxes (2 percent), estate taxes (2 percent), and cigarette taxes (1 percent). Figures are for FY 1994–1995.

2. Lawsuits were filed and, as a consequence, the implementation of this amendment has been delayed for several years. The problem was that the wording of the amendment did not include an implementation date.

3. For a discussion of this vote, see Susan A. MacManus, "Enough is Enough: Floridians' Support for Proposition 3 Limiting State Mandates on Local Government," *State and Local Government Review* 24 (Fall 1992):103–112.

4. For a discussion of the problems of the revenue raising problems of Florida's small cities and counties, see Susan A. MacManus, "Local Government Revenue Diversification: A Comparison of High-Growth and Low-Growth Rural Jurisdictions in Florida," in Advisory Commission on Intergovernmental Relations, *Local Government Revenue Diversification: Rural Economies* (Washington, DC: U.S. Advisory Commission on Intergovernmental Relations, March 1990, SR 13), pp. 31–65.

5. For a comprehensive overview of changes in Florida's partisan landscape, see the collection of articles in Susan A. MacManus, ed., *Reapportionment and Representation in Florida: A Historical Collection.* (Tampa, FL: Intrabay Innovation Institute, University of South Florida, 1991).

6. Susan A. MacManus and Lesa Chihak, "The 1992 State Legislative Reapportionment: An Overview of the Outcomes Under the New Plan," *Governing Florida* 4 (Fall/Winter 1993):21–27.

7. William Earle Klay, Joanne R. Snair, and Gloria A. Grizzle, "Tax Reform in Florida: Lessons From the Past," *Governing Florida* 2 (Spring 1992):12–17.

8. According to 1992 figures, the service sector is Florida's largest employer, constituting 31.6 percent of total nonfarm employment. The second largest sector is wholesale and retail trade, 26.4 percent, followed by government, 16.3 percent; manufacturing, 9.0 percent; finance, insurance, and real estate, 6.6 percent; transportation, communications and public utilities, 5.1 percent; construction, 4.9 percent; and mining, 0.1 percent. State of Florida, *Official Bond Statement for State Board of Education Full Faith and Credit Public Education Capital Outlay Bonds, 1992 Series E*, January, 18, 1994.

9. See Florida TaxWatch, *How Florida Compares* (Tallahassee, FL: Florida TaxWatch, November 1992). The study reported that on the basis of per capita taxes, Florida usually ranks between thirty-seventh and thirty-ninth. However, it is important to note that the state is also regarded by some as a low-tax state only for the wealthy. A study of taxes from 1985 to 1991 by the Citizens for Tax Justice, a private, nonpartisan group, found Florida to be among the ten states with the lowest state and local tax burden on the wealthiest. Its tax burden on the poorest is the same as the national average. The major reason for the inequity is the absence of a state personal income tax and heavier reliance on sales taxes (a more regressive tax source). David Dahl, "Rich Reap Tax Benefits in Florida," *St. Petersburg Times*, April 23, 1991, pp. 1–2A.

10. The governor vetoed the prison building plan and called the legislature back into special session to expand the number of prison beds. He again pushed for the cigarette tax hike but it again failed because additional revenues emerged as a consequence of the state overestimating Medicaid costs.

11. Mary Kay Falconer, Lynda K. Barrow, and Steven O'Cain, "Local Government Revenues Post 1993 Legislative Session: A Combination of New and Improved," *Florida State University Law Review* 21 (Fall 1993): 585–616.

12. The state budget director acknowledged that since the introduction of the lottery, the proportion of state tax dollars going to education dropped from 62 to 53 percent. Charlotte Sutton, "'We Don't Know What We're Doing,'" *St. Petersburg Times*, October 10, 1991. Also see Susan A. MacManus, "State Lotteries Aren't a Windfall for Education," *The Wall Street Journal*, February 14, 1989; and David R. Williams, "Florida's Lottery: An Education Shell Game," *Florida Trend* 34 (February 1992): 9–10.

13. One of the proposals seriously considered by the Florida Taxation and Budget Reform Commission was to offer voters the chance to adopt a state income tax in exchange for reductions in the local property tax.

14. In March of 1993, the Florida Supreme Court ruled that the legislators had broken a contract between the state and the unions when they took back an agreed-upon 3 percent raise. The court also ruled that the pay agreement contract was only binding for the FY 1992 budget year, limiting the amount

of money workers could retrieve and greatly reducing the state's obligation. Phil Whillon, "Court Rules State Can't Renege on Wage Increase," *The Tampa Tribune*, March 12, pp. 1,9.

15. Barton Wechsler, "The Failure of Reform: Reinventing Florida's Civil Service System." *Review of Public Personnel Administration* 14 (Spring 1994): 64–76.

10

Massachusetts: Downsizing State Government

Bruce A. Wallin*

The Commonwealth of Massachusetts has garnered a lot of attention since 1988. The presidential bid of Governor Michael Dukakis called attention to the so-called "Massachusetts Miracle," the period of unprecedented growth in the state's economy and income that occurred in the 1980s. The "miracle," like most biblical miracles, was unfortunately not long lasting, and the defeated presidential contender returned home to find the state's economy in a free-fall, with state revenues in rapid pursuit.

In the gubernatorial campaign of 1990, Boston University president John Silber, the Democratic nominee, brought an "angry man" approach to the stump, promising to rock the boat of state government if elected. If Silber wanted to rock the boat, his long-shot Republican opponent, former federal prosecutor William Weld, wanted to sink it, or to use his own rhetoric, "steer rather than row the ship of state." He promised to cut $2 billion out of a $13 billion budget should the tax-cutting voter-initiated Question 3 pass.

For Massachusetts, the unthinkable happened—the Republican won and carried in a "veto-proof" senate to boot. Since January of 1991, all eyes have been focused on Weld's attempt to "reinvent government" in Massachusetts and shed it of its reputation as "Taxachusetts."

This chapter evaluates the progress of that attempt. It begins with a discussion of the causes of Massachusetts' fiscal problems and an overview of actions taken for fiscal years 1989 through 1994. It reviews expenditure trends in general and in specific budget categories before considering revenue policies. It summarizes the more innova-

---

*Bruce A. Wallin is an Assistant Director of Political Science at Northeastern University.

tive budget policies the state (and the governor in particular) have pursued in their attempts to make Massachusetts government more productive and efficient before concluding with an analysis of budget winners and losers.

CAUSES OF THE MASSACHUSETTS FISCAL PROBLEM

To paraphrase Charles Dickens, Massachusetts in the 1980s experienced "the best of times, the worst of times." The tremendous economic growth in the state, the Massachusetts Miracle hawked by presidential contender Michael Dukakis, raised incomes and expectations, only to have them both dashed by the national economic downturn. While the short-term fiscal problem can largely be attributed to the recession, Massachusetts voters and elected officials made things worse.

Throughout the 1970s, Massachusetts trailed the rest of the nation in employment growth, with nonagricultural employment increasing 19.1 percent compared to the national average of 27 percent.[1] From 1971 to 1977, Massachusetts unemployment averaged 1.25 percent higher than the nation, and in 1980 average earnings in the manufacturing sector were 10 percent below the average.

All this changed drastically in the early 1980s, as outlined in a McCormack Institute report:

> The unusually strong growth that the Massachusetts economy experienced from 1980–87, evidenced by low unemployment and high personal income, resulted from both a fortuitous series of favorable events and the historical development of the New England region, which provided the economy with a unique opportunity for expansion. The initial impetus came from the federal military buildup, beginning the late 1970s, and accelerating through the first half of the 1980s. During this period, orders for defense goods tripled, and Massachusetts received more than double the national average of prime contracts awarded by the U.S. Department of Defense. At the same time, the demand for minicomputers accelerated, benefiting the computer companies in this region that had a dominant position in the market.
>
> As the surge from the computer and defense industries was slowing, the financial services segment of the state economy

began its own boom. The stock and bond bull markets, financial product innovation, and deregulation of the financial markets all combined to create an enormous increase in the demand for financial services. Growth in medical services and in research and development and large increases in revenue flowing into the colleges and universities also bolstered the region's economy.[2]

What goes up, often comes down. A drastic slowdown in federal expenditures in the state, combined with some bad business decisions by some of the state's largest employers (Wang thought personal computers would never make it), pushed the state economy into a free-fall. The recession compounded matters. Between 1988 and 1991, the Massachusetts economy lost approximately 350,000 jobs.

If state government had been more frugal during the 1980s, the effect of the economic downturn on the state fiscal condition would have been greatly moderated. However, Massachusetts elected officials had their party hats on for much of the 1980s. The increase in state spending per capita in Massachusetts between 1981 and 1988 was 47 percent, the second largest increase in the nation. This helped lay the foundation for a structural budget deficit.

Much of the increase in spending was in the form of increased state aid to local governments, an attempt to lessen the local impact of Proposition 2½. A voter-initiated ballot measure, it required that a city or town's property taxes not exceed 2½ percent of total assessed value. Many locales were above that percentage. Further, no matter what the current effective tax rate, property tax revenue was not to increase by more than 2½ percent per year. As a result, the property tax yield fell by $311 million, or approximately 10 percent, the following year.

The state helped fill the gap by increasing state aid by $243 million in fiscal year 1982, a 21.3 percent increase. The state largesse continued throughout most of the decade, with aid growing 136 percent in nominal dollars between fiscal year 1981 and fiscal year 1989. While this generosity was welcomed by local governments and local residents, it placed a burden on the state budget once the economy and revenue growth slowed.

The rise in Medicaid spending also produced a structural gap. Massachusetts was among the most generous states in terms of the options it offered recipients, and the general level of medical costs is extremely high. The economic downturn expanded the caseload from 445,509 in 1988 to 650,000 in 1993. Annual increases in the Medicaid budget were over 15 percent from fiscal year 1988–1992. Overruns occurred nearly every year, with the largest in fiscal year 1989.

In the short run, then, it was the economy that really propelled the state into a fiscal corner. In the medium term, the increase in Medicaid spending pressure was an important factor. But over the decade, the strong increase in state spending, compounded by the Proposition 2½ tax limit, made matters much worse.

OVERVIEW BY FISCAL YEAR

Fiscal Years 89 and 90: The Recession Hits Early and Hard

While battling in the Democratic primaries, Michael Dukakis saw the clouds gathering as his office shepherded his fiscal year 1989 budget through the legislature. By the New York primary on April 15, he was called back to Boston and told by his Department of Revenue that revenues were slowing. With the legislature, Dukakis cut about $200 million from his original budget proposal, approximately $90 million of it from local aid. By the time of his defeat in November, the prospective deficit for fiscal year 1989 had nonetheless climbed to $130 million in a $12.8 billion budget, led by overruns in Medicaid expenditures.

The excess of expenditures over revenues for fiscal year 1989 was $672 million, and after applying the prior year's fund balance, the commonwealth ended fiscal year 1989 with a $319 million deficit. In response to a related cash deficit, the state treasurer deferred until fiscal year 1990 certain fiscal disbursements, including approximately $305 million in local aid.[3]

In July of 1989, the legislature authorized borrowing of up to $475 million due January 31, 1991, and Medicaid borrowings and expenditures to pay $488 million previously owed Medicaid providers. Local aid was cut $210 million, although eventually the Massachusetts Supreme Judicial Court ordered it reinstated. Cities and towns, however, didn't begin to receive this money until June 1990.

A large tax package was also enacted at this time to help close the present and future gaps. Legislation raised the flat income tax rate from 5 percent to 5.375 percent for tax year 1989 and to 5.75 percent for tax year 1990. The funds from these increases were to be credited to two non-budgeted funds, to be used solely for deficit reduction and Medicaid-related borrowings. These tax changes were estimated to increase commonwealth tax receipts by approximately $445 and $298 million for fiscal year 1990 and fiscal year 1991, respectively.

The governor also vetoed certain provisions of the fiscal year 1990 budget, including $273 million in appropriations, one of which caused the commonwealth to default on a payment of $2.5 million due on a general obligation bond to the Massachusetts Community Development Finance Corporation.[4] While a supplemental appropriation to cover the payment was made about two weeks later, Wall Street took notice.

It still wasn't enough. With job losses mounting, revenues continued to fall. The state ultimately experienced a statutory budget deficit of $1.1 billion dollars for fiscal year 1990. Approved in July of 1990, deficit resolution bonds of $1.416 billion were issued to redress the situation in the near future, sending the amount borrowed over two years to over $2 billion. The debt was initially to be paid in seven years, placing a strain on the budget and making future state debt payment a "budget buster." In order to conserve cash, the commonwealth deferred until fiscal year 1991 the payment of approximately $1.26 billion in local aid due in fiscal year 1990.

The Acts of 1990 further raised the income tax rate to 5.95 percent for tax year 1990 and then to 6.25 percent for tax year 1991, with a return to 5.95 percent for tax year 1992 and subsequent years. The legislature also expanded the sales tax base to a variety of services, including professional services such as legal, accounting, engineering, and architectural services, and more than 500 smaller repair, personal, and business services. The tax was viewed by many as unwieldy, as it was designed to hit only businesses, and not individuals, making it difficult to administer. An exemption for small businesses further complicated its administration. While most of this sales tax expansion was later repealed, the tax on telecommunications services and on electricity, gas, and steam for certain nonresidential uses remains in effect. The legislation raised the motor fuels tax six cents in 1990 and four cents in 1991. Finally, the commonwealth's tax on interest from non-Massachusetts banks, dividends, and net capital gains was raised from 10 percent to 12 percent (after a 50 percent deduction). The increases were estimated to add $700 million and $894 million to state revenue for fiscal year 1991 and fiscal year 1992, respectively.

The fiscal year 1991 budget projected expenditures and revenues of approximately $13.7 billion. The budget cut $337 million in local aid, including the previously reinstated $210 million. Soon more pessimistic revenue reports rolled in, with income tax proceeds revised to be $980 million less than budgeted, and sales revenue off $210 million.

As deficit estimates kept increasing during his final months, Dukakis made nearly monthly spending cuts, mostly across the board, as he went out the door. He "takes credit" for cutting 11,000 positions, of which 8200 were full time. By not filling vacancies, "only" 1200 real people were terminated.

In retrospect, Dukakis feels that the state should have been a little more frugal during the good times.[5] In particular, he cites the fact that he and the legislature should have set aside more in "rainy day funds," although no one could see the economic handwriting on the wall. He also feels that the state may have been too generous with local aid, although they felt it necessary given the constraints put on cities and towns by 1980's Proposition 2½. In particular, several commentators have noted that, since much of this increase in local aid went to enhance the salaries of teachers and public safety workers, at least union contract concessions should have been obtained.

Massachusetts critics of Dukakis feel that he was less than candid with the citizens of the commonwealth during his 1988 run for president—that he withheld information on the growing deficit and failed to take the painful action necessary to remedy it, in order to further his electoral hopes. While many wanted to blame the governor turned losing presidential contender, the economy of Massachusetts would have gone into decline whoever was in office. The commonwealth lost 350,000 jobs between December of 1988 and 1991 (4 percent of its nonagricultural base in 1989–1990, and another 5½ percent in 1990–1991), and therein lies the primary cause of its budget problems. And while many wanted to blame Dukakis, he was not governor of New Hampshire, Rhode Island, and Maine, whose economies and budgetary health were soon to follow.

In sum, the major response to the fiscal year 1989 and fiscal year 1990 budget deficits was on the revenue side—tax increases and borrowing, with a fairly substantial reduction in local aid and some other relatively minor expenditure cuts. The budget problem was seemingly perceived to be short term.

Fiscal Years 1991–1994: The Weld Era

In November of 1990, William Weld won a close victory over Boston University President John Silber. Weld painted himself as a "new Republican," liberal on social issues such as abortion and the environment, yet fiscally conservative. Running on the same ballot as a Citizens for Limited Taxation voter initiative, Question 3, which would have repealed the 1989 tax increases, Weld promised to enforce it entirely through spending cuts (approximately $2 billion) should he be elected. Trailing substantially in the polls in September, he benefited from a series of missteps and angry outbursts from his opponent to win the election. While Question 3 lost handily, Weld won and reaffirmed his "no new taxes" pledge.

To the victor went the fiscal spoils. Even with the cuts Dukakis had made during the last months of his term, Governor Weld's new team estimated in January that the commonwealth needed $850 million in budget balancing measures to finish fiscal year 1991 in balance. The governor proposed administrative and legislative actions to address the deficit. Included was the use of Section 9C of Chapter 29 of the General Laws, which allows the governor to reduce allotments, where legally allowed.

The legislature also approved a state employee furlough program, with onetime savings estimated at $71 million. Employees were offered three choices, depending upon their level of compensation. Employees would not be paid for anywhere from two to fifteen days. In June of 1991 state employees took their furloughs. In the next fiscal year, fiscal year 1992, the legislature used a supplemental budget to pay back $10.8 million to certain, generally higher-paid, employees who had opted to work without pay.

In sum, it was estimated that Weld's spending reductions totaled $484 million for fiscal year 1991, and when added to those of the departing Dukakis, produced a total reduction of nearly $850 million. The Massachusetts Taxpayers Foundation estimated that approximately $800 million of the expenditure reductions and revenue increases (including the much ballyhooed $230 million projected from the sale of state property that never happened), were onetime shots, thus postponing the inevitable restructuring.

The new administration also took advantage of the now widely known loophole in Medicaid reimbursement. By filing an amendment to its state Medicaid plan, it could claim 50 percent reimbursement on uncompensated care payments provided to certain hospitals. The resulting $513 million infusion of federal funds was timely. It is worth noting that Governor Weld rewarded the state worker who found the loophole with a $10,000 bonus, an interesting and innovative idea, and one which naturally flows from a private sector/entrepreneurial/ motivational perspective.

The commonwealth ended fiscal year 1991 with a surplus of $237 million, even though spending ballooned from a budgeted $13.7 billion to $13.9 billion, and Governor Weld was indeed able to claim that he accomplished it without a tax increase. Further, he could take credit for pushing the legislature into repealing most of the controversial extension of the 5 percent sales tax to a variety of services the day after it took effect in March of 1991. The repeal legislation called for vendors who had collected any sales or use taxes on the one day the tax was in effect to make a reasonable effort to return the taxes to purchasers of the services.

Before enactment under Dukakis, the tax's constitutionality had been challenged in court; it was ultimately determined to be legal. Weld, however, considered the proposal antibusiness and pushed for its repeal. This roughly $113 million tax cut for fiscal year 1991 ($166 million in fiscal year 1992) was the only reported state tax cut in the nation that year.

It is also important to emphasize that a good part of the success in producing a surplus was due to the huge tax increases passed by Dukakis and the legislature in 1989, most of which were *not* offered for repeal by the Weld administration, and the $513 million Medicaid windfall.

In putting together his first budget from scratch, Governor Weld took an interesting tack. Using the most pessimistic economic projections he could find (a 7.7 percent decrease),[6] Weld introduced a budget that he said must address a projected $781 million deficit. He pegged the overall expenditure target at $13 billion, roughly an 8 percent cut from the previous year. He wielded the sword of "looming junk bond status" (Massachusetts had the lowest credit rating in the country) to repel talk of tax increases or further borrowing.

Thus pledging sober management, painful cuts, and a resolute opposition to taxes, Weld pursued several expenditure reductions, including a major cut in the state's General Relief welfare program, removing ex-offenders, undocumented immigrants, persons over 45 without a significant work history (Dukakis also tried to eliminate this category in 1980, 1982, and 1990), and families with stepparent or grandparent income, with estimated savings of $55 million, nearly a 30 percent cut; further local aid cuts; cuts in higher education; an increase in fares in the MBTA (public transit);[7] and furloughs, deferred pay raises, and increased contributions for health care from state employees.

The legislature, while cooperative on most issues, did override the governor's reduction for state employee health care, which would have resulted in increasing employee and retiree shares from 10 to 25 percent of the premium, noting that these workers had not received a pay raise in three years. But the two items that really covered the alleged deficit were a cut of $348 million in local aid, and the use of $462 million of gas tax revenue supposedly earmarked for highways to cover the general fund shortfall. Budgeted expenditures were approximately $13.4 billion.

In general, then, the losers were local governments, who had their state support reduced yet again, welfare (General Relief) recipients, who were cut off the rolls, state employees who had pay raises deferred and faced furloughs, and higher education students, who had their tuition raised to help make up for cuts in state support. The governor can't take all of the credit (or blame): the legislature cut even more than the governor on both local aid and welfare, waiting for a backlash that never came. Peter Nessen, Weld's Secretary of Administration and Finance, was amazed at the lack of criticism from local officials.[8] While Weld did have a veto-proof senate, it seems that the prevailing political winds were blowing in a fiscally conservative direction.

With DRI estimating that the Weld administration revenue estimate for fiscal year 1992 could be $1 billion low, and the conservative Massachusetts Taxpayer Foundation estimating in January 1991 that tax revenues were already $462 million ahead of the amount budgeted, the spending dike was bound to break. And with some expenditure accounts going out slower than appropriated, there was room for more spending. Supplemental appropriations included $33 million as emergency aid to schools, $20 million for health programs, and $10 million for tourism and convention purposes. Medicaid expenses were $269 million over the amount budgeted, but that still totaled to a mere 1.9 percent increase over fiscal year 1991, compared to what had been a 19 percent annual growth rate for fiscal years 1988–1991. Tax revenues finally came in a positive 5.4 percent, as opposed to the administration's estimate of minus 7.7 percent.[9]

Fiscal year 1992 ended with the commonwealth having spent $13.9 billion, a very modest decline in nominal terms from the previous year, but a decline, nonetheless. The ending balance of $549 million was better than fiscal year 1991. Indeed, the Massachusetts Taxpayer Foundation noted that "1992 was the first year since 1987 that the state spent within its annual revenue stream."[10]

The bond rating, which had suffered from the need to borrow to cover operating expenses, improved. The state's ratings had been slashed seven times in 1989, to BBB, causing significant increases in the state's borrowing costs. In 1991, although the threat was there, the state's bond rating never did fall to junk bond status.

Critics pointed out that little meaningful expenditure reform had been put in place, and that the budget had been balanced by moving from the across-the-board cuts of Dukakis to the "across the state" cuts (local aid) of Weld. While the state's bond rating did improve, nine cities and towns had theirs downgraded. Medicaid reform was on the way, however.

On January 22, 1992, Governor Weld submitted a fiscal year 1993 budget recommendation of $13.992 billion, a negligible increase from the actual fiscal year 1992 budget, but nearly $1 billion more than he had proposed for the previous year.

In projecting tax revenues of $9.15 billion, or .8 percent less than the previous year, the budget was partly constrained by the scheduled drop in the personal income tax rate, from 6.25 percent to 5.95 percent, which took effect January 1, 1992, and that would cost the commonwealth $210 million in revenues; Governor Weld's budget proposal to roll it back to 5.75 percent, which would have cost another $140 million; and proposed new tax credits for college tuition and elderly health insurance premiums, which would have further reduced revenues by approximately $52 million.

The legislature balked at both the economic model, wary of last year's "trick estimate," and the proposed income tax cut, and adopted a revenue estimate of $9.685 billion.

Among Governor Weld's spending initiatives were $186 million in local aid targeted for education reform; an increase of $72 million (11.4 percent) for state police and prisons; and $28 million in additional spending for human service programs.

On the revenue side, the budget again assumed sale of assets that would generate $45 million, which for the second year in a row failed to happen. The budget also assumed payment of $80 million from the MWRA (water authority) in return for future commitments.

Governor Weld, a self-proclaimed "filthy supply-sider," submitted an "economic stimulus plan," in an attempt to attract and retain businesses. As noted above, included was a cut in the personal income tax rate from 5.95 percent to 5.75 percent, which did not pass. The legislature did agree to triple the investment tax credit (from 1 percent to 3 percent), costing $50 million; to an emerging technology fund of $15 millon; and to $500,000 for youth service corps job training.

On November 17, 1992, the legislature approved a three-year increase in wages for state employees, 6 percent during the remainder of fiscal year 1993, and approximately 7 percent for fiscal year 1994. This added $39.8 million to the commonwealth's budget for fiscal year 1993, and an estimated $173.8 million for fiscal 1994. The governor vetoed this, offering a smaller increase, but his veto was overridden on December 21, offering state employees a nice holiday gift.

Real spending rose substantially in fiscal year 1993, up about 8.8 percent for fiscal year 1993, vs. a 2.4 percent estimate for the other states. Final expenditures were $15.2 billion, and the state ended the year with a surplus of $562 million, the third surplus in a row.[11]

The bad news for Massachusetts as it entered calendar 1993 was that it had lost 420,000 jobs since 1988; the good news was that the Massachusetts economy had stopped losing jobs in June 1992. Indeed, for the first time in many years the unemployment rate in the commonwealth dropped below that of the nation. During fiscal year 1993, the commonwealth's credit rating was upgraded by Standard and Poor's and Moody's to A, upgrades from BBB and Baa respectively. (On October 13, 1993, Standard and Poor's and Fitch Investors Service would raise the state bond rating to A-plus, putting Massachusetts ahead of Louisiana and New York and tied with West Virginia out of the forty-one states that issue general obligation bonds.[12])

The bad news for Governor Weld? In the fall elections he had lost a veto-proof state senate.

Governor Weld's budget proposal for fiscal year 1994 sounded the first shot in the 1994 gubernatorial campaign. The $15.2 billion budget represented a 1.6 percent increase ($232 million) over budgeted expenditures for fiscal year 1993, but had some new spending proposals, with a little bit for everyone, as well as some spending cuts. The proposal was structurally balanced, not using any leftover revenues from fiscal year 1993 and reflected a reduction in the reliance on onetime measures.

Some spending additions could be seen as politically motivated, including $175 million more on human services, and although $128 million of it went to Medicaid increases, much of the rest was in response to one of the most vocal anti-Weld lobbies, the human services advocates. He also added $122 million to the higher education budget, where his previous cuts had also drawn much negative press.

For the blatantly political, he proposed a $20 million tax credit for college tuition (with a $70 maximum), $35 million for a tax credit for health insurance premiums for the elderly (about $25 each), and a reduction in driver's license fees of $28 million (about $10 each). A little for all, in other words.

A positive direction in the governor's budget proposal was an emphasis on prevention programs, totaling $84.5 million in new spending. Included were an additional $7 million for the Women, Infants and Children program; $7.7 million in domestic violence prevention; $8.7 million for the homeless mentally ill; and $5 million for AIDS prevention, mostly for increased education. The governor's budget also called for $19 million in new antismoking spending, using some of the earmarked money from the cigarette tax (increased from twenty-six cents per pack to fifty-one cents), a voter initiative in November 1992. This represents a small portion of the $107 million the tax increase was expected to produce.

The Office of the Treasurer estimated that the governor's budget recommended $313.8 million in increased spending for priority program expansions, maintained current service levels for most programs, which—along with increased medical costs, entitlement growth, higher debt service payments, and salary increases—added approximately $733 million in new spending.[13] It also estimated that the governor's proposed budget reflected aggregate spending reductions of $517 million.

What helped fund this generosity? The bottoming out of job losses and some refinancing of state bonds, which took advantage of much lower interest rates, seemed to play a part, but the upcoming 1994 campaign seemed to have lessened the governor's spending phobia.

For the third consecutive year the governor's budget included revenues from the sale of certain state assets ($51 million), including the state transportation building in Boston. For the third time, this did not occur. He also included $50 million from the establishment of new video poker and keno games, which the legislature approved. The most recent estimate is that keno will produce between $7 to $10 million. Finally, there was a onetime revenue estimate of $20 million for corporate tax amnesty.

One thing originally left out of the governor's budget was $175 million in additional funds for fiscal year 1994 for elementary and secondary education reform. He also cut the $185 million he had offered for fiscal year 1993, since the legislature had been unable to reach agreement on school reform. When the legislature did finally pass it, the state had to come up with $360 million.

The final budget approved by the legislature was $15.5 billion, higher than the governor's recommendation by approximately $200–$300 million. It included the $360 million in school aid the governor omitted. Support for colleges and the university system was not increased, home care for the elderly was cut below current services, and state employees were to increase their share of health care premiums from 10 percent to 15 percent.

As the Massachusetts Taxpayer Foundation noted, spending for all other programs was $100 million *below* what the governor recommended.[14] This represents a remarkable turnaround for the legislature from previous years, and suggests that at least for the moment, fiscal sanity may be the norm. The governor and the legislature restrained themselves to "only" $250 million in supplemental spending, down from $400 million and $900 million in extra spending the previous two years. It was reported on July 2, 1994 that fiscal year 1994 preliminarily closed with estimated expenditures of $15.7 billion and a $28 million surplus. Three consecutive years of budgets in the black is a long way from 1988. The fiscal year 1995 budget as passed by the legislature calls for spending $16.38 billion, an increase of approximately 4 percent.

Adding up the estimated current year operating deficits encountered during fiscal years 1988 to 1991 produces a sum of −$2.5 billion (Table 10–1). On a statutory basis, two years, fiscal year 1989 and fiscal year 1990, ended with a combined actual deficit of $1.4 billion. Most of this was made up on the revenue side, initially with borrowing, followed by the Dukakis era tax increases, the Medicaid windfall, and a stronger revenue stream due to an improving economy. Governor Weld and the legislature showed great fiscal restraint in the

TABLE 10–1   Massachusetts Budgeted Operating Funds, Statutory Basis
(in millions)

	FY88	FY89	FY90	FY91	FY92	FY93 (est)
Total Revenues and Other	11,467	12,308	12,223	13,913	14,226	15,205
Total Expenditures and Other	11,837	12,981	13,474	13,934	13,913	15,192
Excess (Deficiency) of Rev. and Other Sources Over Exp. and Other Uses	(369.9)	(672.5)	(1,251.5)	(21.2)	312.3	(13.0)
Ending Fund Balances	353.2	(319.3)	(1,104.4)	237.1	549.4	562

Source: Fiscal 1988–1992, Office of the Comptroller. Estimated Fiscal 1993, Executive Office for Administration and Finance.

fiscal year 1992 budget, but expenditure growth bounced back in fiscal year 1993, and slowed again in fiscal year 1994. It is difficult to find a pattern.

While Governor Weld has a reputation as a big tax cutter, it is overblown. The biggest cut was the already scheduled rollback of the personal income tax rate. It is the tax increases of 1990 and the improving economy that keep the budget in balance, as the state treasurer estimates that they produced $865 million for fiscal year 1993 alone. Details of important expenditure and revenue trends follow.

EXPENDITURES

Table 10–2 highlights the overall budget trend for the Commonwealth of Massachusetts from fiscal year 1988 to fiscal year 1994, and selected accounts. The overall annual increases were as follows:

Fiscal year	
1988–1989	9.6%
1989–1990	3.8
1990–1991	3.4
1991–1992	−0.1
1992–1993	9.2
1993–1994 (est)	5.5

TABLE 10–2 Massachusetts Expenditures, Total and Selected (in millions)

Est.	FY89	FY90	%CH	FY91	%CH	FY92	%CH	FY93	%CH	FY94	%CH
Total Exp. & Other	12,981	13,475	3.8	13,935	3.4	13,914	(.1)	15,193	9.2	16,032	5.5
Direct Local Aid	2,961	2,937	(.8)	2,608	(11.2)	2,359	(9.6)	2,547	8.0	2,734	7.4
Medicaid	1,834	2,121	15.7	2,765	30.4	2,818	1.9	3,151	11.8	3,268	3.7
Public Assis.	924	1,001	8.3	1,092	9.1	1,065	(2.5)	1,075	0.9	1,107	3.0
Debt Service	650	771	18.6	942	22.2	898	(4.7)	1,140	26.9	1,171	2.8
Pensions	660	672	1.8	704	4.8	752	6.8	868	15.5	941	8.4
Higher Education	743	702	5.6	609	(13.3)	534	(12.5)	545	2.0	669	22.8

Source: Fiscal 1989–1993, Office of the Comptroller. Estimated Fiscal 1994, Executive Office for Administration and Finance.

A 1993 report by the Massachusetts Taxpayers Foundation notes that between fiscal year 1988 and fiscal year 1994, the largest increases were in the following spending categories:[15]

	1988	1994	% Change	1988 %	1994 %
Debt					
Service	$570.7	$1305.0	128.7%	4.9%	8.5%
MBTA	248.6	504.3	102.9	2.1	3.3
Medicaid	1591.2	3228.0	102.7	13.7	21.0
Corrections	283.7	478.8	68.8	2.4	3.1

Overall state spending grew 32.5 percent during this period. Among those losing ground during this period were:

	1988	1994	% Change	1988 %	1994 %
General Local					
Support	$1161.9	$915.5	(20.3%)	10.0%	6.0%
Education					
Local Aid	1685.5	1418.5	(15.8)	14.6	9.2
Higher Ed	757.2	669.7	(11.6)	6.5	5.4

In Massachusetts, like most states, Medicaid was the fastest growing budget buster. Unlike most, however, debt service also increased dramatically, while corrections costs were manageable. State aid to local governments, both for general purposes and K–12 education, was the big loser.

Medicaid

Medicaid spending represents the largest item in the state budget, $3.2 billion, or approximately 21 percent of all expenditures for fiscal year 1994. Its cost has risen by 100 percent since fiscal year 1988, in contrast to a 32 percent increase for the budget as a whole. Growth in expenditures increased at an annual rate of 15 percent between 1988–1992 but slowed to 7 percent for fiscal year 1993 and was estimated to climb by only 4.1 percent in fiscal year 1994. The Massachusetts Taxpayers Foundation gives credit to "aggressive rate setting and contracting by the Medicaid Department. Average hospital contracts will increase Medicaid rates by only 3.35 percent, and nursing home rates are constant."[16] Major reform efforts will be discussed below.

Corrections

Corrections spending in Massachusetts, like other states, has grown, from $284 million in fiscal year 1988 to a projected $479 million in fiscal year 1994, for a 68 percent increase. While there were no plans for new correctional facilities in fiscal year 1994, the governor filed a capital request for $565 million for new beds. The system is overcrowded, with 19,660 prisoners in a system whose capacity is supposed to be 15,000.[17]

Debt

As the above table shows, payments to service debt have grown the most of any category from fiscal year 1988–1994 (even greater than Medicaid), with payments in fiscal year 1994 2.3 times higher than they were in fiscal year 1988. The growth of capital expenditures during the 1980s accounts for the significant rise in annual debt service. The debt service also includes the cost of financing the debt to cover the 1990 state deficit.

Lower interest rates and a better bond rating allowed refunding $1 billion of bonds in September and October of 1991, producing a onetime reduction in debt service payments of $261 million.[18] Nevertheless, debt service payments represent a glaring 8.5 percent of the commonwealth's estimated expenditures for fiscal year 1994.

Legislation was enacted in January 1990 to impose a limit on debt service in commonwealth budgets. No more than 10 percent of the total appropriations in any fiscal year may be expended for payments of interest and principal. However, the law may be amended by the legislature or superseded in the General Appropriation Act for any year.

Governor Weld instituted a five-year capital spending plan in August 1991 to reduce the rate of growth in state borrowing.

MBTA

The Massachusetts Bay Transit Authority, while only 3.3 percent of the fiscal year 1994 budget, has also seen dramatic growth between fiscal year 1988 and fiscal year 1994, an increase of 102.9 percent. The commonwealth guarantees its debt service, provides certain contract assistance, and pays the difference between fare revenues and ridership cost. Recent actions by the authority, including staffing reductions, tightening operations management, and a savings of $4 million in electric costs, have reduced the rate of increase in its budget from 12 percent between fiscal year 1992 and fiscal year 1993 to 4 percent between fiscal year 1993 and fiscal year 1994.

Cash Assistance

Cash assistance, including Aid to Families with Dependent Children, Supplemental Security Income, and Emergency Assistance for the Elderly, Disabled, and Children (EAEDC)—formerly General Relief, grew 31.3 percent between fiscal year 1988 and fiscal year 1994, about the rate of overall budget growth. It is important to note that most of this growth has been in the two federally reimbursed programs; funding for the state program, EAEDC, fell from a high of $190 million in fiscal year 1991, to an estimated $92.4 million in fiscal year 1993.[19] There was a major reform in this program enacted in 1992, with many removed from its rolls. This will be discussed below.

Local Aid

Proposition 2½, passed by the voters in November of 1980, put in place a statewide limitation on property taxes, as noted above. When it went into effect, local aid to cities and towns stood at $1.856 billion. Then began an amazing roller coaster ride for the recipients. The commonwealth steadily increased its contribution from 1981 to 1989, with notable increases of 13.4 percent in fiscal year 1982 and 13.7 percent in 1987, at the height of "the miracle."[20] In 1981 constant dollars, total direct local aid expenditures increased by 58.5 percent between fiscal years 1981 and 1989, or 5.9 percent per year. During the same period, the total of all other local revenue sources declined by 5.87 percent or .75 percent per year.[21] The ride slowed in fiscal year

1989 before plummeting 11.8 percent, 8.6 percent and 13.9 percent in the next three years.

The Massachusetts Taxpayers Foundation breaks out education local aid from general local government support. Education local aid dropped 15.8 percent between fiscal year 1988 and fiscal year 1994, bouncing back up a little in fiscal year 1992. It fell from 14.6 percent of the state budget in 1988 to 9.2 percent in fiscal year 1994. The Massachusetts Supreme Judicial Court has ordered the state legislature to redress inequities in funding among districts.

General local government support fell 20.3 percent between fiscal year 1988–1994, from 10 percent of the budget to 6 percent. Clearly "share the wealth, share the pain" has been the operating principle in Massachusetts.

Higher Education

One of the biggest losers after general local support and education local aid is higher education. State university support peaked at $355 million in fiscal year 1988 and bottomed out at $273 million in fiscal year 1992. This drew a lot of criticism from those who had sought to make the University of Massachusetts a world class system. Overall, funding for higher education dropped 11.6 percent from fiscal year 1988–fiscal year 1994, shrinking from 6.5 percent to 4.4 percent of the state budget.

In response, the public higher education system decreased its state-funded payroll by 1711 full time equivalent employees. Between 1987–1988 and 1993–1994, tuition rose an average of 48 percent at all public universities and colleges, and fees rose 240 percent. Together, fee and tuition increases raised the cost of attending a state school 113 percent during this period, compared to a 45 percent increase from 1983–1988. Data on the impact on class sizes and course offerings is not available.

Other Spending

Some other services that have been cut between fiscal year 1988 and fiscal year 1994 include Conservation and Recreation, off 15.1 percent; Day Care Services, off 12.6 percent; the Massachusetts Department of Highways, off 16.5 percent; and Public Health Hospitals, off 11.4 percent. Programs not mentioned above that grew faster than the overall budget involved Services to Children, including Family Preservation, Adoption, and Protection programs; Mental Retardation; Public Health Services, mostly for prevention; and Environmental Protection.

State Work Force

Since 1988, the commonwealth has reduced its work force and payroll quite substantially. Methods used included attrition, layoffs, and an early retirement program. As a share of total spending, the state payroll has shrunk from 20 percent of the total budget in 1988 to under 15 percent. The state work force has decreased by approximately 16,000 jobs.[22] It is interesting to note that about one-half of the decline occurred during the Dukakis administration.

Full-Time Equivalent Work Force

June 1988	January 1991	January 1993
80,339	72,193	64,570

Weld, upon coming into office, committed to reducing the payroll significantly. His goal was to reduce the statewide work force by at least 7,500 FTEs between 1991 and 1993.[23] To that end, between July 1, 1991, and September 1, 1991, 300 layoff notices were issued. Through attrition and eligibly retirement, another 700 positions were eliminated. Another 3,000 employees were expected to take early retirement. The State Retirement Board said 3700 state employees applied for and were approved for an early retirement package, and 319 took advantage of the court employee's retirement package. The school reform package incorporates provisions to fund early retirement for teachers. A proposed higher education early retirement package was vetoed by the governor on July 19, 1993. Clearly Weld has not been able to meet his goal. In fact, from August 1991 to January 1993, the state work force *increased* slightly, from 63,941 FTEs to 64,570 FTEs, leading Weld to institute a sixty-day moratorium on hiring at the start of the 1994 fiscal year.

As noted above, in November 1992 the legislature (over the governor's veto) agreed to fund a 13.9 percent pay raise for state employees, estimated to have cost the state $225 million in fiscal year

1993.[24] However passage of the fiscal year 1994 budget increased state employee contributions for health care from 10 percent to 15 percent.

Collective bargaining agreements with all but one of the commonwealth's employee unions have expired over the past five years, and have not been renegotiated. The only one in force is that of the Massachusetts Correction Officers Federated Union.

Massachusetts, probably to the surprise of most state taxpayers, ranks forty-eighth in the United States in number of state and local employees per 10,000 residents. It last matched the national average at the time of passage of Proposition 2½ in 1980.

REVENUES

As recounted above, the most important aspects of tax policy in Massachusetts over the past five years include the large increases of the 1990 Economic Stability and Recovery Compact (needed to compensate for the deficit caused by the economic downturn), the repeal of the sales tax extension to certain services, the voter-initiated hike in the cigarette tax with revenues earmarked for public health, and an adamant "just say no" approach to tax increases from the Weld administration.

Tax revenues were volatile during this period, as Table 10–3 shows. They fluctuated as follows over the period fiscal year 1990–1994:

	FY 1990	FY 1991	FY 1992	FY 1993	FY 1994 (est)
	$8518.	8995.	9484.	9930.	10694.
% chg	(3.4)	5.6	5.4	4.7	7.7

Income Tax

The state has traditionally taxed personal income at a flat rate, with 5 percent applied to income from employment, professions, trade, etc., and 10 percent applied to interest (other than that from Massachusetts banks), dividends, and net capital gains (after a 50 percent deduction). In 1989, the legislature increased the personal rate to 5.75 percent, with the additional revenues initially earmarked for a Liability Reduction Fund and the Medical Assistance Liability Fund (to pay for

TABLE 10-3 Massachusetts Tax Revenues, Total and Selected (in millions)

Est.	FY89	FY90	%CH	FY91	%CH	FY92	%CH	FY93	%CH	FY94	%CH
Total	8,815	8,518	(3.4)	8,995	5.6	9,484	5.4	9,930	4.7	10,694	7.7
Cigarettes	159	151	(4.9)	144	(4.2)	140	(3.1)	190	36.0	238	25.1
Corporations	887	698	(21.3)	612	(12.3)	644	5.2	737	14.5	875	18.7
Income	4,287	4,465	4.2	5,045	13.0	5,337	5.8	5,375	0.7	5,747	6.9
Motor Fuel	307	302	(1.6)	464	53.8	541	16.6	557	3.0	560	0.5
Sales	2,084	1,956	(6.0)	1,909	(2.0)	1,979	3.6	2,124	7.4	2,333	9.8

Source: Fiscal 1989–1993, Office of the Comptroller. Estimated Fiscal 1994, Executive Office for Administration and Finance.

the 1989 deficit and Medicaid related borrowings, all of which have now been paid off).

The personal rate was to increase to 6.25 percent for tax year 1991, and was scheduled to return to 5.95 percent for tax year 1992, which it did. Governor Weld tried unsuccessfully to reduce it further to 5.75 percent. The tax rate on unearned income was increased permanently to 12 percent. Due to these tax hikes, personal income tax revenues increased at an average annual rate of 8.2 percent over the period fiscal year 1988–1991, even with an economy in steep decline. Massachusetts obtains a highly disproportionate share of its taxes from the income tax, accounting for 54 percent of all tax revenue for fiscal year 1993, compared to 22 percent for sales and use taxes.[25]

Although a flat tax rate is used, the result is a fairly progressive tax system because of exemptions and credits at the lower incomes, the deduction structure, and the 12 percent tax on interest and dividend income, which tends to hit those at higher incomes. According to the March 1994 Massachusetts Department of Revenue report "Massachusetts Statistics of Income," the top 20 percent of income taxpayers pay approximately 5.8 percent of their income in taxes, versus 4.7 percent for middle income earners and 1.3 percent for low income earners.

Sales and Use Tax

Massachusetts imposes a 5 percent sales tax on retail sales and a corresponding 5 percent use tax on the storage, use, or other consumption of tangible properties. Food, clothing, and prescribed medicine lead the long list of items exempt from the sales tax.

As discussed above, the 1990 deficit reduction tax plan established a sales tax on certain services, but at Weld's lead it was for the most part repealed the day after it was to have gone into effect. The tax had also been challenged as unconstitutional. Ultimately, while some portions of the tax would have been constitutional, the extension that would have applied to newspaper and other media production was ruled unconstitutional by the Supreme Judicial Court. The extension to sales and uses of electricity, gas, and steam for nonresidential use and to telecommunication services for both residential and nonresidential uses did go into effect, yielding an additional $113 million in fiscal year 1991 and $180 million in fiscal year 1992.[26] While this might have injected a very little balance into the system, it is outweighed by the increase in revenue from the higher income tax rates.

Business Corporations Tax

Most corporations doing business in the commonwealth are subject to an excise that has a property measure and an income measure. Property is taxed at $2.60 per $1000 value; net income is taxed at 9.5 percent. Annual revenues posted big declines from fiscal year 1989 to fiscal year 1991, from $887 million to $612 million.

Other Taxes

Included are motor fuels excise taxes, cigarette and alcohol beverage excises, estate and deeds excises, and other tax sources. Motor fuels were taxed an additional six cents per gallon (from eleven to seventeen cents) by the 1990 Economic Recovery Act.

A voter initiative in 1992 increased the cigarette tax by twenty-five cents a pack. The revenues are credited to a new Health Protection Fund, and appropriated to pay for health programs and education relating to tobacco use. Governor Weld has threatened to use these funds in whatever manner he likes, yet can claim he has held to his "no new taxes" pledge, since it was the voters who approved the increase. Weak earmarking provisions has allowed him to do the same with gas tax funds, using them to cover shortfalls in the general budget.

The legislature also doubled the deeds excise tax in January of 1993 over the governor's veto. Expected to produce $15.25 million in fiscal year 1993, the revenue is retained by county governments, allowing the commonwealth to reduce its expenditures by a similar amount.

Finally, in response to fears of driving elderly citizens out of the state, the Massachusetts estate tax is scheduled to be phased out by 1997, and replaced with a "sponge tax," based on the maximum amount of the credit for state taxes allowed for federal estate tax purposes. The phaseout began on January 1, 1993, at $300,000, and goes up $100,000 a year until 1997. The revenue loss is expected to be recouped through higher income and sales tax revenues.

Economic Stimulus

"Filthy supply-sider" that he is, Governor Weld has consistently pushed for tax cuts and tax breaks for individuals. As noted, he was successful in obtaining repeal of the sales tax base extension, but was not successful in getting the income tax rate lowered to 5.75%. He was behind the phasing out of the estate tax, and has consistently pushed for a cut in the capital gains tax.

Parts of his "Economic Stimulus Package" were approved in March 1993, including a tripling of the investment tax credit, from 1 percent to 3 percent, although this provision is subject to a sunset provision after three years. There is much skepticism over whether the change will have any job-generating effect.[27]

Tax Forecasting

The Weld administration clearly used the underestimation of revenues in its fiscal year 1992 budget to restrain spending initiatives. It does not appear that the legislature will fall for this again. Slavet and Baressi of the McCormack Institute at the University of Massachusetts, Boston, note that "The legal formalization through legislative resolution of publicly announced revenue estimates has led to more reasonable Massachusetts tax revenue numbers about which the public can have greater assurance."[28] They are not as kind in their characterization of nontax revenue forecasting.

Fiscal Year 1994 Tax Credits and Fee Cuts

The motor vehicle registry fee cut that Weld implemented was rescinded by the legislature. The rescission was vetoed by the governor. The tax credits proposed for elderly health insurance premiums and college tuition discussed above did not make it to the governor's desk.

Local Government

In November 1990, the voters approve by a 54-46 margin ballot question 5, which would devote 40 percent of all state general purpose revenues to local governments. The "flaw" in the bill from the point of view of cities and towns, however, were the words "subject to appropriation by the legislature." This loophole has allowed the governor and legislature to ignore it, although the Massachusetts Municipal Association notes that it was approved by a bigger margin than was Governor Weld.

In both 1992 and 1993 the legislature, mindful of the squeeze put on local governments by declining state aid, voted to allow cities and towns to add the amount in their "overlay" accounts (amount to cover appeals to property assessments) to their limit under Proposition 2½, thus producing a onetime revenue increase; both times the governor has vetoed them. A proposal was also made for fiscal year 1994, which would have allowed municipal officials to raise the auto excise tax and property taxes by the rate of inflation. These were not forwarded to the governor's desk by the conference committee.

The legislature also adopted a provision that would have allowed cities and towns to levy new property taxes on businesses that currently operate commercial enterprises on public authority property, such as fast food establishments at Logan Airport and on the Massachusetts Turnpike. The governor vetoed this provision as antibusiness and inflationary.[29]

Graduated Income Tax

A citizens group qualified for the 1994 ballot a proposal to make the personal income tax subject to a graduated rate. Four times in the past such proposals have failed to meet the voter and legislative approval necessary to amend the constitution.

If voters choose to amend the constitution, the legislature must approve the amendment in two successive sessions and a separate ballot question defining the income tax rates would also require voter approval. If approved, a graduated income tax would not become effective until 1998. As currently proposed, the tax will replace the flat rate income tax, cutting taxes for low and middle income residents (91 percent would pay lower taxes) but increasing them on the wealthy, while remaining revenue neutral.

REVENUE GIMMICKS

The Weld administration has consistently included revenues in its budget proposals that are onetime shots, some that carry an unlikely chance of passage, and some with overly optimistic projected yields.

Medicaid Reimbursement

As discussed above, the commonwealth took advantage of the loophole in the Medicaid reimbursement regulation to collect a $513 million windfall in fiscal year 1991, $164 million in fiscal year 1992, and an estimated $213 million in fiscal year 1993.

In fiscal year 1994, the governor further signed a "municipal Medicaid" program that allows municipalities to receive Medicaid reimbursement through the state and the Health Care Financing Administration for health-related special education costs. The program is projected to save cities and towns an estimated $30 million.[30] The state became eligible for 50 percent reimbursement for medical services for special education students with the Medicare Catastrophic Coverage Act of 1989. The state will turn over the money to municipalities that experienced the costs associated with providing services. Massachusetts is one of the first states to take advantage of the reimbursement.

Asset Sales

One of Governor Weld's emphases in reinventing government in Massachusetts has been privatization, and one of the most ballyhooed elements of privatization is the sale of state assets.

Some of the assets that have been proposed for sale or long-term lease include:

- Lakeville Hospital, a facility that was closed under the governor's facility consolidation plan. Although advertised, the two proposals for development that were received lacked key details or were only conceptual in nature. Regulatory approvals and Determination of Need certificates were not assured. Presumably, once these hurdles are settled, the property will be readvertised.
- Two Department of Mental Health barrier-free residences. These residences were rented to a municipal housing authority.
- A former satellite facility of the University of Massachusetts. Although advertised in February, 1993, no developer has been closed.[31]

- The State Transportation Building. This building houses the headquarters of several quasi-public and public transportation departments and if sold might generate $100 million. Discussion of the long-term costs of leasing space for all of the afcted agencies has essentially pushed aside the governor's roposal to gain revenue from sale or sale-leaseback of this building.
- Boston State Hospital. This facility has essentially been closed since 1985. The state has attempted to develop the parcel many times, with no takers.

At various times the administration has also floated the ideas of selling the Massachusetts Turnpike and Tobin Bridge.

Revenue estimates related to state buildings have been included in the governor's budgets. In the fiscal year 1994 budget, for example, the governor estimated $51 million in revenue will be gained from sale or lease of state assets. In fiscal year 1993, $45 million was to be received, although by May 12, 1993, the treasurer reported that "There are currently no agreements to sell such assets, and the market for some or all of such assets is unfavorable."[32] The governor's budget for fiscal year 1992 included an original estimate of $230 million in asset sales; only $16 million was actually realized. The reality of asset sales has not come close to matching the rhetoric.

Asset sales of certain properties and facilities may make sense, but the downturn in the New England economy has inhibited its development.

Gambling

House Bill No. 1 for fiscal year 1994, at the governor's request, called for the state to develop $100 million of revenue from keno and video gambling. The final appropriation bill included an estimate for only the keno revenue, an estimated $50 million.[33] As of June, 1994, keno revenue was estimated to fall far short, in the $7–$10 million range.

July 1994 the governor filed legislation to fund a "megaplex" stadium and convention center, with partial reliance on revenues to be realized from river boat casino gambling. This was never seriously considered by the legislature.

Other

As noted above, the state has delayed aid to local government payments to finish a fiscal year in the black, and has further raided reserve and dedicated funds, most notably lottery and gasoline tax revenues, to avoid being in deficit, and more recently cigarette tax revenues, to pad the surplus.

In sum, Governor Weld's reputation as a tax cutter exceeds his performance. While he did lead the effort to repeal the sales tax extension, and made sure the already scheduled income tax rate cut occurred, little else on his "supply side agenda" has been accomplished.

INNOVATIONS

While a large part of the fiscal problem Massachusetts has faced has been remedied by short-term tax and expenditure actions, the Weld administration along with the state legislature has enacted or put in place many innovative programs, some more controversial than others. The discussion that follows focuses primarily on the major initiatives, especially Medicaid, privatization, welfare, and school reform.

Medicaid

With a caseload expanded from 445,509 recipients in 1988 to 650,000 in 1993, the Medicaid population involved approximately 11 percent of the commonwealth's population. The resulting $3.2 billion budget is quite naturally a cause of concern, and has drawn the attention of state policymakers.

As discussed above, annual increases of over 15 percent from 1988–1992 were halved to 7 percent for fiscal year 1993, and an estimated 4.1 percent for fiscal year 1994. As the Massachusetts Taxpayer Foundation notes, "The major reasons that program costs have come under control is aggressive rate setting and contracting by the Medicaid Department."[34]

For the longer term, Governor Weld offered, and the legislature passed, a plan to achieve $400 million in savings over two years. Perhaps most notably, the commonwealth has received waivers of federal regulations to implement a managed care system for Medicaid recipients. All, other than the elderly, the blind, those in long-term care institutions, or with some other form of health insurance, must take part. Elements include recipients being assigned to a primary care clinician who determines appropriate specialty and inpatient care, including the enrollment in a managed system of those in need of mental health or substance abuse care, and selective contracts with certain service providers to obtain lower cost care.

To reduce nursing home costs, the most costly element of Medicaid, waivers have been received to allow use of nursing home pre-screening and community service planning, concentrated in twenty-seven Home Care Corporations, "to provide a single entry point and coordinated nursing home diversion services for elderly Medicaid recipients."[35] The state Medicaid program now covers more in-home services in an attempt to reduce the number of obviously costly nursing home referrals.

Finally, a proposed change moved the Executive Office of Human Services from the Welfare department to an expanded Executive Office of Health and Human Services. When the primary concern of Medicaid was the poor seeking medical services, it made sense to run all cash assistance programs out of Welfare. With the changing composition of Medicaid expenditures, the administrative consolidation of health care services seems to make sense. The Welfare Department would still determine eligibility. Promotion of generic drugs and expanded audits of Medicaid providers have also been implemented in an attempt to lower costs.

The treasurer's office concluded in 1993 that "This comprehensive managed care approach to Medicaid administration, combined with other discrete saving initiatives, such as the repricing and buy-in to Medicare services for Medicaid recipients, and restrictions, both financial and clinical, on nursing home eligibility were assumed in the fiscal 1993 budget to produce savings of $100 million."[36]

The Massachusetts Human Services Coalition has compiled an estimate of Medicaid cost-cutting measures, and it finds $175 million in savings for fiscal year 1992, and $159 million for fiscal year 1993.[37] It has voiced concern that some of these cutbacks will result in increased costs in other areas.

Managed care. As noted above, a large part of the savings in Medicaid is a result of the managed care program. To receive the federal waiver, Massachusetts had to assure the federal government that managed care would not restrict access for recipients. The original waiver application was denied, but was later accepted in January 1992 for a two-year period, and has been twice renewed.

There are two primary aspects of managed care. First, Medicaid is referring AFDC recipients and disabled families to the contracted Foundation Health Company (of California). Foundation's health benefits managers help recipients choose the most relevant package of health benefits, either through an HMO or a Primary Care Clinician. Second, Medicaid has set up a managed care program for substance abuse and mental health illness treatment through hospitals and free-standing clinics. This has been done by Mental Health Management of America, a Tennessee firm.

Medicaid was successful in working out contracts with HMOs, many of which had not had dealings with the program before. They have had difficulty in securing participation of enough primary care clinicians (PCCs), however. At the outset, there was to be a limit of 500 Medicaid patients per PCC; after it became clear that this was impossible, the ratio was readjusted to 1500. The federal waiver prohibits assigning anyone to an HMO without their approval, thus putting more pressure on the PCCs.

As of May 1994 the administration claims 350,000 Medicaid recipients are in the managed care program, with 71 percent belonging to the Primary Care Clinician Program. Savings are estimated at $80 million by the administration. It is interesting to note, however, that while the Medicaid waiver application estimated 405,818 participants in the PCC program by March 1994, only 241,995 were enrolled.

The state offers two commissioned studies to support its positive evaluation of the programs. The first, issued in January 1994 by the Heller School at Brandeis, found the mental health/substance abuse section of managed care to have saved $47 million in fiscal year 1993, with generally favorable overall comments. The second, issued in June 1994 by the McCormack Institute at the University of Massachusetts, Boston, found the Primary Care Clinician Program has saved the state $19.9 million, less than the $27.5 million estimated by the state, but a savings nonetheless. Critics of the report note that the disability population was not included.

Social service advocates question why the number of physician visits is down in a program that is supposed to encourage patient-doctor contact. The House Human Services Committee also expressed its concern about shortages of PCCs in certain geographic areas and the disruption of existing doctor-patient relationships when the doctor is not a PCC.[38]

For fiscal year 1994, Medicaid estimated further savings of $45 million from increased utilization review and third-party liability recoveries. Legislation to increase estate recoveries is being developed. The Massachusetts Taxpayer Foundation estimates that "Changes to eligibility and improvements in payment review from earlier years are ongoing and expected to save an additional $200 million on an annual basis in fiscal 1994."[39]

Privatization

The theme that has come to most characterize the Weld administration's approach to state government is privatization. When Governor Weld took office in January 1991, he set his sights on using privatization as an essential tool for reinventing government, to lower costs and improve the quality of services.

In November 1993 the Weld administration put out a report entitled *Privatization in Massachusetts: Getting Results*,[40] which claims that privatization efforts have saved the commonwealth $273 million ($203 million as a result of facility consolidation in human services), a number open to dispute, especially by the Massachusetts House Post Audit Committee. Overall, the privatization effort has occurred with great controversy.

The Weld administration report offers useful perspectives on the process of privatization. In a section entitled "Evaluating Privatization Initiatives," it lists and discusses the ideal conditions for privatization, including:

- competitive marketplace
- potential for savings
- promise of enhanced quality or responsiveness
- satisfactory assurance of government control and accountability
- minimal risk
- no insurmountable legal, political, or practical barriers
- minimal adverse employee impact.

It follows by offering a seven point guide to "mitigating imperfect conditions." Detailed instructions follow on how to compare costs between privatized and in-house operation.

The Executive Office for Administration and Finance developed a privatization manual to guide agencies in their efforts to privatize. Included in the "Privatization Checklist" are sections dealing with:

- minority business participation
- affirmative action
- work force transition
- quality assurance
- public employee participation in bidding
- conflict of interest provisions
- cost comparison
- implementation.

In sum, this report details the care with which the issue of privatization has been approached. Several specific examples of implemented privatization in Massachusetts are worthy of discussion.

The biggest money saver has come through the consolidation of Department of Health and Human Service facilities. A Special Commission on Facility Consolidation issued a report in June 1991 that suggested "[t]he Commonwealth's inpatient facilities system, which was build to accommodate over 35,000 individuals at its peak, today cares for 6,200 clients."[41] The Commission recommended that eleven of thirty-four state-run facilities under the Executive Office of Health and Human Services (EOHHS), including Department of Mental Health (DMH), Department of Public Health (DPH), and Department of Mental Retardation (DMR) facilities be closed and services transferred to other facilities (both public and private), for net savings of approximately $60 million annually.

Despite opposition from some clients' parents, advocate groups, and state employees, as of October 1993 the facility consolidation program had resulted in closures of 3 DPH facilities, 4 DMH hospitals, and 2 DMR schools, with a phasedown of 2 other DMR schools.

Another goal of the consolidation program, besides the potential for savings and better care, was maximization of federal reimbursements. For example, "although not reimbursable by Medicaid in a psychiatric institution . . . treatment for mental illness . . . is reimburseable when carried out in a general hospital. . ."[42] The state has moved many clients to general hospital affiliated facilities.

The privatization of prison health care also appears effective. In 1991, Massachusetts had the highest per inmate costs in the nation for prison health care, due to lack of cost controls, weak central accountability, lax controls of malpractice claims, and few standards for evaluation. Since privatization, the Weld administration claims that expenses are down, and quality of care is up. Health care costs went from $4300 per inmate per year to $2600, with half of the facilities accredited for the first time. Total savings were estimated at $8 million.

The single largest project involves the privatization of the entire maintenance function of a district office of the Massachusetts Highway Department (MHD). In September 1992, the MHD contracted with a Massachusetts-based company for highway maintenance and drawbridge operation for the County of Essex. The A & F report notes that before privatization maintenance was spotty, the ratio of foremen to laborers was 1:2.15, and overtime costs were very high. After privatization savings after the first year of the contract are estimated to be $2 million in operating costs (in a roughly $7 million budget), $1 million in reallocated equipment, and $1.5 million in reallocated personnel, with improved quality of services.

The Massachusetts House Post Audit and Oversight Bureau (the bureau) has attempted to analyze the privatization effort. The bureau cites many instances where privatization has clearly worked in Massachusetts: food services at some state colleges, snow removal, and home care for the elderly. However, with respect to the overall effort, the bureau is concerned that in their opinion no comprehensive plan exists to evaluate the true costs and benefits of each initiative. It concludes that some types of services are easier to privatize than others.

The bureau has reviewed in depth three privatization initiatives: the Essex County Highway initiative, the Pharmaceutical Services at EOHHS, and the Charles River Hospital West (CRHW) initiative, which is part of privatization at DMH.

With regard to the highway initiative, the bureau was critical of the contract's drafting, the lack of provisions for overview, and the freedom given the contractor for prioritizing and oversight. In the pharmacy initiative, the bureau found a rush to judgment at the planning stage, with unnecessary costs and "fractured functions" a result. In the CRHW case, that hospital took over care for patients resulting from the closure of the Northampton State Hospital. The bureau found the former to be in a weak financial position, and expressed concern that the quality of care was hurt by the speed of the decision. In all cases, the bureau found "lack of planning, inappropriate oversight, and deficient management."[43]

Perhaps most disparaging, through interviews, site visits, information requests, and even subpoenas, the bureau has been unable to document the savings claimed by the Weld administration—"The Administration could not provide the documents necessary to prove the savings were as stated." In the case of highway maintenance, "based on repeated visual and photographic inspection, the $1.9 million the administration counts in additional services was never done, and in fact, the Bureau questions whether all the basic services were provided." In the pharmaceutical case, "the information provided to the Bureau was not supportive of the $3 million savings claim."

The bureau further states that completed cost comparison worksheets, like the one in the administration report, were not submitted to the bureau. The bureau further points out that $143 million of the total $273 million in savings are derived from capital avoidance costs— projected capital requirements to meet federal regulations—not direct savings. They also note that some of the savings, especially in DPH, were in part due to a reduced census (fewer people served). In addition costs that should have been included do not appear, including:

- cost of employees working on privatization
- printing costs for promotional materials
- cost of consultants paid to promote privatization.

No information on the cost of displacing employees were offered, including unemployment costs.

In sum, the bureau finds $267,701,000 of the $273,507,000 in claimed savings unverifiable, disputed, or unsubstantiated.

Needless to say, the privatization efforts have provoked an outcry from state workers and their unions, culminating in passage over the governor's veto of the Pacheco bill, which regulates further privatization decisions. The law outlines responsibilities for the privatizing state agency, the contractor, and the state employee. The agency must

- prepare a written statement of services; a management study to determine how the service could be provided in-house in the most cost-efficient manner;

- prepare an in-house estimate to reflect the cost of agency employees providing the service;
- calculate the most efficient in-house provision;
- provide adequate resources for the purpose of encouraging and assisting present agency employees to organize and submit a bid on proposed services;
- prepare a comprehensive written analysis of the cost of the designated bid;
- and certify in writing to the state auditor the validity of the process.

The state auditor must certify that these conditions have been met, and that savings would result, before privatization may proceed.

The effect of this law's implementation on privatization remains to be seen.

Welfare

Shortly after taking office in 1991, Governor Weld moved to do away with the General Relief Program, the one cash assistance program funded entirely by the state, that provides aid to needy individuals who are not eligible for the federal welfare program. The revamped program is called Emergency Aid to Elderly, Disabled and Children (EAEDC). This ended General Relief's status as an entitlement and eliminated benefits to ex-criminal offenders, undocumented immigrants, persons over forty-five without a significant work history, and families with stepparent or grandparent income. On July 19, 1993 Governor Weld vetoed $12.3 million of the fiscal 1994 allocation, by eliminating eligibility for eighteen to twenty-one year-old students and adults enrolled in rehabilitation programs. The legislature overrode the veto.

The new, stricter eligibility requirements of EAEDC were applied to all disabled persons receiving General Relief (by far the largest category of recipients) by a private, for-profit medical review team, HealthPro. A successful 1992 legal challenge to their method forced the Department of Public Welfare to revise its disability determination process, accepting a medical doctor's determination of disability, to provide benefits while reviews are pending, and to provide retroactive benefits to people wrongly denied.

As a result of tightened eligibility, caseloads have fallen sharply from 38,000 early in fiscal 1992, to 22,000 in June 1994, with expenditures falling from $189 million to $104.7 million in fiscal year 1994. Critics find this harsh. In fact, when the change from General Relief to EAEDC took place, the Department of Public Welfare estimated that 28,200 people would qualify. As of June 1994, only 22,015 were enrolled.[44] Many may have been lost in the transition. Further, the number and length of stays in homeless shelters are up.

The Department of Public Welfare has also implemented automated systems to redetermine eligibility for benefits. The project, creating the Family Assistance Management Information System (FAMIS), seeks to decrease program errors, reduce fraud, and increase employee productivity. Funding has been authorized through bond issuance, and more than 65 percent of the costs will be paid by the federal government.[45] The Department of Revenue has gotten more aggressive and thus improved its collection of child support payments.

In fiscal year 1993, the Department of Welfare undertook a scattered-site housing initiative to reduce the number of families in hotels and shelters, and to provide families previously staying in hotels with a more stable environment and appropriate services, including housing search. The Department is leveraging federal funds for scattered-site and transitional shelters. These units provide temporary apartments with social services to homeless families at a lower cost than placement in a hotel without social services.

Specifically, thirty scattered-site transitional housing units were funded entirely through the federal McKinney Emergency Shelter Grant in fiscal year 1993, with a projected 100 more for fiscal year 1994.[46]

Over the governor's veto, the legislature has allowed AFDC families to keep up to $193 in monthly earnings without a reduction in grants, adding $10–$12 million, but encouraging recipients to work.

Governor Weld filed legislation on April 27, 1993 to reform the state's $1.5 billion Aid to Families with Dependent Children program. Included were time-limited benefits and community service for long-term welfare recipients. As a symbol of his proposals, Weld also wanted to change the name of the Department of Welfare to the Department of Transitional Assistance.[47]

Weld claimed his plan, which he refrained from calling workfare, would affect only recipients who have been on welfare for more than two years and whose children are in school. Those recipients would be required to attend job training sessions or perform community service during the hours when their children are in school. The proposal would have also required recipients to sign a contract with the state, pledging to care properly for their children by making sure they are immunized from disease and that they attend school.

If recipients did not adhere to the terms of the contract, resisted job training, or declined to perform community service work, the state could significantly reduce the adult portion of the benefits and eventually initiate proceedings to have their children taken away from them.

Opponents of the plan included members of the Massachusetts Chapter of the National Organization for Women, who claim it would have punished women and children and create "make-work" jobs as opposed to increasing high skill job opportunities.[48]

As a result of the legislature failing to send Weld elements of his welfare reform proposal contained in the house-approved budget that were similar to the comprehensive welfare proposal that he filed in April, the governor vetoed the ultimately approved "hollow welfare proposal that would actually cost money and does not contain any of the provisions to help welfare recipients to transition themselves off the rolls."[49]

In its fiscal year 1995 budget, the Massachusetts legislature passed a welfare reform plan that includes a family cap (no additional benefits when women have additional children on welfare) and a provision that parents under twenty must live at home or in state-supervised homes, must have received or be pursuing a high school diploma, and must take parenting and life-skills classes. Recipients would lose $90 a month in benefits if they refuse to sign up for training, school, or a state-subsidized employment program; are still on AFDC after two years; fail to get young children immunized; or fail to ensure their children under fourteen meet school attendance requirements. The bill also subsidizes $4.50 per hour private sector jobs for welfare recipients and provides day care and Medicaid for up to a year. Employer pays $2 per hour for the first nine months, and $3 per hour the last three.[50] Governor Weld vetoed the bill because the two-year limit was "full of holes," and he worried about the estimated cost of the state subsidized job program ($70 million). His own plan, a revision of his 1993 proposal, called for recipients to find work now after only sixty days or do community service, with day care provided.

School Choice

In 1991, a state Executive Office of Education was established, with a new cabinet-level position, the Secretary of Education, responsible for developing, directing, and coordinating comprehensive educational policy in the Commonwealth from preschool levels through university postgraduate studies.

In March 1991, the first statewide school choice program was created to instill elements of competition and accountability into the public school system. The cost to the receiving district is reimbursed by the commonwealth from funds withdrawn from the sending district's Chapter 70 allotment. Reimbursements are made to sending communities up to 50 percent of the lost funds, unless a community has lost more than 2 percent of its school budget, in which case 75 percent of the lost funds are reimbursed.

The School Choice legislation does not provide for transportation. Consequently, parents who elect to enroll their children are responsible. In 1992–1993, 3,209 students participated in the program, .4 percent of the state's K–12 population. No systematic review of the effects has yet been performed or authorized.

School Reform

Capping a two and one-half year legislative battle, Governor Weld signed "The Education Reform Act of 1993," promising historic changes in how Massachusetts funds, operates, and evaluates its public schools.[51] The bill promises $1.3 billion more for state schools by 2000 to ensure minimum per student spending in every community. Other elements include new statewide performance standards to judge schools, a statewide core curriculum for kindergarten through twelfth grade, state funded early retirement for "dispirited" teachers, measures to hold principals and superintendents more accountable for performance, and a call for "charter" (experimental) schools.

Conservative critics see it as not going far enough in allowing interdistrict school choice and the establishment of innovative, publicly funded charter schools; and warn that the bill's new teacher dismissal system, replacing tenure, may make it "more difficult, rather than easier, to remove an underperforming or noncompetent teacher."[52]

The bill's centerpiece is a promise to double state school aid by the year 2000, so that every community can spend at least $5,550 per student per year. Many local governments opposed the bill, as it will require many of them to spend a total of $700 million more a year of their own revenue on schools. Some cities, like Boston, also complain that it does not account for the different (higher) costs of providing education to certain populations.

Preliminary estimates of the use of the additional revenue shows most going for professional staff rehiring (35.5 percent) and personnel raises (17 percent).[53]

The department continues to pursue the expansion of preschool early childhood education to 8,920 at-risk four-year-old children in the commonwealth, and funded in fiscal year 1994 three new prevention initiatives: new teen suicide counseling programs for high-risk students and their families, a statewide plan for violence protection programs, and $9 million for smoking prevention and smoking cessation programs.[54]

WINNERS AND LOSERS

A look at how Massachusetts responded to its budget problems finds the winners to be primarily the commonwealth's taxpayers, who have benefited from a stable state tax burden after several years of large increases. Beneficiaries of fiscal sanity never draw as much attention, however, as those whose programs suffer. The losers are easy to identify.

Students/Education

Clearly big losers include children and young adults. State aid to local governments for educational purposes dropped dramatically in the early years of the state's fiscal problem. Fewer resources at the K–12 level results in overcrowded classrooms, less equipment, fewer new materials, and the termination of extracurricular activities. While the Education Reform of 1993 seeks to remedy the situation, it will take a while to catch up.

At the higher education level, the results are more easily measured. As noted above, due to lessened state support, tuition rose an average of 48 percent at all Massachusetts public universities and colleges from fiscal year 1988 to fiscal year 1994, while fees rose 240 percent. Together, fees and tuition raised the cost of attending a state school 113 percent over five years.[55] The state's most needy students were the hardest hit, with a 25 percent drop in need-based grant programs from fiscal year 1988 to fiscal year 1993. The number of state supported students dropped by 10.6 percent between 1988 and 1991. During this same period Massachusetts higher education lost 342 teachers, a 4.2 percent loss.

Local Governments

Other big losers included local governments, who experienced local aid cuts of approximately $300 million in fiscal year 1991 and $250 million in fiscal year 1992. Property taxes and fees have increased steadily since 1987. Beside the burden this places on local governments, the shift is from a progressive revenue-raising system to a regressive one. As the state government bond rating improved, many local governments had theirs lowered as a result of the increased financial strain.

Welfare Recipients

The removal of many from the General Relief category has certainly had an adverse impact on the needy in Massachusetts. As noted above, the transition has resulted in more being removed from the rolls than anticipated. There has been an increase in homeless shelter stays.

Medicaid Recipients

The switch to managed care is offering cost control savings to the state and has the potential to provide more preventive medicine, but it has also disrupted some doctor-patient relationships, which may be especially important in mental health treatment.

State Workers

State employees went several years without pay raises, and then had an increase in their share of health care from 10 percent to 15 percent. Further, some were forced to take furloughs in 1991.

In sum, Massachusetts budget responses, as elsewhere, have tended to hit local governments, and those who do not vote as regularly as others: students and the poor.

CONCLUSIONS

Back in March of 1992, Peter Howe summed up the first thirteen months of the Weld administration in the title of his *Boston Globe* article: "Weld's image overshadows his impact."[56] He noted that much of his "budgetary success" in his first two budgets was due to fortune (a slowly rebounding economy), the revenues generated by the Dukakis and Democratic legislature's 1989 tax increases, a Medicaid windfall due to a loophole, and big cuts in local aid. Few of these were likely to repeat.

It would appear that since then, the Weld administration, with the cooperation of the legislature, has put in place some policies that may effect meaningful long-term reform. Most of these are too recent to have their ultimate success determined. While many will disagree with some of the new directions, no one can deny that for Massachusetts, "the times they are a'changin'." Whether they stay changed remains to be seen.

The author wishes to extend his most sincere gratitude to research assistants Erin Keaney, Mary Kolesar, Jack Moynihan, Jesse Decker, and Bill Cole, for excellent work, fine detail, and dedication. Their willingness to persevere, and cheerfulness while doing it, will not be forgotten.

NOTES

1. Slavet, Joseph, et al, "After the Miracle: A History and Analysis of the Massachusetts Fiscal Crisis," The John W. McCormack Institute of Public Affairs, University of Massachusetts at Boston, May 1990, p.2.
2. Ibid. p. 1.
3. Office of the State Treasurer, *Series B General Obligation and General Obligation Refunding Bond Prospectus: Information Statement*, May 12, 1993, p. A–15.
4. Ibid., p A–16.

5. Interview with Michael Dukakis, April 15, 1991.

6. Slavet, Joseph S. and Joseph R. Barresi, "Fiscal Smell Tests: A Mid-Term Reality Check of Massachusetts Finances," The John W. McCormack Institute of Public Affairs, April, 1993.

7. The state government is responsible for covering the difference between MBTA expenditures and revenues.

8. Speech by Peter Nessen to Boston Municipal Research Bureau.

9. Slavet and Barresi, op. cit.

10. Massachusetts Taxpayer Foundation, "Program Budgeting in Massachusetts: Promise and Prospects," January, 1993, p.1.

11. Office of the Comptroller, Commonwealth of Massachusetts, "Comprehensive Annual Financial Report for the Fiscal Year Ending June 30, 1993," December 1991, p. 7.

12. See Comptroller's FISCAL YEAR 1991 Ending Financial Report, p. 18, and Peter J. Howe, "Massachusetts' bond rating is raised by two Wall Street Agencies," Boston Globe, October 14, 1993, p. 35.

13. Office of the State Treasurer, Commonwealth of Massachusetts, Preliminary Official Statement, General Obligation Bonds, Consolidated Loan of 1993, Series B, October 1, 1993, p. A–20.

14. Massachusetts Taxpayers Foundation, "1994 State Budget: A New Clear Challenge and a Potential Achievement," July 15, 1993.

15. Massachusetts Taxpayers Foundation, "State Spending 1988–1994: Recovering From Crisis," May 1993. Figures for 1994 are the governor's recommendations.

16. MTF, p. 14.

17. Massachusetts Taxpayer Foundation, "Corrections: The High Cost of Punishment," May 1993.

18. Office of the State Treasurer, op. cit., p. A–33.

19. Office of the Treasurer, Prospectus, p. A–32.

20. Massachusetts Taxpayer Foundation, "Local Government Revenue: The Big Squeeze," June 1993.

21. General Obligation Bonds, Preliminary Official Statement Dated October 7, 1993.

22. Ibid., p. A–37.

23. General Obligation Bonds, Official Statement Dated October 1, 1991, p. A–35.

24. Governor William F. Weld, Message to the Senate and House of Representatives, July 19, 1993.

25. Slavet and Barresi, op. cit., p. 53.

26. Ibid., p.53.

27. Ibid., pp. 47–49.

28. Ibid., p. 46.

29. Governor William F. Weld, Message to the Senate and House of Representatives, July 19, 1993, p. 11.

30. Weld message, July 19, 1993, p. 6.

31. The Asset Management Board, "Project Report for all Projects Considered in FISCAL YEAR 1993," September 14, 1993.

32. Treasurer, op. cit., p. A–19.

33. State House News Service, "Roundup," July 8, 1993.

34. MTF, "State Spending," p. 14.

35. Treasurer, p. A–31.

36. Ibid.

37. Massachusetts Human Services Coalition, "Poor People's Budget, fiscal year 1993."

38. Joint Committee on Human Services and Elderly Affairs, Massachusetts House of Representatives, "Programs and Issues Addressed by the Legislative Committee on Human Services and Elderly Affairs," February 1993.

39. MTF, "State Spending," p. 14.

40. Executive Office for Administration and Finance, Commonwealth of Massachusetts, "Privatization in Massachusetts: Getting Results," November 1, 1993.

41. Governor's Special Commission on Consolidation of Health and Human Services Institutional Facilities, "Actions for Quality Care: A Plan for the Consolidation of State Institutions & for the Provision of Appropriate Care Services," June 1991, p. i.

42. Ibid., p. 36.

43. House Post Audit and Oversight Bureau, "Privatization Savings: Where's the Beef," December 17, 1993, p. 5.

44. Massachusetts Social Services Coalition, "Poor People's Budget."

45. Office of the Governor, House No. 1, "Investments in Success, Financial Stability, and Economic Growth," vol. 1, p. V–1990.

46. Ibid.

47. Frank Phillips, "Weld Aims at Welfare Overhaul: AFDC Plan Would Require Some to Work or Train for Jobs," *Boston Globe*, April 27, 1993, p. 1.

48. Toni Lucy, "Critics Say Weld Welfare Reform Plan Deals in Stereotypes," *Boston Globe*, May 21, 1993, p. 16.

49. William Weld, "Veto Message," July 19, 1993, p. 8.

50. Peter Howe, "Weld Waves Veto Threat Over Welfare," *Boston Globe*, July 1, 1994.

51. Peter Howe, "Weld Puts Lukewarm Pen to Education Reform Bill," *Boston Globe*, June 19, 1993.

52. Ibid.

53. Massachusetts Board of Education, memo, December 14, 1993.

54. "Investments in Success. . . ," p. V–129.

55. Massachusetts Higher Education Coordinating Council.

56. Peter Howe, "Weld's image overshadows his impact," *Boston Globe*, March 29, 1991, p. 1.

11

Michigan: Rethinking Fiscal Priorities

Robert J. Kleine*

INTRODUCTION

Michigan, like most states, struggled to balance its budget in the early 1990s. Michigan's problems were both cyclical and structural in nature. The recession and the slow economic recovery restricted available resources sharply. At the same time corrections, health care, and retirement costs soared. However, Michigan's problems were worsened by a long-running failure to reduce expenditures to match revenues on an annual basis. The Michigan constitution requires a balanced budget, but the state has long made use of onetime revenues, funding delays and shifts, and creative accounting to get by each year. In almost every year since the late 1970s, these adjustments have been used to balance the budget. One consequence is that the state did not put enough money in its rainy day fund when times were good to protect the budget during an economic downturn[1].

Unlike most states, Michigan did not rely on tax increases to balance the budget. Governor John Engler (R) has received national attention for his refusal to support tax increases, but this has been standard practice in Michigan since two state senators were recalled in 1983 after a temporary increase in the state income tax was enacted.

Michigan was able to avoid tax increases by reducing expenditures,[2] transferring funds from the Budget Stabilization Fund (BSF) and other funds, capturing additional federal aid—mainly for Medicaid—through the use of creative financing arrangements, changing the method of accounting for property tax credits, and delaying pay-

---

*Robert J. Kleine is the Senior Economist of Public Sector Consultants, Inc. in Lansing, Michigan.

ments to school districts, colleges and universities, and local governments.

The major fiscal change in Michigan in recent years was the reform of the school finance system, which was not related to the fiscal crisis of the early 1990s. The new system replaces a large share of the local school property tax with state level taxes, mainly an increase in the sales tax rate from 4 percent to 6 percent and a new statewide school property tax. This new financing system provides a more equal distribution of resources to school districts, but threatens to add more uncertainty and instability to state funding.

This chapter discusses the causes of Michigan's budget problems, the actions taken to balance the budget (with an emphasis on innovative measures that saved money and/or improved service delivery), the consequences of the budget reductions on the citizens of the state, and the new school finance system.

Background

The state budget is the blueprint, or spending plan, for state government; it reflects the program priorities of the governor and the legislature. The budget is a complete financial plan; it encompasses all revenues and expenditures (both operating and capital outlay) of the general fund and special revenue funds for the twelve-month period, the *fiscal year*, extending from October 1 of one calendar year through September 30 of the next.

The total state budget was about $22 billion in FY 1994, with expenditures from state sources (excluding federal aid) totaling about $15 billion. The largest spending category is education, about 37 percent of the total, with social services a distant second at 16.6 percent (state spending from state revenue sources). The state budget is divided into three major funds: general fund/general purpose (commonly referred to as the *general fund*), general fund/special purpose, and special revenue. The accounts of the GF/GP fund reflect the major share of transactions. The budget process concerns mainly the general purpose portion, as only these monies are subject to the complete control of the governor and the legislature. The GF/GP budget totaled $7.8 billion in FY 1993 and $8.1 billion in FY 1994. A key special revenue fund is the state school aid fund, which includes restricted revenues from the sales, cigarette, and liquor taxes, as well as a grant from the school aid fund. The fund totaled $3.7 billion in FY 1993–94.

Spending priorities change over time because of altered economic, social, and political conditions. This certainly has been the case in Michigan during the last twenty-five years. The major changes in the budget since FY 1968 have been the sharp increase in funds allocated to social services, corrections, and health, and a corresponding drop in the share allocated to education. K–12 education fell from about 33 percent of the state budget in FY 1968 to 20.5 percent in FY 1993 and higher education declined from 11 percent to 7.4 percent, while social services increased from 17 percent to 31 percent, health from 7.2 percent to 8.6 percent, and corrections and safety from 2.3 percent to 6.6 percent. These alterations have been caused in large part by higher unemployment in Michigan (until 1993), increased federal requirements for human service programs, a massive prison construction program, and declining enrollment in elementary and secondary schools. This trend toward higher relative welfare spending and lower education spending, however, has been reversed since FY 1983.

Table 11–1 presents general fund spending trends for the last few years. From FY 1990 to FY 1994, general fund spending increased only 7 percent, as large increases in Medicaid and corrections spending were offset by declines in AFDC expenditures and other expenditures, particularly general government and regulatory agencies.

In 1991, state-local general government expenditures were $3,612 per capita, 5 percent below the U.S. average; Michigan ranked twentieth among the states. As recently as 1988, Michigan was 9.1 percent above the national average and ranked eleventh. As a share of personal income, state-local spending was 19.7 percent, ranking Michigan twenty-sixth in 1991; Michigan ranked seventeenth in FY 1988. Michigan ranks high in spending for welfare, education, and health and hospitals but low in highways, interest payments, and parks and recreation.

One criterion for a good state-local tax system is the balanced use of the major revenue sources; income, sales, and property taxes. A rule of thumb is that each should contribute 20 to 30 percent of total state-local taxes. The Michigan tax system has been somewhat unbalanced for a number of years, with too much reliance on property taxes and too little on the sales tax. Property taxes accounted for 39.6 percent (35.7 percent adjusted for property tax credits) of state-local taxes, well above the U.S. average of 31 percent. The sales tax provided

TABLE 11–1   Growth of Major Michigan General Fund Budget Categories, FY 1991 to FY 1994

	FY 1991	FY 1992	FY 1993	FY 1994	Percent Change FY 1990– FY 1994
Elementary-Secondary Education	6.0	7.4	2.6	2.4	17.9
Social Services	0.6	−10.9	−2.4	6.5	−16.7
Medicaid^a	32.4	5.7	19.7	8.4	49.0
AFDC	−3.0	−14.7	5.9	−2.2	−14.0
Corrections	9.1	7.5	12.7	13.1	50.3
Higher Education	4.5	4.4	1.0	0.2	10.4
Mental Health	1.4	2.6	−1.1	8.6	11.2
Public Health	−0.7	−1.5	4.6	4.1	6.5
State Police	1.4	7.1	0.7	0.5	9.6
Capital Outlay	−32.6	6.2	−22.2	18.0	13.0
Other^b	−6.7	−13.0	0.8	−0.2	−21.0
Total	1.8	3.3	0.6	2.1	7.1

Note: Percent changes adjusted for funding delays and other financing shifts. The actual K–12 appropriation for FY 1994 was down 19.2 percent due to the transfer of $225.8 million from the teacher's health care reserve fund to cover increases in health care benefits.

^aFigures include hospital voluntary contributions. Actual general fund increases are smaller due to shift of funding to federal aid.
^bIncludes general government, natural resources, agriculture, labor, and commerce.

only 16.6 percent of state-local taxes, well below the U.S. average of 24.2 percent. The personal income tax provides 22.3 percent (26.3 percent adjusted for property tax credits), compared with the U.S. average of 21.1 percent. (FY 1991 data are used, the latest available for all states.) Unlike most states Michigan does not levy a corporate income tax. The state's main business tax is the Single Business Tax (SBT), a modified value-added tax.

Michigan's total tax burden is about average. Total state-local own-source revenue is 16 percent of personal income, or $3,012 per capita; Michigan ranks twenty-sixth and sixteenth respectively, in these categories (FY 1991 data).

Michigan's rank on many of these comparative statistics will change when FY 1994–95 data become available as a result of the recently enacted change in the school financing system (see discussion below). For example, the state-local property tax burden will be lower and the sales tax burden higher, and the overall tax burden will be slightly lower. On the expenditure side state support for education as a share of total support will be dramatically higher and school aid will be a much higher share of the state budget.

The Engler Agenda

In 1990 the Republican candidate, John Engler, ran on a platform to reduce property taxes, downsize government, revitalize the economy, and improve education. He defeated governor James Blanchard by only 17,000 votes, due, in large part, to a low voter turnout in Detroit, where Mayor Coleman Young and many blacks were not enthusiastic about the governor, who had not been as friendly to Detroit as was Governor William Milliken, his Republican predecessor.

When John Engler took office he inherited a large budget deficit and an economy that had been sluggish for several years, due in large part to downsizing in the auto industry, and in recession since early 1989. The Blanchard administration had used several bookkeeping adjustments to balance the FY 1990 budget, but the Engler administration reversed these adjustments partly for political reasons and partly because they were based on questionable accounting procedures and added to the structural deficit.[3]

The Michigan constitution requires that the governor present and the legislature enact a balanced budget. Until FY 1990 the budget had always been balanced, on paper. However, it had become practice in Michigan in the last two decades to balance the budget with onetime revenues, fund shifts, and accounting adjustments. These onetime adjustments averaged about $580 million from FY 1980 to FY 1990, about 10 percent of general fund expenditures.

The first budget for which John Engler had any responsibility was the FY 1991 budget. The FY 1991 budget was first adopted in July 1990 with general and school aid fund (SAF) revenues estimated at $10.1 billion. When John Engler took office in January 1991, the projected deficit had ballooned to nearly $1 billion and would subsequently exceed $1.9 billion.

Governor Engler initially ran into strong opposition from the Democrats, who controlled the House of Representatives, in his efforts to balance the budget without increasing revenues. Engler's major campaign promises were to reduce property taxes and downsize state government. Most Democrats were convinced that he was using the fiscal crisis as an excuse to reduce expenditures, particularly for social programs, and to make room for cuts in property taxes. The Democrats offered a number of alternative plans that attempted to spread the cuts over a longer period of time and to raise revenues, largely through eliminating so called "tax expenditures," which are tax deductions, exemptions, and credits. The Democrats also included a number of onetime revenue and spending adjustments in their proposals. In the end, the fiscal crisis was so severe and the opposition to tax increases so strong, the governor prevailed with most of his proposals, including the most controversial, which was the elimination of the General Assistance program.

Before looking in some detail at the actions taken to balance the state budget it is instructive to examine the factors that created the fiscal crisis.

Causes of Michigan's Budget Problems

The fiscal crisis in the early 1990s was caused by several factors: 1) the slowdown in the Michigan economy that began in 1987 and accelerated in 1989; 2) the phaseout of the income tax rate increase, which was increased from 4.6 to 6.35 percent in 1983 to deal with the budget problems created by the 1980–1982 recession; the rate was gradually rolled back to 4.6 percent in 1987; 3) the explosion in spending for state prisons; 4) the declining elasticity of the state tax structure; 5) the propensity to use onetime revenues and accounting gimmicks to avoid tough decision on taxation and spending, which resulted in a structural budget deficit; and 6) the failure to put enough money into the Budget Stabilization Fund, or rainy day fund, when the economy was strong.

Economic slowdown. Real personal income, one of the best indicators of an economy's health, grew slowly from 1987 to 1991, before showing improvement beginning in 1992. In 1990 and 1991, real personal income declined, but not nearly as sharply as in the 1979–1982 period. Weakness in real income translates into weakness in state revenues. GF/GP and School Aid Fund revenues (adjusted for policy and accounting changes) increased only 1.1 percent in FY 1990, declined 2.7 percent in FY 1991 and increased a modest 2.9 percent in FY 1992.

Michigan also suffered from a longer term economic problem brought on by the decline of the U.S. motor vehicle industry and a shift in production to other regions. U.S. motor vehicle production as a share of world motor vehicle production declined from about 80 percent in the early 1950s to about 20 percent in 1992. Michigan production fell from about 26 percent of the world total in 1950 to 6.2 percent in 1992; as recently as 1979 Michigan's share was 8.5 percent. This decline, along with a general nationwide decline in manufacturing, sharply reduced the number of manufacturing jobs in Michigan—a decline of about 280,000 or 24 percent from 1978 to 1992. At the same time service jobs have grew rapidly, 58.3 percent from 1978 to 1992.

Manufacturing employment as a share of total wage and salary employment fell from 32 percent in 1979 to 23 percent in 1992, while service employment rose from 17 percent to almost 25 percent. For the first time in history, the service industry in Michigan employs more workers than the manufacturing sector. This has had major economic consequences for Michigan. Because manufacturing jobs pay about twice as much, on average, as service jobs, Michigan has become a poorer state. Michigan's per capita income was about 20 percent above the national average in the early 1950s, and 6–8 percent above the national average in the late 1970s. In 1993 Michigan per capita income was about 2 percent below the national average. Michigan has become a poorer state and the state has just begun to face up to the fact that you cannot have Cadillac services with a Chevrolet budget. This has been a painful realization and the slow adjustment to this new, more austere world has contributed to Michigan's budget problems in the early 1990s.

Income tax increase. In 1983 the state income tax rate was increased from 4.6 percent to 6.35 percent, on a temporary basis. The rate was rolled back in stages, returning to 4.6 percent in 1987. This reduction in the rate during a strong economic recovery prevented the state from building up large balances in the rainy day fund, which could have been used to soften the budget crisis in the early 1990s. Just as important was the change in the political landscape that resulted from the income tax increase. As a result of the increase two state senators were recalled from office and an attempt was made to recall the governor, James Blanchard. The two recalled senators were Democrats, which swung control of the house to the Republicans. Ever since, Michigan politicians have been terrified about raising the income tax. As discussed later, this income tax phobia helped shape the 1993 debate on school finance reform and property tax relief.

Eroding tax base. In addition to the slowdown in revenue growth due to the weak economy, the state has reduced resources by granting deductions and exemptions from the tax base, which are known as tax expenditures. These expenditures have eroded the tax base, increasing by more than $2 billion, or about 50 percent in the last decade. The erosion continued with the July 1993 repeal of the state inheritance tax, which will reduce FY 1994 revenues by about $95 million, and 1994 cuts in income and single business tax revenues of about $200 million.

State tax structure. State revenue has also become less responsive to economic growth. In the 1970s, a 1 percent increase in personal income would produce a 0.9 to .95 percent increase in revenues. Today a 1 percent increase in income results in about an 0.8 percent increase in state revenue. A portion of this decline is cyclical, but most is likely due to structural changes in the economy and the state's failure to levy the sales tax on most services, which is the fastest growing sector of the economy. (The SBT taxes service firms, but a number of special credits and deductions limit the burden on the service sector.)

Spending pressures. The major problems on the spending side of the budget have been the Department of Corrections and health care, including Medicaid. Many of the current problems with corrections spending began with the decision in the 1980s to build a large number of new prisons. Michigan's prison capacity increased from 13,162 in 1984 to an estimated 26,882 in 1993, a 104 percent jump due to the most extensive building program in state history. However, the growth in the prison population has outpaced the building program, and in 1993 the population exceeded capacity by about 8,000 beds. In FY 1979–1980, the Corrections budget was $175 million (GF/GP), 3.6 percent of the general fund budget. The FY 1994 appropriation was $1,137 million, 14 percent of the general fund budget. This explosion continued in the 1994 budget with an increase of $129 million; the state total budget increased only $163 million, although a $300 million reduction in retirement costs helped fund increases of $375 million in the nonretirement portion of the budget. This increased share came from other state programs and is destabilizing other budgets.

As in every state, health care has eaten up resources. Michigan health care costs (includes Medicaid, programs in other departments such as corrections, and cost for state employees and retirees, including teachers) increased $2.6 billion from FY 1981 to FY 1991, a 129.7 percent increase compared with a 72 percent increase for the GF/GP budget. As a share of the total state budget, health expenditures rose from 21 percent in 1981 to 26 percent in 1991—a shift from other programs of about $550 million. However, as shown in Table 11–2, Medicaid has not been a drain on the state's general fund, largely because of the sharp increase in federal aid (see discussion below). From FY 1989 to FY 1994, total Medicaid expenditures increased at an annual rate of 18.2 percent. However, because of a 19 percent annual increase in federal aid, general fund expenditures increased at an annual rate of only 3.7 percent. The point is, however, that the growth in Medicaid spending in the 1980s crowded out other state programs and only creative federal financing arrangements prevented further crowding out in the 1990s.

TABLE 11–2 Michigan Medicaid Expenditures, FY 1986 to FY 1994 (dollar amounts in millions)

Fiscal Year	Total ($)	General Fund ($)	Federal Aid ($)	Federal Aid as % of Total	Hosp. Vol. Contributions ($)
1986	1,458.6	617.6	832.6	57.1%	
1987	1,568.5	665.2	895.2	57.1%	
1988	1,623.5	714.9	899.7	55.4%	
1989	1,727.7	780.1	940.1	54.4%	
1990	2,070.9	956.3	1,107.1	53.5%	
1991	2,756.6	865.0	1,483.4	53.8%	400.9
1992	3,068.0	886.0	1,711.0	55.8%	451.6
1993	3,672.0	848.0	2,056.0	56.0%	451.6
1994	3,982.0	935.0	2,242.0	56.3%	489.0
Percent Change (Annual Rate)					
1986–1989	5.8%	4.1%	4.1%		
1989–1994	18.2%	3.7%	19.0%		

Source: Michigan Department of Social Services, 1993.

All these factors contributed to Michigan's budget problems and required the governor and the legislature to make numerous reductions and adjustments in the state budget for the period from 1990 to 1993. The actions taken by the state fall into four main categories; 1) reductions in expenditures, including elimination of some programs; 2) actions to increase federal aid, mainly in the Medicaid program; 3) onetime revenue or expenditure adjustments, such as changing the method of accounting for tax credits and delaying state payments to colleges and universities; and 4) transfers from other funds, such as the Budget Stabilization fund. The specific actions that were used to balance the budget for fiscal years 1991 to 1993 are summarized below.

BUDGET AND TAX STRATEGIES: FY 1991–1993

Michigan's approach to the budget problems created by the economic downturn in the early 1990s was to take all possible actions to avoid a tax increase. Expenditure reductions were the first option, but when the problem grew to the point that additional cuts were not politically possible and the rainy day fund was depleted, the governor and the legislature resorted to other strategies. The first was to capture as much federal aid as possible, which was largely used to replace general fund support. For example, federal aid to Michigan increased $1.6 billion or 38 percent from FY 1990 to FY 1993, with about 60 percent of this amount in the Department of Social Services. Federal aid increased from 24.1 percent of total state revenues in FY 1990 to an estimated 28.8 percent in FY 1993. Federal support for Medicaid rose from $940 million in FY 1989 to $1.9 billion in FY 1993, an increase of over 100 percent. This represents about 44 percent of the total increase in federal aid during this period. There were also large increases in federal aid for other social services programs such as foster care, child and adult care programs, and child support enforcement, as well as for job training programs.

The next approach was to make accounting changes, such as switching property tax credits from the revenue to the expenditure side of the budget, and delaying payments for school districts, local governments, and school districts. These onetime adjustments were an important part of the strategy to avoid tax increases, since it was not possible politically to solve the entire problem with budget cuts.

These adjustments amounted to 12 percent of the budget in FY 1991, 9.2 percent in FY 1992, and 6.2 percent in FY 1993.

Michigan's serious budget problems began with the FY 1991 budget. Although revenue increased only 1.2 percent in FY 1990 and the year ended with a $300 million deficit, no major budget reduction actions were taken in that year. The outgoing governor, Jim Blanchard, did approve several bookkeeping adjustments to show a balanced budget for FY 1990, but these were reversed by the Engler administration.

The legislature and the governor enacted the FY 1991 budget during the summer and fall of 1990. The general fund budget appropriated $7.6 billion based on the assumption that general and school aid fund revenue would increase 6.9 percent. Early in the fiscal year it became clear that revenues were falling well short of estimates and the budgets for several departments, mainly corrections and social services, did not have adequate funding to meet the policies mandated in the budget. To summarize the FY 1991 experience, the shortfall in revenues, supplemental expenditures, and a carryover deficit of $310 million from FY 1990 turned a budget originally balanced into a potential deficit of $1.994 billion. This deficit was equal to about 20 percent of the original statutory estimate of revenue. Only 40 percent of the problem was solved by permanent reductions in spending. Other large adjustments were onetime revenues (28.2 percent), rainy day fund withdrawal (12 percent), and increased federal aid from hospital voluntary contributions (10.1 percent). The remaining 10 percent consisted of various funding transfers and delays in payments.

Michigan's budget problems continued in FY 1992, requiring another round of expenditure reductions and onetime revenue and spending adjustments. The governor's original budget was based on a general and school aid fund revenue estimate of $10.0 billion (an increase of 4.9 percent) plus $131.3 million in accounting changes. The governor recommended a GF/GP appropriation level of $7.6 billion plus $278 for a property tax reduction program. Actual revenues for the fiscal year increased only 2.9 percent (on a lower than estimated FY 1991 base) and ended up $588 million lower than estimated in the governor's budget. Adding to the budget were supplemental expenditures of $130 million, about one-half for school aid. In addition, the year began with a deficit of $169.4 million.

The actions taken to balance the FY 1992 budget totaled $888 million. Only 27 percent of this problem was solved by permanent spending cuts. Other large adjustments were funding delays (39 percent), onetime revenues (13.3 percent), and a withdrawal from the rainy day fund (19 percent).

The budget problems in FY 1993 were less serious than in the previous two years, but reductions were still required. In the spring of 1993, the legislature and the governor agreed on and enacted a $374 million deficit reduction package. The originally enacted FY 1993 budget projected a year-end balance of $18.5 million. The original budget assumed $342 million in onetime revenues (less $20 million in tax reductions).

There were also three changes in state-financed retirement programs. First, an increase in the number of years used to amortize retirement fund earning reduced retirement contributions by $9.3 million. The second change transferred $7.9 million of pre-funded reserves in the state employee dental and vision health plans to the general fund. The third change utilized a maximum of $89.6 million of the pre-funded health reserve in the Public School Employees Retirement System to pay for the current year cash cost of retiree health benefits. (These changes did not endanger the solvency of retirement system as there was a substantial surplus in the health reserve.)

The only significant tax increase was $14.3 million in additional liquor revenue due to a 9 percent increase in the price of liquor effective May 1, 1993 (Michigan is a control state).

For the first time since the new consensus revenue estimating process began in 1991, state revenue in FY 1993 exceeded the consensus revenue estimates. The budget was built on a estimate that revenue would increase 4.1 percent; the actual increase was 7.5 percent. As a result, the year ended with an estimated surplus of about $312 million, of which all but $26 million was transferred to the state's rainy day fund.

Table 11–3 presents a three-year summary of the budget shortfalls and the actions taken to eliminate the potential deficit. Expenditure reductions accounted for only 37.2 percent of the total budget adjustments. The other major actions were funding shifts and delays (12.5 percent), onetime revenues (19.6 percent), and rainy day fund withdrawals (12.5 percent).

The changes in the various budget categories since John Engler took office are presented in Table 11–4. Total state spending from state sources (excluding federal aid) increased only 4.2 percent from FY 1990 to FY 1993. The changes in the various program areas vary

TABLE 11-3 Changes from the Michigan General Fund Budget as Originally Enacted, FY 1991-FY 1993 (millions of dollars)

	FY 1991	FY 1992	FY 1993	Three-Year Totals
Assumed Ending Balance	15.0	0.4	18.5	33.9
Revenue Shortfall	(927.4)	(587.9)	(40.0)	(1,555.3)
Expenditure Increases	(766.5)	(130.1)	(161.0)	(1,057.6)
Change in Beginning Balance	(315.1)	(170.2)	0.0	(485.3)
Potential Deficit	(1,994.0)	(887.8)	(182.5)	(3,064.3)
Actions to Reduce Deficit				
Appropriations Reductions	791.7	238.5	162.0	1,192.2
Funding Shifts	194.5	0.0	157.2	351.7
Funding Delays	114.4	345.7	45.5	505.6
Retirement Changes	0	15.2	115.6	130.8
Budget Stabilization Withdrawal	230.0	170.1	0.0	400.1
One-Time Revenue Items	494.0	118.3	14.3	626.6
Total Adjustments	1,824.6	887.8	494.6	3,207.0
Remaining Balance	(169.4)	0.0	312.1	142.7

Note: The FY 1993 budget as originally enacted included $342 million in onetime revenue items.
Source: Senate Fiscal Agency, 1993.

considerably and are, in part, a reflection of the governor's priorities. There have been particularly large reductions in capital outlay, a normal occurrence when resources are limited, regulatory (departments of commerce and labor), and social services. In most of these areas a significant share of general fund monies have been replaced by federal aid.

The largest increases in the budget were for corrections, school aid, natural resources, and higher education. The governor ran on a platform that emphasized support for education, and he largely spared education from budget cuts, although, adjusted for inflation, resources declined. Law enforcement is traditionally a Republican priority, but the large increase in corrections spending is largely the legacy

TABLE 11–4 Growth of Michigan Spending from State Resources, FY 1990 to FY 1993

Category	Percent Change
Corrections	33.9%
School Aid	13.1
Natural Resources	12.4
Higher Education	10.0
Public Health	7.0
State Police	4.8
General Government	4.4
Mental Health	3.0
Social Services	−12.7
Medicaid	−7.3[a]
Regulatory	−16.5
Capital Outlay	−49.9
Total Budget	4.2%

[a]The total Medicaid budget increased 67.4 percent, but a large increase in federal aid, due in part to creative financing, resulted in a decline in general fund expenditures.
Source: Senate Fiscal Agency, 1994.

of a prison construction program that started in the Milliken and Blanchard administrations.

Table 11–5 a summarizes the expenditure reductions by department for fiscal years 1991 to 1993. The largest dollar reduction, $645.8 million, was in the Department of Social Services. However, the largest percentage reduction, 29.1 percent, was in the appropriations for the Public School Employees Retirement System. The largest department reductions were labor, 27.3 percent, agriculture, 13.5 percent, and commerce, 13.3 percent. Education (community colleges, higher education, and school aid) largely escaped significant cuts.

FY 1993–1994 Budget

Because of the improved economic and revenue picture, the FY 1994 budget was relatively trouble free, despite the need to cover onetime revenues used to balance the FY 1993 budget. The governor's FY 1993 budget used about $428 million in onetime revenues and included a $59 million reduction in retirement costs. The FY 1994 general fund

TABLE 11–5 Michigan Budget Reductions as Proportion of Total State Appropriations, FY 1991–FY 1993

Program/Department	Total Reductions (thousands of $)	Percent of Appropriations
School Employees Retirement	343,649	29.1
Labor	63,625	27.3
Agriculture	20,602	13.5
Commerce	102,624	13.3
Education	19,362	11.3
Capital Outlay	58,488	9.9
Social Services	645,774	9.7
State Police	43,914	6.5
Natural Resources	44,172	6.1
Civil Service	4,339	6.1
Revenue Sharing	168,380	5.2
Library of Michigan	4,293	5.2
Management and Budget	19,215	4.6
Civil Rights	1,553	4.4
Public Health	22,470	4.3
Military Affairs	5,138	4.1
Legislature	10,582	4.0
Mental Health	108,844	3.8
State	5,541	3.0
Higher Education	104,191	2.7
Attorney General	2,388	2.7
School Aid	185,657	2.1
Judiciary	8,127	2.0
Corrections	48,753	1.8
Treasury	8,428	1.4
Executive	145	1.1
Transportation	35,300	0.9
Community Colleges	2,255	0.3
Total (State Spending from State Sources)	2,087,810	5.2

Source: Senate Fiscal Agency, 1993.

budget, as approved by the legislature in September 1993, was up only 1.9 percent from FY 1993. However, subsequently about $170 million in supplemental expenditures were added to the budget, and taxes were reduced by $155 million (effective in FY 1994–95). Because of the strong economic recovery, for the first time in several years, no mid-course budget corrections were required. A surplus of nearly $300 million is estimated for FY 1994, and it would be even higher except for an $107 million reduction in revenue due to school finance reform.

INNOVATIONS

Much of what was done to balance the budget in the 1990–1993 period involved elimination of programs, across-the-board budget cuts, one-time revenues, and payment delays. There were few actions that could be classified as innovative that had a significant impact on the budget, although there were a number of changes that could result in significant savings in future years.

The innovative action that had the biggest budget impact was the hospital voluntary contributions program, and this was not unique to Michigan. Many states took advantage of a loophole in federal law to increase their federal Medicaid revenues. This was done by appropriating money to hospitals for Medicaid with the understanding that the money would be returned to the state. This had the impact of increasing expenditures on Medicaid, on paper, thereby increasing the federal Medicaid match, and reducing general fund expenditures on Medicaid. Michigan saved $200–$250 annually in general fund expenditures in fiscal years 1990 to 1994. The federal government changed the law in 1992 to prevent voluntary contributions from hospitals as a means of earning additional federal aid. However, the law did not prevent transfers to university hospitals, and the state has taken advantage of this loophole by setting up an intergovernmental transfer with the University of Michigan hospital, allowing the state to continue to capture additional federal aid for the Medicaid program.

Michigan has been a leader in establishing a system to begin privatizing state services. However, this had yet to have an impact on the state budget. The only privatization actions approved have been the sale of the State Accident Fund, which provides worker's compensation insurance, and the contracting out of the state's liquor distribution system. The state is expected to receive up to $200 million for the fund. The governor has already included about $70 million of this amount in the FY 1995 budget to establish an endowment for state parks and for a civilian conservation corps. A large portion of the remainder is expected to be transferred to the rainy day fund. A number of companies have bid on the state liquor contract, which will be awarded in 1994 or 1995.

The privatization process, known as PERM (Privatize, Eliminate, Retain, and Modify) is being implemented throughout state government. The governor began the process by appointing a Public-Private Partnership Commission. The commission recommended adopting the PERM process and called for all state services to apply this structured method for reviewing agency services for possible privatization. The governor then established a Privatization Division in the Department of Management and Budget (DMB) to manage the process. Their first major action was to issue a call for private firms that wished to conduct privatization studies to submit proposals. This resulted in eight firms qualifying to conduct these studies. In 1993 DMB began to issue requests for proposals (RFPs) to the eight firms to prepare studies on the feasibility of privatizing specified services. To date the RFPs have been limited to data processing services.

The state also made a number of changes in the process for letting state contracts that are expected to achieve substantial savings in future years. A central contact office was established in DMB and a statewide computer-based control system for contracts was set up.

The Department of Social Services also instituted some changes that have the potential to save significant amounts of money over the longer term. These include a change in welfare rules in June 1992 that permit recipients to keep the first $200 a month they earn, plus 20 percent of earnings above that amount. Welfare recipients who work are allowed to collect the federal earned income credit each month. The department also started a voluntary agreement program, known as a "social contract" that strongly encourages welfare recipients to devote at least twenty hours a week to volunteer work, job training, or education. These programs are credited with increasing the number of AFDC recipients with jobs to about 51,000, 50 percent higher than three years ago. This is 23.3 percent of all AFDC parents, the highest percentage in the nation according to the Department of Social Services. These programs are part of the governor's "To Strengthen Michigan Families" welfare reform initiatives. Other important components are programs to enhance the lives of children and families, prevent child abuse and neglect, protect children, and prevent the unnecessary separation of children, and the Healthy Kids program that expands health care for kids in low-income families not eligible for Medicaid. Most of these programs cost money in the short run, but are designed to reduce welfare caseloads and social problems and save money over the longer term.

Although the Department of Corrections is the fastest growing general fund program, cost saving measures were undertaken. From 1990 to 1994 the department increased the use of double bunking by 33 percent and closed more costly prisons, resulting in estimated cumulative saving of about $50 million. Community placement, electronic tether, and bootcamp programs were instituted to reduce state prison populations.

The Department of Public Health has taken several innovative actions to reduce costs and/or provide more efficient delivery of services. First, a new rebate agreement was reached with Wyeth-Ayerst laboratories for infant formula. This agreement provided for a public-private partnership in cooperation with the State of Indiana, generating over $30 million in savings. Second, a Medicaid Cost-Based Reimbursement project in cooperation with the Department of Social Services was initiated. This allows local health departments to receive federal Title XIX funding for the full cost of delivering Maternal and Child Health clinical services. This project is generating $5 million per year in added funding for local health departments. Michigan was among the first states in the country to implement such a project. Third, at the Department's request, the legislature approved $3.4 million in additional fees to support the Michigan drinking water program and retain primary enforcement authority for the Safe Drinking Water Act. The value of the projected savings far exceeds the cost of the annual fees.

The Department of Natural Resources took a number of actions to reduce costs. Two are particularly significant. The Department determined it could become more efficient by implementing a "cluster plan." This is a means of providing a system of core parks responsible for their own operation and other state parks assigned to the cluster. The plan resulted in a reduction of twenty-four administered parks, about forty-four positions, and a net savings of $0.5 million. Also the State Parks Division and the Recreation Division were merged. The consolidation plan is still being developed, but significant savings will be realized from the elimination of several supervisory positions.

It is too early to determine the long-term saving and effects on services of many of the innovations, particularly privatization. However, it is clear that the state expenditure base in Michigan has been reduced and that efforts to improve the efficiency of government service delivery through privatization and other means will continue, and likely accelerate in the future.

CONSEQUENCES OF BUDGET CUTS

Budget reductions do not occur without consequences. While it may be true that the majority of Michigan's citizens have not been noticeably affected by the cuts, there are several groups that have felt the impact: college students and their parents, K–12 school districts, the poor, state employees, and local governments.

Higher education did relatively well in the 1980s, increasing from 16.7 percent of GF/GP spending in 1980 to 19.3 percent in 1989. However, in the early 1990s universities were one of the victims of Michigan's fiscal crisis. In FY 1994 higher education spending was only 16.7 percent of the GF/GP budget. In FY 1992, public universities nationwide received 41.2 percent from state appropriations, while Michigan universities received only 36.5 percent of their revenue from state appropriations. One consequence is high tuition rates that are well above the national average. In 1990–1991 the average tuition rate at a four-year university in Michigan was about 40 percent above the national average, seventh highest in the nation. The average tuition at community colleges was 36 percent above the national average, ranking Michigan seventeenth. Tuition rates at Michigan's public universities increased at an annual rate of 9 percent from 1990 to 1993, well above the rate of inflation, but about the same rate as nationally. Enrollments have not suffered, increasing significantly since the mid-1980s. University enrollments increased from 190,000 in 1985 to 216,000 in 1993, while community college enrollments rose from 113,000 to 130,000. Although higher education was affected by budget reductions, it fared relatively well compared with other areas of the budget and compared with other states (see discussion in Chapter 5).

Although Governor Engler has made K–12 education a priority of his administration, and that area of the budget has largely avoided cuts, sufficient resources have not been available to help many fiscally distressed school districts. This was most vividly illustrated by the Kalkaska school district, which attracted national attention by closing its doors ten weeks early in 1993, rather than reduce its programs to match its resources. There were at least fifty school districts (out of 559) in similar financial distress, and the governor and the legislature had been struggling to find a solution for a number of years. In 1993 state government provided about 35 percent of the total resources spent on K–12 education in Michigan. The national average was 51 percent and only six states provided a smaller share than Michigan. In the early 1970s, the state provided about half the resources for K–12 education, and in the late 1970s the state share was over 40 percent. State support has risen since the deep recessions of the early 1980s, when it fell below 30 percent. In the past the lack of resources pitted the poorer, "in-formula" school districts, against the richer, "out-of-formula" school districts, as the state resorted to reducing categorical payments to the richer districts in order to increase support for the in-formula districts that receive equalization payments from the state. This division in the school community made it difficult to build sufficient support for school finance reform, and is a major reason it took so long the resolve the issue. As discussed below the legislature and the governor have taken a bold new approach to this problem, after the voter rejected a proposal in June 1993 to reduce school property taxes, raise the sales tax from 4 percent to 6 percent, and guarantee $4,800 for each pupil. This proposal received a yes vote from 59 percent of the voters outside of Metro Detroit, but in wealthy Oakland County, where most of the school districts are out-of-formula, the proposal lost 3–1. The proposal also lost by a large margin in Wayne County (location of City of Detroit) and bordering Macomb County.

Budget reductions clearly had a major impact on the poor. During the recessions of the early 1980s, public assistance grants were reduced on seven separate occasions. Those reductions have not been restored, and there have been minimal increases in recent years. The average AFDC grant, adjusted for inflation, declined 16 percent from 1990 to 1993. In FY 1990, the AFDC maximum grant for a family of three living in Wayne County was $5,748, equal to 58 percent of the poverty threshold (not including food stamps).[4] In FY 1993, the maximum grant was $5,508, only 49.2 percent of the poverty threshold. The poverty gap, the difference between the maximum grant and the poverty threshold, increased from $4,671 in FY 1990 to $5,679 in FY 1990, a 21.6 percent increase. In addition the number of Michigan families living in poverty increased from 9.4 percent of total families in 1979 to 13.1 percent in 1989 and 13.5 percent in 1992.

The largest reduction in any program in the FY 1990–1993 period was the elimination of 84,000 individuals from the General Assistance program, resulting in an income loss to recipients of about $250 per month. The policy was to eliminate all able-bodied adults from the program for an estimated budget savings of $300 million. This was the governor's most controversial action during his tenure and caused many Democrats and welfare groups to label the governor as "mean spirited." According to a 1993 report by the University of Michigan[5]:

> Conflicting reports from the administration, strong disagreement in the legislature, heated public debate, and court cases challenging the termination led to confusion on the part of recipients and local service providers. The program ended with little awareness of and planning for the needs of the population, widespread belief that the government had no other budgetary options, and an ideology that employment was somehow undermined by the GA program. When the program was terminated two new programs were created (State Family Assistance and State Disability Assistance) to continue supporting some GA recipients. About 30,000 people were transferred to these other programs. The rest of the population, more than 80,000 people, were terminated from public assistance. Many of them still qualify for Food Stamps and medical coverage from the state or Wayne county. The medical programs for which they qualify are less comprehensive than either Medicaid or the former GA-Medical program (which was also terminated in October, 1991).

AFDC caseloads increased moderately from FY 1989 to FY 1991, rising from 211,700 to 227,400, but leveled off in the next three years. General Assistance caseloads had begun to grow after falling sharply in the mid-1980s, until the program was largely eliminated in FY 1992.[6] The conclusion is that welfare caseloads were a minor contributor to the fiscal problems of the early 1990s.

The reductions in the state budget did not result in massive layoffs of state employees, but employment was significantly reduced through attrition and early retirement programs; a hiring freeze has been in effect for most departments. As shown in Table 11–6, state classified employment declined by 5,804 or 8.7 percent from FY 1990 to FY 1993. The reductions were across the board, but the sharpest declines were in health and human services. In addition most state employees were required to take off four days without pay in the summer of 1991. The state has also been successful in holding down pay increases for state employees. Most of the unions signed contracts

TABLE 11-6 Average Number of Michigan State Classified Employees, Selected Departments, Various Years

Department	FY 1984–85	FY 1989–90	Percent Change	FY 1991–92	FY 1992–93	Percent Change FY 1990–1993
Corrections	6,352	13,822	117.6%	13,437	14,128	2.2%
Social Services	13,336	14,141	6.0%	13,208	13,410	−5.2%
Mental Health	11,266	10,195	−9.5%	7,398	6,489	−36.4%
Natural Resources	3,457	3,513	1.6%	3,616	3,596	2.4%
Public Health	1,724	1,984	15.1%	1,373	1,345	−32.2%
State Police	2,891	3,183	10.1%	2,941	2,889	−9.2%
All Other	19,257	19,953	3.6%	19,530	19,130	−4.1%
Total State	58,283	66,791	14.6%	61,503	60,987	−8.7%

Source: Michigan Department of Civil Service, 1994.

providing for no pay increase in 1992, a 0–1 percent increase in 1993, a 0–2 percent increase in 1994 plus a lump sum payment of $750, and a 0–3 percent increase plus a lump sum payment of $600 in 1995 and 1996. The percentage pay increases in 1993–1996 are tied to success in controlling health care costs. The pay increases for 1993 and 1994 averaged about 1 percent.

The Michigan constitution requires that 41.6 percent of the state budget be allocated to local units of government (including school districts and community colleges). This provision provides some protection against large reductions in aid, but local governments have been affected by the state's budget problems. First, revenue sharing payments were reduced by $10.7 million in FY 1991, $45.5 million in FY 1993, and $49.6 million in FY 1994. In addition, revenue sharing payments were delayed in FY 1992 until the next fiscal year, saving the state $112 million in that fiscal year. Second, a number of grant programs have been reduced or eliminated, such as aid to cities with racetracks and cultural and arts grants, which were cut about 40 percent. Third, although not directly related to the budget situation local governments lost an estimated $150 million in revenue in FY 1992–93 due to a state imposed freeze on 1992 property tax assessments.

SCHOOL FINANCE REFORM

In July 1993 the legislature in a stunning move voted to repeal all school operating property taxes as of December 31, 1993 (affecting FY 1994–95 school budgets), nearly $7 billion of about 60 percent of all local property taxes. The legislature took this action after over twenty years of failure to change the system, including the defeat of ten school finance ballot proposals, the latest in June 1993. The legislature did not provide for any replacement revenue, although it was understood that most of the revenue would be replaced. In October 1993 the governor presented his school finance plan to the legislature. It provided for a $4,500 grant per pupil beginning in FY 1994–95 and guaranteed that all school districts spending $6,500 per pupil or less would receive up to a 2 percent increase above FY 1993–94 revenue. Districts spending in excess of $6,500 would be required to ask voters to approve local millages. Future increases in per pupil revenue would be limited to the rate of inflation. The governor also recommended a number of education reform measures including schools of choice and charter schools.

The governor recommended replacement of all but $300 million of the lost revenue. The governor's proposed revenue package included a 2-cent increase in the state sales tax (from 4 cents to 6 cents), a 16 mill property tax on nonhomestead property, an 0.5 percent increase in the single business tax rate to 2.85 percent, a 4 percent real estate transfer tax, a 50-cent increase in the state cigarette tax to 75 cents, the elimination of the state-financed circuit breaker property tax credit, and the elimination of state revenue sharing (excluding money from the sales tax that is guaranteed by the constitution), with the revenue sharing funds of about $700 million to be replaced by constitutionally establishing additional local property tax millage of from 2 to 6 mills. The governor proposed that the package be placed on the ballot for a February vote. The defeat of the proposal would have required the legislature to start over and put school funding for FY 1994–95 in jeopardy.

In a twenty-six hour session ending on Christmas Eve 1993, the legislature, after twenty-five years of failure, agreed to a school finance reform package, including the replacement of the majority of the $7 billion in school property taxes repealed in July 1993. The plan would put into effect by law various tax increases grounded by an income tax hike but allow voters, in a special March 15 referendum, to substitute a different tax plan, grounded by a 2-cent increase in the sales tax. Either way, K–12 funding in FY 1994–95 would total $10.5 billion, an increase of about $600 million over the FY 1993–94 level. The distribution of funds was the same under both proposals. All districts were brought up to $4,200 per pupil, with this foundation grant increased gradually to $5,000. Districts spending from $4,200 to $6,500 were guaranteed the FY 1993–94 level plus an additional $160 to $260 per pupil. Districts spending in excess of $6,500 will have to ask voters for additional millage. All districts will be allowed to ask voters for an additional 3 mills. Also a $230 million categorical grant was set up to provide $385 per pupil based on a district's number of students whose parent's income is sufficiently low to qualify the child for free school lunches.

On March 15, 1994, 69 percent of the voters opted for the ballot plan, which includes a 6 percent sales tax (up from 4 percent), a 6 mill property tax on homesteads, a 24 mill tax on nonhomesteads, a 2 percent property transfer tax (subsequently reduced to .75 percent), a 50-cent increase in the cigarette tax (to 75 cents), and a reduction in the income tax rate from 4.6 percent to 4.4 percent. This negated the backup statutory plan, which included a 6 percent income tax, a 12 mill property tax on homesteads, a 24 mill tax on nonhomesteads, a 2.75 percent SBT (up from 2.35 percent), a 1 percent property transfer tax, a 15-cent increase in the cigarette tax (to 40 cents), and a $900 increase in the personal income tax exemption (to $3,000).

The ballot plan provided a net tax cut of about $700 million. After adjusting for the impact of federal deductibility, taxes declined by about $300 million. Because of improved revenue growth, the use of onetime revenues, and the collection of new revenues beginning May 1, 1994, the school finance plans will have a minimal impact on the FY 1994–95 general fund budget. However, because school property tax revenues were not fully replaced, monies will have to be appropriated from the general fund to the school aid fund to fully fund the new formula. This will create budget problems when the surplus from the early collection of the new taxes is gone and the economic growth slows, possibly as early as FY 1997.

The approval of the ballot proposal ended twenty-five years of debate and frustration over property tax relief and school finance reform that generated ten statewide ballot issues, with all going down to defeat. The success of this measure (Proposal A) was a victory for Governor Engler, who pledged to reduce property taxes in his 1990 campaign and who strongly supported the ballot proposal, and won against strong opposition from the labor unions, including the powerful Michigan Education Association, and from the tobacco industry, which spent millions on an ad campaign designed to mislead voters.

The new funding plan is an improvement on the current system. In FY 1994, the state provided only 35 percent of the support for public schools, with local school taxes making up the rest; nationwide state support is over 50 percent. This results in an inequitable distribution of resources, with some districts spending $3,000 per pupil and others $10,000 per pupil. State support for education will now jump to nearly 80 percent, second highest in the nation, and the lower spending districts will be brought up to at least $4,200 per pupil in the first year, while increases for the higher spending districts will be limited. Also Michigan previously had an unbalanced tax system, with a property tax burden about 35 percent above the national average and a sales tax burden about one-third below the national average. The new funding plan reduced property taxes about 33 percent, reducing the property tax burden to the national average, while the increase in the sales tax also moved Michigan to near the national average.

There are two other less publicized changes that may be beneficial. First, the new funding plan eliminated separate payments to school districts for retirement and Social Security and rolled them into the foundation grant. This may result in smaller pay increases for school employees in the future, which have been outpacing increases for private sector workers, as the districts will be picking up all the retirement and Social Security costs rather than the state picking up the costs. More importantly this has an equalizing effect as direct funding provided more per pupil aid to richer districts with higher average salaries, and now all districts receive the same per pupil support. Second, the plan includes a limit on assessment increases, the lower of 5 percent or the rate of inflation. In Michigan, assessment increases have caused more taxpayer anger than anything else. This combined with lower property taxes should mollify most taxpayers.

Also included in the package are several educational reforms including a mandated core curriculum for all schools, an increase in required classroom instruction from 900 hours to 1080 hours annually by the year 2000, and authorization for public schools, community colleges, and universities to establish charter schools. Although schools of choice was strongly supported by the governor, they were not included in the final package. The governor vowed to bring up the issue again.

What Michigan did was not revolutionary. The state corrected some longstanding inequities and imbalances. Hopefully, the long-term result will be better schools, a stronger economy, and happier taxpayers. Most importantly, after twenty-five years the state will be able to move on to other important issues.[7]

CONCLUSION

John Engler has taken Michigan in a new direction. Historically Michigan has been a high tax, high spending state with a progressive tradition, similar to Wisconsin and Minnesota. Michigan now has average levels of taxes and spending and is beginning to look more like Ohio and Indiana.[8] There will still be political barriers to hurdle, but, as discussed above, Michigan could be well on its way to becoming a leader in the privatization movement. The returns to date have been meager, other than the funds from the sale of the State Accident Fund, but potential savings in the future could be significant.

It is also noteworthy that Michigan did not adopt any significant tax increases in the last three years despite the state's serious fiscal problems. Michigan is one of a handful of states that has not enacted a permanent increase in a major tax since 1971, other than as a replacement for a reduction in other taxes. However, the budget outlook has been complicated by the school finance reform legislation discussed above. There could be future implications for the budget as several of the revenue sources proposed to replace school property taxes are unstable and these replacement sources, in total, are likely to grow slower than the economy, which could result in resources being shifted from the remainder of the budget to fund K–12 education. Particularly at risk are higher education and social services.

There is a strong commitment to making government more efficient, as well as limiting the role of state government. The latest proposal is to change the state retirement system for state employees and teachers hired after January 1, 1994 from a defined benefit plan to a defined contribution plan. Currently, retirees are guaranteed a certain monthly pension based on years of service. Under the new plan the state would contribute 5 percent of payroll and employees could contribute as much as they wanted and would decide how the money should be invested. This change would sharply reduce state retirement costs in the future, as the current system cost the state about 12 percent of payroll. This proposal was not approved in the FY 1994 or FY 1995 budgets, but is likely to be proposed again in the future. As discussed above the governor has recommended and obtained approval for the privatization of state liquor warehouses and the sale of the State Accident Fund. Clearly Governor Engler and many legislators want to make major changes in how state government provides services.

There are proposals to make government more efficient every few years, and they generally amount to nothing. However, it may be different this time. The economic and political environment has changed to the point that government must fundamentally change if it is to effectively address the nation's problems. Government budgets will continue to be very tight, due mainly to the huge federal budget deficit, global competition, an aging population, an influx of immigrants, and soaring health care costs. At the same time the public's faith in government has never been lower. Not only must government learn to provide services more efficiently, but it must sort out the services it should provide and those that can best be left to the private sector. This opens the door for privatization, contracting, subsidies to the private sector, user charges, joint ventures, and other nontraditional ways of conducting government business. Much of the growth in resources into the next century will be claimed by rising health care costs, retirement costs, inflation, caseload increases, and property tax relief. Without a more efficient delivery of these services there will be little money for other important areas, such as education and infrastructure investment, that are critical for future economic growth. This is only the beginning of a revolution that will fundamentally change how government operates.

The following excerpt from *The Economist* (August 15–21, 1992) provides a good description of future choices.

From now on governments will find public spending even harder to control, let alone reduce. Over the past decade budget cuts have fallen heavily on investment in infrastructure. Pot-holed roads cannot be ignored much longer. As populations age, spending on health care and pensions will rise. And there is the clamor for more spending on education and cleaning up the environment. Unless something changes, public spending will rise remorselessly. If governments are to keep budget deficits in check they face a difficult choice. They can raise taxes—but that will blunt incentives and brake economic growth. Or they can return to first principles and rethink the role of the state. Discharging the state's existing tasks more efficiently, crucial though that is, will not do. New priorities must be set, with more tasks handed to the private economy. Governments must strive to aim welfare benefits more accurately at those who are really in need. Above all, public subsidies to the comfortable middle classes—starting with the unaffordable commitments to universal state pensions—will need to be pared back ruthlessly.

It appears that future budget choices in Michigan will be just as difficult, if not more difficult, than past choices. The question is whether state government is better equipped to deal with these choices in the future than during the most recent fiscal crisis. Unfortunately, the answer is probably no. On the one hand, the expenditure base has been reduced, and there seems to be a long-term commitment to making government more efficient. On the other hand, it will be more difficult to make budget cuts during the next economic downturn as many of the "easy" cuts have already been made, and the cookie jars have been emptied. The next round of cuts may actually be felt by the average citizen. Also the will to build up reserves to reduce the necessity for future budget cuts is not present as evidenced by the legislature and governor's recent decision (June 1994) to cut taxes and add supplemental expenditures to the FY 1994 budget. This action was taken in light of an expected budget surplus in FY 1994, despite warning that the new school aid system is underfunded and the budget may again be in deficit as early as FY 1997.

The lesson of the recent fiscal crunch is that responsible fiscal management always loses out to political considerations. The only way to overcome this endemic problem may be to make the tax system more responsive to economic growth and to pass a constitutional amendment requiring that if revenues, adjusted for inflation, increase more than 2 percent, for example, the excess be placed in a rainy day fund. After the fund balance reached 10 percent, for example, of general fund expenditures, the excess could be refunded to the tax-payers.

For the last thirty years or more, state and local governments have been able to cover up poor fiscal planning by raising taxes. I believe those days are over in most states, at least for the foreseeable future, as the tolerance for government taxes and spending is as low as it has ever been. This is going to force government to become more efficient and to adopt more responsible, longer-term fiscal policies. This should have been a major lesson learned from the experience of the early 1990s. Unfortunately, many politicians and state and local officials are slow learners. In Michigan, the terms of the governor and state legislators are now limited (eight years for the governor and senators, six years for members of the house). It is difficult to forecast the impact of term limits, but there is a good chance that shorter terms will not increase legislators' willingness to take a longer view. They may not worry about reelection, but they will worry about leaving their mark, and better fiscal planning is not likely to be high on the list. There is some hope for fundamental changes in state spending and tax policies, but a more severe crisis than recently occurred will probably be required to force state and local governments to plan beyond the current upturn in the economy.

NOTES

1. In 1977 the state established the Budget and Economic Stabilization Fund (BSF). Monies are deposited in the fund when Michigan personal income increases more than 2 percent and transferred to the general fund when real personal income declines. The law also provided for withdrawals when the Michigan unemployment rate averages more than 8 percent for a quarter; these monies are to be used for economic stabilization purposes, such as job training or summer youth employment. In FY 1991 and 1992, a total of $405 million was transferred to the general fund to help balance the budget. The balance in the fund at the of FY 1993–94 was about $300 million, following the pay-in of about $283 million from the FY 1992–93 budget surplus.

2. For example, the FY 1991 budget was reduced by 9.2 percent across the board, a number of promotion and economic development programs in the Department of Commerce were eliminated, and in FY 1992, the general assistance program for able-bodied single persons was eliminated, and grants to Detroit for cultural institutions were reduced from about $47 million (FY 1991) to $28.5 million.

3. For a discussion of the structural deficit, see Michigan House Fiscal Agency, *Solving Michigan's Budget Deficit: Opportunity From Crisis* (December, 1990). This report estimated the FY 1991 budget deficit at about $1 billion, of which $559 million was characterized as structural and $448 million as economic.

4. In FY 1980 the maximum AFDC grant was equal to 77.7 percent of the poverty threshold and the poverty gap was $1,465.

5. *Michigan's General Assistance Population: An Interim Report of the General Assistance Termination Project*, (Ann Arbor: University of Michigan School of Social Work, February 1993).

6. AFDC caseloads fell from 240,100 in 1984 to 211,700 in 1989. General assistance caseloads decreased from 148,700 in 1984 to 101,000 in 1989 and then rose to 112,200 in 1991 before dropping to 16,100 in 1992, 12,200 in 1993, and 11,600 in 1994.

7. For a detailed description of the new school finance system see, C. Philip Kearney, *A Primer on Michigan School Finance*, (Ann Arbor: University of Michigan School of Education, 1994).

8. Michigan taxes and expenditures actually had been declining to nearer the national average before John Engler took office. In FY 1986, Michigan state-local revenue was 9.4 percent above the national average, ranking the state fourteenth highest. In FY 1989–90, state and local revenue was only 1.7 percent above the national average, ranking Michigan twenty-sixth highest. On the expenditure side Michigan fell from 12.3 percent above the national average in FY 1986 to 1.7 percent above the average in FY 1990. Welfare spending declined form 46.7 percent above the national average to 11.1 percent above the average.

12

Minnesota: Innovation in an Era of Constraint

Thomas F. Luce, Jr.*

INTRODUCTION

Minnesota entered the 1990s with a relatively robust economy and a state budget cushioned by a large cash reserve that was accumulated during the 1980s. The cash reserve, at nearly $1 billion, represented nearly 15 percent of an annual budget at that time—a level clearly in excess of needs. However, the 1990s began with a series of unbalanced budgets that drew down roughly a third of the reserves and the 1992–1993 biennium began with a projected deficit exceeding $1 billion. The imbalance was met with a combination of a moderate increase in state taxes and a planned drawdown of reserves. However, subsequent improvements on the revenue side of the budget as a result of the improving economy generated a large (and unexpected) surplus in the FY 1993 budget that brought the state full circle. At the beginning of FY 1994, the reserve had been rebuilt to nearly $900 million.

Projections for the period from 1994 through 1997 revert to the norm for the 1990s, showing current account deficits that would consume more than two-thirds of the refreshed reserves. The pattern does not represent an immediate or serious crisis. However, at a minimum, the next budget cycle (1996–1997) is likely to present the state with the need for new revenues in order to maintain its cash reserve fund at its currently agreed-upon level ($500 million). If economic trends undermine state revenues further during the next few years, Minnesota could face another relatively serious budget crunch in the late 1990s.

---

*Thomas F. Luce, Jr. is an Assistant Professor of Public Affairs and Planning at the Hubert H. Humphrey Institute of Public Affairs at the University of Minnesota.

True to its reputation, Minnesota has pursued a relatively ambitious agenda of institutional reform. The state prides itself on good government, and the late 1980s and early 1990s brought a series of initiatives in education, health care, budget procedures, state-local relations, and welfare reform. The extent to which the state has delivered on its reform agenda varies by policy areas. In education, several school choice programs have actually been implemented and are serving substantial numbers of students. Welfare reforms affecting large numbers of recipients have also been implemented during the period. In health care, the state has yet to fully fund a relatively ambitious program originally intended to provide universal insurance coverage by 1997. The targeted date for universal coverage has been pushed back into the next century and there have been serious discussions about significantly reforming the program. The state has also increased its reliance on performance measures in the budgeting process. However, current reforms fall short of full performance budgeting and it is not clear how far policymakers want to go in this area. Finally, there have been some failed initiatives. In particular, efforts to rationalize the state's very generous state aid programs met with very little success.

BACKGROUND

The Public Sector in Minnesota

Minnesota is a state known for progressive public policies and sound fiscal practices. In the early 1970s the "Minnesota Miracle"—a series of policies that enhanced the balance and elasticity of the state's revenue system and increased the state role in financing local services—put the state at the forefront of the "professionalization" of state government. In the 1980s the state enacted a series of institutional reforms that made it an exemplar "laboratory of democracy" to many analysts. These innovations included a variety of school choice programs, a charter school project, and an ambitious health care access program (MinnesotaCare).

The ambitious nature of the state's public sector is reflected in its size and complexity, as well as in its innovations. The state ranks near the top in state and local spending. In 1990, state and local general expenditures were $3,914 per capita, seventh highest in the country. The state government supports local governments with a myriad of aid programs that add to a total that placed the state fifth in 1990 in (nonschool) state aid per capita at $981.[1] The state's local sector is among the nation's most fragmented, at six local governments (municipalities and townships) per 10,000 in population.[2] Perhaps because of this complexity, the state has a history of innovation in this dimension. Minnesota was among the first to regionalize responsibility for selected urban services (with the establishment of the Twin Cities Metropolitan Council in the late 1960s) and to institute tax-base sharing for a portion of the commercial and industrial tax base in the Twin Cities metropolitan area (with the Fiscal Disparities Program in the early 1970s).

The revenue system supporting this structure is relatively balanced and elastic. Income, sales, and property taxes represented 30 percent, 22 percent, and 31 percent of total state and local revenues respectively in 1991.[3] The most significant tax change since that time enhanced the balance by increasing the role of the "underused" instrument, the sales tax.

Consistent with what one sees in most states, the tax system as a whole is mildly regressive. The state income tax is mildly progressive with rates ranging from 6 percent to 8.5 percent. Reforms in the middle and late 1980s reduced the progressiveness of the rate structure, but an earned income tax credit was instituted in the early 1990s. The progressivity of the income tax is offset by mildly regressive sales and property tax systems. The state sales tax, raised to 6.5 percent in 1992, excludes food and clothing but is still mildly regressive. The state government controls local property taxes to a greater extent in Minnesota than in most states. Property tax rates are set by the state for twelve separate classes of property.[4] The system includes both progressive and regressive elements. Tax rates on owner-occupied properties are progressive—in 1993 homes were taxed at 1 percent up to $72,000 in value and at 2 percent above $72,000. In addition, the state income tax includes a circuit breaker and property tax deductibility for both owners and renters. However, rental units and apartment buildings (used disproportionately by lower income households) are taxed at higher rates, ranging from 2.3 percent to 3.4 percent in 1993. On balance, the property tax system is regressive.[5]

As noted above, the state is very generous in its support of counties, municipalities, and townships. In 1990, Minnesota ranked second among the states in the percentage of its state budget allocated to local revenue sharing (at 14.7 percent), fifth in the per capita magnitude of that aid (at $350.65) and fifteenth in growth in that figure between 1985 and 1990 (at 56.3 percent).[6] Two programs represent more than half of this aid—Local Government Aid (LGA) and Homestead and Agricultural Credit Aid (HACA). Both provide unrestricted aid to counties and municipalities with the bulk going to the latter. The distribution of the funds is in a state of transition from a system driven largely by local tax capacity and effort to a more modest (although still generous by national standards) system based less on local effort and more on some measure of expenditure needs. The transition has been slow and is discussed further in the section on institutional innovation and reform.

By national standards, the state is less involved in local education finance. The share of state aid in elementary and secondary education spending declined during the 1980s to roughly 55 percent (from more than 70 percent in the 1970s). The state's general education aid program combines elements of foundation aid and power equalization. Stagnancy in the foundation aid portion of the formula explains the decline and the (in)equity of the system was the object of litigation in the early 1990s.[7] The 1994–1995 budget includes a class size initiative and other changes in aid formulas that increase state funding significantly, but the state share is not expected to change dramatically during the biennium.

The state operates on a biannual budget cycle with a four-year planning horizon. Odd-year legislative sessions generate the subsequent biennial budget and two-year plan—the 1993 session generated the FY 1994 and 1995 budgets and the FY 1996 and 1997 planning estimates. Off-year sessions are meant to be supplemental, affecting the budget only at the margin or in response to forecast errors. In practice, however, major budget items have often been raised in off years. For instance, the 1992 session included significant changes in sales tax coverage of local government expenditures and major health care initiatives.

Minnesota politics are relatively competitive. During most of the 1980s the Democratic-Farm-Labor (DFL) party controlled the executive and legislative branches, but the Independent-Republication (IR) party provided active opposition. An IR governor ushered in the 1980s, the party actually controlled one house of the legislature from 1984 to 1986, and IR candidate Arne Carlson won the governorship in the 1990 election. Carlson's first term was a period of conflict with a DFL legislature. The DFL maintained strong majorities in both houses of the legislature but the majorities were not veto-proof and Governor Carlson used his line-item veto power liberally.[8] This was especially true late in the term when Carlson's ability to push his agenda and maintain vetoes was enhanced by scandal within the DFL.[9] However, the IR could not be described as a unified party at the end of Carlson's first term. Despite his high profile and spirited competition with the DFL legislature, Carlson failed to win the endorsement of his party at the 1994 caucuses, forcing him to face a serious challenge in the IR primary from a more conservative opponent.

The Fiscal Situation Entering the 1990s

The State of Minnesota entered the 1990s in a relatively strong fiscal position. The reasons for this were both economic and policy related. The state's economy fared relatively well during the 1980s. Personal income per capita grew at roughly the national rate during the decade and exceeded the national level by 15–20 percent throughout the period. Employment also grew at national rates, but unlike most of the country, Minnesota's manufacturing sector expanded during the decade. While the national economy lost 6 percent of its manufacturing employment, Minnesota gained 6 percent. State policymakers therefore did not have to deal with the major structural changes in the state's economy that many states faced.

On the policy side, a variety of changes during the decade resulted in a broadened base for state revenues. The sales tax was increased from 4 percent to 6 percent in two steps in 1981 and 1983, and the base was broadened to include some services in 1987. The state thus significantly increased its reliance on the least-used leg of the income-sales-property tax triad. The income tax also went through several changes during the decade. Early in the period a temporary surtax on income was used to bolster revenues. In 1985, after the surtax expired, tax rates were cut to improve the state's business climate. In response to federal tax reform in 1987, the state avoided a windfall by reducing and flattening tax rates.[10] Finally, gasoline and motor vehicle tax rates increased in several steps. The gasoline tax increased from 11¢ per gallon to 20¢ and motor vehicle excise taxes increased with the sales tax.

The net effect of all of these changes was that the state ended the decade with nearly $1 billion in cash reserves. This represented 15 percent of an annual budget at that time, a level of reserves clearly in excess of needs. The budgets of the early 1990s should be viewed in this context. Much of the explicit debate regarding those budgets was about the appropriate size of the reserve fund and how to divide excess reserves between revenue reductions and expenditure increases. Implicit in the debates was the problem of distributing the excess reserves in a way that would not generate a long-run structural deficit—i.e., doing it in way that would avoid a budget crisis once reserves were down to reasonable levels.

STATE GOVERNMENT BUDGETS IN THE 1990s

Overall Budget Trends

Table 12–1 summarizes current revenue and expenditure data for the State of Minnesota for fiscal years 1990 through 1993, the approved budgets for fiscal years 1994 and 1995 and the planning estimates for the 1996–1997 biennium. As noted above, the state started the period with a very large cash reserve—$946 million dollars carried forward into FY 1990 from prior years. Roughly a third of this reserve was drawn down during the 1990–1991 biennium, mostly in FY 1991. The FY 1991 deficit of $330 million occurred despite the fact that the 1990 legislature devoted much of its time and energy to closing an expected 1991 deficit then forecast at $145 million. The solution was designed to use only $16 million from reserves while cutting spending (from previously approved levels) across many categories. These efforts were subsequently undermined by the effects of the recession.

The recession of the early 1990s was comparatively mild in Minnesota. However, the state experienced a decline in employment between November 1990 and February 1991.[11] It was at this point—the beginning of the 1991 legislative session—that the state faced its most significant crisis of the period. Revised forecasts for the remainder of FY 1991 showed the greater-than-expected shortfall in that year and forecasts for the 1992–1993 biennium predicted a deficit of $1.1 billion over the two years.

The 1991 legislative session was the first for the newly elected governor, Arne Carlson. Carlson, an Independent-Republican, faced DFL majorities in both houses of the legislature. Much of the 1991 session was devoted to bargaining between the governor and the legislature regarding the extent to which the deficit would be dealt

TABLE 12-1 Minnesota State Finances, Summary Budget Data 1990–1997 ($ million)

	1990	1991	1992	1993	1994 budget	1995 budget	1996–1997 planning estimate
Current Revenues	6,358	6,613	7,065	7,754	8,133	8,476	17,568
Current Expenditures	6,419	6,943	7,171	7,326	8,260	8,595	17,957
Current Balance	-61	-330	-106	428	-127	-119	-389
(% of current expend.)	(-0.9)	(-4.8)	(-1.5)	(5.8)	(-1.5)	(-1.4)	(2.2)
Balance from Prior Year	946	885	555	450	878	750	632
Budget Reserve	550	400	400	360	500	500	243
Other Reserves	335	155	49	518	250	132	0
Balance Carried Forward	885	555	449	878	750	632	243

Note: Federal aid is excluded. Data for 1991 through 1993 are based on actual revenues and expenditures; 1994 through 1997 data are from the budget of the 1994 legislative session.
Source: Minnesota Department of Finance.

with through expenditure restraint, new revenues, or spending of remaining reserves. Carlson pushed for expenditure reductions but, in the end, the deficit was erased with a .5 percentage point increase in the sales tax (to 6.5 percent), a .5 percentage point increase in income taxes on incomes above $172,920 (for a married couple filing jointly), increases in other smaller taxes, and further drawdowns from reserves.[12] The sales, income, and other tax increases represented additional revenues over the biennium of about $370 million, $150 million, and $90 million respectively. The governor attempted to veto an additional $114 million of expenditures, but roughly $30 million of the funds were restored by the courts for various reasons. (An additional $23 million was later restored by the 1992 legislature.) The remainder of the shortfall was to be met with spending from reserves.

Revenues and expenditures matched these expectations through much of the biennium. As late as November 1992 (nearly halfway through FY 1993), the FY 1993 budget was expected to be balanced—the November 1992 forecast showed just a $9 million surplus. The picture changed dramatically during the next seven months. In March 1993, the forecast surplus was $225 million and the actual surplus ended up at $428 million (as shown in Table 12–1). At the same time, the forecast deficit for the 1994–1995 biennium moved from $986 million in November 1992 to $376 million one year later to $246 million at the end of the 1994 legislative session (June 1994). However, the timing of these changes (coming in late 1993 and early 1994 for the most part) was such that the 1994 legislative session began at a time when there was still a relatively high level of alarm about forecast imbalances in the 1994–1995 biennium. This led to a great deal of discussion early in the session about proposals to increase taxes on the rich or on gasoline. Various tax increases passed either the house or the senate, but when more favorable revenue forecasts began to come in, the governor vetoed all tax increases that had been passed and promised to veto any other increases that reached his desk. Instead, he proposed a wage freeze for state workers and all employees of the higher education system, actions that would cut more than $100 million from the November 1993 estimates of the 1994–1995 deficit (to the level shown in Table 12–1). The governor's proposals were very well received in public opinion polls and carried the day.

The state's financial position thus changed dramatically over the twenty months from November 1992 to June 1994. In November 1992, FY 1993 was expected to add nothing to reserves and the following biennium was forecast to more than deplete all remaining reserves. One year later, reserves had actually been replenished to nearly $1 billion and deficits for the subsequent biennium were expected to draw down only about a third of this total. Subsequent actions by the legislature decreased the drawdown further, to just a fourth of total reserves.

These dramatic changes were due largely to changes in revenue forecasts, especially for income taxes. Increases in actual or forecast income tax revenues between November 1992 and June 1994 represented about 60 percent of both the $400 million increase in the FY 1993 surplus and the $740 million decrease in the projected FY 1994 and 1995 deficits.

Tax revenues in general were so robust during the fiscal year that it is interesting to compare the actual situation with what it would have been had the income and sales tax increases of 1991 not been enacted. Without the changes (which increased revenues by a total of roughly $500 million over the biennium), the state would have ended the period with a cash reserve of about $375 million. This is close to both the often cited benchmark for reserves (5 percent of expenditures) and the agreed-upon level of the budget reserve account at that point in time ($360 million). The inevitable uncertainties associated with revenue forecasting therefore undermined an important element of fiscal policy in the period—the orderly drawdown of reserves to a reasonable level. Without the 1991 tax rate increases, the state would have faced larger projected deficits for fiscal years 1994 and 1995, of course. But hindsight shows that the 1991 increases could have been delayed by a full biennium without serious budgetary problems.

At the end of FY 1993, the state had thus come full circle. The situation entering FY 1994 was much the same as it was in 1990. Cash reserves in excess of 10 percent of the annual budget were on hand but planned deficits during the next four years were forecast to draw down a substantial portion of those reserves. At the beginning of FY 1991, the best guess had been that the budget would be in crisis in 1993—i.e., cash reserves would be exhausted and the budget would be in deficit. At the beginning of FY 1994, forecasts implied that the budget would be nearing crisis again at the end of 1997, when cash reserves were forecast to be nearly depleted and the budget to be in structural imbalance.

The state's official budget reserve, broken out in Table 12–1, had also come full circle. At the beginning of the decade, the state maintained an unusually large official reserve—$550 million against annual expenditures of $6.4 billion. The level of the reserve fell to $400 million during fiscal years 1991 and 1992 and to $360 million in FY 1993. Whether to increase the reserve back to $500 million in FY 1994 was a serious point of contention between the IR governor (who favored the increase) and the 1993 and 1994 legislatures. In the end, the large 1993 surplus made the debate moot for the 1994–1995 biennium. However, the planning estimates for the subsequent biennium show the reserve falling below $500 million, implying that the issue will resurface in future years.[13]

Revenues by Category

Table 12–2 shows annual percentage changes in revenues disaggregated into major categories for the period from 1991 to 1995. Also shown are budget shares by category at the beginning and end of the period. The state relies very heavily on income and sales taxes for its revenues—roughly 75 percent of current revenues throughout the period. Other taxes represent about 18 percent of revenues, leaving only 7 percent to a few small nontax categories.

Growth rates across the revenue sources were relatively uniform. Revenues from sales and "other" taxes grew more quickly than average while growth rates for personal income taxes were less than average. The differences did not result in any major shifts in the importance of the different instruments, although the share of the sales tax increased from 29 percent of total revenues to 31 percent.

As discussed above, the major tax changes during the period involved income and sales taxes. Although the primary motivation for the sales tax increase was the $1.1 billion shortfall facing the 1991 legislature, the sales tax change was not imposed as a simple rate increase. Technically, the increase to 6.5 percent was instituted statewide only from July 1, 1991 through December 31 of that year. During that period, revenues from two percentage points of the tax were earmarked for the newly formed Local Government Trust Fund (discussed further below). Beginning January 1, 1992 the statewide tax was to drop back to 6 percent with 1.5 percentage points earmarked for the trust fund. Counties would then have the "option" to impose

TABLE 12–2 Growth of Minnesota General Fund Revenue in Major Categories

	1991	1992	1993	1994	1995	Cumulative	1990 % Share	1995 % Share
Total Current Revenues	4.0%	6.8%	9.8%	4.9%	4.2%	33.3%	100%	100%
Taxes	3.3	7.0	10.3	5.6	4.5	32.8	93	94
Income	3.4	5.8	10.4	2.2	4.3	28.7	45	44
Sales	5.0	11.6	8.4	6.9	4.3	41.7	29	31
Corporate	−4.4	−8.2	21.2	8.7	13.3	31.1	8	7
Motor Vehicles	−7.9	14.2	9.6	10.6	5.8	34.9	4	4
Other	10.7	6.2	8.8	14.8	−1.4	44.8	7	8
Nontax Revenue	13.2	5.1	3.1	−4.1	−0.3	17.3	7	6
Interest	−24.3	−59.8	−15.1	23.0	−42.3	−81.7	1	0
Lottery			4.6	−4.3	0.0	0.0	0	0
Depart. Earnings	8.8	75.7	−18.8	−20.0	10.4	37.1	1	1
Other	26.7	−8.2	15.7	−0.5	−0.1	29.4	4	4

Note: Federal aid is excluded. Revenue changes for 1991 through 1993 are based on actual revenues; 1994 and 1995 changes are from the budget of the 1994 legislative session.
Source: Minnesota Department of Finance.

a .5 percent local sales tax, the revenues from which would go into the trust fund. The local "option" was accepted by all eighty-seven counties but was not viewed as a real choice by local officials since opting out would have been associated with a decline in aid from the trust fund greater than the tax savings. The bottom-line effect of the changes was a statewide increase of .5 percent in the tax. However, it was not until two years later, when the local government trust fund was abolished, that the increase was technically acknowledged as a permanent increase in state (as opposed to local) taxes.

The sales tax was also modified in a significant way in FY 1993 when many purchases by county and local governments were brought into the tax base. (State government purchases were already subject to the tax.) The change was expected to raise nearly $70 million per year.

The income tax changes in FY 1992 were also motivated by more than the need for new revenues. The changes removed the rate "bubble" that existed as a result of federal tax law changes in prior years. The existing rate structure had a rate "bubble" that imposed a higher tax rate (8.5 percent) on income in intermediate ranges (between $79,130 and $172,920 for a married couple filing jointly) than on income above the range (which was taxed at 8 percent). The changes raised rates at the high end to match the "bubble" rate. The income tax was also changed in FY 1992 to provide an earned income tax credit equal to 10 percent of the federal credit. Under the provisions, families earning less than $21,245 could receive a credit against state taxes of up to $502. The credit was subsequently increased to 15 percent of the federal credit by the 1993 legislature for FY 1994.

Expenditures by Category

Table 12–3 shows annual percentage changes and budget shares by expenditure categories between 1991 and 1995. Categories representing intergovernmental flows dominate the expenditure side of the budget. K–12 education and local aid (aid to municipal governments for the most part) represented roughly half of expenditures throughout the period. By the end of the period, higher education and Medicaid showed roughly equal shares at 13 percent and 15 percent, respectively.

The data also show some significant reshuffling of priorities over the period. Intergovernmental aid was shifted from local governments

TABLE 12–3 Growth of Minnesota General Fund Spending in Major Categories, 1991 to 1995

	1991	1992	1993	1994	1995	Cumulative	1990 % Share	1995 % Share
Total	8.2%	3.3%	2.2%	12.8%	4.1%	33.9%	100%	100%
Education	19.2	2.2	−1.9	19.1	3.8	47.7	41	45
K-12	26.9	3.6	−2.5	25.1	4.1	66.9	26	33
Higher Education	5.6	−0.8	−0.5	5.9	3.0	13.8	15	13
Univ. of Minnesota	4.5	−2.5	−3.1	3.1	3.8	5.6	7	5
Other	6.5	0.7	1.6	8.2	2.5	20.9	8	7
Medicaid	15.8	61.5	8.3	16.3	11.4	162.2	7	15
Income Maintenance	33.8	38.1	−3.1	2.5	−7.8	69.4	3	3
Corrections	12.5	11.5	9.1	10.3	4.4	57.7	1	2
Total Local Aid	−10.9	−12.9	5.7	8.2	3.3	−8.4	26	18
Local Govt. Aid (LGA)	−18.2	−13.4	7.3	−4.8	14.4	−17.3	6	4
Homestead Aid (HACA)	1.9	−25.2	8.3	13.9	−1.9	−7.8	10	7
Other	−19.7	3.8	2.5	9.8	3.2	−3.2	10	7
Other	5.0	−5.0	4.7	3.9	2.5	11.1	22	17

Note: Spending financed with federal aid is excluded. Expenditure changes for 1991 through 1993 are based on actual expenditures; 1994 and 1995 changes are from the budget of the 1994 legislative session.
Source: Minnesota Department of Finance.

to school districts. Some of this shift is an artifact. In FY 1991, a portion of Homestead Aid that was earmarked for education was transferred into the K–12 accounts. Because of overlapping fiscal and planning years, the decline in Homestead Aid showed up in FY 1992 while the K–12 increase occurred in FY 1991. However, even without this accounting change, the education share would have increased by four percentage points to 30 percent in 1995 (rather than to 33 percent) and the local aid decline would have been six percentage points, to 20 percent, in 1995 (instead of to 18 percent).

Nearly all of the K–12 increase (beyond the accounting change) occurred in fiscal years 1994 and 1995. Early in the period education aid was actually reduced from previous budgets due to slower than expected enrollment growth and funding under the state's general education aid program was relatively stable over the whole period. The 1994 increase resulted from an initiative to decrease class sizes in elementary grades. $112 million of additional aid over two years was earmarked to reduce student-teacher ratios to 17:1 in kindergarten through third grade classes throughout the state.

The state's generous aid programs for municipal governments were under attack throughout the period. The Local Government Trust Fund was created in FY 1992 in an attempt to stabilize and rationalize the programs but succeeded at neither and was discontinued by the 1994 legislature. (See the following section for discussion of attempts to reform local aid programs.) Thus, with the exception of funds allocated for a very specific educational purpose—the class-size initiative—the state was steadily decreasing its role in financing locally provided services during the period.

Other categories showing substantive changes were Medicaid and higher education. The Medicaid share leapt from 7 percent of expenditures in 1991 to 15 percent in 1995. In four of the five years, Medicaid spending increases were consistent with national trends. However, FY 1992 showed an extraordinary increase of more than 60 percent. Much of this was due to the way the state reacted to changes in federal regulations regarding the use of provider taxes to finance the state portion of Medicaid. In July 1991, Minnesota followed the lead of other states and took advantage of a loophole in federal regulations that allowed states to artificially increase the federal share of funds for Medicaid. The state assessed a new provider tax on hospitals. The revenues from the tax were returned to hospitals as payment for Medicaid services but the new payments were associated with no change in supplied Medicaid services. Nonetheless, they showed up as increased state spending in the state budget. The federal government accordingly matched the spending increase at the going rate. The net result was that hospitals and the state broke even, but the federal government was sending more money to the state for Medicaid. Total spending for Medicaid was increased but only by the amount of the increased federal support. However, payments from the provider tax showed up on the expenditure side of the state budget as increased spending and when the loophole was closed by the federal government in 1992, the previous spending "increases" (both real, from the increased federal match, and illusory, from the provider tax) were taken over with state funds. In effect, the program's constituency was able to use the state's prior claims for the provider tax (that it generated a real increase in spending) both to retain the real increases due to the extra federal funds and to convert the accounting artifact into an actual increase.

Higher education was a clear loser over the period. This was especially true for the University of Minnesota, which was forced to absorb an absolute decline in funding between 1990 and 1993 and a planned increase over the full five years that was roughly one-sixth of the rate for total expenditures. These trends were reflected in both student tuition and employee compensation in the university system. Tuition increases and compensation restraint were greatest at the University of Minnesota. Between 1990 and 1993 tuition increases were 35 percent, 20 percent, and 23 percent (compared to 12 percent for the cost of living) for the University of Minnesota, the state university system, and community colleges, respectively.[14] Similarly, University of Minnesota employees were forced to accept wage freezes in two years (fiscal years 1992 and 1994) while wages were frozen only in FY 1994 for state university and community college employees.

Spending in the remaining smaller categories—income maintenance and corrections—grew at greater than average rates, but did not have a large impact on the budget. Income maintenance spending moved countercyclically, increasing in the early years of less robust growth and falling off in later years as the economy picked up. Although welfare reform has been a much debated topic in the state and a significant new program was initiated in FY 1994, reform efforts had little effect on spending levels. Growth in corrections spending was largely attributable to penalty increases instituted during the 1980s. The adult prison population in the state grew from 1,886 in

1981 to 3,699 in 1992, with further increases to roughly 4,500 expected by 1995. However, Minnesota still ranks very low among the states (forty-seventh) in prison costs with spending of roughly $25 per capita.[15]

INSTITUTIONAL INNOVATION AND REFORM

Innovation in public service delivery was a much studied and discussed topic in Minnesota in the late 1980s and early 1990s. This continues a long tradition of good government and innovation in the state. Indeed, the state began the 1990s with a prototypical "good-government" reform bill. The 1990 legislature passed a "taxpayer bill of rights." The legislation regulates the behavior of taxing entities in the state, requiring that taxpayers be informed in simple nontechnical terms of their assessments, tax rates, and collection, appeal, and refund procedures. The law also provides legal remedies to taxpayers for losses resulting from public employee negligence and clearly spells out the rights of taxpayers with regard to seized property and tax court appeals. To most taxpayers, the most important result of the bill is that they receive a clear statement each year of the past and present year assessed value of their home and the taxes paid and payable to all public agencies that assess a property tax.

However, the extent to which study and discussion led to real policy changes in other areas and the degree to which those changes succeeded has varied in recent years. In education and welfare, important innovations were actually implemented with some success during the period. In other areas, like health care and budgeting procedures, major reforms are in the works, but are still incomplete and in political difficulty. Finally, in some areas, state aid programs in particular, reforms have been attempted without success. This section describes reform and innovation efforts in Minnesota in five policy areas: school choice; health insurance reform; budget and management procedures; state-local relations; and welfare.

School Choice Programs

Several programs intended to enhance the quality of education by increasing the choices available to parents and students were implemented in Minnesota between 1985 and 1993. Included are programs that increase the availability of advanced courses to high school students, encourage "problem" students to complete high school by changing schools or curricula, allow parents to transfer their children to public schools outside their district, permit groups of teachers and administrators to establish charter schools, and provide students with a variety of within-district school or curriculum options. The effects of the programs on the quality of education provided to the state's children are inherently difficult to measure or evaluate and many have been in existence only for very short times. There have therefore been very few efforts to evaluate the programs rigorously. However, participation rates and other indirect measures of success are available for some of the programs.[16]

Post-secondary options. This program allows eleventh and twelfth graders attending public schools to enroll either full-time or part-time at an eligible postsecondary institution prior to graduation from high school. If the courses count toward high school graduation, all tuition and fees (including textbooks) are picked up by the state and financed by a reduction in state aid to the student's high school. Begun in 1985, participation in the program has increased from 3,600 in 1985–1986 to more than 7,000 in 1991–1992, or roughly 6.5 percent of eligible students. The program provides direct competition with public schools and many high schools responded by increasing in-house access to advanced courses. The availability of advanced placement courses in Minnesota high schools doubled between 1985 and 1993 and more than 100 schools implemented "College in the Schools" programs. "College in the Schools" offers students access to college-level courses in their high schools. Participating colleges control the curriculum, but the courses are taught by district teachers. Students get both high school and college credit, but the school district keeps the state aid that would have been lost had the student enrolled at the college or university.

Area learning centers and high school graduation incentives. The programs, begun in 1987, are designed to encourage certain students (ages twelve–twenty-one) to complete high school after experiencing problems at their original public school. Criteria determining eligibility include low test scores or grades, chemical dependency, pregnancy or parenthood, and excessive truancy. Most participants enroll in either a public high school in another district or an Area Learning

Center (ALC). ALC's are state-approved individualized programs offered by one or more districts that focus on both academics and preparation for work. By the early 1990s there were roughly forty ALC's serving nearly 12,000 students per year at about seventy sites around the state. Roughly a third of the participants are drop-outs. Although there have been no studies of actual graduation or achievement rates, early surveys of participants show dramatic differences in the pre- and post-participation percentage of enrollees who plan to graduate from high school.

Enrollment options program. The open enrollment program, begun in 1987, allows students to transfer to public schools outside their district, provided that the receiving district has room and that the transfer does not adversely affect desegregation efforts. The program was operated on a limited basis from 1987 to 1990 when participation by school districts was phased in (based on several criteria). By the 1990–1991 school year the program was statewide. Participation grew from just 440 students in 1988–1989 to more than 12,500 in 1992–1993, or approximately 1.6 percent of all students. One early survey found that the most commonly cited reasons for using the program to select a new school were academic reputation and convenience. However, most administrators (from 62 percent to 89 percent depending on the question) reported no substantive changes in instructional programs or administration as a result of school choice and more than 60 percent reported that they expected no future effects on school-level decision making or instructional strategies.[17] Some analysts have cited these surveys and the scale of the program—use by less than 2 percent of students—as indicators that the impacts of the program are likely to be minimal. In addition, a significant percentage of students in the state's largest and, by most accounts, most troubled school district are excluded from participation. School desegregation requirements in Minneapolis limit the extent to which white students in the city are permitted to participate.[18] The bottom line is that the jury is still out on this central component of Minnesota school choice programs. Demand for the program is growing, but from low levels and it is difficult to cite other concrete measures of success or failure.

Charter public schools. The program, passed in 1991 and revised in 1993, allows for the establishment of up to thirty-five charter schools.[19] The program is intended to allow interested parents and teachers to design innovative approaches to education. Charter schools must be approved by the Department of Education but are largely free of bureaucratic rules and regulations. In principle, they compete with other public schools for enrollments. A proposal for a charter school goes first to the local school board for review, then to the State Board of Education. Once approved, charter schools receive the same funding guarantee per pupil from the state that traditional schools receive. Because charter schools have no power to levy taxes, they receive all of their funding from the state.[20] However, the law does not provide bonding authority to charter schools for capital costs, special funds for start-up expenses, or money for facility costs.

By the end of 1993, more than twenty-five groups of teachers had submitted proposals. However, there was resistance to the charter school concept by many school boards, administrators, and teacher's unions early in the program and most of the applications were turned down at the local level. The 1993 revisions in the state law made it easier for applicants to appeal such a decision, and eleven plans had been approved by local and state boards of education by the end of 1993. One charter school opened during the 1992–1993 school year, five others opened for 1993–1994 school year, and a seventh opened early in 1994.

The types of schools that have made it through the application process and actually opened for business illustrate the degree of tension that has existed with existing school authorities. Three types of applications dominated submissions early in the program—proposals targeting specific populations, proposals from rural areas, often with the intention of keeping a school open in the community, and proposals from alternative programs already in operation, usually Montessori programs. In general, proposals for schools that would compete directly with traditional schools for a cross section of students were turned down in the early rounds of applications. Five of the six charter schools in operation during the 1993–1994 school year served special populations—usually at-risk or expensive-to-serve groups. The sixth is a Montessori program.

At this very early stage, it is difficult to evaluate the program. However, a set of common characteristics is evident already across the schools. They tend to be small, with very small class sizes. Among the first six, total enrollments ranged from 16 to 195 and average student/staff ratios varied from 4:1 to 20:1 in 1994. Because funding per pupil is at the same level as traditional schools (which have larger class sizes) and there is no funding for facilities, the charter schools must economize. They tend to do so with lower-than-scale teacher salaries and low-cost facilities. Some schools have been able to attract grant funds to supplement state funding, but only one of the six schools in operation in 1994 paid up to its school district's salary scale. Teachers at the charter schools have been noted for their dedication, but burnout is a clear concern. All of the schools operate in relatively ad hoc physical environments, sometimes not well suited to their needs.

Transportation has been a problem at some schools. The local district is responsible for providing transportation. This causes friction with both parties. Some charter schools have expressed frustration with being tied to the traditional school schedule and school districts don't like to be burdened with the relatively expensive task of transporting a small number of scattered students to a single site. Finally, there has been general confusion, and sometimes antagonism, in the relationships between charter schools and their "parent" school districts. The law provided little framework in this regard. The fact that most of the charter schools experienced management problems exacerbated these problems. The charter schools are essentially small teacher-run enterprises, meaning that each school inevitably found itself lacking in one or another management skill.

In general, the charter school experiment is still in its infancy. Outcome-based evaluation of the program is not possible at this point, and it is still an open question whether the existing schools will be able to maintain current effort levels, especially by teachers working at less-than-union scales, given the financial constraints.

A variety of other *Within District Options* are also available to parents and students. These include a range of magnet schools, such as language immersion or Montessori curricula, "schools within schools" where special curricula are made available to subsets of the student body, and ALC's or High School Graduation Incentives programs made available to current enrollees. Outside of Minneapolis and St. Paul, students choosing schools or programs within their district other than the assigned one increased from about 4,000 in 1990–1991 to about 5,400 two years later. Minneapolis and St. Paul also include substantial numbers of "choosers" but it is difficult to measure how many represent truly voluntary choices. Both districts require all students to choose a school at certain grades. St. Paul has had some problems matching students to the chosen schools (because of excess demand for particular schools), and Minneapolis has prevented many students from leaving the district under the open enrollment program for reasons of racial balance. As a result, it is difficult to untangle "free" choices from "forced" ones in those districts. However, both districts more than doubled the number of options available to students between 1985 and 1993.

The overall effects of all of these school choice programs on the Minnesota educational system and its students are extremely difficult to assess, and little work has been done in this regard. For instance, there have been no attempts to evaluate the effects of individual programs on student achievement. In addition, some programs, such as the charter schools, are not "ripe" for study due to their short duration and limited size while others, such as open enrollment, are affected significantly by outside factors like desegregation programs. However, the programs, as a group, have been chosen by impressive numbers of students and parents. Excluding the portion of Minneapolis and St. Paul students who made "forced choices,"[21] school choice programs were used by about 53,000 Minnesota students in 1992–1993, representing more than 7 percent of total enrollments in public schools. This was an increase of more than 60 percent in just two years from 31,000 students (4.5 percent of total enrollments) in 1990–1991. In addition, the reactions of the public schools to the existence of these programs, such as the new courses and programs developed in response to the Post-Secondary Options programs, imply that public schools react with new alternatives when they must compete for both students *and* the state resources associated with them.

Health Insurance Reform

In 1993, Minnesota was at the forefront of the states when it came to health care reform. A large bipartisan coalition in the 1992 and 1993 legislatures passed ambitious bills setting up MinnesotaCare, a program designed to provide universal health insurance coverage to state residents by 1997. Under the plan, insurance would be provided to qualified uninsured and underinsured residents on a sliding scale premium schedule based on income. Cost containment measures for MinnesotaCare were modeled on the state's large HMO sector. Groups of health care providers were to band together into "integrated service networks" (ISN's), HMO-like consortia of providers that would provide an array of services for a fixed price per patient. They were to offer one or more of five benefit packages that could vary by the services offered and the combinations of co-payments and premiums used. The bill also provided for various regulatory, planning, and study commissions to review ISN plans and to formulate (and enforce) policies regarding the regulation of technology and large-scale purchases of equipment or facilities. Provisions for private insurance reform designed to provide pooling mechanisms for small employers and individuals and increased incentives in education financing programs for recipients to locate in rural areas upon completion of training were also included.

Just one year later, in 1994, health care reform was foundering.[22] There were two major problems—funding and concerns regarding the increasingly concentrated nature of the HMO network in the state. The original bill did not provide adequate funding to meet the ambitious schedule for coverage increases. The primary funding mechanism was a 2 percent gross revenues tax on health care providers and insurers. Although this source is expected to eventually generate nearly $200 million per year, this is not sufficient to provide full coverage by 1997. In the original bill the program was expected to generate a surplus of roughly $50 million in fiscal years 1994 and 1995 when coverage was minimal, but to fall more than $230 million into deficit during fiscal years 1996 and 1997. The original bill also required that the Department of Health and Human Services provide a plan to the legislature by February 15, 1994 that would limit expenditures to eliminate this deficit. In the interim, Governor Carlson made it clear that he would veto any new taxes passed by the 1994 legislature and estimates of revenues from the provider tax were scaled down by roughly 25 percent. Not surprisingly, the Department of Health and Human Services could not reconcile universal coverage by 1997 with the existing revenue plan.

During the same period, many legislators were becoming concerned with the increasing concentration in Minnesota's HMO sector. Two major mergers during the early 1990s led to a situation where three HMOs dominated Minnesota's $14 billion health insurance industry.[23] In addition, high profile research by the Congressional Budget Office and the Office of Technology Assessment in late 1993 and 1994 compared health care costs under the systems being debated in the national congress and cast doubt on the cost containment advantages of HMO/managed competition systems like the one envisioned for Minnesota.[24]

In this environment, health care reform advocates in the 1994 legislature were in no position to "fill in the blanks" left by the existing legislation. In particular, they were in no position to find the missing revenues needed to balance the 1996–1997 MinnesotaCare budget. An attempt was made to create a $75 million reserve fund (from general fund revenues) that would have provided another year for the Department of Health and Human Services to devise an expenditure plan consistent with revenues from the provider tax. However, the bill was vetoed by the governor on the grounds that the general fund couldn't afford it. There was also some discussion of a proposal to eventually use the income tax to fill in the gap but, in general, little discussion of substantive issues was possible during the session. By the end of the session, the funding gap had been "filled" by moving the point of universal coverage back into the early 2000s. Health reform advocates were also arguing for caution regarding the plan's reliance on HMOs and HMO-like organizations. Indeed, Minnesota Senator Paul Wellstone, a strong DFL advocate of universal coverage, actually had the national congress hold hearings in Minnesota on the issue of medical insurance consolidations and concentration in the industry.

Thus, by mid-1994, MinnesotaCare was effectively on standby. The program is still on the books and is scheduled to spend about $400 million during the 1996–1997 biennium. But nobody expects the current plan to remain in its present form for that long. In this dimension, much depends on the party of the governor following the 1994 election. An IR governor is very likely to be able to limit the size of the program with vetoes of any significant tax increases passed to cover the costs of universal coverage, while a DFL legislature and governor would be much more likely to fully fund a program much like the one in the 1993 legislation.

Performance Budgeting

Minnesota has a twenty-five year record of concern about changing the focus of state budgets from inputs to outputs.[25] The earliest example was in the late 1960s when, as the result of an executive branch initiative, five state departments submitted "program budgets" for the 1970–1971 biennium. These budgets emphasized program categories and activities rather than input costs. The 1969 legislature also passed a resolution that agency budgets should "be stated in terms of programs and anticipated accomplishments rather than in terms of the objects of expenditure."[26] In subsequent years, the state budget process gradually shifted toward more emphasis on program descriptions and the outcomes of state spending. By the 1974–1975 biennium, several agencies prepared both a traditional budget and an outcome-oriented program budget, and the FY 1977 budget instructions required agencies to include a statement of objectives, performance measures, and an evaluation of accomplishments. Budget instructions continued to encourage the use of various performance measures through the 1980s. However, by the end of the decade, the effort seemed to have lost momentum, and renewed attention to the issue was one of the stated priorities of Governor Arne Carlson when he entered office in 1991.

Three early Carlson initiatives and a bill passed by the 1993 legislature have reconcentrated attention on performance budgeting. The first, "Minnesota Milestones," was initiated by the governor in February 1991 with the intent of generating measurable long-run goals and performance indicators to serve as the framework for executive branch policy and budgeting. The resulting report, *Minnesota Milestones: A Report Card for the Future*, highlighted twenty general goals and seventy-nine indicators meant to measure progress toward the goals. For example, the first goal is: "Our children will not live in poverty." The two associated indicators are percentage of children living in households below the poverty line and percentage of parents who receive full payment of awarded child support. The report cites past trends and sets future targets for many of the indicators. One clearly intended use of the report was as a basis for budget proposals and discussions. However, a subsequent evaluation concluded that Minnesota Milestones had very limited impact in the first budget cycle following its release—the 1994–1995 biennium. The study also concluded that reliable data do not exist for many of the seventy-nine performance indicators and that the legislature and state agencies had shown no sense of "ownership" for the report, undermining its ability to last beyond the current governor's term.[27]

The second initiative was the Commission on Reform and Efficiency (CORE). Appointed by the governor in August 1991 to study ways to increase the efficiency of government in the state, CORE has generated a series of reports on public management issues. These include a report on budgeting and financial management that evaluates the use of performance indicators in the budget for the 1992–1993 biennium. The report, published in early 1993, evaluated nearly

1,000 performance indicators used in agency budgets and found, among other things, that many measures "were inappropriate or not of high quality."[28]

Finally, the governor, through the Department of Finance, issued budget instructions for the 1994–1995 biennium in June 1992 requiring all agencies to submit program-level budgets that included an agency mission statement, the purpose of the program, and performance information.

The state legislature, at least partly because of the problems with the 1992–1993 budget cited by the CORE report and dissatisfaction with measures used in the 1994–1995 budget, responded with an initiative of its own. The 1993 legislature passed a bill that requires most state agencies to develop performance reports that include: a mission statement; performance, output and outcome measures and goals; and data and projections from four years into the past and two years into the future. The reports will be submitted annually for review and evaluation by the Office of the Legislative Auditor and are to be generated *separately from agency budget requests*. This last feature makes it clear that the bill does not institute full performance budgeting. The feedback in the system from performance to budget allocations is very indirect.

The early 1990s thus brought a revival in interest in Minnesota in the use of goal setting and performance measures in the budget process. However, the actual attempts to create a process of performance budgeting have been fragmented and incomplete. They have been fragmented in that there has been little effort to coordinate all of the different initiatives. In particular, there has been little coordination with the governor's vehicle for long-run planning, Minnesota Milestones, by either the Department of Finance in its budget instructions or the legislature in its 1993 bill. It is incomplete in the sense that the procedures now in place do not formally link performance with appropriations.

However, it is not clear at this point if full performance budgeting is what the governor, legislature, or bureaucracy desires. Conflicting signals have come from the executive branch on this question. On the one hand, the governor, the Commissioner of Finance and the Finance Department have all represented current procedures as the first step toward implementing full performance-based budgeting in the state. On the other hand, executive branch officials have also often described the current system as full-fledged "performance budgeting," implying that further steps are not needed.[29] On the legislative side, a major evaluation of performance budgeting by the Office of the Legislative Auditor, an important actor in the procedures laid out in the 1993 bill, recommended against implementing full performance-based budgeting. Included in the report's conclusions is a strongly worded argument for caution in this dimension of public management.

> In our view, with very limited exceptions at the present time, agency performance should not be tied to appropriations in a formal, mechanical way, nor should it be a primary component of funding formulas. In other words, we do not think it is a good idea to have large components of agency budgets that directly depend on the levels of outcomes those agencies help to produce. For many government services, the relationship between funding and outcomes is indirect or not well-documented. Numerous variables can affect outcomes, some beyond the control of agencies. Also it is often very appropriate to consider factors such as caseloads or workloads when setting agency budgets, even though these are not measures of outcomes. Ultimately, we think decisions about appropriations require the Legislature's best judgement based [on] a variety of considerations— including, but not limited to, performance information.[30]

State-Local Relations

Minnesota's system of local governments is highly fragmented and the ties between localities and the state are very complex. Several initiatives in the late 1980s and early 1990s attempted to rationalize state-local relations. Most important among these were changes in the major state aid programs to local governments. Other important changes involved the division of responsibilities for welfare programs and local property tax levy limits.

Minnesota funds a variety of relatively generous aid programs to localities. The most significant are Local Government Aid (LGA) and Homestead and Agricultural Credit Aid (HACA). Aid distributions in both of these programs were originally based in one way or another on local tax capacity, and the LGA formula during the 1980s also rewarded local tax effort. There was a serious attempt in the late 1980s to revise the formulas for both programs, but consensus could not be reached in the legislature about what to include in the formula. In the end, the old formulas were discarded without replacement and, entering the 1990s, the aid from these two programs (totaling more than $600 million) was distributed essentially according to prior year allocations with some adjustments for inflation.

The state also supports a myriad of other small aid programs. These include, but are not limited to, Equalization Aid (budgeted at about $20 million in FY 1994) that is targeted to jurisdictions with very low tax capacity, Disparity Reduction Aid ($30 million) that is targeted to places with very high tax rates, Border City Disparity Reduction Aid ($2.5 million) that goes to various properties and cities near the border with North Dakota to offset the lower tax rates prevailing in that state, and County Social Services Aid ($50 million) that is distributed by a formula based on population, population over 65, and income maintenance caseloads.

This complex system of programs has been under attack from various sources since the mid-1980s and budget allocations reflect this. As noted in the previous section and Table 12–3, growth in nonschool local aid lagged behind all other major categories in the budget during the early 1990s—indeed, aid levels actually declined over the period.

The 1991 legislature made a serious attempt to rationalize and stabilize the system. At the beginning of the session, Governor Carlson proposed severe cuts in LGA (totaling more than $500 over two years) as part of the package to deal with the projected 1992–1993 deficit. The legislature resisted cuts of this magnitude, but there was general consensus that the aid system needed "fixing." The compromise that was struck cut LGA by about $170 million over the biennium and set up the Local Government Trust Fund (LGTF) beginning in FY 1992. The LGTF was financed with earmarked revenue from the sales tax and automobile excise tax (2 percentage points from each, totaling more than $700 million in 1992), and most local aid programs were included in the fund. At the same time, the legislature created the Minnesota Advisory Commission on Intergovernmental Relations (ACIR). It was hoped that the ACIR could take on the task of consolidating aid programs (particularly LGA and HACA) and devising a new formula for more effective targeting of the aid that would potentially reduce the overall cost of the programs. The following two years brought a great deal of discussion of these issues, including significant work on distribution formulas controlling for both local tax capacities and expenditure needs.[31]

In the end, however, the LGTF and the ACIR were unable to serve the functions planned for them. In practice, allocations under the primary grant programs in the LGTF did not move with the earmarked sales tax revenues. Aid levels tended to be set for the major programs, usually based on prior allocations and inflation, then expenditure programs would be moved in or out of the fund in order to balance the account. Discussions of consolidation and new formulas also foundered, as individual places and legislators worried about how simplification of the system would affect them or their constituencies. The 1994 legislature essentially acknowledged failure in this dimension by abolishing the LGTF and disbanding the ACIR. Local government interests were able to negotiate a quid pro quo for the loss of the trust fund. The FY 1994 tax bill included a provision indexing total LGA disbursements to inflation (within a range between 2.5 percent and 5.0 percent). There was also an attempt during that session to tie the LGA program to a new formula and the 1994–1995 budget includes a new LGA formula based on both revenue capacity and expenditure need. However, the formula is to be phased in over twenty years and affects only year-to-year increases. This means, for instance, that less than $16 million of the $330 million allocation for FY 1995 comes under the formula.

The state had more success in reforming other features of state-local relations. Early in the period, the state took action to deregulate a very significant aspect of local governance. The 1989 legislature removed all levy limits on county and local governments. Prior to that time, counties and localities faced levy limits that were determined by the prior year levy limit, the amount of LGA received, inflation, and population growth.[32] One year later, the 1990 session passed legislation that completed the takeover by the state government of county responsibilities for income maintenance and county and local court costs. In 1990, counties were still responsible for between 5 percent and 15 percent of spending for income maintenance. All of this spending, totaling roughly $140 million per year was taken over by the state in FY 1991 along with about $30 million per year for court costs.

In sum, state-local relations received a significant amount of attention during the early 1990s. However, the major initiatives—the

Local Government Trust Fund and the ACIR—must be considered failures. As of the 1994–1995 budget, local aid is still characterized by a confusing array of programs with aid under the most important ones still not targeted effectively. Much remains on the state's agenda in this important policy area.

Welfare Reform

Welfare reform was a much debated topic during the late 1980s and early 1990s in Minnesota. As early as 1985 the state was studying reforms that anticipated the major federal initiatives of the late 1980s. Many of the Minnesota reforms were passed in 1987 and eventually implemented under the auspices of the Job Opportunities and Basic Skills program (JOBS), jointly funded by the federal government and the states under the Family Support Act of 1988. Interest did not end at that point however. After much study, a very sizable five-year demonstration project was launched in early 1994.

The discussion about welfare reform began in 1985 with the passage of the Minnesota Jobs Bill, which included a number of provisions intended to reduce the unemployment rate in the state. Among other things, the legislation reorganized state offices serving the unemployed and called for better coordination between state departments operating employment and training programs and agencies serving welfare recipients. The 1986 legislature then debated a wide range of proposals to reform the Aid for Families with Dependent Children program (AFDC) in ways consistent with the Jobs Bill. The debate created deadlock and DFL Governor Rudy Perpich established a bipartisan Commission to make recommendations to the 1987 legislature. The commission's recommendations emphasized preventive measures targeted for groups of recipients deemed at risk of becoming long-term recipients. Two programs with the potential to affect significant numbers of welfare recipients emerged from the legislature during the next three years—Project Success Through Reaching Individual Development and Employment (STRIDE) and the Minnesota Family Investment Plan (MFIP).

The STRIDE program was passed in 1987 and became the primary vehicle for meeting the federal requirements of the JOBS program. It emphasizes individualized assessment of client needs, integrated case management for targeted AFDC recipients, and activities designed to increase earning capacity over the long term. Three recipient groups are targeted by the program—caretakers (usually single mothers) under the age of twenty-one; caretakers without a high school degree or General Equivalency Diploma; and caretakers who have received AFDC for twenty-four or more of the last thirty-six months.[33] The program emphasizes education and job skills training activities and was serving more than 10,000 families by FY 1993 (out of a total AFDC caseload in Minnesota of roughly 60,000).

MFIP is a program with even greater potential to change the experience of welfare recipients. A five-year, $200 million demonstration was begun in March 1994 after six years of planning, study, and applications for federal waivers. The program is intended to serve about 6,000 participants in seven counties over the five years and is designed to increase the opportunities for AFDC recipients to move into jobs. Unlike many experimental programs around the country, it does this primarily with carrots, rather than sticks. The intent is to eliminate the disincentives to work that exist in the current welfare system. Specifically, the transition from AFDC participation to private employment is eased for MFIP participants by allowing them to keep up to twice the amount of their basic welfare grant in private income plus grants without losing any of their welfare grant, Medicaid coverage, or day care support. (Normally, an AFDC recipient in Minnesota loses a dollar of assistance for each dollar earned in a job after four months on the job). In addition, benefits to MFIP participants are streamlined by including food stamp grants in the monthly AFDC check with no restrictions on how the money is to be spent.

For example, a single mother with one child receiving support through the mainstream AFDC program in Minnesota in 1994 would receive $437 per month in an AFDC check and $180 in food stamps. If she got a job, she would lose AFDC benefits dollar for dollar (after four months) and she would lose all AFDC and Medicaid once her private income reached $424 per month. In the MFIP program, on the other hand, the recipient would receive $617 in a single benefit check and could earn as much as $1,185 per month in total income (assistance plus wages) before losing any AFDC or Medicaid benefits.[34] Recipients who do not take a job within two years of entering the program are required to participate in a job training and employment program. An evaluation (using a full control group) by the New York-based Manpower Research Demonstration Project is built into the demonstration to examine the effects of the program on employment rates and AFDC participation.

The focus of welfare reform in Minnesota has long been on preventive approaches intended to decrease the dependence of long-term recipients on AFDC benefits. STRIDE grew out of this tradition and MFIP continues it. Like many of the other reforms discussed above, it is still too early to know how successful the programs will be. However, with MFIP at least, policymakers and analysts can count on seeing the results of a careful evaluation of the program's outcomes.

WINNERS AND LOSERS IN THE 1990s

Extremely large tax increases or service reductions have not been necessary in Minnesota in the early 1990s. Consequently, state policy changes have not generated major changes in the distribution of benefits and costs of state activities. However, budget policies in the first half of the decade were not completely neutral and some distinct winners and losers are discernable.

Table 12–4 shows how changing priorities affected general expenditure categories during the first half of the decade. The table compares actual 1995 budget allocations to the distribution of funds that would have occurred if all categories had maintained their 1990 share of the budget. A negative number in the "Difference" column signifies a category that lost support during the period relative to other categories.

Clear losers during the period include providers and consumers of higher education and local property taxpayers. Support for higher education in the 1995 budget was nearly 20 percent below what the allocation would have been had higher education maintained its share of the budget. The University of Minnesota alone "lost" $124 million from its annual budget, nearly 30 percent of its actual state funding. State spending for higher education lagged behind inflation as well as other state spending. The result was that real tuition increased for all students and real income declined for most employees in the system. Nor were the real tuition increases offset by state aid to individuals. There has been much discussion in the state about targeting higher education aid more effectively by decreasing general state support for universities and using the savings to increase aid to individual students targeted by income. The decreases in general support have occurred, but without any corresponding increases in targeted aid.[35]

TABLE 12–4   Changing Minnesota Expenditure Priorities, 1990–1995
($ million)

Category	1995 Budget	1995 Budget Assuming Constant Share	Difference	Difference as % of 1995 Budget
K–12 Education*	$2,758	$2,437	$320	12%
Higher Education	1,062	1,250	−188	−18
Univ. of Minnesota	462	586	−124	−27
Other	600	664	−64	−11
Local Government Aid (LGA)	333	540	−206	−62
Homestead Aid (HACA)*	602	649	−47	−8
Other Aid	604	836	−232	−38
Medicaid	1,227	626	600	49
Income Maintenance	275	218	58	21
Corrections	142	120	21	15
Other	1,432	2,130	−698	−49

*K–12 Education and HACA constant share estimates control for the shift of $168 million from HACA Education Aid to K–12 Education Aid in 1991–92.
Source: Minnesota Department of Finance

Local taxpayers suffered from two significant changes during the period. The decline in state aid to local governments and the extension of the state sales tax to many local government purchases each put additional pressure on local tax bases. The state aid declines show up clearly in Table 12–4. LGA was hit especially hard, with a relative decline in funding equal to more than 60 percent of the actual 1995 budget. Effective local property tax rates on residential homesteads increased by 24 percent on average between 1990 and 1994 and by 17 percent for commercial and industrial property.[36] Not all of these increases can be attributed to state aid declines or extension of the sales tax, of course, but it is clear that the net effect of the these two changes in state policy was to increase local property taxes above what they would have been.

There were two significant state tax increases during the period with the potential to create significant losers. Both changes occurred in FY 1992 when the sales tax was increased from 6.0 percent to 6.5 percent and the income tax rate was raised in the highest tax bracket. The impact of the sales tax increase, although mildly regressive, was felt across all incomes—reflecting the overall incidence of the tax. The income tax change was targeted exclusively on high income taxpayers and represented significant revenues—$150 million over the 1992–1993 biennium. However, the rate change eliminated a clear inequity in the rate structure (the rate bubble for upper-middle income taxpayers) and few analysts would regard the resulting rate structure to be excessively progressive—rates vary from 6 percent in the lowest tax bracket to 8.5 percent in the highest. In addition, high income taxpayers benefited in the same year from changes in the state-set rates for local property taxes.

Clear winners are less easy to discern. Some consumers of public education probably came out ahead during the early 1990s. State aid for local education increased at greater than average rates during the period, but much of the real increase was targeted for an initiative with a very specific goal—class size reductions in grades K through 3. The benefits from school choice innovations are much more difficult to trace, because it is difficult to assess the effects of the changes on the total system. However, revealed preference—at least 50,000 students chose schools or programs other than those assigned to them in FY 1993—suggests that many parents and students have benefited from the programs.

Medicaid and income maintenance also show greater than average increases over the period. Many of the changes reflect costs and caseloads, rather than benefit increases, but STRIDE and MFIP have created new opportunities for some welfare recipients. Other potential winners in the late 1990s include the low to moderate income households that are potential participants in MinnesotaCare. 1994 estimates placed the uninsured population in Minnesota at 300,000. If the program is eventually funded to levels consistent with universal coverage, this population clearly stands to gain. However, full funding will also generate losers on the revenue side of the budget.

On balance, policy changes in the early 1990s created some clear winners and losers, although no large class of taxpayers benefited or lost enormously. It was a period of significant ferment in the state, but it is likely that, if one were to assess the distribution of fiscal dividends (the value of benefits from state services minus taxes paid) across taxpayers before and after the changes, the overall pattern would not be drastically different at the two points in time.

CONCLUSIONS

Despite the fact that Minnesota did not face a fiscal crisis of the severity of other states in the first half of the 1990s, the period was one of significant turmoil in the state. On the budgetary front, the state benefited from a very large cash reserve that was built during the 1980s. As a result, it was able to deal with a relatively severe fiscal scare early in the decade—a projected deficit for the 1992–1993 biennium equal to roughly 8 percent of budgeted expenditures—with relatively modest tax increases. Subsequent improvements in the economy rebuilt the reserve back to a level in excess of 10 percent of annual expenditures. The need for a reserve of this magnitude is clearly questionable. A strong case could be made that a significant portion of this money would be used more effectively either as additional disposable income for taxpayers or additional state services. A counterargument might note that the state budget has exhibited some signs of a structural deficit—deficit spending in five of the first six fiscal years of the 1990s. However, a policy of slowly spending down excess reserves is a prudent strategy for any state to follow when reserves reach the levels seen in Minnesota. It is therefore difficult to say that the deficits represent an ongoing imbalance between what the revenue system is able to generate and what voters (and politicians) demand in services in a typical year.

In sum, the dominant factors during the period were a relatively strong economy and the state's historically conservative posture toward risk taking with the budget. Combined, they resulted in the state beginning and ending the early 1990s with a relatively large cash reserve. The inevitable uncertainties associated with forecasting tax revenues and political pressure to spend down excess reserves meant that the state spent from this reserve in most years, but not at excessive rates. Later in the decade, the state is likely to have to make adjustments in either revenue or expenditure rates to bring long-run budget projections into balance, but the required adjustments are likely to be relatively modest—on the order of 2 percent of the magnitude of the planned budget.

Minnesota continued its tradition of innovation in public services during the period. The early 1990s brought the implementation of significant reforms in public schools, health care, and welfare. However, most of the initiatives in these areas originated in the 1980s. Many of the attempts at policy reform in the 1990s—in state-local relations, budgeting procedures, and health care finance for instance—have been either short-lived or incomplete, leaving much on the state's agenda for the second half of the 1990s. How the state will follow through on that agenda is not clear. It remains to be seen if the slowdown in reform efforts represents a "breather" from all of the activity of the late 1980s, a reaction to fiscal uncertainties early in the period, the moderating impact of an IR governor on the DFL legislature, or a long-run change in the state's approach to public services.*

NOTES

1. U.S. Bureau of the Census, *Government Finances in 1989–90* (Washington, DC: U.S Bureau of the Census, 1991).
2. Computed from Advisory Commission on Intergovernmental Relations, *Local Boundary Commissions: Status and Roles in Forming, Adjusting and Dissolving Local Government Boundaries* (Washington DC: U.S. Advisory Commission on Intergovernmental Relations, 1992).
3. Minnesota Department of Revenue, *Model Revenue System for Minnesota* (St. Paul, MN: Minnesota Department of Revenue, July 1992).
4. Localities vary tax rates by taxing different percentages of their "tax capacity"—the revenues generated by applying the state-set rates to the local tax base. e.g. A city might set taxes at 105 percent of capacity, in effect setting local taxes at 105 percent of the state set rates on each class of property.
5. Minnesota Department of Revenue, *Minnesota Tax Incidence Study* (St. Paul, MN: Minnesota Department of Revenue, October, 1991), and Theresa Van Hoomissen, Julia Friedman, and Tamara Hancock, *Minnesota's Property Tax and Local Aids: How Do the System and the 1988 Reforms Measure Up?* (Minneapolis, MN: Hubert H. Humphrey Institute of Public Affairs, University of

*The author wishes to express his gratitude to research assistants Steven Struthers and Julie Urban for very fine work. Special thanks also go to Bob Cline of the Minnesota Department of Revenue and Steve Hinze of the Research Department of the Minnesota House of Representatives for their willingness to spend time bringing a relative newcomer to Minnesota up to speed. Of course, all opinions or errors are the author's.

Minnesota, 1989). The estimates treat the property tax as an excise tax on housing services (rather than as, at least partly, a tax on capital).

6. Steven D. Gold and Sarah Ritchie, *State Policies Affecting Cities and Counties in 1991*, (Albany, NY: Center for the Study of the States, Rockefeller Institute of Government, State University of New York at Albany, 1992).

7. In the first round of the suit, a lower court ruled that the entire financing system for education in the state was unconstitutional. The ruling implied that almost nothing short of full state funding for schools would meet constitutional requirements for equal access to education. However, the state supreme court eventually overturned the ruling, validating the current system and saving the state government from a significant fiscal problem.

8. Carlson's veto total for his first term in office was ninety-nine, more than for the previous four governors combined. See Dennis McGrath, "Carlson Pulls Away in the Veto Derby," *Minneapolis Star Tribune*, May 15, 1994, p. 10A.

9. Of primary importance was "phonegate" in 1993, when the DFL leadership in the House of Representatives was caught up in an incident involving misuse of the house long distance telephone code. The scandal involved the DFL Majority Leader directly and he was forced to resign from the house. Although not directly involved in the scandal itself, the DFL Speaker of the House was perceived to have mishandled the incident. This contributed to dissension that led to her resignation as speaker in 1993.

10. See Helen F. Ladd, "State Responses to the TRA86 Revenue Windfalls: A New Test of the Flypaper Effect," *Journal of Policy Analysis and Management*, 12, no. 1, (1993): 82–103, at 86. Ladd's estimates imply that Minnesota's potential tax windfall was the fourth largest in the country.

11. Steven D. Gold, *Differences among the States in the Impact of the Recession* (Albany, NY: Center for the Study of the States, Nelson A. Rockefeller Institute of Government, State University of New York at Albany, January 1994), p. 17.

12. In an action that no effect on the state budget, the legislature also "paid back" high income taxpayers by eliminating the highest tax bracket for local property taxes, reducing local tax liabilities for higher income homeowners.

13. Minnesota does not have a true "rainy day fund" in the sense of an account that must be maintained at a legally set level. The "budget reserve" is included in the state's cash flow account and the level is set by agreement in budget negotiations. This is why the official budget can show the account falling below $500 million. The agreed-upon level of the reserve actually fell to $240 million for part of FY 1993, but was raised back up to $360 million when it became clear that revenues would be greater than forecast.

14. Minnesota State Legislature, Office of the Legislative Auditor, *Higher Education Tuition and State Grants* (St. Paul, MN, Minnesota State Legislature, Office of the Legislative Auditor, February 1993).

15. State of Minnesota, Minnesota Department of Corrections, as reported in the *Minneapolis Star Tribune*, August 16, 1993, p. 3B.

16. Except where noted, statistics in the following discussion are from: Mike Malone, Joe Nathan and Darryl Sedio, *Facts, Figures and Faces: A Look*

at *Minnesota's School Choice Programs* (Minneapolis, MN: Center for School Change, Hubert H. Humphrey Institute of Public Affairs, University of Minnesota, November 1993); Dana Schroeder, "School Choice Options Drawing Students Throughout the State, Influencing Programs," *Minnesota Journal*, April 13, 1993, p. 1; Mary Jane Smetanka, "Schools Changing Under Student Choice Program," *Minneapolis Star-Tribune*, December 16, 1991; and Joe Nathan and Wayne Jennings, *Access to Opportunity: Experiences of Minnesota Students in Four Statewide School Choice Programs* (Minneapolis, MN: Hubert H. Humphrey Institute of Public Affairs, University of Minnesota, 1990).

17. See Michael C. Rubenstein, Rosalind Hamar, and Nancy E. Adelman, *Minnesota's Open Enrollment Option* (Washington, DC: Policy Studies Associates, for the U.S. Department of Education, 1992).

18. See Dana Schroeder, "School Choice Options Drawing Students Throughout the State, Influencing Programs," *Minnesota Journal*, April 13, 1993, p. 1, and Mary Jane Smetanka, "School Choice: State Leaders Defend Program, Say Foundation Criticism Unfair," *Minneapolis Star-Tribune*, October 27, 1992.

19. Much of the following discussion is based on Susan Urahn and Dan Stewart, *Charter Schools: A Critical Look at Minnesota's Promising Educational Experiment* (St. Paul, MN: Minnesota House of Representatives, Research Department, April 1994), and Maureen M. Smith, "Charter Schools Working Out the Bugs," *Minneapolis Star Tribune*, August 7, 1994, p. 1B.

20. The state aid formula guarantees all school districts $3,150 per pupil in funding (in 1994). School districts levy a state-set tax on the local property tax base and the state then makes up the difference between the amount forthcoming from the local tax base and $3,150 per pupil. Local districts are allowed to spend more than $3,150 from local levies, but only after a special referendum process. Charter schools in districts that spend more than $3,150 per pupil receive only $3,150 per pupil from the state and nothing from the local district.

21. This includes all elementary and high school students in both cities.

22. See Patricia Lopez Baden, "Health Reform Going Nowhere Fast, Despite Lengthy Debate," *Minneapolis Star-Tribune*, March 31, 1994, p. 1B.

23. One estimate is that five large insurance plans represented 74 percent of spending for private health insurance in the state in 1992. Between 1992 and 1994, mergers reduced these five plans to three. See Greg Gordon, "State Health Mergers Stir Fears of 'Monopoly Medicine,'" *Minneapolis Star Tribune*, May 22, 1994, p. 21A.

24. Mike Meyers, "Budget Office Study Says Single-payer Health Plan Would Be the Least Expensive," *Minneapolis Star Tribune*, December 22, 1993, p. 12A; Patricia Lopez Baden, "Single Payer Health Plan Getting New Scrutiny," *Minneapolis Star Tribune*, March 7, 1994, p. 1B; and Mike Meyers and Tom Hamburger, "A Model in Dispute: Study Questions Using Minnesota as Valid Example for Health Reform," *Minneapolis Star Tribune*, July 27, 1994, p. 1A.

25. Much of this section is based on Minnesota State Legislature, Office of the Legislative Auditor, *Performance Budgeting* (St. Paul, MN: Office of the Legislative Auditor, Program Evaluation Division, February 1994).

26. Minnesota Laws (1969), Chapter 889, Section 1 as reported in Office of the Legislative Auditor, *Performance Budgeting*.

27. Office of the Legislative Auditor, *Performance Budgeting*, pp. 70–73.

28. Commission on Reform and Efficiency, *Budgeting and Financial Management in Minnesota State Government: Detailed Report* (St. Paul, MN: Commission on Reform and Efficiency, January 1993), p. 17.

29. See, for instance, John Gunyou, "Permanently Solving Fiscal Problems: A Modern Day Fable for the States," *Government Finance Review*, June 1994, p. 32.

30. Office of the Legislative Auditor, Program Evaluation Division, *Performance Budgeting*, pp. 77–78.

31. See, for instance, Helen F. Ladd, Andrew Reschovsky, and John Yinger, *Measuring the Fiscal Condition of Cities in Minnesota* (St. Paul, MN: Minnesota Legislative Commission on Planning and Fiscal Policy, March 1991). Ladd, Reschovsky, and Yinger showed that LGA distributions at that time were roughly correlated with tax capacities, but showed essentially no relation with the balance between tax capacity and their measure of expenditure needs. The Minnesota Taxpayer's Association was also an active participant in this debate.

32. Income maintenance and social service costs were excluded from the county-level levy limits.

33. See Sharon Patten, *Implementation Study of the JOBS Program for AFDC Recipients: Round I, Part A—State Context and Initial Response in Minnesota* (Minneapolis, MN: Hubert H. Humphrey Institute of Public Affairs, University of Minnesota, March 1991) and Jan L. Hagen and Irene Lurie, *Implementing JOBS: Initial State Choices* (Albany NY: Nelson A. Rockefeller Institute of Government, State University of New York at Albany, March 1992).

34. Jean Hopfensperger, "State Begins Experiment Aimed at Helping Parents Work Free of Welfare," *Minneapolis Star Tribune*, March 29, 1994, p. 1A.

35. Minnesota State Legislature, Office of the Legislative Auditor, State of Minnesota, *Higher Education Tuition and State Grants* (St. Paul, MN: Minnesota State Legislature, Office of the Legislative Auditor, February 1993).

36. Minnesota Department of Revenue, Research Division. The data are for effective property tax rates, not revenues.

PART III

What Next?

13

Lessons for the Future

Steven D. Gold

Many conclusions can be drawn from the diverse experiences of the six states examined in the last part. This chapter uses three approaches. First, it briefly characterizes the experience of each state individually. Second, it describes a number of findings for general readers. Many of these conclusions are not surprising to state officials who have had to wrestle with the fiscal crisis. Third, it distills some lessons that may be useful in confronting the long-term fiscal crisis and mitigating the problems that will be encountered in the next short-term fiscal crisis, which will occur at an unknown time in the not-too-distant future.

SIX STATES, SIX EXPERIENCES: STATES ARE NOT ALL THE SAME

The policies pursued by the states discussed in this book differed significantly. These differences reflected both variations in the problems they confronted and the choices they made.

California faced the most severe fiscal crisis. Exacerbated by defense cutbacks, the recession lasted longer than in the other states. Budget problems were compounded by a high rate of immigration of poor people, and policies were constrained by a series of constitutional initiatives going back to Proposition 13.

California's governor and legislature were unable to come to grips with the fiscal crisis, preferring to enact budgets based on unrealistic assumptions about the economy and federal aid. It rolled over deficits year after year. In part, this failure is due to the exceptional magnitude of its problem, with potential solutions being politically unpalatable. But it also reflects the weakness of California's policy-making culture. Sacramento is more like Washington, DC than other state capitals, with gridlock more of an endemic problem.[1] Because of its booming economy, California could behave until the 1990s as though it were immune from the competitive forces that other states have to respect.

Although it was unable to come close to balancing its budget, California did make some important changes in its policies in response to the crisis. It shifted fiscal burdens to local governments, it raised university fees sharply, it halted indexation of welfare and other benefits (and in fact cut them absolutely), and it began to improve its business climate by cutting corporate taxes and workers' compensation rates. It adopted an important reform of state-local relations, realigning responsibility for health programs with counties. It also enacted the first large state tax increase since the early 1970s. While most of these policies were sensible responses to the fiscal crisis, they were woefully inadequate to restore the state budget to balance.

Connecticut was also hit very hard by defense cutbacks and had a much more severe recession than most other states. But it responded in a particularly dramatic way, overhauling its tax system. It enacted a personal income tax and used the revenue to mitigate spending cuts and reduce general sales and corporate income taxes. The result was to make its tax system more elastic, stable, and progressive.

Connecticut also adopted some other important reforms, establishing a limitation on the growth of expenditures that will prevent a repetition of the wild mid-1980s spending spree that set the stage for its fiscal crisis. In addition, it changed collective bargaining laws to reduce salary increases.

But Connecticut is not altogether a model for other states. It shifted many costs into the future by issuing bonds to cover part of its deficit and by scrimping on contributions to pension funds. It also did little to ameliorate its high property tax burdens.

Florida's governor Lawton Chiles had the most ambitious reform agenda, pushing for major tax increases, increases in services, and spending reforms that embodied many *reinventing government* themes. To place these efforts in perspective, it is important to recognize that Florida's taxes are among the lowest in the United States, and its tax system is extremely inelastic, while its population growth rate is among the highest in the country. Florida's fiscal crisis was due less to a severely depressed economy than to its inadequate tax system and extreme demographic pressures.

Governor Chiles' successes were only limited. Because of legislative opposition, taxes were increased much less than the governor's proposals, with relatively little reform. Consequently, spending on forward-looking investment programs was not raised much. But substantial progress was made in improving state financial management.

Massachusetts, another state hit particularly hard by the recession, raised taxes at the start of the fiscal crisis under Governor Dukakis but cut taxes modestly after William Weld took office in 1991. Spending was severely constrained, with both elementary-secondary and higher education bearing much of the brunt of cutbacks.

Governor William Weld placed considerable rhetorical emphasis on privatization, but it contributed relatively little to solving the state's budget problems in the short run. Much more important was reliance on gimmickry, especially big increases in federal aid for Medicaid.

Michigan is the only one of the six states that did not increase taxes at all to deal with its budget problems. It also stands out because of the priority given to education, both K–12 and higher education. Other programs were severely squeezed, but only 40 percent of the state budget gaps were closed by cutting state spending. The rest of the adjustment was based on fiscal gimmicks that postponed costs or shifted them to others. Michigan was even more effective than the other states in extracting increased aid from the federal government.

Michigan's most lasting accomplishment was overhauling its school finance system in 1994, breaking a stalemate that had bedeviled the state for more than two decades. With revenue mainly from a higher sales tax, this reform enabled Michigan to cut the property tax from one of the highest in the country to close to the national average.

Minnesota had the least severe fiscal crisis. In part this was because its economy was not hit particularly hard by the recession, but other factors were its large rainy day fund balance and its penchant for looking further into the future than most other states when considering budget and tax policy. In retrospect, it appears that Minnesota overreacted to budget projections that turned out to be considerably too pessimistic.

Minnesota stands out for its experimentation with ways to improve schools and efforts to improve health care. It was the first state to establish charter schools and has more students involved in school choice programs than any other state. No other state moved any further in its plans to reform health care.

This synopsis of state fiscal policies illustrates the diversity of the state experiences and policies:

- Two states did not have an income tax in 1990. Governors in both states tried hard to increase taxes substantially, but one succeeded much more than the other. One state adopted an income tax while income tax proponents in the other state did not even try for one, knowing it was fruitless.
- One of the six states completely avoided raising taxes to deal with the fiscal crisis, although it did increase state taxes to cut the property tax.
- One state issued bonds to pay off its deficit gradually over time.
- One state did not come close to balancing its budget, rolling over deficits year after year.
- One state had much less of a fiscal crisis than the others. That state also was ahead of the others in experimenting with changes in education and health programs.

MAJOR FINDINGS

Despite the diversity among states, they have much in common. This section begins with a review of fifteen major findings and then focuses particularly on how reform efforts fared. Although the six states discussed in this book are used as examples, the conclusions apply generally to most states across the country.

1. *The economy is the most important influence on state fiscal conditions, although it is not the only influence.* As these words are written in mid-1994, five of the six states appear to have emerged from the short-term crises that they experienced in 1990–1991. California is the only one that is still mired in deficits, and it was one of the last states where the recession ended. To a considerable extent, the improvement in state

fiscal conditions was due to strong economic rebounds rather than to new policies adopted by state governments.

2. *States do not have to balance their budgets every year.* California has incurred deficit after deficit after deficit. Connecticut "made its deficit go away" by issuing bonds. The relevance of this finding for the debate about a federal balanced budget requirement is discussed below.

3. *States are not limited in balancing their budgets to cutting spending and increasing taxes.* They can avoid tax increases completely if they are willing to cut spending enough, if they shift burdens to the federal government or local governments, and if they are willing to rely heavily on one-shot measures.

4. *The various programs vary considerably in strength as they battle for scarce budget resources at the margin.* Medicaid has been dominant, taking an ever larger share of state resources. Corrections spending is also growing inexorably. Education is not as formidable. Even when enrollment is increasing, many states reduce the share of the budget going to elementary-secondary schools, leaving local property taxes to pick up the slack. For higher education, students and their families can be made to pay a bigger share. Welfare recipients and local governments are two of the weakest budget contenders. The fiscal problems of local governments are a low priority of state policymakers.

    One implication of the above patterns is that education is often a balance wheel of state budgets. It fares well when state finances are healthy but suffers disproportionately during periods of fiscal stress.[2]

5. *States have considerable ability to shift their fiscal problems to others.* That was a common response in the early 1990s, with local governments, the federal government, and college students bearing increased costs. In a sense, deferring pension contributions and incurring debt amounts to shifting costs to future taxpayers.

6. *Increasing taxes by itself is not usually sufficient to eliminate a serious budget problem.* All of the six states did more than merely increase taxes (if they increased them at all). On the other hand, tax increases can help to moderate spending cuts and minimize reliance on fiscal gimmickry. Michigan is the only state that avoided tax increases.

7. *Tax increases are not always permanent.* Among the six states in this study, Massachusetts allowed one to expire and repealed another. In the 1980s, California, Michigan, and Minnesota allowed temporary increases to expire. Connecticut rolled back sales and corporate income tax rates in 1991 when it adopted a personal income tax.

8. *Tax increases are not necessarily political suicide.* Despite the fact that four of these states enacted substantial tax increases in 1991, there were few repercussions in 1992 elections. This was most significant in Connecticut, where adoption of a personal income tax ignited fierce protests in 1991. A year later the great majority of legislators who backed the new tax were reelected. The point is that tax increases are acceptable if political leaders do a good job explaining why they are necessary.

9. *Rainy day funds can help to stabilize state finances.* Michigan and Minnesota both benefited from funds built up in the 1980s. But most states lack the political will to make the funds large enough to provide much of a budgetary cushion.

10. *States have considerable discretion in how they respond to fiscal crises, with the positions of the governor and the legislature both playing important roles.* The governors' firm opposition to tax increases was critically important in avoiding higher taxes in Massachusetts and Michigan, while the governor's stubborn insistence on adoption of an income tax was vital in Connecticut. But the governors of California, Florida, and Minnesota settled for tax policies that were different from those they preferred. In California and Minnesota, tax increases were bigger, while in Florida they were smaller.

11. *Election outcomes matter.* Governors Engler and Weld won narrow election victories in 1990, with the mistakes of their opponents having at least as much impact on the outcome as the popularity of the winner's ideas. (Engler's rival, the incumbent governor, had alienated many Detroit voters, and Weld's opponent lost support because of his arrogant outbursts.) But once in office Engler and Weld set their states on new conservative courses, avoiding tax increases and in fact cutting taxes somewhat. The profound effects of their policies may have surprised many who failed to vote for the Democratic candidates in 1990.

12. *Tax and spending limitations can be highly restrictive.* They are major features of the fiscal landscape in California and Massachusetts, where property tax rates are severely limited. Newly enacted limits could be important in the future in Florida (on property taxes) and in Connecticut (on state spending).

13. *State policies are not static.* Levels of service are rising and falling, as are levels of taxation. A common theme of several governors was to recommend abandonment of the use of current service baselines in presenting their budget proposals. This makes it easier to cut services. While taxes were rising in most of the six states studied, they were falling in Massachusetts (after 1990) and Michigan. Major tax structure changes occurred in Connecticut and Michigan.

14. *Reforms are often difficult to enact and implement, but they are occurring in many states.* As discussed below, they will help to make future budget problems more manageable.

15. *All states are not alike.* They differ in their budget flexibility and priorities, tax structures, demographic pressures, willingness to borrow, run deficits, and innovate, farsightedness, and many other respects. But states have enough in common that they can learn from others' successes and failures.

Assessing Reforms

The fact that all states are not alike implies that the policies they ought to consider are not the same. Connecticut addressed two major problems—an unbalanced state tax system and a history of budgetary shortsightedness that led to large, unsustainable spending increases during the boom of the mid- to late–1980s.

Connecticut policymakers get high marks for dealing with its problems:

- By enacting a personal income tax, Connecticut was able to obtain revenue to balance its budget and simultaneously reduce the rates of its sales tax and corporation income tax, both of which were the highest in the country. The result will be more stable tax revenue that causes fewer economic distortions.

- By enacting a state spending limit, Connecticut created a barrier against future spending increases that exceed the growth of the state's economy or the rate of inflation.

Connecticut also made another change that was important for it and some other states but not for many others: It reformed its local collective bargaining law so that arbitrators have to consider the government's ability to pay when they are deciding how much to increase employees salaries in cases where unions and governments reach an impasse in negotiations. The absence of this provision had helped Connecticut employees achieve salaries among the highest of any public employees nationwide.

Florida also enacted significant reforms but in a totally different way from Connecticut. Although it raised taxes in 1990 and 1991, it did not deal with the structural problems in its tax system. It remains one of the nine states without a broad-based personal income tax.

But instead Florida implemented a series of important reforms to increase efficiency. Governor Chiles had made "right-sizing" state government one of the main themes of his 1990 campaign, and despite the failure or limited success of some of his initiatives (such as civil service reform), others were quietly put into effect. Managerial reforms, such as allowing agencies to invest savings from initiatives that cut costs, helped to increase productivity. In response to demands from private sector representatives serving on state commissions, Florida developed much better information about program activities.

Privatization initiatives had not yet produced obvious significant payoffs as of mid-1994. Massachusetts and Michigan devoted considerable effort to establishing a framework for evaluating privatization options, but the results of these efforts have thus far been relatively meager. In Massachusetts, despite Governor Weld's making this a high priority, efforts to sell state assets often failed because of a lack of buyers. Most of the purported benefits of privatization have been challenged by a legislative study.

Privatization is one element of the Osborne-Gaebler agenda for "reinventing government." Other elements include making government programs more results-oriented, customer-driven, mission-driven, enterprising, preventive, decentralized, market-oriented, empowering, and competitive. Several of these themes were pushed hard by various governors, particularly Governor Chiles in Florida. Some of them led to failed efforts, but a general conclusion is that it is too soon to tell whether such initiatives are producing meaningful results.

Emphasis on prevention was a theme in nearly all states. The austere fiscal climate thwarted efforts to increase spending substantially for preventive programs, so most of them still had relatively small budgets in 1994. Expanding preventive programs by shifting resources from other programs were not particularly successful.

Increased use of performance budgeting, which focuses on the results accomplished rather than inputs or processes, also was not an outstanding successes in these states. Performance budgeting is an old idea that was a fad in the past, but whether it has more longevity now remains to be seen.[3]

Decentralization and making programs more market-oriented and competitive are reinvention themes that have led to some important changes in state programs and interesting experiments. Examples are moving the mentally ill from state institutions to community-based programs, California's realignment initiative, and various school reforms.

Shifting patients out of state mental hospitals is not an innovative policy. All states have pursued it to some extent, especially in the 1970s. But it has often been thwarted by opposition from employee unions, resulting in continued operation of facilities when service could be provided more efficiently through community mental health programs without sacrificing quality (although local programs are often underfunded). When this opposition is overcome, it can be characterized as "abandoning business as usual." During the early 1990s Massachusetts and Michigan each closed a state mental hospital, and California moved many patients out of state hospitals as a result of its program that realigned responsibilities between the state and counties.

California's realignment, while adopted for fiscal reasons, had some other positive effects. (Realignment shifted responsibility for mental health and indigent health care from the state to counties, increased the county share of the cost of many social services, and raised state sales taxes and motor vehicle fees, with the revenue dedicated to help counties pay for these programs.) For example, it resulted in less reliance on high-cost group foster homes and, as mentioned above, fewer patients in state mental hospitals.

Realignment was the most dramatic change in state-local relationships in any state during this period. It was judged a success both by the state and by counties. It helped the state by removing some costly programs from the state budget, and it helped counties by providing a relatively certain stream of revenue from dedicated taxes rather having to depend on annual appropriations. While the taxes produced less revenue than the transferred programs cost, many county officials thought that they fared better than they would have if state aid had been appropriated.

One benefit of realignment was unique to California: It represented a way of increasing state taxes without having to share 40 percent of the revenue with schools. Education is guaranteed a share of all general fund revenue, but realignment was funded out of a new earmarked fund. But other aspects of realignment—simplifying state budgeting, providing a relatively stable source of local aid for transferred programs, unifying responsibility for programs at a single level of government, and providing incentives for better utilization of resources—illustrate the kinds of gains that can occur from reforming state-local policies. That is a lesson that other states can take to heart.

Another area where decentralization and competition took root, even though the roots were shallow, was in reform of elementary-secondary schools. Most of these states experimented with school choice and charter schools. The former allow students to select their school, and the latter permit teachers to establish schools free of state mandates, provided that they satisfy accountability standards.

As with many other reforms, it is too soon to judge how successful these innovations are. But the evidence from Minnesota suggests that they are helpful, not only because many students avail themselves of the choice option but also because the threat of losing students stimulates improvements in school program offerings.

Spending cuts can be reforms in the eyes of some, but that is controversial. Massachusetts and Michigan made large cuts in eligibility for their welfare programs for adults, known as general assistance. The impact of those cuts, although they occurred in 1991, is still uncertain. California and Connecticut also cut welfare benefits, and most of these states obtained federal waivers to experiment with new restrictions of welfare programs. As in other cases, it is too early to tell what their results will be.

Likewise, many states curtailed support for higher education. One result was higher tuition, which some would applaud as appropriate because many students are from relatively affluent families. But the cuts in California and Massachusetts also resulted in significant cutbacks in course offerings and larger class sizes, making it much more difficult if not impossible for many students to complete their course of study in four years. Moreover, most states hurt access to higher education because they did not raise financial aid commensurately with tuition increases.

It is also important to recognize that states developed some significant reforms unrelated to the short-run fiscal crisis. While they may not save a large amount of money immediately, they could help to improve services in the long run. Education has already been discussed. Health is another prime example.

Many health initiatives will cost rather than save money, but they could play a big role in reforming the national health care system. Minnesota is one of the leading states in the country in implementing health reform. On the other hand, Massachusetts claims that its managed care initiative is an important reason why the growth of Medicaid fell sharply in 1993 and 1994.

LESSONS FOR STATE OFFICIALS

What should states do to be better prepared for the next short-term fiscal crisis and to deal with an ongoing long-term crisis?

Short-term crises usually result from recessions, which depress state revenue and boost spending. Minnesota provides the best model of how to minimize the impact of short-term crises. It maintains a large rainy day fund, and its policymakers devote considerable attention to multi-year budget projections, reducing the probability that it will be caught by surprise when economic growth slackens. In 1991 it actually overreacted to the projection of an impending deficit. Most states make the opposite mistake, holding bare bones reserves and focusing on the short-term outlook, paying little attention to projections more than eighteen months ahead.

The long-run fiscal crisis relates to structural deficits. Reviewing the recent record, the bottom-line questions are whether, in dealing with their fiscal crises, (1) states cut spending or changed programs in ways that make government more efficient, and (2) when they increased taxes, did they fundamentally improve the tax system in some regard? The answers vary from state to state, and they are often not black and white. A state may have enacted some worthwhile reforms that had relatively little effect on the overall budget situation while relying largely on old fashioned spending restraint, tax increases and stopgap measures as its main strategies for getting through the crisis. Aside from the small reforms, there are at least three substantial ones:

- *Tax reform*: Connecticut's overhaul of its tax system and Michigan's property tax relief initiative
- *State-local relations*: California's realignment

These three reforms stand like beacons in the first half of the 1990s, providing the important lesson that significant reforms of tax policy and state-local relations can be put into effect.

Unfortunately, no spending reform stands out as clearly as these reforms of taxes and state-local policies. The lesson is that it is more difficult to reform spending fundamentally than to enact reforms in the other areas.

This does not imply that states are standing still in the spending area. On the contrary, a great deal of change is fermenting. The authors of the Connecticut and Florida chapters emphasized that the culture of state government has changed to become more acutely concerned with delivering services and managing programs efficiently and effectively. In Massachusetts and Michigan, the foundation has been laid for a significant expansion of privatization. In many states, schools are facing more competitive threats because of choice and related initiatives.

A possible lesson for states is that they cannot afford to stand still. If they are not working seriously on reform of their programs, they risk falling behind other states. Cynics may reject this lesson on the ground that the reforms are not proven successes; rather, reinvention themes are either old ideas that have been around for a long time or they are good principles that are extremely difficult if not impossible to operationalize on a large scale. Based on the state experiences in this book, such cynics cannot be proven wrong yet, but not enough time has elapsed to prove them right.

Fiscal conservatives may draw another lesson from the experiences of these states—that a state does not have to increase taxes when it is in a fiscal crisis. Michigan did not. Massachusetts resisted further tax increases after 1990 even though its budget was far out of balance. California's crisis continued unabated after big 1991 tax increases, leading some observers to the erroneous conclusion that higher taxes did nothing to alleviate the state's fiscal dilemma.

It is certainly true that higher state taxes can be avoided, but at what price? Not increasing state taxes may have at least six possible effects:

- Greater efficiency in providing services;
- Lower levels of state services;
- Worse compensation of state employees;
- Higher fees for state services (particularly at universities and colleges);
- Lower local services or higher local taxes; and
- Increased reliance on gimmicks that shift costs into the future.

Of these six effects, only the first in unambiguously a good thing. Tax opponents often use rhetoric that assumes elimination of waste and inefficiency will be the only results of not increasing taxes, ignoring the other five effects.

Lower services are often hard for the average citizen to perceive. Most of the general state budget goes for school aid, higher education, and assistance to the sick and poor.[4] It is not difficult for a state to obscure the effects of spending cutbacks from the average citizen.

How did Michigan (throughout), Massachusetts (after 1990), and California (after 1991) avoid tax increases?

- Michigan relied more on gimmicks than on budget cuts. It was particularly successful at obtaining higher federal aid, with a 41 percent increase between 1990 and 1992.
- Massachusetts also benefited from a celebrated $500 million federal Medicaid windfall. In addition, it made drastic reductions in elementary-secondary and higher education spending, although it later replaced much of the reduction in school aid.
- California imposed enormous cuts on cities and counties, resulting in serious reductions not just in services like libraries but even in law enforcement. It also impaired the quality of its higher education system by drastic budget reductions.

An important part of the fiscal strategy of many states in this period was to shift costs to the federal government through creative financing of Medicaid. Nationally, federal aid increased more than three times as much as tax revenue between 1990 and 1992. If the federal government takes steps to curtail entitlement and other spending, this option may not be open to states in the future.

So these three states demonstrate that avoiding state tax increases has many effects other than simply increasing the efficiency of providing services. It entails substantial costs, except to the extent that a state is able to shift costs to the federal government.

To recapitulate, three lessons have been noted:

- Major reforms of tax policy and state-local relations are feasible.
- States cannot afford to stand still. Other states are critically reexamining their programs and how services are delivered, so if a state is not focusing on these issues, it risks falling behind others.
- Avoiding tax increases in a major fiscal crisis entails serious side effects. No state has figured out how to radically improve efficiency.

Each of these lessons has important implications for state policies in the rest of the 1990s. In a competitive, antitax, slow economic growth environment with the federal aid spigot turned down, states would be ill advised to forget the lessons of the early 1990s.

In an important sense, the results of this study are disappointing. By examining six of the states with the best reputations for being innovative or abandoning business as usual, we hoped to learn lessons that would make it easier for other states to cope with future fiscal problems. But over and over we have found either that celebrated departures were not as far-reaching as rhetoric implied or that it was too soon to tell how successful they will be. The quest for a magic bullet is fruitless.

A related lesson is a sober one. Even if a state adopts some of the "right" policies, it may still not escape from fiscal crisis. Realignment helped California, but it did not solve its problems. Closing unnecessary state facilities or allowing students more choice in the schools they attend can make service delivery more efficient, but it is necessary to implement many such policies to make a big difference in the state budget.

LESSONS FOR THE FEDERAL GOVERNMENT

One of the findings noted above is that states can and do run deficits, in some cases repeatedly. All states, with one or two exceptions,[5] are supposed to adopt balanced budgets, but in many cases they are not required to keep the budget balanced if spending unexpectedly exceeds revenues. As California demonstrates, even the requirement to adopt a balanced budget becomes virtually meaningless if unrealistic assumptions are used.

This implies that proponents of a federal balanced budget amendment are misguided if they point to states as always balancing their budgets. The capital markets are more of a discipline on state deficits than constitutional or statutory requirements. California's miserable record of fiscal irresponsibility led to several downgrades by municipal rating agencies and finally to dictation by banks of major parts of the fiscal year 1995 budget.

But there is another lesson for the federal government. While states do not really *have to* avoid deficits every year, they usually do make tough decisions to balance their budgets, involving both spending cuts and tax increases. While gridlock and gimmickry are not unknown in state capitals, they do not reign as they do in Washington, DC.

VITAL MISSING INFORMATION

The six case studies provide a more complete record of state fiscal policies than is generally available, but they fall far short of answering the most important question about the effects of state policies: *What happened to services?* As discussed above, when spending is cut, efficiency may increase, but that is not always the only or even the primary result. Unfortunately, information about service levels is rarely easy to obtain. The widespread efforts to implement performance budgeting and benchmarking could help to fill this gap, but in the meantime a major ingredient needed to assess state policies is missing. This is a major area for future research.

NOTES

1. There are many reasons, including the size and diversity of the state. California's state senators represent more people than do its U.S. representatives.

2. One legislative staffer explained to the author that during boom times it is easier to increase school aid than to expand state-operated programs. When the budget is tight, legislators in his state resist cutting social services because they consider their level already to be bare bones. Although both school aid and higher education can be considered to be balance wheels, higher education is more vulnerable to cutbacks because elementary-secondary education usually has a considerably stronger constituency. Besides, colleges and universities can raise tuition and fees to offset state budget cuts.

3. The Minnesota chapter describes the conclusions of an evaluation of performance budgeting by that state's Legislative Auditor.

4. Another important state service, transportation, is paid for primarily from earmarked motor fuels taxes, so it is somewhat inoculated from state fiscal crises.

5. It is commonly stated that Vermont is the only state that does not require a balanced budget, but a recent federal report concluded that Wyoming also does not have a balanced budget requirement. U.S. General Accounting Office, *Balanced Budget Requirements: State Experiences and Implications for the Federal Government* (March 1993).

14

The Fiscal Agenda of the States to the Year 2000

Steven D. Gold

In order to discuss the fiscal issues facing the states in the next five years, one must first project the environment in which they will operate. This chapter begins by sketching the external conditions that will affect state spending and revenues and then discusses the major fiscal issues facing the states.

This analysis updates the author's book *The State Fiscal Agenda for the 1990s*, which was published in 1990.[1] It is possible to benefit from hindsight in examining the extent to which events unfolded as anticipated and the reasons why they did not.

THE STATE FISCAL ENVIRONMENT

Will the second half of the 1990s be like the first half? It is always tempting to extrapolate trends, but that may be misleading. The main influences on state fiscal conditions, aside from state policies, are the economy, demographic changes, federal policy, and citizen attitudes about taxes and services. Developments in these four areas are likely to result in considerable state fiscal stress.

The Economy

The capacity of the economy is expected to grow at an annual rate of about 2.5 percent. This is relatively low by historical standards because the labor force is growing relatively slowly and the rate of productivity increase is still depressed.

The most important implication of moderate economic growth is that state tax revenue will also grow only moderately, unless states raise taxes by increasing rates or broadening the tax base. In most states, excluding legislated changes, revenue grows somewhat more slowly than personal income.

Another result of relatively slow economic growth is that it contributes to the already intense interstate competition for economic development. If the national economy is growing slowly, the economies of laggard states may actually contract.

It is also important whether the national economy grows steadily or in a volatile fashion, with a recession interrupting periods of expansion. The odds are that there will be another recession within a few years. That recession will precipitate the next short-run fiscal crisis for most states.

Demographic Changes

The most important demographic variable affecting state-local finances is the growth rate of public school enrollment. During the first several years of the 1990s, this enrollment rose about 1.7 percent annually, a relatively high rate. States responded in part by reducing the proportion of school costs that they finance, with the state share of state-local school revenue dropping from 51.6 percent in 1989–1990 to an estimated 49.2 percent in 1993–1994.[2] This of course led to pressure for higher local property taxes.

School enrollment is expected to continue up but at a slightly slower pace. The U.S. Department of Education projects that after a 7.4 percent increase between 1990 and 1994, it will grow another 7.2 percent in the next four years.

Several other demographic developments imply only moderate pressure on state budgets:

- Higher education enrollment is projected by the U.S. Department of Education to increase just 3.5 percent between 1995 and 2000.
- The population between the ages of fifteen and twenty-four, which accounts disproportionately for commission of crimes, will increase 4.1 percent between 1995 and 2000, but the population aged twenty-five to thirty-four will decrease 8.2 percent.

On the other hand, the number of people over the age of eighty-five, many of whom will require nursing home care, will increase 20.5

percent between 1995 and 2000, putting upward pressure on Medicaid spending.

It is important to emphasize that demographic trends differ greatly from state to state. While the school-age population grows rapidly in one state, it may be falling in another state. Immigration is a major issue in some states (particularly California, Florida, and Texas) but of relatively little importance in many others.

Federal Policies

The federal government influences state finances through the aid it provides and the costs that it mandates. A surprise in the early 1990s was the large increase that occurred in federal aid because Washington allowed states to pay for part of their share of Medicaid in ways that did not burden the general state budget. Meanwhile, the imposition of expensive new federal mandates slowed sharply after 1990, although some mandates legislated in previous years had growing effects on state spending.

The outlook for federal policy in the latter half of the 1990s is uncertain, but it is unlikely to be as benign as it was in the first several years of the decade. In fact, it could be considerably more hostile to the states because Washington's "deficit hawks" appear to be gaining strength, and many of them myopically consider it a spending cut when they shift the cost of federal programs to the states.

On the other hand, President Bill Clinton has been more mindful of federal mandates than his recent predecessors, and he is likely to resist imposing expensive new unfunded mandates on states.

A federal balanced budget amendment could have profound consequences. A probably scenario is that the federal government would respond by cutting aid to state and local governments sharply. Depending on the degree to which mandates were also curtailed, this would result in a severe state fiscal crisis and significant reduction in state services and benefits for citizens.

Citizen Attitudes About Taxes and Services

Polls indicate that citizens are increasingly cynical about government at all levels and skeptical that their tax dollars will be spent productively. Meanwhile, an increasing number of high-profile governors (such as John Engler, William Weld, and Christine Todd Whitman) have proposed tax cuts even when their states projected unbalanced budgets.

The next few years are likely to be characterized by more antipathy to tax increases than normal. There might also be numerous tax cuts, although that is less certain. The widespread tax cuts enacted in 1994 were, with few exceptions, relatively small in size and are consistent with the policies adopted by states in 1984–1985 after the recession of the early 1980s.

There does not appear to be a strong public demand for increasing spending to offset the forces pushing for tax cuts. But the public does not seem to want lower services either. Those favoring more spending will have to make a compelling case that it will actually yield significant benefits such as better schools, a safer community, or more effective infrastructure.

Other Influences on the Fiscal Environment

Court decisions and voter initiatives will also add to budget problems in states, as they have in past. Tax revolt initiatives could be a greater problem than previously because tax opponents have recently become more sophisticated in designing their proposals. In particular, four states recently adopted constitutional amendments requiring that tax increases be approved by a popular vote or by more than a simple majority of the legislature. These initiative proposals are more difficult to defeat than proposals that cut taxes by large amounts from existing levels, but they will make significantly increase the difficulty of enacting tax increases.

Summary

The fiscal environment will at best be tranquil. This scenario would unfold if the economy grows steadily close to full employment, federal aid is not reduced and expensive new mandates are not imposed, citizens do not demand significant tax cuts or support stringent new tax limitations, and demographic factors do not result in big increases in service demands. Even in this optimistic scenario, spending will be relatively tight.

But states will have more stress if elements of this ideal scenario fail to unfold. If we have a serious recession, the federal government imposes expensive new unfunded mandates or reduces aid, or citizens demand tax cuts, considerable fiscal stress will exist. This is especially so in states where demographic developments will burden state budgets.

The degree of fiscal stress is not completely beyond the control of the states. If they have modern, responsive tax systems and enlightened spending policies, that will help moderate fiscal stress considerably. Several questions are vital in this regard:

- Will states reform their tax systems to make them more responsive to economic growth, for example, by taxing services more broadly and increasing reliance on the personal income tax and making it more progressive?
- Will states continue to drive up their corrections budgets by adopting stricter sentencing rules for lawbreakers, even when their offenses are nonviolent?
- Will states focus on finding better ways to deliver services, such as by restructuring schools, reducing mandates on local governments, and relying more on market mechanisms rather than bureaucratic solutions?

FOUR AGENDAS

There is no single state fiscal agenda. Rather, there are at least four agendas—an efficiency agenda, an equity agenda, a "do less" agenda, and a "do more" agenda.

The efficiency agenda is likely to be a high priority for states in the antitax environment of the next few years. The message from the case studies in this book is that dramatic increases in efficiency cannot be achieved overnight. Despite extravagant claims by governors of some of the states discussed here, efficiency gains usually come slowly.

There are two aspects of the efficiency agenda. One is the reinvention of government movement popularized by Osborne and Gaebler. The other is simply getting away from "business as usual" and attacking sacred budgetary cows. These two ways of increasing efficiency may overlap, but that is not always the case.[3] Both confront substantial political obstacles, but both are needed.

The *equity agenda* can also be divided into several parts—taxing the affluent more, taxing the poor less or giving them more services, and distributing services more fairly.

- The potential for taxing rich people more varies considerably from state to state. If a state already has relatively high taxes on the wealthy, it risks hurting its business climate by raising their taxes further. But if taxes on the affluent are low, the available options are considerably wider.
- A state can also make its tax system more progressive (or less regressive) by reducing taxes on the poor. If the tax cuts are carefully targeted, as by adopting an earned income tax credit that helps only low-income workers and their families, the cost to the state treasury is relatively modest. Alternatively, the poor can be helped by providing them with more services.
- Another way to improve equity is to reduce inequalities in the distribution of services. This is most often discussed in relation to schools. Changes in that area usually come in response to actual or anticipated court decisions.

A *"do less"* agenda is implicit in many proposals to cut taxes broadly. Proponents often deny this, claiming that spending cuts can target waste and inefficiency, but lower taxes usually result in lower services. California's experience after Proposition 13 demonstrates this starkly.

Privatization is a variant of the "do less" agenda. Although privatization is so widespread that it is really nothing new, considerable momentum appears to have developed to accelerate privatization efforts. The extent to which privatization leads to more efficient service delivery rather than simply less service remains to be seen.

The *"do more"* agenda will face tough going in the next few years because of the sluggish growth of revenue from existing sources and the difficulty of selling large tax increases.

In the next few years the possibility that states will aggressively pursue a "do more" agenda appears scant. This has important implications for the nation. In 1990, Alice Rivlin wrote as follows:

If the United States is to have a world-class economy for the 21st century, state governments will have to take the lead. Infrastructure must be modernized, school systems drastically improved and public services, from child development to adult retraining, made dramatically more effective. The federal government is both broke and unsuited for the role of providing these services which require diverse responses tailored to local conditions, active citizens participation and visible elected officials who can be held accountable for results. Washington is too far from the scene to handle these challenges flexibly and effectively.[4]

The most that can be expected in the next few years is modest expansion of services, not the substantial changes called for by Rivlin. Perhaps states will devote more efforts to expanding children's services or adult retraining, but the political will to do so is not clear as of 1994.

These agendas will compete for primacy in state capitals in the years ahead. While there are conflicts among them, it is theoretically possible for a state to pursue all four agendas at the same time. Some agendas, however, will inevitably dominate others. The various agendas can be mixed and matched:

- Governor Christine Todd Whitman of New Jersey has said that we need "smaller, smarter" state governments. She thus seems to unite the efficiency and the "do less" agendas.
- Advocates for expanded services for poor children bring together the equity and "do more" agendas. They also claim to enhance efficiency because it is cheaper to prevent social problems from developing than to deal with their effects.
- The efficiency and equity agendas come together in condemning wasteful programs that benefit wealthy communities. States can continue to be mindful of equity even as they pursue efficiency by adopting safeguards that ameliorate the problems new policies create. For example, transition assistance can be provided to communities that lose facilities or to employees whose jobs are eliminated.
- It is possible to advocate "doing more" and "doing less" at the same time because cutting some programs is often the best way to pay for expanding others.

To summarize, state officials face major challenges in attempting to balance these four agendas. But barriers to progress should be more feasible to overcome in a competitive environment in which many other states are considering new departures.

CRITICAL QUESTIONS

Many of the state responses to the fiscal crisis of the early 1990s involved shifting burdens to others, to the federal government through maneuvers to increase Medicaid, to local governments through aid reductions and new mandates, to college students through higher tuition, and to future generations through cutbacks in pension contributions and other investments. As they confront the rest of the 1990s, states face the question of whether they can and should continue to pursue these strategies.

- Will the federal government prevent the cost shifting of the early 1990s? It has already moved in that direction.
- Will states adopt a broader view of how their policies affect local governments rather than continue the ad hoc approach of the early 1990s?
- Will they continue to increase reliance on tuition? Will they reconsider higher education policies, providing more financial aid to prevent major decreases in access by those who cannot afford higher tuition levels? Will they take a more discriminating approach to trimming budgets, eliminating duplication among campuses, or will they cut indiscriminately without adopting safeguards to minimize the damage to higher education opportunities available to students?
- Will states continue to push costs into the future? With the proliferation of term limits for legislators, the temptation to defer costs is likely to increase.

State policies toward local governments especially merit more attention than they received in the early 1990s. How long can states continue to push costs down to cities, counties, and school districts before a severe backlash develops? In the first part of this era of "fend-for-yourself federalism," property tax rates rose, but taxpayers rebel when that trend goes too far. In the remainder of the 1990s, states should be considering issues like local revenue diversification, mandate relief, reform of aid programs, and how responsibilities are sorted out between the state and local governments.

ALL STATES ARE NOT ALIKE

The fiscal agenda is not the same in every state. It varies depending on demography, the economy, traditions, the tax system, and existing spending patterns. For example, many states modernized their tax systems in the 1960s, adopting either a personal income tax or a general sales tax, whichever they did not already have. The twelve states that still lack one or both of those taxes will have to grapple with the implications of having an unbalanced tax system, which requires them to rely heavily on the taxes they do employ, often causing economic distortions.

Michigan illustrates the same issue in a less extreme way. Before 1994 it had much higher property tax rates than most states and a very low sales tax rate. Its 1994 tax reform was a major development for it, but it merely brought Michigan's tax system in line with those of most other states.

States differ in the same way in their spending policies. Some states have rigid civil service systems, while others have relatively flexible rules. Some states require students to pay relatively high tuition while others keep tuition low with large state subsidies for universities. Counties in some states still have to help pay for welfare programs, but in most states that is purely a state cost.

Since states differ so much in their tax and spending policies, it follows that their future budget outlooks also diverge widely. Differences in the growth of their economies and the populations needing services reinforce these differences. Thus, some states will have persistent large gaps between their revenues and the spending needed to maintain current services, while other states may not have any gaps at all.

These kinds of differences make it difficult to compare states. It is easy to draw the wrong lessons from developments, but the diversity among states does not make it impossible for states to learn from each other. The case studies in this book provide the kind of information that is indispensable for understanding what has really occurred in states.

THE LAST WORD

The short-term fiscal crisis of the early 1990s ended as state economies recovered from the recession. At the same time the long-term fiscal crisis faded into the background. In early 1994, when very few states had short-term budget problems, the leading organizations of state officials issued a report predicting severe fiscal difficulties unless states overhauled their tax systems. But the message of this report was virtually ignored in the months after it was published.

States do have choices. One is to attempt wholeheartedly to reform their tax systems, spending programs, and budget strategies to make their finances more stable and their services more efficient. The other is to continue muddling along, passing their fiscal problems along to others, and allowing service levels to decline. The first choice requires taking the long view. Unfortunately, a short-term orientation seems to be ascendant in most states. Bold enlightened leadership could change this, but too little of it has not been forthcoming.

A fiscal crisis is the ideal time for rethinking existing policies and undertaking new initiatives. The preliminary verdict on the fiscal crisis of the early 1990s is that states took some important steps in the right direction but not enough to satisfy those who perceive the need for major changes in tax systems and spending practices. The real work has only begun.

NOTES

1. Steven D. Gold, *The State Fiscal Agenda for the 1990s* (Denver: National Conference of State Legislatures, 1990).

2. These statistics exclude federal aid, which contributes about 7 percent of school revenue. National Education Association, *Estimates of School Statistics, 1993–94.*

3. For example, eliminating an ineffective program or closing an unnecessary facility is "getting away from business as usual," but it need not have anything to do with reinventing government in the Osborne-Gaebler sense.

4. Alice Rivlin, "Wanted A New State-Level Tax to Prepare Us for the 21st Century," *Governing* 3 (April 1990): 74.

Index

Contents

Tables